MW00457598

THE SACRED BEE
in Ancient Times and Folklore

Plate I.—RELIEF FROM THE TEMPLE OF THE SUN OF NE-USER-RE
(FIFTH DYNASTY) IN ABUSIR

(By permission of the Director, Egyptian Museum, Berlin)

THE SACRED BEE
in Ancient Times and Folklore

Illustrated

Hilda M. Ransome

THe Parliament is held, Bils and Complaints
Heard and reform'd, with feverall reftraints
Of ufurpt freedome ; inftituted Law
To keepe the Common-Wealth of Bees in awe.

DOVER PUBLICATIONS, INC.
Mineola, New York

Bibliographical Note

This Dover edition, first published in 2004, is an unabridged republication of the work originally published in 1937 by George Allen & Unwin, London.

Library of Congress Cataloging-in-Publication Data

Ransome, Hilda M.
 The sacred bee in ancient times and folklore / Hilda M. Ransome.
  p. cm.
 Originally published: London : George Allen & Unwin, 1937.
 Includes bibliographical references and index.
 ISBN-13: 978-0-486-43494-0
 ISBN-10: 0-486-43494-X
 1. Bees—Folklore. 2. Bees—History. 3. Bee culture—History. 4. Honey—Folklore. I. Title.

GR750.R3 2004
398.24'525799—dc22

2003068757

Manufactured in the United States by LSC Communications
43494X10   2021
www.doverpublications.com

TO THE READER

The chiefest cause, to read good bookes,
That moves each studious minde
Is hope, some pleasure sweet therein,
Or profit good to finde.
Now what delight can greater be
Than secrets for to knowe
Of Sacred Bees, the Muses' Birds,
All which this booke doth showe.

Charles Butler, *The Feminine Monarchie*, 1609

PREFACE

EDWARD LEAR's old man of Tralee was "horridly bored by a bee," a regular brute of a bee, which annoyed him by its buzzing. If, therefore, the buzzings of bees are wearying to anyone, they will hardly care for this book, which is full of their humming and buzzing; if, however, they are interested in folklore it may appeal to them, for the bee excited the interest of man from the earliest times; no creature provided him with so much sweet and wholesome food, which he used largely in his ritual, and around none has such a number of beliefs and superstitions arisen.

My thanks are due to those who have encouraged me in my work: to Mr. Donald A. Mackenzie for many helpful notes; to Dr. Rendel Harris, Dr. R. Campbell Thompson; to Professor M. A. Canney, Rev. T. Fish, and the late Miss W. M. Crompton, who read some of the chapters; to Dr. Guppy of the John Rylands Library, Manchester; to Sir W. Mitchell Ramsay; to Sir Arthur Evans for the Cretan illustrations; to Dr. Alfred M. Tozzer of Harvard University; to Señor Hernandez-Pacheco of Madrid; to Dr. Gaster for the folktales from Rumania; to the late Dr. P. C. Lee of Cork; to Dr. L. D. Caskey of the Museum of Fine Arts, Boston, Mass.; to the heads of various departments of the British Museum, and to all those who have so kindly responded to my request for material.

HILDA M. RANSOME

CONTENTS

LIST OF ILLUSTRATIONS

PLATES

FIGURES

THE SACRED BEE

CHAPTER I

EARLY TIMES

*Honey used by primitive man—Bee regarded with reverence and
awe—Fossil forms—"Apis adamitica"—Rock painting of man and
bees' nest at Bicorp, Spain*

OF bees especially the proverb holds good, "Truth is stranger
than fiction." Among all the members of the insect world bees
and ants have aroused greater interest than any others, but it is
the bees who have been of paramount use to man. As we look
back upon their history we become more and more convinced
that it is impossible to over-estimate their value to man in the
past.

What veneration and yet what fear these tiny creatures excited
in man! They exercise a fascination even on those who fear their
sting, and all who tend them have quite a peculiar love and regard
for them which they do not feel for other animals, and which is a
bond of union between all beekeepers; they feel that they belong
to a fraternity which reckons Vergil among their number. From
the dawn of human society the nature and origin of the bee have
awakened the curiosity and interest of man. For thousands of years
honey was the only sweetening material known, and it is quite
natural that in ancient times the little busy creature who produced
this sweet food should have been regarded with reverence and awe.

Man very early discovered that honey was good for his health,
and that a sparkling, fermented drink could be made from it, so it
can easily be understood that he came to regard honey as a true
"giver of life," a substance necessary to existence like water and
milk. He held the bee to be a creature of special sanctity connected
with those things which seemed to him so mysterious—birth,
death, and reincarnation. Thus have arisen those folktales and
customs relating to bees which are found among so many different
peoples. The very widespread custom of telling the bees of occur-

rences which happen in their owner's family would not have
arisen had they not been credited with almost supernatural powers.
This custom still lingers; quite recently a woman in Sussex said
that the death of her baby was due to her having omitted to tell
the bees of its birth.

The scientific name of the European honey bee is *Apis mellifica*,
the honey-maker,[1] and its history can be traced back to a period
long before man appeared on the earth, as there actually have been
found in various rocks fossil remains of this

> Active, eager, airy thing,
> Ever hovering on the wing,

as Aristophanes called the bee nearly two thousand five hundred
years ago.[2]

Some of the oldest fossil bees are found in the amber of the
Baltic coast, and they so resemble our honey
bee that scientists have regarded them as their
ancestors. A fossil bee, which is illustrated on
Plate II and in Fig. I, was found at Oehningen
in Baden, and it is also so like our bee that it
was named by its discoverer *A. adamitica*,[3]
though pre-adamitica would have been a more
correct name, as this bee lived and gathered
honey before there were any men on the
earth. Its legs and antennae are missing, but its head, thorax,
and abdomen can distinctly be recognized, and also one large eye.

FIG. I.—FOSSIL BEE
FROM OEHNINGEN,
BADEN

Central Europe was probably the region where the different
races of bees developed, for the oldest forms have been found
there.[4] All these fossil bees were as fully developed as the honey

[1] The latter part of the name was given by Linnaeus in 1761; in 1758
he had named it *A. mellifera*, the honey-bringing bee.

[2] Knights, 400, Hookham Frere's translation.

[3] Oswald Heer, *Die Urwelt der Schweiz*, 1864, English translation by
J. Heywood, *The Primeval World*, 1876, vol. ii, p. 43.

[4] Of the eight thousand five hundred varieties of fossil insects known, only
about fifty-nine can be identified as honey bees (Apidae). Among these is
one from Corrent (France), one from Krotten See (Bohemia), eleven from
Oehningen (Baden), one from Orsberg, eleven from the amber forests of the
Samland, three from Radobaj (Croatia), five from Rott (Rhenish Prussia),
and six from Florissant (North America). For a good account of fossil bees,

PLATE II.—FOSSIL BEE FROM OEHNINGEN, BADEN

Now in the Geologischen Institut der Techischen Hochschule in Zürich.

(By kind permission of Professor O. Schneider-Orelli)

PLATE III.—EGYPTIAN HIVES, STILL USED BY THE NATIVES AND
MADE OF NILE MUD

(*Above*) Separate Hives placed in a Pile   (*Below*) Hives Joined with Mud

(Egon Rotter: "Die Biene in Ägypten jetzt und vor 5000 Jahren," *Archiv für Bienenkunde*, III, 1921)

bees of the present day; that is, they built combs, reared their young, looked after the mother-bee just as they do now, and formed the same industrious state whose organization has been for ages the wonder and admiration of man. Man has done nothing to develop them; he has given them modern appliances which help them to store more surplus honey for him, but the character and work of the bees remain the same, and we can never describe them as really domesticated animals; they often, as bee-keepers know to their cost, display independence of character; it has been truly said that "Bees never do any-thing invariably."

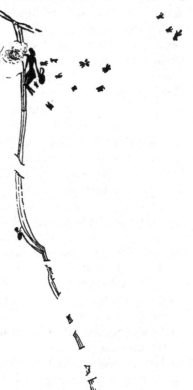

When did early man dis-cover that honey was good for food and drink? We can never answer that question positively, but it must have been long ages ago, for there is definite proof that he was taking honey in late Paleo-lithic times, that is, perhaps ten thousand to fifteen thou-sand years ago. In 1919 a won-derful series of rock paintings were discovered in the Araña (Spider) Cave at Bicorp, near Valencia in Spain, most of

FIG. 2.—MEN GATHERING HONEY. SPANISH ROCK PAINTING IN THE ARAÑA CAVE, BICORP, VALENCIA (From "Escéna Pictorica con Representaciónes de Insectos de Epoca Paleolitica")

which were hunting scenes in which extinct as well as existing animals were portrayed, thus proving their antiquity. One of these drawings represents a unique scene, reproduced on Fig. 2, where

see Professor H. von Buttel-Reepen, *Leben und Wesen der Biene*, Braunschweig, 1916. Also Professor T. A. Cockerell, "A Fossil Honey Bee," in *Entomologist*, vol. 40, pp. 227-229, and "Some European Fossil Bees" in vol. 42, p. 317.

two men are climbing up a very rudimentary ladder, probably made of esparto grass, which grows abundantly in the neighbourhood. One of the men is by a natural hole in the rocks (there are many like it in the rocks around), he is holding on to the ladder with one hand and in the other he carries a basket of some sort, perhaps made of skin, the handle of which can be clearly seen. The figures painted on the wall around him are bees in flight, which have come out of their nest in the hole. The head, abdomen, legs, and extended wings may be distinguished on some of them. The man lower down carries a bag, similar to that the first man holds, but on his back so as to have his hands free. The ropes, on account of his weight, are not vertical, so probably this man is climbing up to bring down the honey which the other man is taking out of the nest. Both men are naked and so without any protection against the stings of the bees, but they seem to have something on their heads.[1]

This scene was drawn when man was still in the hunting stage of civilization, before he had begun to domesticate any animals, except perhaps the dog. His food would be flesh and fish; he would have no bread, for there was no agriculture; no milk, for he had no cattle, but he had found in the wild bees' nests the sweet food which must have been such a welcome addition to his simple fare. Perhaps, too, he had already discovered that an intoxicating drink could be made from it; for mead in some form was certainly one of the earliest, if not the first, fermented drinks known.

Honey must first have been obtained from nests in rocks or in hollow trees within easy reach. The hunters would carefully mark each nest, watching the bees fly in and out, but this picture shows that honey was wanted sufficiently for the men to venture naked up a frail ladder to get it, which seems to imply that it was wanted for very special reasons, which gave them courage. Possibly honey was already used for magical or religious purposes, and man had begun to offer it to the spirits of his dead, a custom which is found in some of the earliest known religious rites.

Many of the pictures of animals found at Altamira and other

---

[1] Francisco Hernandez-Pacheco, "Escéna pictorica con Representaciónes de Insectos do Epoca Paleolitica," in *Bulletin of Real Sociedad Española de Historia Natural,* Madrid, 1921, tome 50, pp. 62–77. See also *The Times,* August 1, 1921.

places in Spain and the South of France seem to have been drawn under a magico-religious impulse. Man appears, even at that early period, to have had a belief in invisible powers, and he probably thought that these paintings somehow helped him to carry out a successful hunt, and this drawing of the bees was therefore possibly made in the belief that it would aid and protect him when really collecting the honey he so much needed. Many natives of Asia and Africa at the present day take honey when only very scantily clad, believing that they are protected by having performed some religious observances, which vary in different tribes, but in all cases have for their object a magical increase in the yield of honey.[1]

After this painting there is a gap in our knowledge of bees for many thousands of years. Possibly the perforated clay vessels which have been found among the Neolithic lake pile dwellings of Switzerland may have been used for straining honey; at certain temperatures the honey would flow through the holes leaving the wax behind.[2] This suggestion is rendered more probable by the fact that a similar way of straining honey is still used in the Emmental and also in the Bernese Jura.[3] If it is true it would prove that Neolithic man had discovered some of the many uses of wax. The writings of the Ancient East will, however, provide the next authentic information of the sacred bees.

[1] See Chapter XXII.
[2] J. G. Bessler, *Geschichte der Bienenzucht*, Stuttgart, 1886, p. 2; A. Gmelin, in Witzgall, *Das Buch von der Bienen*, Stuttgart, 1898, p. 2.
[3] F. Keller, *Lake Dwellings of Switzerland*, London, 1878, p. 564.

CHAPTER II

ANCIENT EGYPT

*Bee used as symbol for king of Lower Egypt from about 3500 B.C.
till Roman times—Relief from Temple of Ne-user-re at Abusir—
Beekeepers' petition—"Wanderbienenzucht"—Use of wax for
magic figures—Burial in honey—How to make a mummy—Honey
as tribute—Honey in religious rites—Given to sacred animals—
Ceremony of "Opening the Mouth"—Bee souls—Origin of bees*

BEES and honey are mentioned in the oldest literatures of the
world, for honey is often alluded to in the Sumerian and Babylonian
cuneiform writings, laws about bees are included in a Hittite code,
the sacred writings of India, the Vedas, contain frequent mention
of bees and honey, and in ancient Egypt, besides many allusions
in its literature, we have the earliest known use of the bee as a
symbol. About 3500 B.C. or even earlier, when the two countries of
Upper and Lower Egypt were united under one ruler, it was used
as the hieroglyph to denote the king of Lower Egypt, that for the
king of Upper Egypt was the reed. In the Kahun papyrus there is a
reference to this union:

> He hath united the two lands,
> He hath joined the Reed to the Bee.[1]

This bee hieroglyph, denoting the king of Lower Egypt, is
found on inscriptions from the First Dynasty down to the Roman
period, that is, for about four thousand years. On Fig. 3 (*a–l*)
are represented types of the hieroglyph used at various periods
(*a, b, i* also show the reed).[2] In nearly all cases the head, antennae,
thorax, and abdomen are clearly distinguishable, and the wings,
only two of the four being shown, are erect. The bee is
always drawn in profile and in the earliest times the number of
legs depicted was usually three, but in the later dynasties and in
Ptolemaic times four legs were drawn, which is strange for an

[1] Kahun Papyri, Pl. III, 1, 2.
[2] Fig. 3 (*m*) shows the earliest recorded bee place-name, "Papyrus Clump
of the Bee"; Fig. 3 (*n*) hieroglyph for "honey"; Fig. 3 (*o*) hieroglyph for
"beekeeper."

FIG. 3.—EGYPTIAN BEE TYPES

a) First Dynasty, King Qa. (*Royal Tombs*, I, Pl. 8, Fig. 9) (*b*) First Dynasty, King Qa. (*Royal Tombs*, I, Pl. 17, Fig. 26) (*c*) First Dynasty, King Azab. (*Royal Tombs*, I, Pl. 26, Fig. 57) (*d*) First Dynasty, King Den-Setui. (*Royal Tombs*, II, Pl. 7, Fig. 8) (*e*) Second Dynasty. Khasekhemui. (*Royal Tombs*, II, Pl. 23, Fig. 211) (*f*) Fifth Dynasty. (Petrie: *Researches in Sinai*, No. 52) (*g*) Old Kingdom. (Murray: *Saqqara Mastabas*, I, Pl. 38) (*h*) Twelfth Dynasty. (Blackman: *Rock Tombs of Meir*, II, Pls. 17, 26) (*i*) Sixth Dynasty. Reed and Bee of Menenra. (Abydos I, Pl. 54) (*j*) Eighteenth Dynasty. Thothmes III. (Abydos I, Pl. 64) (*k*) Fifth Dynasty. (Ptahhotep I, Pl. 14, Fig. 161) (*l*) Eighteenth Dynasty. Thothmes I. (Deir el Bahari, I, Pl. 14) (*m*) Place-name = "Papyrus Clump of the Bee." (Ptahhotep I, p. 23) (*n*) Hieroglyph for *Honey* (*o*) Hieroglyph for "Beekeeper"

observant people like the early Egyptians; they might have shown all six, as their idea of perspective was somewhat faulty.

Egypt is described in the Bible as a land, like Canaan, "flowing with milk and honey."[1] It was probably the first land where agriculture and cattle-rearing were practised, and where there is pasture and fodder for cattle there will be plenty of food for bees. It is not known when the inhabitants began to keep the wild bees in hives, but already in pre-dynastic times they must have known a good deal about bee life, have observed the communal life of the bee-state, and the one large bee among the crowd, before they chose it to denote their king; and as the royal symbol means "He who belongs to the bee," or perhaps, originally, the "beekeeper," and there was as early as the first dynasty an official called the "Sealer of the Honey," it seems probable that it was an industry before the union of the two kingdoms.[2]

It is, however, nearly one thousand years after the introduction of the bee as a symbol before we have direct evidence of the existence of beekeeping. In 1900 a German expedition, excavating at Abusir, found a relief which shows the industry in such an advanced condition that it must have been practised for a very long period.[3]

This relief, which is illustrated by the Frontispiece, belongs to a series representing the seasons found in the Temple of the Sun, built about 2600 B.C. by Ne-user-re of the Fifth Dynasty. The hieroglyphs, which divide the relief into four groups, reading from left to right, have been translated as "Blowing or smoking, filling, pressing, sealing of honey." On the extreme left a man is kneeling before the hives, taking out honey. He has something in his hand, possibly a block of dried cow dung, like those still used by Egyptian beekeepers of the present day for smoking the bees. The hives are nine in number, placed one above the other, and were probably pipes made of burnt clay, tapering slightly towards the end, very similar to the hives made of pipes of clay or Nile mud which are

---

[1] Numbers xvi. 13.

[2] The Egyptians called the bee *âfa-bat* = fly-of-honey; honey = *bat* or *bati*. In Coptic, honey is *ebiô*; beekeeper, *ebiate*.

[3] The relief is described by Dr. Ludwig Armbruster in *Archiv für Bienenkunde: Die Biene in Aegyptien, jetzt und vor 5000 Jahren*, pp. 68–80 (1921); and by Frau Luise Klebs, *Die Reliefs des alten Reiches*, Heidelberg, 1915 p. 58. It is now in the Berlin Egyptian Museum, No. 20037.

used in Egypt to-day (see Plate III). The same type of hive has thus persisted for over four thousand five hundred years.[1]

The next scene shows three men who are filling various-shaped jars with honey. The third group, depicting the "pressing," is unfortunately damaged, but it evidently consists of two men who must be squeezing the honey into some jars. The last scene contains one figure only, a man who is kneeling and sealing up a curiously shaped vessel. He is probably sealing it at the top with the owner's seal. Two other jars of the same shape are already sealed above him, and between him and the last group are the hieroglyphs which describe the scenes.

Until lately it was not known if the ancient Egyptians practised what the Germans call *Wanderbienenzucht*, that is, moving the hives to different districts in order to take advantage of the earlier or later flowering plants, as our beekeepers take the hives to the heather when the ordinary honey flow is over. However, in 1914–15 a number of papyri were found which belonged to Zenon, a Greek official who lived at Philadelphia in the Fayum, about the middle of the third century before Christ. One of these documents is a "Petition from the Beekeepers," which runs:

To Zenon greeting from the Beekeepers of the Arsinoite nome. You wrote about the donkeys, that they were to come to Philadelphia and work ten days. But it is now eighteen days that they have been working and the hives have been kept in the fields, and it is time to bring them home and we have no donkeys to carry them back. Now it is no small impost that we pay the king. Unless the donkeys are sent at once, the result will be that the hives will be ruined and the impost lost. Already the peasants are warning us, saying, "We are going to release the water and burn the brushwood, so unless you remove them you will lose them." We beg you then, if it please you, to send us our donkeys, in order that we may remove them. And after removing them we will come back with the donkeys when you need them. May you prosper![2]

---

[1] Beekeeping, showing hives and bees, is also depicted on a later tomb of Pa-bu-sa (*c.* 625 B.C.), and there is a good representation of an offering of honeycombs on an Eighteenth-Dynasty tomb at Thebes. Both these are reproduced by H. Malcolm Fraser, *Beekeeping in Antiquity*, 1931, University of London Press.

[2] C. C. Edgar, "Selected Papyri from the Archives of Zenon," No. 106, p. 41, in *Annales du Service des Antiquités de l'Égypte*, vol. xxiv.

This interesting document proves that it was customary to move hives in the third century B.C., so it was probably a custom which had long been in use. In 1740 a French traveller, De Maillet,[1] wrote that the people of Lower Egypt, recognizing that all plants flowered earlier in Upper Egypt than with them, sent their hives at the end of October up the Nile. When they arrived at their destination, they were numbered and placed in pyramidal form on rafts, specially built for this purpose. The bees were released and collected honey from the fields near by. When the flowers there were over, the rafts were moved a few miles farther down. Thus they passed through the whole of Egypt, arriving at Cairo at the beginning of February, where the produce of the expedition was sold. The removal of hives is practised to-day in Upper Egypt, either in boats or by land on camels and donkeys.[2] The conservative Egyptians have thus preserved the usage of their forefathers to the present day.

Beekeeping must have been practised on a large scale in ancient Egypt, for honey was required by all classes. It was used in every household as a sweetening material; there is a marriage contract in existence which states: "I take thee to wife . . . and promise to deliver to thee yearly twelve jars of honey."[3] The physicians and magicians (in early times there was no great distinction between the two) were aware of its healing properties, and it figures largely in recipes in the Medical Papyri. Many of these prescriptions were handed down from generation to generation; the Greeks took them to Europe, and some are still in use among the peasantry of the present day.

Beeswax was used by the sorcerers for making figures of men and animals. One of the earliest instances of the magical use of wax is related in the Westcar Papyrus. A man named Aba-aner, who lived in the time of the Third Dynasty, that is, about 2830 B.C., and who held the important priestly office of Kher-heb, kept a box of materials and instruments always ready to make such figures. He once made a wax image of a crocodile which was to be put

[1] *Description de l'Égypte*, tome ii, p. 24, quoted by T. Wildman, *A Treatise on Bees*, 1768, pp. 88–9; cf. Bessler, *Geschichte der Bienenzucht*, p. 12.

[2] Dr. H. von Buttel-Reepen, in *Archiv für Bienenkunde*, 1921, p. 45.

[3] H. K. Brugsch, in "Deutsches Rundschau," 1889, quoted by J. Ph. Glock, *Die Symbolik der Bienen*, Heidelberg, 1891, p. 126.

into the pool where his wife's lover bathed. This wax crocodile, when thrown into the water, became alive and seized upon the man and dragged him into the pool, where he remained seven days. On the seventh day Aba-aner invited the king to come and see a wonder. They went together to the pool, Aba-aner called to the crocodile to bring up the man, and it appeared with him in its mouth; Aba-aner took the crocodile in his hand, and it became a wax one as before. When the king had heard Aba-aner's reason for making the crocodile, he said to it, "Take that which is thine and begone." Immediately the wax figure was thrown into the water again it became alive, seized upon the man, and disappeared into the depths of the pool.[1]

One of the most ancient beliefs is that if a figure of a man, made by a wizard or witch, was injured or destroyed, the man would also suffer or die. This custom, which was practised by the magicians of Egypt, Babylonia, and India, passed from Egypt to Greece and Rome, and continued until quite recent times in our own island. Wax images played a prominent part in certain of the daily services performed in the temple of Amen-Ra at Thebes.[2] It was said that if a wax figure of Apep, the enemy of Ra, were made and his name cut upon it, Apep would be consumed.[3] In the Graeco-Roman period wax figures were used in the performance of magical ceremonies of every kind.

Wax was sometimes employed in mummification, and the coffins in which the embalmed bodies were placed for transport were made airtight by means of beeswax.

The dead were also sometimes preserved in honey. A story is told that once some men were seeking for treasures in graves near the Pyramids. They came upon a sealed jar, which they opened and found it contained honey, which they began to eat. One of the party noticed that a man who was dipping his bread into the honey had a hair on his fingers, and they then discovered in the jar the body of a small child in a good state of preservation. It was well dressed and had on various ornaments.[4]

In later times it is said that great healing powers were attributed to Egyptian mummies, which were, however, difficult to obtain.

[1] Sir E. Wallis Budge, *Egyptian Magic*, p. 68. [2] Ibid., p. 77.
[3] Ibid., p. 81. [4] Idem, *The Mummy*, p. 183.

In an old Persian manuscript there is a method given for making
an artificial one:

> Find a ruddy, red-haired man and feed him till he is thirty years old
> on fruit; then drown him in a stone vessel which is filled with honey
> and drugs, and seal up the vessel. When it is opened after the lapse of
> one hundred and fifty years, the honey will have turned the body into
> a mummy.[1]

History does not relate if the recipe was ever carried out! In any
case the man who began it would hardly live to benefit by it!

Honey was so much valued that it was exacted in tribute. Many
jars of honey were paid annually by the chief of the Retenu (a
people in Syria) to the great conqueror Thothmes III. It is mentioned as one of the spoils on the Carnarvon tablet, which records
the defeat of the Hyksos by Kamose, and later it was one of the
rations allowed to the king's messengers and standard-bearers.[2]

The priests required large quantities of honey for their religious
rites. Taxes of honey were collected for this purpose, and some
of the Pharaohs, especially Rameses III, presented enormous
amounts of honey to the priests for their great festivals.[3]

It was also used to feed the sacred animals. Diodorus Siculus,
who lived at the time of Augustus, says that the sacred bull Apis at
Memphis, the Mnevis at Heliopolis, the he-goat at Mendes, the
lion at Leontopolis and the crocodile at Crocodilopolis were all
kept in sacred enclosures and tended by the priests, who fed them
on fine flour, milk, and cakes sweetened with honey.[4] These honey-
cakes were used in many other ceremonials. On one of the reliefs
in the tomb of Rekhmara, vizier of Hatshepsut and Thothmes III,

---

[1] Nirzami's "Alexander's Exploits," quoted by F. Berger in *Von Biene,
Honig und Wachs*, Zürich, 1916, p. 44. N. W. Thomas, in an article on
"Burial Rites of West Africa in Relation to Egypt," mentions honey as one
of the materials used by the natives where mummification is practised; see
Ancient Egypt, 1921, p. 10.

[2] Petrie, *History of Egypt in Seventeenth and Eighteenth Dynasties*, pp. 46
and 112; Paton, *Egyptian Records of Travel*, vol. ii, p. 60; Breasted, *Ancient
Records*, III. 208.

[3] One record states that he gave 20,800 jars, each containing $\frac{1}{2}$ *hin*, and
1,040 jars of 1 *hin* for the Nile god (a *hin* = about $\frac{1}{2}$ litre), besides 7,050
jars of honey for cakes. See Breasted, *Ancient Records*, II. 571; IV. 228;
IV. 239; IV. 300; IV. 344, 350, 390.   [4] Ibid., I. 84. 5; Strabo, XVII. i, 38.

men are depicted baking them for use in the Temple of Amen. The four-handled jar in which the honey was kept is also shown (Fig. 4).[1]

Nearly all the religious rites of the Egyptians were concerned with the after-life of man; they believed that the dead wanted his body in the next world—hence the custom of mummification—and that therefore he needed food and drink. In order that the mummy could make use of the food offering, a ceremony was performed, known as the "Opening of the Mouth." It consisted of a number of elaborate episodes, in many of which honey was offered. The priests had special instruments with which to "open

FIG. 4.—BAKING HONEY-CAKES. TOMB OF REKHMARA
(Newberry, Pl. xii, Fig. 13)

the mouth" of the statue. The ceremony was performed on the statue of a god, and on the statue or mummy of the king or other great nobles; it is frequently represented on reliefs.

In the ritual used at the ceremony there are some passages whose meaning it is very difficult to explain. In one, the Kher-heb, the officiating priest says, "*Going about as a bee, thou seest all the goings about of thy father.*"[2] There is an ancient belief, found in many parts of the world, that *souls* take the form of bees, and it is just possible that this text may contain the germ of this belief. The Egyptians believed that a man possessed a *ka* or double, who had to be fed after death, and this *going about like a bee* may refer to this *ka*. It is to be remembered that the symbol for the Pharaoh as the king of Lower Egypt was the bee, so it would be natural for

[1] P. E. Newberry, *Life of Rekhmara*, Pl. xii and p. 35; W. Wreszinski, *Zeitschrift für aegyptische Sprache und Altertumskunde*, Band 61, s. 10.

[2] Wallis Budge, *Book of Opening the Mouth*, vol. i, p. 31.

the people to think of his *ka*, or that of one of his subjects, appearing
as such. There is also a text from another ritual known as the
"Book of Am-Tuat" (the Otherworld) which compares the voices
of souls to the hum of bees:

> This god crieth out to their souls after he hath entered the city of the
> gods who are on their sand, and there are heard the voices of those who
> are shut in this circle which are like [the hum] of many bees of honey
> when their souls cry out to Ra.[1]

The Egyptians often represent souls as birds, and from these texts
it seems probable that they held, though perhaps somewhat vaguely,
that the soul could also assume the form of another winged
creature, the bee.

Another passage in the ceremony of "Opening the Mouth" is:
"*The bees, giving him protection, they make him to exist.*"[2] In the
hieroglyphic text there are three bees in a row, and it has been
suggested that they refer to the four sons of Horus (three of them
here in the form of bees and the fourth as a praying mantis), whose
heads were often carved on the lids of the jars in which the heart,
liver, and intestines were placed, and which were arranged round
the mummy at the four cardinal points to guard it. The passage
seems to mean that the sons of Horus gave the *ka* the power to
live, perhaps by feeding it with honey, for another text which
refers to "opening the mouth" of a god, mentions honey as one of
the oblations offered to "*thy ka at each of thine appearances.*"[3]
In the ceremony the Kher-heb recited special formulae, which
were believed to change the foods (bread, honey, etc.) offered to
the statue into divine substances, and these material elements were
then eaten sacramentally by the priests and relatives of the dead
man. This belief was certainly held during the Fifth Dynasty,
and probably much earlier.

There are two other very interesting texts which throw a
little light on the subject of how the Egyptians regarded the origin
of bees and honey. One is found in the same ceremony of "Opening
the Mouth," which was performed daily in the Temple of Amen-
Ra. One part of the service was called the "Chapter of the Festal

[1] Wallis Budge, *Egyptian Heaven and Hell*, vol. i, Book of Am-Tuat, p. 171.
[2] Idem, *Opening the Mouth*, vol. i, p. 158, and vol. ii, p. 14 n.
[3] Breasted, *Ancient Records*, 329.

Perfume in the Form of Honey," and in it the Kher-heb recited the following passage:

Hail, Amen-Ra, Lord of the Throne of the Two Lands! I present unto thee honey, the Eye of Horus, the Sweet One, the exudation from the Eye of Ra, the Lord of Offerings, Amen-Ra, the Lord of the Two Lands is flooded therewith, for it is sweet to thine heart, and it shall never depart from thee.[1]

The other passage is found in the Salt Magical Papyrus:

When Ra weeps again the water which flows from his eyes upon the ground turns into working bees. They work in flowers and trees of every kind and wax and honey come into being.[2]

The Sun-god Ra was in the creation myths of the Egyptians the framer of the earth and sea, and the god who caused the Nile flood. His right eye was the sun, his left the moon, and when he opened his eyes there was light. In these two texts bees and their products, honey and wax, are said to have come from *water*, which there is good reason for believing the Egyptians regarded as one of the principal sources of life, one of the "Givers of Life."

In Egypt, then, we find myths about the origin of bees and honey, the bee used as a symbol to express royalty, beekeeping practised many thousands of years ago, and honey and wax used by all classes. The bee and her products thus played no mean part in the life of those wonderful people, the Ancient Egyptians.

NOTE TO CHAPTER II

Some Egyptologists have been doubtful whether a bee or a hornet were represented in the hieroglyphs. Dr. Samuel Birch in his edition of Wilkinson's *Ancient Egyptians* states that the bee is not represented on the monuments, the insect, the symbol for the king so often found, being the hornet or wasp, though honey is often mentioned. Sir E. Wallis Budge has, or had, doubts as to the identity of the hieroglyph with the bee, but in his books, though he sometimes puts the word *hornet* in brackets after *bee*, when

[1] Wallis Budge, *Opening the Mouth*, vol. ii, p. 206.
[2] British Museum, No. 10051, recto 2, 5-6.

translating the passages where the word appears, yet he more often omits it. Sir Flinders Petrie, in his early books, alludes to the sign as a "bee or hornet," but in his later books he omits the latter word. For instance, in *Social Life in Ancient Egypt* (1923, p. 9) he writes: "The king acquired the dominion of Sais, figured by the bee *(bati)*." Mr. Warren R. Dawson, in a letter dated April 1924, writes, "I do not think there is any doubt whatever as to the identity of the hieroglyph with the bee, there is no evidence at all for hornets." Professor Breasted writes: "The king himself was designated by a bee." The discovery of the Abusir relief depicting beekeeping seems to end all doubt on the subject, as the bee hieroglyph carved there is identical with that used for the royal title. The qualities of bees would be much more likely to impress the unwarlike Egyptians as suitable to express their king than those of the hornet. The Latin writer Ammianus Marcellinus (xvii. 4, 11), and the Greek writer Horapollo (Hieroglyphica), who lived in the fourth century A.D., both state that the Egyptian symbol for the king was the *bee*.

CHAPTER III

SUMERIA, BABYLONIA, AND ASSYRIA

*Early use of wax—Honey in ritual about 2450 B.C.—Gudea of
Lagash—Honey in exorcisms—Honey-god—"Opening of the
Mouth"—Formulae for consecrating butter and honey—Honey as
propitiating offering to gods—Used for preserving the dead—Wax
figures used by sorcerers—"Syriac Book of Medicines"—Beekeeping
introduced into Suhki—Assyria a land of milk and honey—
Whistling to attract bees—D. Wildman*

THE great civilizations of Sumeria and Babylonia were contemporary with the early dynasties of Egypt, and that of Assyria with the Empire. Unfortunately there is no allusion to beekeeping in any of the early records, but the ancient inhabitants must have had some notion of apiculture, for the existence of bees in the lower Euphrates valley is certain. Honey is frequently mentioned in inscriptions, as it was much in request for religious rites, and wax was used as early as 2050 B.C. for the casting of bronze images, by the process known as *cire perdu*, that is, modelling on a coating of wax which is afterwards melted out.

Honey was poured over thresholds and stones bearing commemorative offerings, and honey and wine were poured over bolts which were to be used in some sacred building. Temples were erected on ground which had been consecrated by libations of wine, oil, and honey The earliest record we have of this use of honey is found on cylinders which describe the building of a new temple for the god Ningirsu by Gudea, the ruler of Lagash, about 2450 B.C.

Gudea made offerings of honey and butter when the foundations were laid; when the building was finished an auspicious day was waited for, and when it came the image of the god was removed to the new temple, and Gudea sprinkled the ground with oil and set out offerings of honey, butter, wine, dates, grain mixed with milk, foods untouched by fire, for the gods.[1] This record shows that honey was a customary offering in these religious ceremonies,

[1] Gudea cylinder; see L. W. King and H. R. Hall, *Egypt and Western Asia*, 1907, p. 209.

and so its use must go back farther than the time of Gudea, and it continued to be used in the same rites for centuries after him. Esarhaddon, who began to rebuild Babylon in the first year of his reign, 682 B.C., records that he sprinkled its foundations with oil, honey, and wine;[1] and another of his inscriptions says that he poured honey on the foundation-stone of the House of Wisdom in Asshur.[2] Date-wine, oil, and honey were poured by Nabonidus, king of Babylon from 555–538 B.C., on the walls and woodwork of the temple of the god Sin in Harran.[3]

The triad, honey, butter, and wine, mentioned so often together on inscriptions, occurs in one dated about 2398 B.C.:

"Bursin, King of Ur, King of the Four Regions of the World, erects a House of Honey, of Butter, and of Wine at the place of his sacrifices," to the great god, En-lil.[4]

Honey was largely used by the priests in the elaborate rites for exorcizing evil spirits and demons. A number of these rituals have been found inscribed in two languages, Sumerian and Babylonian, and the fact that in the great library of Ashur-bani-pal, king of Assyria from 669 to 625 B.C., cylinders have been found on which these ceremonies were still written in Sumerian, at that time a liturgical language only, probably show that the prescribed ritual goes back to Sumerian times, earlier even than Gudea of Lagash and Sargon I of Babylon (2870 B.C.). At any rate, by the time of the great Hammurabi (2123–2081 B.C.) the priests necessary for performing these ceremonies were so powerful as to form a sort of guild.[5]

The ritual was so arranged as to propitiate the invisible powers and thus accomplish the healing of the person exorcized. One record gives a very full ritual for the exorcism of a king. In it the exorcizing priest anointed himself with a salve of honey and curdled milk. Seven altars were prepared in the palace yard on which

[1] Harper, *Assyrian and Babylonian Literature*, p. 89.
[2] A. T. Olmstead, *History of Assyria*, New York, 1923, p. 349.
[3] Harper, *Assyrian and Babylonian Literature*, p. 165.
[4] *Die Sumerischen und Akkadischen Königsinscriften*, bearbeitet von F. Thureau-Dangin, Leipzig, 1907, Gudea cylinder.
[5] Dr. Otto Weber, "Dämonenbeschwörung bei den Babylonien und Assyrien," in *Der Alte Orient*, Jahr VII, heft 4, p. 20.

were placed different kinds of bread, dates, meal, honey, oil, butter, and milk. After reciting a special formula the priest sprinkled a mixture of honey and butter to the quarters of the four winds. He then went to an open field near the palace where seven vessels were placed filled with honey, oil, butter, and wine, and the king was washed with water. Sunrise was then waited for and libations, in which honey played a part, made to the gods.[1]

Many of the substances used in these ceremonies were identified with some special god, as the god Adad with cypress, which was used to propitiate him. A bilingual text mentions a "Honey-god," but unfortunately no indications are given as to which god it was connected with. In this text the exorcizer placed an image of Nergal at the head of the sick person, and images of other gods in various parts of the room. Then the text continues:

> So that nothing evil can come near, I placed the Honey-god and the *Lāl-arag* in the doors in order to drive away every evil thing.[2]

In Babylonia there was also a ceremony known as "Opening or Washing of the Mouth." In Egypt the rite was performed on the statue of a god, and on the mummy or statue of a dead man. In Babylonia it was performed on the statue of a god and on living persons, on priests at their consecration, and also if they had lost their power over demons or the favour of the gods.[3] On some fragments in the British Museum which describe the ceremony on a god, honey water and date-wine mixed with honey are used.

Each substance employed in the rite had its own special form of consecration. A tablet, also in the British Museum, contains some of the formulae used to consecrate various materials. One of these for consecrating the butter begins:

> The pure butter, the clean butter, which was born from the cow of the cattle stall.[4]

Another, called in the rubric "An Incantation for washing a God's mouth with Honey," runs:

[1] Dr. Otto Weber, "Dämonenbeschwörung bei den Babylonien und Assyrien," in *Der Alte Orient*, Jahr VII, heft 4, p. 17.

[2] Ibid., p. 20. The *lāl-arag* was possibly a vessel which contained honey. *Lāl* = honey.

[3] Aylward M. Blackman, "The Rite of Opening the Mouth," in *Jour. of Egypt. Arch.*, 1924, p. 59.   [4] Ibid., p. 49.

Fruit that is plenteous in the garden, fruit that is born in the midst
of mountains, plenteous honey, rich in butter, the Sun-god, Lord of
Heaven and Earth, rises from the hill; in holy wise he approaches . . .
he comes to me. The Water-god (Ea), Lord of the Abyss, may he make
the honey sweet . . . may it be pure for me, may it be bright for me.
Let the evil tongue stand aside.[1]

Honey was also used as a propitiatory offering to the gods. When
Shamash-shum-ukin, king of Babylon, rebelled against his brother
Ashur-bani-pal, king of Assyria in 648 B.C., and was besieged by
him in Babylon, he first prayed to Shamash, the Sun-god from
whom he had received his name, but as things did not go so well
with him as he wished, he prayed to Sin, the Moon-god; honey,
wine, and butter were made ready, and then the king cried aloud:
"I am thy servant, Shamash-shum-ukin. I have presented unto thee
a pure oblation, I have poured out before thee the best wine and
honey"; but his prayers were of no avail, and refusing to surrender
he had his palace set on fire and threw himself on the flames.[2]

Honey was sometimes used for preserving the dead.[3] Herodotus
states, "They [the Babylonians] bury their dead in honey and
have funeral lamentations like the Egyptians";[4] and Strabo says
that "The Assyrians bury the body in honey, first smearing it with
wax."[5] It is recorded that Alexander the Great on his death-bed
commanded that he should be buried in honey and that his orders
were obeyed; his body was placed in "white honey which had not
been melted."[6] No confirmation of this custom, however, has been
found recorded on any inscription.

As in Egypt, the custom of making magical wax figures of a
desired victim was a very ancient and popular one in Babylonia
and Assyria. An Assyrian tablet states that if a hostile wizard lays
a waxen image of a man near a corpse, subsequent evil is sure to
befall the victim.[7] Wizards and witches were therefore greatly

---

[1] British Museum, No. 78, 7-8, K3511. Translated for the writer by
Mr. Sydney Smith of the British Museum.

[2] Olmstead, *History of Assyria*, p. 473-475. Nebuchadrezzar was very
lavish in his honey offerings.

[3] L. W. King, *Babylonian Religion and Mythology*, 1903, p. 49.

[4] I. 198.   [5] XVI. i, 20.

[6] Wallis Budge, *Life and Exploits of Alexander*, vol. ii, p. 349.

[7] R. Campbell Thompson, *Semitic Magic*, p. 115.

feared. A series of Exorcism Rituals has been preserved called
"Maklu" (burning), because the chief topic in them is the burning
of the images made by the sorcerers and the incantations to use
when doing this. One is:

> May her mouth be wax, her mouth honey, may the word causing
> my misfortune that she has spoken, dissolve like wax. May the charm
> that she has wound up, melt like honey.[1]

Honey was constantly used as an offering when imploring the
aid of Marduk, Istar, or other gods to avert the evil caused by
witchcraft. It was also largely used in medicine. In the *Syriac
Book of Medicines* there are many recipes whose origin must be
very ancient, and in a great many of them honey and wax are
used. Many are quite useful, but we should doubt the efficacy of
these:

> *A Medicine to prevent the hair from becoming white.* Take a handful
> of bees, roast them in oil and smear on the hair, and it will become black.[2]

Four others refer to bees and hives, but will hardly be adopted
by a modern beekeeper:

> (1) *To prevent bees leaving.*—Heat water and wine and rub the
> mixture on the hives, or fumigate them with burnt asses' dung.[3]
> (2) *To keep moths from hives.*—Sprinkle fresh milk and the urine of
> children over the legs of hives and the bees will make honey.[4]
> (3) Bury the liver of a white falcon in a beehive, and the bees will
> thrive.[5]
> (4) Whosoever shall place the eye of a bear in a hive of working bees,
> the bees shall prosper.[6]

Honey and wax, then, were used in large quantities by the
Sumerians, Babylonians, and Assyrians, but it is not known when
they began to practise beekeeping, although the Sumerian words
for honey, beekeeper, and honeycomb are known,[7] which shows
that it must have been an ancient craft. The first direct mention

---

[1] M. Jastrow, *Religion of Babylonia and Assyria*, p. 284.
[2] *Syriac Book of Medicines*, ed. Budge, vol. ii, p. 691.   [3] Ibid., p. 689.
[4] Ibid., p. 689.   [5] Ibid., p. 702.   [6] Ibid., p. 704.
[7] Sumerian: Honey = *lál*, beekeeper = *lu-lál*, honeycomb = *gab-lál*;
Assyrian: Honey = *dišpu, dašpu*, mead = *duššupu*.

of it which I have been able to find occurs on a provincial monument discovered in Babylon, which commemorates the principal achievements of Shamash-resh-usur, governor of the land of Suhki, probably between the years 783 and 745. Shamash-resh-usur records that he dug out the Suhki canal and planted palm-trees, but the act of which he seems most proud was the introduction of bees into Suhki:

> Bees which collect honey, which no man had ever seen since the time of my fathers and forefathers, nor had brought to the land of Suhki, I brought them from the mountains of the Khabkha tribe and I put them in the garden of Gabbari-ibni. . . . They collect honey and wax. The preparing of honey and wax I understand and the gardeners understand it.

He adds that in days to come a ruler will ask the elders of his land, "Is it true that Shamash-resh-usur, governor of Suhki, brought honey-bees to the land of Suhki?"[1]

About fifty years after the events recorded in this stele, in 701 B.C., Sennacherib, king of Assyria, sent an army against Hezekiah, king of Judah, and one of his officials, the Rab-shakeh, spoke to the people of Jerusalem telling them not to trust in their king's promises, but to listen to the message of Sennacherib, who would take them to a land like their own, "a land of corn and wine, a land of bread and vineyards, a land of olive oil and honey" (2 Kings xviii. 32). This shows that Assyria was a fertile land, where flowers and trees abounded and where bees prospered.

Some have thought that the saying of Isaiah (Isa. vii. 8),

> The Lord will hiss for the fly that is in uttermost part of the rivers of Egypt, and for the bee that is in the land of Assyria,

alludes to the custom of whistling or making a noise to attract bees. Cyril, the Patriarch of Alexandria, who died in A.D. 444, comments on this passage:

> Isaiah took this picture from the custom of Assyrian beekeepers who understand how to call the bees out of their hives and drive them in again. This is a well-known custom in the East, which I have often seen with my own eyes.[2]

---

[1] L. W. King, *History of Babylon*, p. 267 et seq.; A. T. Olmstead, *History of Assyria*, p. 79.　　[2] Quoted by Bessler, *Geschichte der Bienenzucht*, p. 22.

This is rather a doubtful interpretation, though it is said that an Englishman, Daniel Wildman, who had travelled much in the East, could tame whole hives of bees and send swarms wherever he wished. He travelled through Europe and exhibited his art at various Courts. At his command a swarm of bees would settle on him where he wanted, either on his beard, wig, or any other place.[1] In Siberia there is said to be a custom of whistling for bees, and in East Africa there is a clan with a bee totem, whose members seem to have the power of making bees follow them (see Chapter XXII).

A more modern interpretation of the passage is that it means that God would call upon the fly of Egypt—there are many flies in the Nile Valley—and for the bee of Assyria—which must have been a land of bees—to punish the Israelites; or, in other words, that the Egyptians and the still more dangerous Assyrians would attack Israel in great numbers.[2] Before discussing other allusions to bees in the Bible, we turn our attention to India.

NOTE TO CHAPTER III

Some scholars think that the honey of the Babylonian rites was not always bees' honey, that it consisted of elaborate mixtures, and that date-honey was often used. It is possible that in later times artificial honey might sometimes be used, but we have no authority for it. Herodotus, who mentions artificial honey in Lydia and Libya, says nothing about its use in Assyria, though he mentions the honey there. It is still a moot point whether the references to honey in the Bible may sometimes refer to artificial honey (Heb.: debash, the modern dibs); certainly the honey mentioned in the medical books of Babylonia and Assyria would be bees' honey. In the Syriac Book of Medicines, honey is mentioned in over three hundred prescriptions and wax in over fifty. Wax is not obtainable from artificial honey, and the properties of the artificial would be

---

[1] Quoted by Bessler, Geschichte der Bienenzucht, pp. 23 and 133. Daniel Wildman wrote in 1775 A Complete Guide for the Management of Bees. In Herzog's Theologischen Realencyclopedie, under heading "Bienenzucht," it is stated that bees are enticed by whistling, the beekeepers understand how thus to attract them. [2] See Peake, Commentary on the Bible, p. 442.

very different from those of the real honey. Many passages in the
texts allude to "date-wine mingled with honey," or to "honey
and dates"; if the honey were date-honey both would hardly have
been required. Professor Sayce (in *Religion of Ancient Egypt and
Babylon*, p. 466) distinctly says that among the offerings of first-
fruits in Babylonia was "honey from the hive." Professor Deimel,
a great authority on Sumeria and Babylonia, wrote to a friend of
the author that he knows of no proof of artificial honey among
the Babylonians, and that he does not believe that they made it.
Dr. Mingana (of Rylands Library, Manchester) told the writer that
when in Nineveh (Mosul) from 1900–9 there were many hives
in the town, in the villages near the river, and in those of the plains
which had water. In the villages in the mountains there were hives
of bees everywhere, and honey was sent from them to those where
bees were not kept. He also said that wax candles were always used
in all the churches for lights, there being no other illumination.
Assyria and Babylonia were also much more fertile in ancient times
than they are now, and that therefore there would be likely to
be more bees.

We may conclude, then, that bees' honey was used in these
rites, certainly in the earliest times, and later, as a substance once
used in religious ritual is very rarely replaced by another, it seems
improbable that the priests would use artificial honey, even if it
were used for domestic purposes. The early use of wax also shows
that the Sumerians and Babylonians were well acquainted with
bees, and the quantity of this material which would be required
for the bronze casting proves that there must have been plenty of
honey to be had. Whether it was from wild or domesticated bees
we cannot say at present.

CHAPTER IV

INDIA AND CHINA

THE classical writers about the beginning of our era believed that there were no bees in India. Strabo wrote that there were none to be found there, though there were reeds and trees which yielded honey (XC. 20); and Aelian (XV. 7) records that:

> In spring it rains with honey, which is deposited on the grass and reeds, and this prepares wonderful pastures for the cattle and sheep. The shepherds lead their herds to these pastures and the animals in consequence give such milk that there is no need to mix it with honey, as the Greeks do.

Both these writers seem to be giving a confused account of sugar-cane, but the statement that there were no bees in India is quite unfounded, for our honey-bee (*Apis mellifica*) is indigenous there as well as three other species.[1]

The oldest of the sacred books of India, the Rig-Veda, contains many allusions to bees and honey.[2] It was probably written or compiled between 2000 and 3000 B.C., and many of its hymns may have been written before the Aryans settled in India. These Aryans spoke the language known as Sanscrit, and they and their

---

[1] *Apis indica, A. dorsata, A. florea.*

[2] Hillebrandt, *Vedische Mythologie*, vol. i, p. 239, writes: "The idea of the sacredness of the bees, the considerable rôle which honey plays in the mythology, is not Indian, nor Indo-Iranian, but, according to the showing of the Greek beliefs, is really prehistoric; its occasional intrusion in the Vedas must rest on ancient tradition."

kinsfolk, the Iranians of Persia, are connected in language, and probably also in race, with the principal European nations, and it is therefore not surprising to find some resemblances in their mythology and literature.

The Sanscrit word for honey is *madhu*, which is etymologically identical with the Greek *methu* and the Anglo-Saxon *medu*, mead.[1] The gods Vishnu, Krishna, and Indra were called *Madhava*, the nectar-born ones, and their symbol is the bee. Vishnu is represented as a blue bee, resting on a lotus flower (Fig. 5). The lotus flower is an ancient symbol of life, of resurrection, of Nature whose power slumbers until the warmth and light of the Sun calls it to life. An old poem contains these lines:

FIG. 5.—VISHNU, AS A BLUE BEE ON LOTUS FLOWER

(F. Creuzer: *Symbolik*, Pl. IV, Fig. 23A)

> When the Sun rises, the lotus flower opens
> And frees the bees from their prison.[2]

In the Rig-Veda Vishnu is said to have three "steps." These are sunrise, zenith, and sunset, and the highest "step" is connected with life after death. There the pious are happy and there is a spring of mead:

> In the wide-striding Vishnu's highest footstep,
> There is a spring of mead. (R.-V., I. 154, 4–6)

Krishna, the popular incarnation of Vishnu, is often represented with a blue bee on or above his forehead; it, like the bee connected with Vishnu, is blue, because blue is the colour of the ether from which the god issues.

Sacred to these gods, Vishnu and Krishna, is a plant, the *Tulasi*, or holy basil (*Ocymum sanctum*).[3] According to a Sanscrit legend the tulasi was once a beautiful maiden, beloved by Krishna, who to perpetuate her memory changed her into this plant and ordained no worship to him should be complete which was not graced by her presence. For this reason, and because they hold honey to be

---

[1] Sanscrit names for the bee are: *madhva*, the honey-fly, *madhu-pa*, honey-drinker, *madhu-kara*, honey-maker, *madhu-lih*, honey-licker, and also *Brahmara*, the wanderer.

[2] Quoted by J. Ph. Glock, *Die Symbolik der Bienen*, p. 108.

[3] E. Thurston, *Castes and Tribes of Southern India*, vol. i, p. 1316. The plant is also called toolsey. It is very aromatic.

the food of the gods, the Hindus to the present day hold a piece of this herb in their hand when taking honey from the hive.[1] Thus honey-taking has become a religious cult, for the god himself is enclosed in the bees.

Vishnu, as one of the great Indian triad, Brahma, Vishnu, and Siva, is generally known as the "Preserver" and Siva as the "Destroyer," but Siva has also a less terrible form when he is known as "*Madheri*," the suave one, and he is then represented in the form of a triangle surmounted by a bee (Fig. 6).

FIG. 6.—SIVA, AS TRIANGLE AND BEE

(F. Creuzer: *Symbolik*, Pl. 11, Fig. 12)

Another divinity connected with the bee is Kama, the Indian god of Love. Like the Greek Eros, he carries a bow, whose string is composed of a chain of bees, perhaps symbolizing that the arrows of the god cause pains, though they may be sweet ones. Kalidasa, one of India's most famous poets, writes:

> A stalwart soldier comes, the spring,
> Who bears the bow of Love;
> And on that bow, the lustrous string
> Is made of bees. . . .[2]

and again, that Kama

> Weaves a string of bees with deft invention
> To speed the missile when the bow is bent.[3]

In Fig. 7 Kama is represented as a young god with a string of bees behind his back; he is being carried on his quiver, out of which comes a lion, and underneath is a bee supporting the whole group. Bees and lions are both symbolical of Vishnu; in an ancient poem of the Jagadeva bees on the lotus flower are compared with the claws of a lion.[4] There was some mysterious connection, difficult to explain, between these two creatures, so unlike each other; we shall come across it in Western Asia, among the Hebrews and Greeks, and in the religion of Mithra.

[1] E. N. Falaise in Hastings's *Ency. Rel. and Ethics*, vol. vi, p. 700; G. A. Addison, *Indian Reminiscences*, 1837, p. 40. *Tulasi* leaves and honey are also thrown into a new well before the water is used.

[2] Kalidasa, *Shakuntala*, Everyman edition, p. 215.

[3] Ibid., p. 163; cf. p. 200. Kalidasa's date is uncertain, probably about A.D. 375.   [4] J. Ph. Glock, *Die Symbolik der Bienen*, p. 115.

Several gods have been mentioned who are connected with the bee, but it is the Asvins, the twin horsemen, the lords of light, who seem first to have been associated with the *madhu* (honey) cult. In the Rig-Veda there are many hymns in which they are mentioned in connection with honey. It was *their* chariot only which was called *Madhuvahana*, honey-bearing; in it, drawn by white horses which are compared with ambrosial swans, they carry "honey to the bee" (R.-V., I. 112, 21). The horses are friendly, rich in store of mead, and they come like the bee to the mead (R.-V., I. 45, 4). The Asvins had a honey-goad or whip, *Madhukasa*, which instilled sweetness, food, and strength in the sacrifices and in men: "Dripping with honey is your whip, O Asvins . . . sprinkle therewith the sacrifice" (R.-V., I. 22, 3). In another hymn they are invoked to come in their car, the car laden with mead, and sprinkle the people with their whip, and so prolong their life (R.-V., I. 157, 2–4).

Fig. 7.—KAMA, THE INDIAN GOD OF LOVE SUPPORTED BY A BEE
(F. Creuzer: *Symbolik*, Pl. XIX, Fig. 107)

In the Atharva-Veda there is a special hymn addressed to the honey-whip of the Asvins. We give a few verses from it:

(1) From heaven, from earth, from the atmosphere, from the sea, from the air, from the wing, the honey-lash hath verily sprung.

(2) When the honey-lash comes bestowing gifts, there life's breath, and there immortality has settled down.

(5) The gods begat the lash of honey, from it came an embryo having all forms.

(16) As the bees carry honey upon honey, thus in my person, O Asvins, lustre shall be sustained.

(19) O Asvins, lords of Brightness, anoint me with the honey of the bee, that I may speak forceful speech among men.

(22) He that knoweth the seven honeys of the whip, becomes rich in honey. . . .

(24) Rich in honey becomes he, rich in honey becomes his appurtenances, worlds rich in honey doth he win, he that knoweth this.[1]

[1] Sacred Books of the East, *Hymns of the Artharva-Veda*, vol. 42, hymn IX.

Several attempts have been made by scholars to explain this honey-lash of the Asvins. One thinks it signifies the life-giving morning breeze which accompanies the first appearances of the Asvins, the lords of Light, for in the Rig-Veda (III. 61, 5) the morning red is the honey-bringer; others suggest it means the rain[1] or the lightning which whips the clouds and produces the rain. None of these explanations is entirely satisfactory; all that can be said is that there was a connection in the minds of the compilers of this ancient hymn between the Asvins and real honey, for in it they are implored:

> Anoint me with the honey of the bee,
> That I may speak forceful speech among men. (v. 19)

Here we come upon the belief which we shall find later in many European myths that the bees, the "Birds of the Muses," give the gift of eloquence and song to men. The same belief is found in the Rig-Veda:

> To you, O Asvins, the bee took honey in its mouth
> As a woman goes (with honey in her mouth) to an assignation (R.-V., x.40, 6)

and another hymn says that the poet Kahsivat was assisted in his art by the honey which dropped from the honey-vat of the Asvins (R.-V., I. 106, 10); the Asvins themselves were compared to bees ("like two bees ye procure honey," R.-V., x. 106,10), and were entreated to salve the singer with honey, so that he could speak happily before men (A.-V., VI. 2, 19). Thus in India, as in Greece, it is the bee who gives the poet the gift of sweet speech.

In the ancient writings known as the Laws of Manu, there are many allusions to bees and honey. By this time, about 1000 B.C., the caste system was in existence, and a Brahman, the highest of the four castes, was not allowed to sell or trade in honey and wax; if he did he was degraded for seven days to a lower caste, that of the agriculturists. Stinging insects, like mosquitoes, ants, and bees, are said to come from hot moisture, and the bees are animals who reach heaven by means of fasting. The meaning of this is obscure,

---

[1] See R. T. H. Griffith, *Hymns of the Artharva-Veda*, p. 427, 3rd ed., Benares, 1920; H. Oldenberg, *Religion des Vedas*, 1917, p. 208; Sacred Books of East, vol. 42, p. 597 ff.; cf. Dr. Rendel Harris, *Picus who is also Zeus*, 1916, pp. 57–8.

unless we may think of the bee as a "soul." In parts of India it is still believed that the souls of the departed enter into flies and bees.[1]

Regulations are given as to the amount of honey a king might claim from his subjects; he is warned that as the leech, calf, and bee take their food little by little, even so must the king draw a little from his subjects. He was, however, allowed a sixth part of the honey produced, a fairly generous allowance! Honey was so valued that if a man stole it, in his next life he became a gadfly. In certain cases honey was tabooed. A novice for the priesthood was ordered to abstain from honey, meats, perfumes, and women. Every month a feast was held in honour of the gods and of the souls of the departed, and if a novice ate honey at the feast he had to fast for three days and spend one day standing in water! It must have been difficult for the novice not to eat honey at these feasts, as it was one of the foods which the sacrificer, "being pure and attentive," had to offer to each guest, "successively inviting them to partake of each dish, proclaiming its qualities."[2]

This taboo against honey did not find favour with all students. Another writing, the *Satapatha Brahmana*, says that as honey is the supreme essence of plants, so the eating of it is like the absorbing essence of the Vedas, therefore let the student freely eat of it.[3] We see here the high value set upon honey, and in another passage of the *Satapatha Brahmana* it is said to be a life sap of the sun:

"Honey the winds pour forth for the righteous, honey the rivers; full of honey may the plants be for us! Honey by night and morn, rich in honey may the region of the earth be for us, honey the father Heaven! Rich in honey may the tree be for us, rich in honey the sun, full of honey the kine." This triplet, then, is honey; and honey being life sap, it is life's sap he thus puts into him [Agni].[4]

Honey was thus regarded as a "life-substance," and it was much used in ritual. In the *Satapatha Brahmana* the priests are compared to the bees and the sacrifice to the honey:

[1] See W. Crook, *Folklore of Northern India*, vol. ii, pp. 152, 257.
[2] For the Laws of Manu, see vol. xxv of Sacred Books of the East.
[3] Sacred Books of the East, *Satapatha Brahmana*, vol. 44, p. 90.
[4] Ibid., vol. 41, VII. 5, 1, 4.

"It is bees' honey," they say; for bees' honey means the sacrifice, and the bees that make the honey are no other than the officiating priests; and in like manner as the working bees make the honey increase, so do they [the priests] thereby strengthen the sacrifice.[1]

Here bees' honey is distinctly mentioned, but in the Vedas it is sometimes difficult to distinguish when *madhu* means honey and when it means the sacred drink *Soma*. In certain passages it might mean either. At one rite both are mentioned. In it the chief officiating priest takes the honey-cup, the *madhu-graha*, in a golden vessel and deposits it in the middle of the *soma-graha*, and afterwards the cup of honey is presented to the Brahman.[2] The Asvins also have a special ritual cup; the priest when presenting the *Asvina-graha* recites:

Mix ye the sacrifices, O Asvins, with that goad of yours, rich in honey and joyfulness;[3]

and they are invoked in another hymn to come in their chariot to the sacrifice, so that they may drink the honey drink.[4]

At many rites a honey mixture called the *madhuparka* was used. In the Grihya-Sutras, which are rules of Vedic domestic ceremonies, and also in the Laws of Manu, a householder is told to offer the *madhuparka* to certain visitors of importance. When the guest received the mixture, he recited this formula:

What is the honeyed, highest form of honey, and the enjoyment of food; by that honeyed highest form of honey and by that enjoyment of food, may I become highest, honeyed, and an enjoyer of food.[5]

There were certain rites connected with birth, marriage, and burials in which honey played a part. In the Laws of Manu (II. 29) a birth-rite is ordered to be performed for a male child, and, while special sacred formulae are being recited, he must be fed with gold, honey, and butter. Here the child is to be *fed* with gold. From the Grihya-Sutra, in a sort of commentary on the above

[1] *Satapatha Brahmana*, III. 4, 3, 14.
[2] Ibid., V. I, 2, 19, and V. I, 5, 28.   [3] Ibid., IV. I, 5, 17.
[4] Sacred Books of the East, *Vedic Hymns*, Mandala IV. 14, 1–4.
[5] See Sacred Books of the East, *Grihya-Sutras*, vol. xxix, pp. 89, 173, 197, *Laws of Manu*, vol. xxv, III. 119, 120.

rite, we learn that the child is only to be fed with honey and butter after they have been touched with a golden spoon or a piece of gold. The father in offering them says:

I give thee this honey food so that the gods may protect thee and that thou mayst live a hundred autumns in this world.[1]

It is also stated that the first solid food of children, given in the sixth month, is curds, honey, and ghee.[2]

These customs still exist. The Karnâtak Jains feed the new-born child with honey, but the father is not allowed to give this, as the idea prevails that the infant is likely to receive demoniacal influences through the father.[3] In the Deccan Brahmans drop honey into the mouth of new-born children; the high-class Hindus do the same, but use a gold spoon or ring, which is the same custom as that used in Vedic times. In the Punjab honey is sometimes used amongst the Mohammedans as the chief ingredient of *ghutti*, which is given to a new-born child by the most respected matron of the family during the birth ceremonies. In the rites following birth among the Hindus of the Punjab, honey and sweetmeats are passed round the head of the child in order to drive away the evil spirits.[4]

The influence of evil is also specially dreaded at marriage, and therefore honey is used to propitiate the malignant spirits. One of the sacred laws of the Aryas ordered that the *madhuparka* was to be offered at a wedding sacrifice. Among the Deccan Hindus at the present day, honey and curds are given to the bride-groom when he comes to the bride's house. In other districts of modern India honey is offered at a marriage ceremony, and when the newly married man kisses his bride he says:

Honey, this is honey, the speech of thy tongue is honey; in my mouth lives the honey of the bee, in my teeth lives peace.[5]

Sometimes also the mouth, brow, and other parts of the bride are smeared with honey.

1 Professor K. Knortz, *Die Insekten in Saga, Sitte und Literatur*, 1910, p. 2. Cf. L. D. Barnet, *Antiquities of India*, 1913, p. 138.
2 Grihya-Sutras, II. 1, 5.
3 W. Crooke, *Folklore of Northern India*, vol. i, p .277.
4 See Hastings, *Ency. Rel. and Ethics*, vol. vi, under "Honey."
5 Knortz, *Die Insekten in Saga, Sitte und Literatur*, p. 1.

Honey appears occasionally in burial rites. In the great funeral hymn of the Rig-Veda (x. 14) the priests are directed to pour to Yama, the god of Death, the oblation "most rich in honeyed sweetness." In a ritual described in the *Taittiriya*, the bones of the corpse were collected and placed in an urn filled with curds and honey, which was then hung on the branch of a tree. Another ancient book relates that a Brahman washed his mother's body with the five pure fluids—milk, curds, ghee, honey, and sugar.[1]

As in Egypt and Babylonia magical charms were much used. A number are given in the Artharva-Veda. The following was recited as a charm against snake poison:

With the charm that was found of yore by the Brahmans . . . with honey do I mix the rivers; the mountain peaks are honey. Honey are the rivers, Parushni and Sipala. Prosperity be to thy mouth, prosperity to thy heart. (A.-V., vi. 12, 3)

Another is a charm against the poison of scorpions and insects.

This herb, born of honey, dripping honey, sweet as honey, honeyed, is the remedy for the injuries. Moreover, it crushes insects. (A.-V., vii. 56,2)

A hymn to all magical and medicinal plants contains the following verse:

Honeyed are the roots of this herb, honey are their tips, honeyed are their middles, honeyed are their leaves, honeyed are their blossoms. They share in honey, are the food of immortality. (A.-V., viii. 7, 12)

In order to win and secure a woman's love this charm was used with licorice or sugar-cane:

This plant is born of honey, with honey do we dig for thee. Of honey art thou begotten, do thou make us full of honey. At the top of my finger may I have honey, my tongue's root sweetness of honey. Sweet as honey is my entrance, sweet as honey my departure. With my voice do I speak sweet as honey, may I become like honey! (A.-V., i, 34)

Honey has always been a symbol of sweetness, but here we get rather a surfeit of it!

In ancient India, as in Greece and Rome, there were many

---

[1] Govind S. Ghurye, "Egyptian Affinities of the Indian Funerary Practices," in *Anthropos*, vol. 18–19 (1923–4), Vienna, pp. 429 ff.

superstitions connected with bees, and swarming was anxiously observed, for if by chance a swarm went into a house, it denoted misfortune, which could only be averted by burning some pieces of the Udumbaba-tree. In the Grihya-Sutras a man is told that if bees make honey in his house, he must fast and sacrifice 108 pieces of Udumbaba wood, which had been smeared with curds, honey, and ghee, and recite: "No harm to us in our offering."[1]

To dream of bees resting on a building denoted that some evil would befall it, and the man who dreamed that bees entered his house would either soon lose his life or suffer some great misfortune. Nearly all the allusions to bees and honey in the *Dream Wisdom of the Jagadeva* denote some disaster as in Rome, except that he to whom a Brahman presents honey will become a king,[2] which is somewhat similar to the belief found in classical times that a swarm of bees settling on or near a man meant that he would attain sovereignty.

In all these allusions to bees and honey in the ancient writings of India we find no allusion to beekeeping, though it must have been a very ancient craft there, and the peasant of yore probably kept bees like the peasant of to-day near his bamboo hut in hives made of reeds.

There seems to be little to note about bees and honey in China and Japan. In the latter country we have not come across any mention of them in myths or folklore; in Japanese art bees are occasionally represented, and then always in connection with peony flowers.

In China in the seventeenth century there seem to have been plenty of bees, for Samuel Purchas writes in 1657:

There is great abundance [of honey] in China, for they wonderfully delight in keeping of Bees there, there is also very much wax, you may lade ships, nay Fleets therewith.[3]

The bee is mentioned in Chinese literature in the *Erh Ya*, a work assigned by the Chinese to the twelfth century before Christ, but notices of honey do not occur until some centuries after our era.

[1] Sacred Books of East, vol. xxix, p. 139.
[2] Julius von Negelein, "Der Traumschlüssel des Jagadevas " in *Religionsgeschichtliche Vorsuche und Vorarbeiten*, vol. xi.
[3] S. Purchas, *A Theatre of Politicall Flying Insects*, p. 140.

The word *fêng*[1] means both wasps and bees, but distinction is made by additional words, as honey-fêng, the honey-bee, family fêng, the domesticated bee, etc. The earth-fêng, the ground-bee, is said to carry off small caterpillars to feed its young, but the Chinese believe it has no offspring and trains these caterpillars to become young bees! On the K'un-lun mountains there is said to be a bee 10 feet long, with a sting that will kill an elephant. A hive of these bees would be unpleasant neighbours!

In the seventh and eighth centuries honey was mixed with opium. A short poem in praise of honey was written by Kuo P'o, who lived A.D. 276 to 324.

In the great *Chinese Encyclopedia* of 1727 there is a section on bees and a further section of about thirty pages on honey. Honey here includes "wood honey," sweet juices from dates, sugar-cane, etc., but "bees' honey" is dealt with fully. The Chinese have a few popular sayings about bees, as, "Bees make honey and men eat it," and "When the nest is destroyed, others [than the makers] get the honey."[2]

In ancient Chinese literature the line of demarcation between man and animal is so faint as hardly to exist at all. Man and beasts alike, both mentally and bodily, are said to be composed of *yang* (the good) and *yin* (the evil) substance. In their folktales man is often represented in all sorts of animal forms. Among insects there are many of man in *ant* form, and De Groot says there are similar stories with respect to bees and wasps.[3]

Beekeeping is a common industry in China at the present day. For hives the people mostly use a kind of basket smeared with mud; these are sometimes placed on pieces of wood driven into the side of the house fairly high up from the ground. The Chinese still destroy the bees in order to take the honey. They take swarms in one of their hats, which they smear inside with honey. The gentleman to whom the author is indebted for this information said he was told that the bees only understood Chinese, so when he took swarms he was careful to address them in that language!

[1] *e* as the *u* in "sung."
[2] For the above information I am indebted to Professor H. A. Giles of Cambridge.
[3] J. J. M. de Groot, *The Religious System of China*, Leyden, vol. iv, p. 280. I have been unable to trace any story in which man appears in bee form.

There are a few superstitions with regard to bees. According to the reports of missionaries, in some parts of China the beehives are turned round after the death of the owner,[1] a custom which we shall find in Britain; and the following passage from Wang Shi-Chin's *Chi-pei-yau-tan*, a work which was completed in 1553, shows that the Chinese believed swarms to be lucky.

The inhabitants of certain mountains south of Yau-yue are all in a lifelong ignorance of the calendar, but in its stead they observe punctually every morning and evening the hives which the family keeps. Whatever day the bees happen to swarm, is deemed unfailingly lucky. Should some business chance to be unfinished in the day, it is put off till another occasion of bees swarming. On such a day are also celebrated ordinarily the ceremonies of marriage and of beginning buildings. Thus, swarm in whose house the bees may, the servants and neighbours go round the place with the news; indeed the people never attempt to conceal the fact. Once upon a time a trading stranger came and sojourned in the locality for a year, and during that time he attentively recorded the days on which the bees swarmed, although numbering one hundred odd. On his return home he examined the calendar, and was astonished on finding those days without exception marked *dies albi*; whereas all other days on which the bees did not swarm were either marked unlucky or of no import. So wonderful is the mystic instinct of these animals which enables them to communicate freely with the Creator.[2]

Bees must, indeed, have been important to the people of this district! Probably when the literature and folklore of China is better known in the West, we shall learn more of how the people regarded the bee, and when they began to practise beekeeping.

We now turn to peoples of Western Asia, among whom we know that beekeeping was practised in the second millennium before our era.

[1] J. Ph. Glock, *Die Symbolik der Bienen*, p. 251.
[2] *Notes and Queries*, Series X, vol. x, p. 285. The quotation is signed "Kumagusu Minakata, Tanabe, Kii, Japan."

CHAPTER V

THE HITTITES, WESTERN ASIA, AND CRETE

*Cuneiform tablets—Bee legislation—Honey used in ritual—Great
Mother-goddess—Artemis of Ephesus—Bees on her statues—Gold
bee and plaques with bees' bodies found in Artemisium—The
Essenes—Chastity of bee—The Melissae—Bee jewellery found on
Aegean islands—"Bee-goddess"—Ephesian tesserae—Bees and lions
—Crete—Bee hieroglyph—Beekeeping*

ONE of the connecting links between the ancient civilizations of
India, Babylonia, and Assyria and those of Greece and Rome was
that of the Hittites. Excavations during the last thirty years have
shown that they were the leading power in Western Asia from
about 2800 to 700 B.C.; their influence extended eastwards to the
Euphrates, westwards to the Aegean, and southward to the country
of the Philistines. Unfortunately the Hittites' hieroglyphs have not
yet been deciphered, but among the discoveries at one of the
explored sites, Boghaz-keui in Cappadocia, were a number of clay
tablets, inscribed in Babylonian cuneiform writing, which com-
prised part of the archives of the Hittite kings about 1300 B.C.

Some of these tablets contain a code of laws, and among its
clauses two refer to bees. The first states:

If anyone steals bees out of a hive, formerly he had to pay 1 mina of
silver, now he need only pay 5 shekels, then he is set free.

The second says:

If anyone steals two or three beehives (*lit.* beehouses) he formerly
had to have his own hives destroyed, now he needs to pay 6 shekels of
silver. If anyone steals a hive and there are no bees in it, he needs to pay
3 shekels of silver.[1]

From these we learn that beekeeping was an established in-

[1] P. Maurus Witzel, *Hethitische Keilschrift-Urkunden*, Fulda, 1924, p. 171;
J. Friederich und H. M. Zimmern, "Hethitische Gesetze aus dem Staats-
archiv von Boghaz-keui," in *Der Alte Orient*, 1922, Jahrg. 23, Heft 2; Sir
Flinders Petrie, in *Ancient Egypt*, 1924, p. 24. 1 mina = 60 shekels; a shekel
equals roughly £2 now.

dustry, and that it was even then an ancient craft, for the clauses refer to other and greater penalties which had been enacted by an earlier code. The fact that the penalty was lessened probably shows that the number of hives was greater than in past times, and therefore they were proportionally not so valuable, though of course it might also denote that the later code was not so severe. These are the earliest bee-laws known, as no legislation on the subject has yet been discovered in Egypt or Babylonia.

As in Egypt, Babylonia, and India, honey was used in some of the religious rites of the Hittites. On one of the tablets directions are given for a ritual to be used when administering an oath. Meal was put into the man's hands and strewn about, then the text says:

> They are given a honeycomb and sheep's fat in their hands, it is put into a vessel, now he speaks, "As this fat is melted, he who breaks his oath to the gods, he shall be pressed out like a honeycomb, melted like fat."[1]

Among the substances to be prepared for another rite are two bowls of honey, and during the sacrifice the priest placed on a table little bowls, sixteen of which were filled with honey, olive oil, figs, grapes, and olives.[2] Honey is also mentioned in a ritual which has some points of resemblance to that of the Hebrew scapegoat. In it two jars of honey were placed by the sacrificing priest on the altar, and a number of other vessels were filled with honey and covered with figs.[3]

Scholars are agreed that the main feature of the religion of Western Asia, that is, of the countries which came under the Hittite influence, was the worship of a Great-Mother goddess, a fertility goddess, who appears under various names at different periods—Ma, Anaitis, Rhea, Cybele, Istar, Atergatis, Artemis, and many others—but her Hittite name is not known, although she is represented on the sculptures at Iasily-Kaya, near Boghazkeui, riding on a lioness and followed by a youth similarly mounted.

When the Hittite confederation broke up between 1200 and 700 B.C., many other religious influences were at work, but the ancient worship of the Great-Mother persisted, and became very

[1] P. Maurus Witzel, *Hethitische Keilschrift-Urkunden*, Fulda, 1924, p. 69.
[2] Ibid., pp. 99, 107.   [3] Ibid., p. 125.

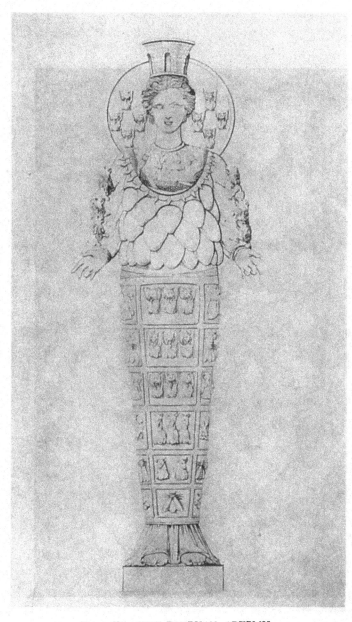

PLATE IV.—THE EPHESIAN ARTEMIS

(Naples Museum)

PLATE V.—GOLD JEWELLERY. EIGHTH TO THIRD CENTURY B.C.
(From British Museum)

1. Oak-leaf Wreath with Bee-clasp in Centre (not clearly seen in print). Cat. No. 1628
2. Three Rosettes with Bees' Bodies. Eighth to Seventh Century B.C. Cat. Nos. 890, 892, 897
3. Bee from Crete. Cat. No. 1239
4. Eros, holding a Plaque on which is a Bee. Cat. No. 1914–15

pronounced at Ephesus, which had been one of the Hittite har-
bours. Here she was known to
the Greeks as Artemis, and
later to the Romans as the great
"Diana of the Ephesians" (Acts
xix. 29). This Artemis, however, is not the Greek Artemis, but the old Asiatic Great-
Mother, as is clearly shown
in her archaic cult statues with
their many breasts, which are
the symbol of fertility. These
archaic statues have been found
not only at Ephesus but in
many other cities of Western
Asia, which shows that her cult
was widely spread.

Attempts have been made to
show that the rude shape of
the Mother-goddess was intended to represent that of a
bee, but they are so far without
direct evidence. The Hittites
were undoubtedly beekeepers,
and must have had a fairly
good idea of life in the hive,
yet there is no proof that their
Great-Mother had any con-
nection with a bee.[1] It is, however, an undisputed fact that
the bee figures in the worship
of the Ephesian Artemis. The
two statues of her which are
shown on Plate IV and Fig.
8, and on which the bee is
clearly seen, only date from the
Roman period, but various

Fig. 8—THE EPHESIAN ARTEMIS
(C. Menetrius: *Symbolica Dianae*,
Roma, 1657)

[1] See Sir W. Mitchell Ramsay, "Greek Religion," in Hastings's *Dictionary of the Bible*, vol. v, pp. 114 ff.

ornaments, connecting her worship with the bee, found among the ruins of the celebrated Artemisium, date back to the eighth or seventh century before Christ. Among these were a beautiful gold pin head, in the form of a bee, illustrated on Plate VI, Fig. 5 (*a*, *b*), and three small plaques composed of flowers or leaves alternating with bees' bodies (see Plate V, Fig. 2).[1]

The head of the priestly hierarchy at Ephesus was for centuries known as the *Megabyzos*, who was a eunuch, and Strabo says he was obliged to appoint virgins as his colleagues in the priesthood.[2] There were also officials connected with the worship of Artemis, who were called *Essenes*. The word Essene means a *King Bee*, and Pausanias mentions in his well-known work (written about A.D. 150) that these Essenes were bound to observe chastity for a year.[3]

It is at this point in our study of the history of the bee that the belief in her chastity begins to emerge, a belief which lasted through classical times, through the Middle Ages down to quite modern times, and which, of course, as regards the worker bee, has a foundation in fact.

There has been much discussion as to the original title of the virgin priestesses of the Ephesian Artemis. It is well known, as we shall see in Chapter IX, that the priestesses of several of the Greek Mother-goddesses, as Rhea, Demeter, and others, were called the *Melissae*, the *Bees*, and at the beginning of our era the priestesses of the Great-Mother Cybele were still known by that title,[4] but we have no authentic use of this name at Ephesus. The only reference is the following line from a lost tragedy of Aeschylus, the "Priestesses," but it is doubtful whether the quotation refers to the Ephesian goddess or to Artemis of Tauris:

Hold your peace! The Beekeepers are at hand to open the house of Artemis.[5]

It seems probable that the virgin character of the priestesses

---

[1] G. Hogarth, *Excavations at Ephesus*, London, 1908, Pls. V. 5; VIII. 22; v. 26, 31. Numerous crude female figures were also found, clearly representing the Mother-goddess.   [2] Strabo., XIV. 1, 23.

[3] Paus., VIII. 13, 1. Pausanius was a great traveller and antiquary.

[4] Lactantius, *Div. Inst.*, I. 22. Greek, *Melissa* = bee.

[5] The line is quoted by Aristophanes, *Frogs*, 1283.

of the Great-Mother had its origin in Asia, not in Greece, and if the priestesses of the Ephesian Artemis were *Melissae*, they could be paralleled with the *Essenes*, whose existence at Ephesus is undisputed.

At Camiros in Rhodes several articles have been found which were evidently connected with the worship of Artemis Ephesia. One is a series of seven gold plaques (illustrated on Plate VI), on each of which is a winged figure of the goddess with a lion on each side of her. Several other examples of this winged Artemis with lions were found, as well as gold plaques on which she is represented not only with wings but also with the body of a bee, the "Bee-goddess," as it has been named, which is illustrated on Plate VI (centre).[1]

In a grave on Thera, an island much influenced by Aegean culture, other pieces of jewellery were found on which is depicted a female head with a bee's body, very similar to those of Camiros; they have been named "Bee-demons," but they were probably also connected with the worship of Artemis. They are represented on Plate VI (top row).[2]

Had this "Bee-goddess" priestesses at Ephesus named after her in the seventh or sixth century B.C.? It is possible, but the name *Melissa* disappeared there, and in later times her priestesses were known by other names.[3] The Bee-goddess may, however, have been one of the many divinities which helped to form the very complex type of Artemis Ephesia, and the bee, which figures on her statues, may be a reminder of this. It is certainly an undoubted fact that from the earliest times when coinage first began to be used, the *bee* figures on Ephesian coins. It appears on electron money before 545 B.C., and continued until late Roman times· Several of these coins are figured on Plate VIII.

There is another link between the bee and Ephesus. In early Imperial times are found some curious bronze *tesserae*, with a

[1] These specimens are in the Museum of Fine Arts, Boston, U.S.A. There are similar ones in the British Museum; they are dated to the seventh century.

[2] E. Pfuhl, *Mitteilungen des kais. deut. arch. Institut, Athen. Abteilung*, vol. 28, p. 225.

[3] For discussion of priestesses of Artemis, see C. Picard, *Éphèse et Claros*. Bibliothèque des Ecoles Françaises d'Athène et de Rome, Paris, 1922, pp. 231, 522 ff., etc. Picard mentions a Phrygian town named *Melissa*, where Alcibiades was killed in 404 B.C.

stag on one side and a bee on the other, both of which are among the most ancient symbols of the Ephesian cult. No satisfactory explanation has been given why these tesserae were minted, for numismatists are agreed that they were not current coins. One of them is represented in Fig. 9; the bee has round it a mysterious inscription, which has been variously interpreted.[1] It contains an allusion to beeswax, and one scholar has suggested that the tesserae were druggists' tokens for the purpose of advertising the sale of beeswax. Another explanation is that the inscription might be one of the mysterious magic formulae used as charms,

and that the tokens might be charms to call the bees home when swarming; but the most plausible solution seems to be that the tesserae were connected with the secret rites of Artemis, especially as the stag of the goddess is on the reverse side of the tokens.[2]

FIG. 9.—
EPHESIAN
TESSERA

One of the most important animals connected with the worship of the Asiatic Great-Mother was the lion, and it is a curious fact that we often find a connection between bees and lions. At the old Hittite town of Carchemish sculptures have been found of the goddess on her lion throne and behind her a long line of priestesses bearing various articles. We do not suggest that these were called *Melissae*, but in the jewellery illustrated on Plate VI we see how the goddess with her lions merges in or is connected with the "Bee-goddess."

In a grave in the north-west Peloponnesus were found two pin heads, dated fifth century B.C., which are now in the Boston Museum of Fine Arts. They are of most beautiful workmanship, and are reproduced on Plate VIII. The larger one consists of an Ionic capital with a central cone made of acanthus leaves. From the volutes spring four *lions*, their forepaws resting on the cone, and between the forepaws of each rises a spiral ornament; in the spaces between the spirals are four *bees*, modelled with absolute realism,

[1] This was drawn from a specimen lent to the writer by Dr. A. B. Cook of Cambridge, who suggests that the legend, in which there is evidently a word missing, might be translated something like: "This is how Mistress Beeswax looked at the Hive-shaker."

[2] See article by B. V. Head in *Numismatic Chronicle*, 4th series, vol. viii (1908), pp. 281 ff.

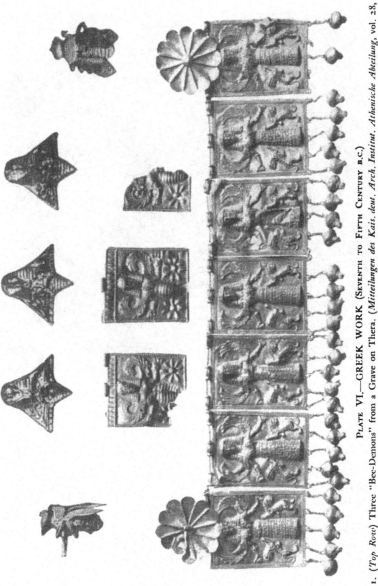

PLATE VI.—GREEK WORK (SEVENTH TO FIFTH CENTURY B.C.)

1. (*Top Row*) Three "Bee-Demons" from a Grave on Thera. (*Mitteilungen des Kais. deut. Arch. Institut. Athenische Abteilung*, vol. 28, p. 225, 1901)

2. (*Centre*) Three Plaques of "Bee-Goddess" from Camiros, Rhodes. Seventh Century. (Museum of Fine Arts, Boston, Mass.)

3. (*On Sides*) (*a, b*) Pin Head from Ephesus. (Eighth to Seventh Century B.C.)

4. Artemis and Lions. From Camiros, Rhodes. Seventh Century. (British Museum Catalogue of Jewellery, No. 1128)

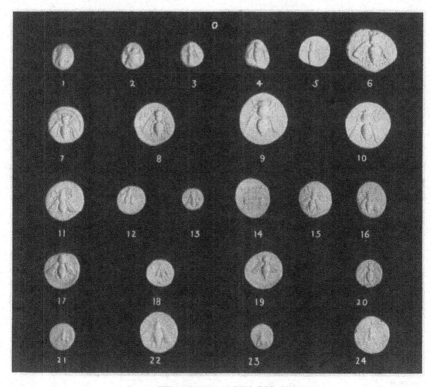

Plate VII.—COINS WITH BEE TYPE

(From the British Museum)

Figures 1 to 16.   Coins of Ephesus

    Figs. 1 and 2. Electron. Sixth Century
    B.C. or earlier.

    Figs. 3 and 4. Silver before 480 B.C.

    Fig. 5. 480–450 B.C.

    Fig. 6. 450–415 B.C.

    Fig. 7. 415–394 B.C.

    Figs. 8 and 9. 394–387 B.C.

    Fig. 10. 387–295 B.C.

    Figs. 11–14. 305–288 B.C.

    Figs. 15–16. 280–258 B.C.

Figures 17 to 20.   Coins of Crete

    Fig. 17. Elyrus. 400–200 B.C.

    Fig. 18. Aptera. 200–76 B.C.

    Fig. 19. Hyrtacina. 400–300 B.C.

    Fig. 20. Praesus. 400–300 B.C.

Figures 21 to 23.   Coins of Aegean
Islands

    Fig. 21. Julis. Second to First Century
    B.C.

    Fig. 22. Coressia. Second to First
    Century B.C.

    Fig. 23. Syros. Third to First Century
    B.C.

Coins of Troas

Fig. 24. Gentinus. Fourth Century B.C.

even to the veining of the wings. The smaller pinhead is not quite so elaborate; the centre is a conventionalized rosebud, with three of the petals turned down, so that they rest on a small globe below. Between them are three *lions*, and on the bud itself there are three *bees*, each sucking from a small bud, and between the bees are three tiny sphinxes. As these pinheads were found in Greece it cannot be proved that they had anything to do with the worship of the Ephesian Artemis, but as they were found in a grave, they would have some religious significance, and were probably connected with the worship of one of the "Great-Mothers," if not with that of Artemis.[1]

Another link between the lion and the bee is found on an Etruscan gem (Fig. 10). The inhabitants of Etruria are held by scholars to be connected with those of Western Asia, and this gem may be a remembrance of the link with their original home.

The Great-Mother goddess was also worshipped by the early inhabitants of Crete, whose position in the Eastern Mediterranean brought her into contact with the Hittites and other Western Asian peoples. The Cretan Great-Mother is also accompanied, like the Hittite goddess, with lions who

Fig. 10.—ETRUSCAN LIONESS AND BEE, FROM CORNUTO
(Furtwängler: *Antike Gemmen*, Pl. xviii, Fig. 7)

guard her on each side, and from Crete these guardian lions passed over to Greece, where they are to be seen on the Lion Gate at Mycenae. Some of the earliest Greek myths about bees and honey, which appear to be indigenous in Crete, are those connected with the Mother-goddess Rhea and the birth of her son Zeus. A small golden bee, found in Crete and now in the British Museum (see Plate v), is of Greek workmanship, and may possibly be connected with these myths, which will be discussed later.

---

[1] G. Perrot and C. Chipiez, *History of Art in Phoenicia*, 1885, vol. ii, p. 385, Illustrate a pendant on which two heads of a somewhat Egyptian type alternate with bulls' heads and *bees*. It is said to have beeen found in Milo; the workmanship resembles that found at Camiros.

In Chapter IV the lion and bee were noted in connection with Kama, the Indian God of Love. Other connections will be noted later.

Besides her intercourse with Western Asia, Crete had early relations with Egypt, probably from pre-dynastic times (see Fig. 11). Unfortunately the key to the Cretan script has not yet been found, but though it developed independently of Egypt, yet there are some signs which much resemble Egyptian hieroglyphs,

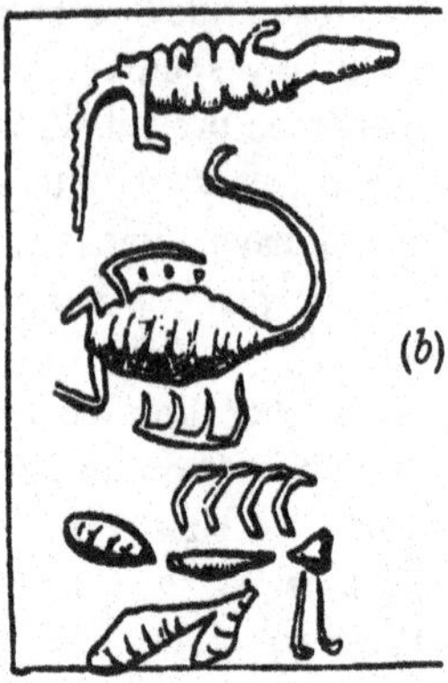

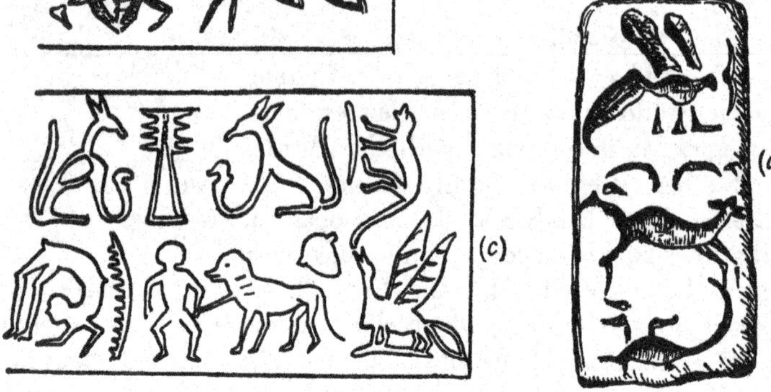

FIG. 11.—(a, b, c) EGYPTIAN CYLINDERS WITH CRETAN CHARACTERISTICS
(d) PRISM SEAL FROM KARNAK
(Sir Arthur Evans: *Scripta Minoa*)

and which Sir Arthur Evans, one of the first excavators in Crete, thinks may be due to direct borrowings. Among these are the *bee* and the *palace* sign in a simpler form, which are grouped together in such a way that they probably denote a royal title (Fig. 12).[1]

Several bee hieroglyphs have been found on Cretan sealings

---

[1] Sir Arthur Evans, *Palace of Minos*, 1921, p. 281.

(see Fig. 13 (*a*)); within the abdomen of one of these bees there are some grains, and as these same grains appear in jars (Fig. 13 (*b*)), it is possible that they denote honey.[1] The early existence of bee-

(*a*) Minoan   (*b*) Egyptian

FIG. 12.—"PALACE" AND "BEE" SIGNS

(Sir Arthur Evans: *Scripta Minoa*, p. 240)

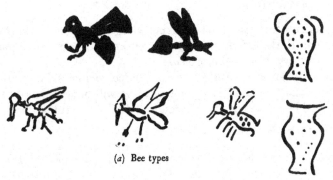

(*a*) Bee types

(*b*) Jars (containing honey)

FIG. 13.—CRETAN BEE HIEROGLYPHS

keeping in Crete has been proved by the discovery of a terra-cotta beehive at Phaistos (Fig. 14), which is of the same type as those still used on the island.[2] The wax was probably used for making

[1] Evans, *Scripta Minoa*, p. 212.
[2] Angelo Mosso, *Palaces of Crete*, 1907, p. 154.

candles, for in rooms without windows candlesticks or sconces
have been found, which are too small to have held torches.[1] A
sealing of a funnel-shaped vessel also has the "honey" grains in it,
and it may have been used for straining honey. Sir Arthur Evans
suggests that another sealing of a hand in connection with a bee
(Fig. 15) might possibly stand for a glove used in extracting honey
from the hive.[2] If so the Cretans must have been expert beekeepers,

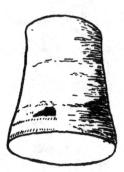

FIG. 14.—CRETAN BEEHIVE
FROM PHAISTOS
(Angelo Mosso: *Palaces of Crete*)

FIG. 15.—HAND, OR GLOVE,
AND BEE ON CRETAN SEALING
(Sir Arthur Evans: *Scripta Minoa*)

and perhaps they passed on their knowledge to the mainland, for
it is through the Greeks that we owe our knowledge of the Cretan
words for bee, hive, and propolis.[3]

Before, however, passing on to Europe to inquire what the
Greeks and Romans knew about bees, we will notice allusions to
bees and honey among the Hebrew and Mohammedan writers.

[1] G. Glotz, *The Aegean Civilization*, 1925, p. 183.

[2] *Scripta Minoa*, p. 184. Professor Glotz goes so far as to say that "professional beekeepers had an emblem, a bee together with a glove, and they
possessed secrets which they taught the Greeks" (*The Aegean Civilization*,
p. 169).

[3] *Sphex* = bee; *simblos* = hive; *kerinthos* = propolis.

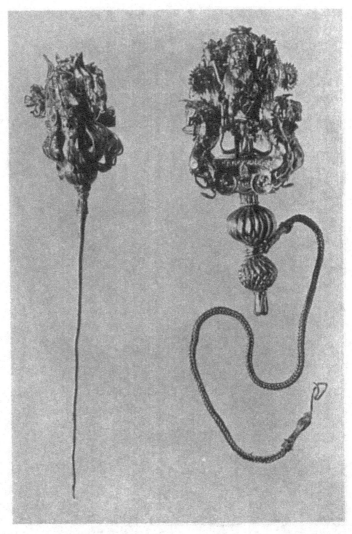

PLATE VIII.—TWO PIN HEADS WITH LIONS AND BEES. FOUND IN
NORTH-WEST PELOPONNESUS. FIFTH CENTURY B.C.

(Museum of Fine Arts, Boston, Mass. By kind permission of Dr. L. D. Caskey)

PLATE IX.—GREEK BLACK-FIGURED AMPHORA FROM VULCI,
SHOWING LAIOS, KELEOS, KERBEROS, AND AIGOLIS, AND THE
SACRED BEES IN THE DICTAEAN CAVE

(British Museum Catalogue of Vases, II, No. B177)

CHAPTER VI

THE HEBREWS AND MOHAMMEDANS

Wild bees numerous in Palestine—Earliest mention of beekeeping—
Honey as article of export—First-fruits of honey—"Wild honey"
—Samson and bees—Notices of bees and honey in Bible—Honey
not allowed in sacrifice—Saul's taboo on honey—Honey as present
—Septuagint rendering of Proverbs vi. 6—Bodies preserved in
honey—"Curds and honey"—Beekeeping in Talmud—Hives—Regu-
lations about hives—Beekeeping in Arabia—The Koran—Sura XVI,
"The Bee"—Stories of Mohammed—Natural History of Ad-Amiri
—Bees compared to the Faithful—Honey a remedy for all illnesses—
Allusions to bees in early Mohammedan poetry—Queen of Sheba
and Solomon

THOUGH the land of Palestine was so often alluded to as the land
"flowing with milk and honey," which shows how valued those
articles were, yet there is no direct mention of beekeeping in the
Bible, and therefore it is impossible to say at what stage in their
history the Hebrews domesticated the wild bees which from time
immemorial have lived in the numerous clefts and cavities of the
limestone rocks of their land.

Beekeeping was of great antiquity in the neighbouring lands of
the Hittites, and therefore it is probable that it was an old craft
among the Jews, although Philo the philosopher (born about
20 B.C.) is the first to mention it. He says the sect of the Essenes,
who lived not far from the Dead Sea, kept bees.[1] There are many
allusions to bees in the Talmud, which was compiled in the first
centuries of our era, and Josephus mentions honey as a product
of the Plain of Jericho, both honey "from bees" and artificial
honey, the modern "dibs."[2]

It is possible that beekeeping was not practised till after the
Exile, though it was probably earlier, for in Genesis (xliii. 11)
and in Ezekiel (xxvii. 17) honey is mentioned as an article of
export; this might be honey from wild bees, but in 2 Chronicles
(xxxi. 5) it is said that the people brought the "first-fruits" of honey

[1] *De Vita Contemp.*, II. 663. In Chapter V it was noted that priestly officials
at Ephesus were called *Essenes*. Whether there is any connection between them
and the Jewish sect would be difficult to say.   [2] *De Bell. Jud.*, 4, 8, 3.

to Hezekiah, which seems to support the view that the craft was an established one at that period.

John the Baptist is stated to have eaten *wild* honey in the wilderness, which has been taken to infer that honey was also obtained from domesticated bees. Diodorus Siculus, however, who lived about the same time, calls the honeydew, which exudes from trees and shrubs, by the name of "wild honey," and Suidas (A.D. 1000) in his Lexicon wrote that "the forerunner also ate locusts and wild honey, which is gathered from the trees and commonly called *manna*"; so the "wild honey" of the Gospels may either refer to honey taken from the wild bees' nests or to this honeydew.[1]

Among the Hebrews there are no mythological stories about bees such as we find among many peoples, no beliefs that they were divine or semi-divine creatures, and this is easily understood when we remember that the Hebrew religion was henotheistic from very early times—the Jews were forbidden by the Mosaic Law to make any graven images—and therefore they have no myths like those of the Egyptian, Babylonian, Indian, and Grecian divinities, and they do not seem to have absorbed many of the folk-beliefs of their neighbours.

There is one story, however, in the Book of Judges, that of Samson, which scholars now consider as a collection of myths, perhaps connected with solar worship. The name Samson has been connected with "Shamash," the Sun-god of the Babylonians; his father, Manoah, lived near Beth-Shemash, the house or temple of the Sun. As the cult of the sun was non-existent among the Hebrews the place must be related to an older worship. The episode of the lion and the bees in its dead carcase may belong to the original myth, but the fact that Samson, a Nazarite, touched the body of a dead animal shows that the *Nazarite* is an addition to the original story. Riddles were a very favourite occupation in the East, and Samson's riddle, "Out of the eater came forth meat, out of the strong came forth sweetness," with its answer, "What is sweeter than honey, what is stronger than a lion?" is probably one of the oldest known.[2]

---

[1] E. J. Jenkinson, *The Unwritten Sayings of Jesus*, 1925, pp. 80–81.

[2] For the Samson myths, see S. Reinach, *Cultes et Religions*, Paris, 1912, vol. iv, pp. 148–166. Cf. O. Gruppe, *Griech. Mythologie*, vol. i, p. 248.

It has been suggested that underlying this story is the belief in the reproduction of bees from decaying carcases, for though bees will never enter a decaying carcase, yet in that hot country the lion's body would soon become desiccated enough for a swarm to take possession of it, and hence the belief might have arisen. But the story is probably much older than the belief, and it is more probable that if we could trace it farther back, we might find a connection between the lion of the Mother-goddess and the bees, that mysterious connection between the two animals which we noted in the last chapter.[1]

One other story in the same Book of Judges may show some link with bees. The name "Deborah" signifies in Hebrew a *Bee*, and the name "Barak," *lightning*; Deborah sat under a tree to judge the people, and it was Barak whom she chose to lead the forces of Israel against Sisera; it has been suggested that this may be a dim remembrance of the tree, struck by lightning, in which resided the sacred bees.[2]

In Hebrew literature bees and their products are often used in a metaphorical sense. In Psalm 118 (verse 12) the enemies of Israel are compared with angry bees, who surround him; in Deuteronomy (i. 44) the Amorites attack the Israelites like angry bees issuing from the rocks. In other cases the bees are thought of as fierce creatures, using their stings—the Palestinian bees are said to be much fiercer than ours—but usually it is the good qualities of bees and their sweet honey which are emphasized. In Ecclesiasticus (xi. 3) Jesus, the son of Sirach, says:

The bee is smalle among the fowles, yet doth its fruits pass in sweetness.[3]

The judgments of the Lord are "sweeter than honey and the honeycomb" (Psa. xix. 10), his words are "sweeter than honey to my mouth" (Psa. cxix. 103), and the wise son of Sirach says the

---

[1] On the so-called "Ring of Nestor" two insects are depicted which Sir A. Evans takes to be butterflies (see his article in *Jour. Hell. Studies*), but M. P. Nilsson (*The Minoan and Mycenaean Religion*, pp. 549 ff.) says that they are hymenoptera, and thinks that the scenes on the Ring represent some cult rites. If it were possible to identify the insect with a *bee*, we have here another example of the bee and lion, for the latter occupies one of the divisions of the Ring.

[2] For theories connecting bees and sacred trees, see Dr. Rendel Harris, *Boanerges*, p. 330.   [3] From a translation of 1603.

same of wisdom (Ecclus. xxiii. 20). Friendly words are as honey-combs (Prov. v. 3; xvi. 24); and both honey and honeycomb are mentioned in connection with the bridegroom (v. 1), and the bride (iv. 11) in the Song of Solomon.

In these passages there is no doubt that bees' honey is meant, but in other passages it may denote not only bees' honey but also the syrup of figs and dates, which under the name of "dibs" is still common in the East; but considering the large quantity of real honey produced in Palestine, there seems to be no reason for supposing that *debash* (Heb. = honey) means anything but bees' honey.[1]

The Mosaic Law forbade the use of honey as a sacrifice (Lev. ii. 11). There are several views as to the reason of this prohibition. Philo thought it was forbidden because the bees came from decayed flesh, and therefore the honey was unclean. More probable are the opinions that it was forbidden either because it was a customary offering among the heathen to their deities or that it was liable to ferment and was therefore prohibited like milk and leavened bread. The fact, however, that the Promised Land was one of "milk and honey" shows that the Hebrews valued honey as a food, and the son of Sirach enumerates honey as one of the "principal things for the use of man's life" (Ecclus. xxxix. 26).

In his struggles against the Philistines, Saul, in order to propitiate Yahveh and secure his help, laid a solemn taboo on the people forbidding them to take food that day. His men, weary and discouraged for want of food, came to a wood where they found bees' nests so full of honey that it was dripping on the ground, but none dared touch it. The king's son, Jonathan, who had not heard of his father's prohibition, tasted the honey and was much refreshed, "his eyes were enlightened." The soldiers told him of the taboo, but he replied that they would have done much better if they had also eaten some (2 Sam. xiv).

That honey was considered suitable as a present to those from whom a favour was to be asked is to be gathered from the passage in Genesis (xliii. 11), where Jacob sends honey among his other presents to the mighty governor of Egypt, Joseph; and Jeroboam sends his wife with a cruse of honey to Ahijah the prophet, entreating him to heal his sick son (1 Kings xiv. 3). In this latter case

[1] See Hastings, *Dictionary of the Bible*, p. 264.

honey may have been sent as an acceptable medicine; it was a favourite ingredient in remedies for the eyes, and Ahijah suffered from blindness.

It is strange that there is no mention of the industry of the bee in the Hebrew version of the Old Testament, it is from the ant that the sluggard has to learn, "consider her ways and be wise" (Prov. vi. 6). In the Septuagint version, however, we read the addition:

Go to the bee, and learn how diligent she is, and what a noble work she produces, whose labours kings and private men use for their use, she is desired and honoured by all, and though weak in strength she values wisdom and prevails.[1]

Wax is only mentioned a few times in the Bible, and then only in a figurative sense. Josephus states that the body of Aristobolus was preserved in honey for some time before his burial in Jerusalem; and Herod I is said to have kept the body of Marianne for two years in honey, for he loved her even after she was dead.

The passage in Isaiah that the Lord will hiss for the bee that is in the land of Assyria (vii. 18) has already been commented upon (see Chapter III). In the same chapter of Isaiah is an account of a sign that shall be given to King Ahaz that his enemies will not prevail; a child will be born, who is to be fed with curds and honey (v. 15). This feeding with curds and honey has been given various interpretations; one of the most interesting is that it alludes to the custom, which has its origin in mythology—particularly in Iranian mythology—of feeding infants with honey and curds, a custom which possibly descended through the Babylonians to the Hebrews, and by another line to Greeks, who described the food of the infant Zeus as milk and honey.[2] However this may be, milk (or curds) and honey have been used as the first food of children in many nations. Milk was the child's natural food, honey endowed him with sweetness, and the gifts of eloquence, wisdom, and song; among the Germanic peoples if a baby's lips had once been smeared with honey, its life might not be taken (see p. 160).

[1] This addition also exists in Arabic versions, and it is quoted by Origen, Clement, Jerome, and others.

[2] See G. B. Gray, International Critical Commentary, Isaiah, Edinburgh, 1912, p. 160.

From none of the passages quoted above do we learn anything about beekeeping among the Hebrews, but some facts concerning it are to be gleaned from the Talmud. The hives were made of straw or reeds, and were of different forms, some square, some round, and one is mentioned with a small window. This may have been an observation hive like the one attributed to Aristotle (see next chapter). In one book a bee-house is spoken of as big as a room; the hives were placed one above another, flight holes pierced on two or four sides, and they were protected from the sun by a straw roof.

Some passages allude to regulations about hives; they must be at certain distances from the villages so that the bees do not sting the inhabitants. A man might go into a neighbour's field and cut off a bough on which his swarm had settled, and only had to pay the value of the bough. The Mischna attributes to Joshua the regulation that no water must be given to bees on the Sabbath, because they can fetch it for themselves. If this statement is true, beekeeping could be traced back to the early occupation of Canaan, but there is no confirmation of it. In buying honeycombs from a hive the two outside ones must be left, so that the bees may have food during the winter. In one passage it is said that the *medaph* must be kept clean; the *medaph* is explained by one commentator as a vessel in which burning cowdung was put for use in smoking the bees when taking honey; another says it was a board which was placed before the hives so that the bees might rest on it when weary on their homeward flight.

The Talmud also states that manna was six times sweeter than honey (just as the Greeks said that ambrosia was nine times sweeter), that honey was a remedy for various diseases, as gout and heart troubles, for healing wounds of man and beast, and that it was good for mixing with wine.[1]

To-day apiculture is carried on in Palestine to a considerable extent, and honey and bees are exported. Some of the hives used are still very primitive; they are made of hollow cylinders of earth, mixed with chopped straw, about thirty inches long and ten across, much like the Egyptian hives illustrated on Plate III.

---

[1] For these Talmud references, see Bessler, *Geschichte der Bienenzucht*, pp. 16–20; Glock, *Die Symbolik der Bienen*, p. 148; Gmelin, in *Witzgalls Buch von der Biene*, pp. 14–15.

There are also cylindrical hives made of basketwork, pitched inside and out with a composition of mud and cowdung. These hives are piled tier above tier, pyramid fashion, and roofed over with thatch or covered with a mat. At the end of last century it was the custom in many parts to move the wickerwork hives higher up the mountains in summer in order to take advantage of the later flowers.[1] It would be interesting to know if this custom came from Egypt; if it did it would be an argument in favour of beekeeping among the Jews in early times.

We have no notice of beekeeping in the neighbouring country of Arabia earlier than the testimony of Pliny that one tribe there was noted for its ample supply of honey and wax,[2] which seems to imply beekeeping at that period—first century A.D.; and it appears probable that the Arabians derived their knowledge of it from Greco-Roman sources. It is not until the time of Mohammed and his successors that we learn anything definite about it.

As Mohammedanism is monotheistic no traces are to be found of any mythological or cult reverence for the bee, but its work and industry was held in high honour, and Mohammed named one of the books of the Koran (Sura xvi) "The Bee." Here we read:

Thy Lord has taught the bee saying, "provide thee houses in the mountains, and in the trees, and in the hives which men do build for thee. Feed, moreover, on every kind of fruit, and walk the beaten paths of the Lord." From its belly cometh forth a fluid of varying hues, which yieldeth medicine for men. Verily in this is a sign for those who consider.

Other chapters of the Koran are called the "Ant" and the "Spider," but the Bee is the only animal whom Mohammed says is addressed by the Lord himself. An old Arabic commentator on the above passage says that honey is of various colours according to the flowers which the bees visit; and he also adds that honey is not only good for eating, but is very useful in illnesses, and relates the following story:

A man went to Mohammed and told him his brother had violent pains in his body, and the Prophet told him to give the sick man honey. He did as he was told, but soon came back to say his brother was no

---

[1] W. M. Thomson, *The Land and the Book,* vol. ii, p. 465.
[2] *Nat. Hist.,* VI. 32.

better. Mohammed answered, "Go back and give him more honey, for
God speaks the truth, thy brother's body lies." When the honey was
taken again, the sick man, thanks to the grace of God, recovered
immediately.[1]

In the "Sunna," the traditions of Mohammed, which is regarded
by his followers as a canonical book, it is related that in a visit to
Paradise the Prophet saw a tree, which bore fruit sweeter than
honey. There in the seventh heaven Mohammed found Christ,
who commanded the angel Gabriel to hand him three goblets,
one of which was filled with honey. From this we gather that it
must be a Muslim belief that there are bees in Paradise; also
the Koran (Sura xlvii. 17, 18) says there are rivers of honey in
the Paradise promised to the god-fearing.

There is a curious book on Animals, written in 1371 by Kam
al nil-Din ad-Amiri, which gives a picture of the beekeeping
of that period. His beelore seems to have largely derived from
Aristotle and Vergil, though he quotes other Arabic writers.
Ad-Amiri remarks that bees, the "honey-flies," are the only flies
who go to heaven, all the other flies go to hell. The bees are
obedient to the orders of the Lord, they build their houses in
three places, the mountains, the trees, and lastly the hives which
man prepares for them (referring to the passage in the Koran
quoted above).

Look, then, how they yield obedience, even to the taking of their
houses before they eat, for they take to them first and when they have
established their houses they go and eat of the fruits.

Honey is the sweet matter which the bees find sprinkled on
the flowers and leaves; they take their young from the plants in
their mouths. This is evidently from Vergil (Geor. IV. 200),
for Ad-Amiri is not clear how bees are generated, and though
he knows that the workers are female and the drones, who do
no work, male, yet he says that the eggs are placed by the bees
in the cells and that they then brood over them like birds over eggs.
The bees obey their leader, who only leaves the hive with a
swarm and who has no sting (of course a mistake). If the king is
no use, the bees conduct him out of the hive and kill him. The

[1] Al Beidawi, quoted by Bessler, *Geschichte der Bienenzucht*, p. 21.

slaughter of the drones is noted, and a story told of a wise Greek who said to his pupils, "Be like the bees in their hives." They asked him how the bees acted in their hives, and he replied, "They suffer no lazy men in it, but turn them out, because they only occupy room, devour honey, and teach sloth to the others."

The bees hate uncleanness, and therefore carry all their refuse from the hive; they only drink pure waters and eat only as much honey as will satisfy their hunger. If the store of honey is low, they put water into it so that it may go farther. The colour of the honey varies according to the kind of bee and its pasturage, the taste also varies for the same reasons. The best honey is in the comb, and it is excellent as a medicine, but if it is cooked in water it loses its healing properties. It is specially good for the eyes, and it is a good thing to give a dog if bitten by another!

Dreaming of and appearances of bees had their significance among the Arabs as well as in most other nations. Ad-Amiri relates that Abdulmumin bin Ali when a boy was once asleep in the house when his father, who was making clay jars, heard a swarm of bees, saw them envelop his son, lift him up, and then without hurting him, put him down again. A soothsayer said it meant that the peoples of the East would gather round him; which thing came to pass.

Another Arabic writer, Ibn al-Athir, who died in 1232, compares the bees with the Faithful, for they were intelligent, wise, did little harm, did good to fruit blossoms, produced useful articles, worked in the daytime, disliked dirt and evil smells, did not eat of food gathered by others, and were obedient to their prince. Also there were certain things like darkness, clouds, storms, smoke, water, and fire which prevented bees from working; in like manner there were hindrances to the work of the Faithful, the darkness of indiscretion, the clouds of doubt, the storm of revolt, the smoke of the prohibited water of superfluity, the fire of lust.

Another writer, Ibn Magih, relates that the Prophet said:

Honey is a remedy for every illness, and the Koran is a remedy for all illnesses of the mind, therefore I recommend to you both remedies, the Koran and honey.

The Arabians were great lovers of honey, and not honey only, for they liked to pull off the hinder part of the bees' bodies and then suck the honey, a custom still to be found among some African tribes. This practice was strongly condemned by Ad-Amiri, who says that the Prophet did not approve of it.

In the *Arabian Nights' Tales* there is a story of a bee which carried crumbs from the Sultan's table to feed a poor blind sparrow, and the poet Nazimi (*c.* 1200) tells the following tale:

A hornet seized a bee, intending to devour it. The bee begged for its life and said, "My hive contains so much honey, I myself am of so little worth, why do you not go to the hive and leave me in peace?" The hornet replied, "The hive is sweet because of the honey in it, but you must be sweeter as you are the source and spring of the honey."[1]

We end this chapter with one more story:

It is said by the Rabbis that when the Queen of Sheba visited King Solomon she held out to him two wreaths, one of artificial, the other of genuine flowers. Unable to discover which were the real flowers, the king caused the casement to be opened, when, lo! a flight of bees entered and lighted on the natural flowers.[2]

So the bees were wiser than the wise king!

[1] For references to Ad-Amiri, see Gmelin, in *Witzgalls Buch von der Biene*, pp. 15–20; and W. C. Cotton, *My Bee Book*, London, 1842, pp. 346–349. Gmelin says that Ad-Amiri's book was in manuscript until 1875, when it was published at Bulak near Cairo.

[2] E. J. Jenkinson, *The Unwritten Sayings of Jesus*, 1925, p. 155.

CHAPTER VII

BEEKEEPING IN GREECE

Allusions to bees in Homer—No beekeeping—Hives mentioned by Hesiod—Legislation of Solon—Honey of Hymettus—Pythagoras— Democritus—Herodotus—Xenophon and poisonous honey—Xeno-phon's Economics—Aristotle—Observation hives—Alexandrian writers—Honey and wax merchants—Uses of honey and wax— Honey much used in food

IF the Cretans did take the knowledge of beekeeping to the mainland prior to the coming of the various Greek peoples,[1] it practically disappeared and when the Greeks emerge into the light of history they are still in the "wild honey" stage, for their earliest writer, Homer (*c.* 1000 B.C.), apparently knew nothing of the craft, though he often alludes to bees and honey.

In the *Iliad*, when Nestor calls upon the Achaeans to assemble for the fight, they hasten to obey him,

Even as when the tribes of thronging bees issue from some hollow rock, ever in fresh procession, and fly clustering among the flowers of spring, and some on this side and some on that fly thick." (*Iliad* II. 87)

Homer uses many expressions which refer to the sweetness of honey; wine is "honey-sweet," Diomedes gives his horses "honey-sweet" barley, and many other instances. He also alludes to it as a food. When Hekamede prepared a meal for Nestor and Machaeon,

She drew before them a fair table . . . and set thereon a vessel of bronze, with onion for a relish to the drink, and pale honey, and the grain of sacred barley. (*Iliad* XI. 631)

Oil and honey in two-handled jars were placed by the great-hearted Achilles near the funeral pyre of his friend Patrocles; for the foods which men loved in life were burnt on the pyre, so that the shades might enjoy them in the nether world.

[1] We find traces of it in the name *Melikertes*, said to mean *Honey-cutter*, who was connected in prehistoric times with Corinth—Corinth is a *Cretan* name—and in the myth of *Melissa*, priestess of Demeter at Corinth (see Chapter IX).

After the fall of Troy it is possible that the Greeks obtained a knowledge of beekeeping from Western Asia, for the earliest writers on the subject, whose works have unfortunately been lost, were natives of Ionia. The first extant writer to mention hives, thus showing that bees were domesticated, was Hesiod, whose date is uncertain, but he can hardly have lived later than 750 B.C. His works show that in his time a considerable amount was known about the inmates of the hives, for in his *Theogony* he compares women to drones:

Women, a great source of hurt, dwell along with mortal men, help-mates not of consuming poverty but of surfeit; and when as in close-roofed hives bees feed drones, sharers of bad works, the former the whole day long are busy till sunset day by day, and make white combs, whilst the latter, remaining within the close-roofed hives, reap the labours of others.[1]

It was not, however, only women whom he compared to drones, for in the *Works and Days*, which Hesiod wrote to exhort a useless brother, he says that:

Gods and men are indignant with him who lives a sluggard's life, like in temper to stingless drones, which lazily consume the labours of the bee.[2]

By the time of Solon, the great Athenian legislator (*c.* 639–599 B.C.), beekeeping was so widespread an industry that he ordered that if anyone would raise stocks of bees he was to place them 300 feet from those already raised by another.[3] Attica was the goal of the Greek *Wanderimker*, the bee-masters who moved their hives so as to take advantage of another "Honey-flow," and they came to it from all parts, especially from Achaia and the north-west of the Peloponnesus. The best honey in Attica was that obtained from the lower slopes of Mount Hymettus, which were covered with thyme, and it is possible that the laws of Solon referred to these stocks which came to Attica from other districts.

There are said to have been twenty thousand stocks of bees in Attica in the time of Pericles[4]—about 400 B.C.—and later the

---

[1] *Theogony*, 596, trans. J. Banks.   [2] *Works and Days*, 304.
[3] Plutarch, *Life of Solon*, 23.
[4] Gmelin, in *Witzgalls Buch von der Biene*, p. 21.

fame of the Attic honey spread to other lands. In the Papyri of Zenon mentioned in Chapter III, a man named Dromon writes to Zenon:

> Order one of your people to buy me a kotyle of Attic honey, for I need it for my eyes, by command of the god;

and in another letter the importation of Attic honey into Egypt is mentioned.[1]

Athenaeus, the learned Greek grammarian, tells how much the Attic honey was appreciated:

> Praise the cheese-cakes which from Athens come,
> And if there are none still of any country
> Cheese-cakes are to be eaten; also ask
> For Attic honey, the feast's crowning dish.[2]

Honey was much esteemed by the Greek philosophers. The philosophy of Pythagoras, who lived in the sixth century B.C., included a life of moral abstinence and purification. He lived to a great age, and is said to have attributed it to his constant use of honey. His doctrine was the transmigration of souls; the pure were raised to higher modes of life. Centuries later Porphyry,[3] teaching the same doctrine, taught that those souls who lived justly were called bees, "for the bee is just and sober."[4] Athenaeus states that:

> Bread and honey were the chief food of the Pythagoreans according to the statement of Aristoxenes, who says that those who eat this for breakfast are free from disease all their lives. And Lycus says that the Cyreans (and they are a people who live near Sardinia) are very long lived because they are continually eating honey.

Athenaeus also relates the story of Democritus, the philosopher of Abdera, who lived about 460 B.C., which shows how long life was attributed to the use of honey.

---

[1] No. 89.

[2] Athen., III. 59. Athenaeus lived about A.D. 230. In his *Deipnosophistae* or *Banquet of the Learned* are many quotations from ancient Greek writers. Cheese-cakes always contained honey. [3] A.D. 233–304.

[4] Porphyry, *De ant. nym.*, 8. Plato also held that the souls of quiet and sober men came to life as bees and ants. See Frazer, *Golden Bough*, VIII. 308.

Democritus determined to rid himself of life on account of his extreme
old age, and he had begun to diminish his food day by day when the
day of the Thesmophorian festival came round and the women of his
household besought him not to die during the festival; so he was persuaded and ordered a vessel full of honey to be set near him, and in this
way he lived many days with no other support than the honey; and then
some days afterwards when the honey had been taken away, he died.
But Democritus had always been fond of honey; and once he answered
a man who asked how how he could live in the enjoyment of the best
health, that he might do so if he constantly moistened his inward parts
with honey and his outward man with oil.[1]

Herodotus (c. 482–428 B.C.), writing as an historian, does not add
to our knowledge of beekeeping. He mentions two districts where
artificial honey-making was carried on, one in Africa: "On the
Libyans border the Gyzantians, in whose country a vast deal of
honey is made by bees, very much more, however, by the skill of
man";[2] and again in Lydia, "where the men live who make honey
out of the fruit of the tamarisk."[3] This mention of artificial honey
in those regions only, shows that in Greece at that time the honey
used was entirely bees' honey, in fact artificial honey-making in
Europe seems to be quite a modern introduction. Herodotus also
relates that one of the burial customs of the Scythians was to
enclose the dead bodies of their kings in wax.[4]

Xenophon (born c. 430 B.C.) in his account of the retreat of the
ten thousand Greeks from Persia, states that just after sighting
the longed-for sea near Trapezus his soldiers found,

Great quantities of beehives in those villages and all the soldiers who
ate of the honeycombs lost their senses and were seized with vomiting
and purging, none of them able to stand on their legs. Those who ate
little were like men very drunk, and those who ate much like madmen,
and some like dying persons. In this condition they lay on the ground
as if there had been a defeat. The next day none of them died, but
recovered their senses, and the third day they got up as if they had taken
medicine.[5]

Strabo, writing just before the Christian era, mentions this
poisonous honey of Pontus. He writes:

[1] Athen., II. 26.   [2] Herod., IV. 194.   [3] Ibid., VII. 31.
[4] Ibid., IV. 71.   [5] Anabasis, IV. ch. 8

The Heptakometes cut off three of Pompey's cohorts, as they were passing through the mountains, by placing on their road vessels filled with poisonous honey, which is procured from the branches of trees. The men who tasted the honey and lost their senses were attacked and easily dispatched.[1]

Modern scientists who have visited these regions believe that this honey must have been obtained from *Rhododendron ponticum* and *Azalea pontica*, which are found in great abundance there, and it is said that the honey got from these plants to-day is thrown away and only the wax used.[2]

In his *Economics* Xenophon makes Ischomachus relate how he trained his young wife, who was only fourteen when he married her:

"I think," he said to her, "that the mistress bee is an excellent example for the wife." "What is the business of the mistress bee?" asked the young wife. "The mistress bee," replied Ischomachus, "keeps always in the hive, taking care that all the bees which are in the hive with her are duly employed in their several occupations; and those whose business lies abroad she sends out to their several works. These bees, when they bring home their burden, she receives, and appoints them to lay up their harvest, till there is occasion to use it, and in the proper season she dispenses it amongst those of her colony according to their several offices. The bees who stay at home she employs in disposing and ordering the combs, with a neatness and regularity becoming the nicest observation and the greatest prudence. She takes care likewise of the young bees, that they are well nourished and educated to the business that belongs to them, and when they are able to go abroad and work for their living, she sends them forth under the direction of a proper leader."[3]

Ischomachus also tells his wife that in his opinion it was a great favour of the gods to give them such an excellent example as that shown by these little creatures, of the duty of husband and wife to assist one another in the good ordering of affairs.

---

[1] Strabo, XII. ch. iii, 18.

[2] Poisonous honey is found in other countries. In North America, near Philadelphia, a great number of people are said to have been fatally poisoned by it in 1790. This was attributed to honey from *Kalmia latifolia*. In the Russian-Turkish war of 1878, Walters, the correspondent of the *Daily News*, was stupefied and ill after eating honey near Batum, which is the same region where Xenophon's soldiers suffered two thousand years before. See Professor K. Sajo, *Unsere Honigbiene*, Stuttgart, 1909, p. 83.   [3] *Econ.*, VII. 32.

None of the writers we have mentioned were students of Natural History, but we now come to one whose name over-shadows all others in every branch of science for many centuries, that of the teacher and friend of Alexander the Great, Aristotle (384–321 B.C.). Before his time there had certainly been writers on Natural History, but though we know the names of a few of them their works are lost. Anaxagoras, a contemporary of Hero-dotus, was one to whom Aristotle owed much; another was the philosopher Democritus, already mentioned as a lover of honey, who is quoted several times by Aristotle.

When we consider under what handicaps the men of his time laboured when investigating the life history of a small animal like the bee, the marvel is, not that Aristotle made mistakes, but that he made so few. In his work on Natural History he devotes an extraordinarily large part to the subject of bee life. He studied bees more from the theoretical than the practical side, and was especially interested in their reproduction, a subject to which he gave much thought, but never reached a solution which satisfied him; in fact, the real functions of the "mother bee" were not understood until two thousand years after Aristotle wrote.[1]

There is an interesting anecdote of Aristotle related by the Arabic writer, Ad-Amiri, mentioned in the last chapter. He says that Aristotle had an observation hive made of glass, in order to see how the bees worked, but the bees did not approve of this, and did no work until they had smeared the inside of the glass with clay. Strange to say, the only other place where I have found this story is in Ireland. Lady Gregory, in a note to her play *Aristotle's Bellows*, writes:

Aristotle's name is a part of our folklore. The wife of one of our labourers told me one day as a bee buzzed through the open door, "Aristotle of the Books was very wise, but the bees got the best of him in the end. He wanted to know how they did pack the comb, and he wasted the best part of a fortnight watching them doing it. Then he made a hive with a glass cover on it and put it over them, and thought

---

[1] He treats very fully of it in *Hist. Animalium*, Book V, and in *De Genera-tione Animalium*, Book III; Book IX of the *Hist. Animalium*, which also has a long section on bees, was not written by Aristotle, but after his time. Another book which bears his name, *De Mirabilibus Auscultatibus*, contains interesting items about bees.

he would watch them, but when he put his eye to the glass, they had covered it with wax, so that it was as black as the pot, and he was as blind as before. He said he was never rightly killed until then. The bees beat him that time surely."[1]

There are no other extant writings on bees for centuries after Aristotle. Theophrastus (372–287 B.C.) wrote botanical and zoological works, but the latter are lost; Nicander (c. 185–135 B.C.) is said to have written a poem on beekeeping, and there are allusions to the industry in the works of the Greek writers of Alexandria. Aristophanes of Byzantium, who lived in Egypt and had charge of the great library of Alexandria, relates that the beekeepers had their heads shaven because the bees dislike perfume; from which statement we may perhaps infer that there was a sort of beekeepers' guild, the members of which were so distinguished.[2]

It can certainly be definitely stated that the Greeks had a flourishing bee industry. In his plays Aristophanes (c. 444–380 B.C.) mentions the *melitopoles*, the honey merchant, and the *keropoles*, the wax merchant. The wax was used for modelling, for writing tablets, for sealing, for covering metals to prevent oxidation, and in many other ways. Honey was occasionally used for preserving bodies in the case of those Greeks who died far from home, as we saw in the case of Alexander the Great. The body of the Spartan king, Agesipolis, who died in Asia, was placed in honey to preserve it until it could be brought to Sparta. The honey-loving philosopher, Democritus, was also buried in honey.[3] The chief uses of honey, however, were in religious rites, which will be discussed later, and for food.

Athenaeus tells of many dishes and drinks in which honey played a part. Cheese-cakes, in which honey was always used, seem to have been a specially favourite food of the Greeks. He quotes a

---

[1] *Three Wonder Plays*, 1921, p. 156.

[2] See Dr. Klex, "Bienenkunde des Aristoteles und seiner Zeit," in *Archiv für Bienenkunde*, 1919, p. 44.

[3] Sir Thomas Browne, *Urn Burial*, Chapter III. Dr. Adolf Bastian, *Völker des Östlichen Asien*, vol. ii, p. 27, states that in Burmah the bodies of important men were placed in honey for a year, because the preparations for the funeral took that time. It was an effective and economical method as the honey which had been given for the purpose was afterwards sold! A Burmese student in Manchester in 1925 said that this custom is still in use, but only for monks.

passage from Euripides' *Cretan Women*, which says that at dessert
would be offered

> Cheese-cakes, steeped most thoroughly
> In the rich honey of the golden bee;

and another from Eubulus:

Everything is sold in Athens . . . cheese-cakes, honeycombs.[1]

Of drinks Athanaeus writes:

there is a kind of cup called *celebe*. Meander the Colophonian in his
Dialects says that the *celebe* is a vessel used by the shepherds in which
they preserve honey. For Antimachos the Colophonian in the Fifth Book
of his Thebais says:

> He bade the heralds bare to them a bladder
> Filled with dark wine, and the most choice of all
> The celebea in his house which lay
> Filled with pure honey . . .

and again:

> And golden cups of wine, and then besides
> A celebeum, yet untouched by man,
> Full of pure honey, his most choice of treasures.[2]

[1] Athen., XIV. 46.   [2] Ibid, XI. 50.

CHAPTER VIII

BEEKEEPING AMONG THE ROMANS

Apiculture an important industry—Varro, "De Re Rustica"—
Vergil, "Geor. IV"—Story of Vergil and his bees—"The Aeneid"
—Columella, "De Re Rustica"—Palladius—Pliny the Elder—
Seneca—How is honey made?—Dioscorides, "De Materia Medica"
—Ovid—Corsican honey—Wax tablets—Hives—Smoking used
when taking honey—Honey used in large quantities—Imported from
other countries—Wax of Corsica—Honey in food and drinks

BEEKEEPING in Italy does not appear to have been practised at such an early date as in Greece. Possibly the knowledge of bee-keeping was first gained from the Phoenician or Greek settlers in various parts of Italy. There are many extant Latin works on agriculture, and in several of these beekeeping is fully treated. The Romans were a practical people, and we must not forget that before the introduction of sugar bee-culture was a most important industry, and quite worthy of a place among the other activities of a farm. To-day, if mentioned at all in works on agriculture, it would be dismissed in a few lines.

The most important writers on apiculture were Varro (116–28 B.C.), Vergil (70–19 B.C.), Columella (c. A.D. 1–68), and Pliny the Elder (A.D. 23–79). A lost work, often quoted by these writers, in which beekeeping had been treated, was one by the Carthaginian Mago. His date is uncertain, but his work was translated into Latin by the order of the Senate in 146 B.C.

Varro was a most accomplished man; he wrote many works—it is said seventy-four—on a variety of subjects, which gained for him the title of "most learned of Romans." In his eightieth year he wrote his work on agriculture, *De Re Rustica*, in three books in the form of a dialogue, and it is the most important ancient work of its kind extant. In the Italy of Varro's time thoughtful men noted with sorrow that men were leaving the land and flocking to the cities. The great landowners were dispossessing the peasant small-holders, who were thus forced to seek a livelihood in the towns, while the landowners lived in luxury, leaving the management of their estates largely to slaves. Varro observed this with regret, so at the end of his long life he wrote this work on agriculture to show how much better it would be if men stayed in the country. The cry of "back to the land" is no new one.

Varro treated very fully of apiculture in Book III, Chapter XVI, of his work. He discusses the position and the various kinds of hives, the work and pasturage of bees, and said they must be fed on food made from figs or grapes if they are not able to get sufficient for themselves. He notes many plants which provide good food for the bees, and gives many other practical suggestions. It is in this work that Varro remarks of our sacred bees:

It is with good reason that the bees have been called the "Birds of the Muses," for if they are flying away, they can quickly be recalled by clapping of hands and tinkling of symbals. Nature has also given the bees the undisturbed flower-covered hills for their habitation, just as men say that those divinities [the Muses] live on Helicon and Olympus. (III. 16, 7)

Vergil's father must have been a man of character and energy. He meant to get on and he succeeded. He was not content with one occupation, but by keeping bees and speculation in timber he made money.[1] When Vergil wrote about bees in the *Georgics*, he enters into their life so heartily that we feel he must have been brought up among them. It was Vergil who, once for all, centuries before Maeterlinck, wrote the Epic of the Bees. He who has read the Fourth Book of the *Georgics* will never forget his wonderful account of the bees; their home life, their valiant fighting, their loyalty to their king; their nature and wonderful gifts, which Jupiter gave them as a reward for their following the sounding clang made by the Kuretes on Mount Dicte when they fed the King of Heaven there[2]; the swarms which escape into the clear summer air, like a dark cloud trailing along in the wind, and which must be recalled by shaking the cymbals sacred to the Mother-Goddess (Cybele); their illnesses and the remedies to be given, all this is marvellously described. The first half of the book is practical; the second gives the story of Aristaeus and how bees

[1] T. R. Glover, *Studies in Vergil*, London, 1904, p. 33.
[2] Alluding to the old Cretan myth of the birth of Zeus; see below, p. 92. Vergil had the greatest admiration for the intelligence of the bee, and maintained that she possessed a portion of divine reason (*Geor.* IV. 220).

can be procured if all your stocks have perished, a tale which will be told later.

There is a charming little story told of Vergil and his bees, which we hope is true. It is said that some soldiers tried to plunder his property; his servants rescued his valuables and placed them among the beehives. They then made the bees swarm on to the invaders, who, attacked by the angry creatures, fled away. Vergil calmly watched them, and then cast a grateful look on his beloved bees.[1]

In other poems Vergil often uses different facts of bee life as illustrations, for instance in the *Aeneid* in describing the building of Carthage:

"As when in the early summer o'er the flowery mead beneath the sun the honey bees are at work, when they lead forth the full-grown young of their race, or when they pack the liquid honey and fill their combs full of sweet nectar, or receive the burdens of those that come in, or form a martial line and drive forth from the hives the drones, a lazy tribe; hotly glows the work, and the sweet-scented honey is fragrant with thyme," even so work the Carthaginians.[2]

Columella was a native of Cadiz in Spain. He wrote a long work on agriculture, *De Re Rustica*, founded partly on the study of previous works on the subject, partly on his own experience gained in Spain, Italy, Asia, and on his own estates. The work was written in A.D. 60, and consists of twelve books, the ninth of which is devoted to the care of bees. Another Latin writer, Palladius, who lived in the fourth century, collected the knowledge of the early authors, and his main authority was this work of Columella, which also formed the basis of the English books on bees in the sixteenth and seventeenth centuries.[3]

Pliny the Elder, who was born in A.D. 23, and lost his life whilst watching the eruption of Vesuvius which destroyed Pompeii and Herculaneum in the year 79, wrote a comprehensive Natural History, comprising thirty-seven books. In Books XI and XXI he gives consecutive accounts of bees, the materials for which he had

---

[1] Bessler, *Geschichte der Bienenzucht*, p. 88.

[2] *Aeneid*, I. 430 ff., trans. Lonsdale and Lee. In Book XII. 590, he alludes to the practice of using smoke for taking honey from wild bees' nests.

[3] There is an English MS. translation of Palladius in the library of Colchester Castle, which was printed by the Early English Text Society in 1873.

assiduously collected from many sources, Latin and Greek. He also gives little items of interest which he himself had learnt in the course of his travels over the Roman Empire. For example, he relates:

There is a strange fact worthy to be mentioned which I have ascertained about the food of bees. There is a village called Hostilia on the banks of the river Po. The farmers of this settlement when the flowers of the neighbourhood are over, place their hives on ships and take them during the night about five miles up the river. In the daytime the bees fly out and bring their booty to the ships, whose position is changed daily until it is noticed by the sinking of the ship lower in the water that the hives are full; then they are taken home and the honey extracted. This custom is also carried out in Spain, the hives being carried on the backs of mules.[1]

Pliny alludes to poisonous honey, which produced madness, found in the district of the Sanni in Pontus—the same region where the soldiers of Xenophon suffered from the honey. The people had to pay a *wax* tax to the Romans, but not of honey on account of its poisonous qualities. He also states that in Pontus a white bee was occasionally found which made honey twice a month.[2] Aristotle mentions a very light-coloured bee, but there are no white bees, except in the old folktales, which are given in Chapter XIX.

Besides these five writers, who made special mention of bees in their works on agriculture or natural history, many other Latin authors allude to bees.[3] Seneca, the tutor and counsellor of Nero, gives an interesting account of the similarity between the bee-state and the human monarchy:

It is really nature who invented the monarchy, as can be seen among social animals, especially the bees. The king is here lodged in the most

[1] Book XXI. 73.

[2] Book XXI. 77. Poisonous honey was also found in Persia and Mauretania (XXI. 74).

[3] Celsus, who lived under Augustus and Tiberius, wrote a work, now lost, which is quoted largely by Columella. Hyginus, a freedman of Augustus and librarian of the Palatine Library, wrote a bee-calendar, which Columella incorporated in his work. Saserna, father and son, who lived between the times of Cato and Varro, and Tremellus Scrofa, a friend of Varro, made observations of bees in their works. Aelian, second century, wrote on natural history and has much to say about bees.

spacious cell, he is placed in the centre, the most secure spot; then he, freed from all work himself, surveys the labour of the others, and if anything happens to him, the whole hive is disorganized; the unity of power is the absolute rule, and in case of competition, a fight serves to discover the most worthy. Besides this, the exterior aspect of the king attracts the eye, he differs from the others in his body, as well as in the brightness of his colouring. But this is what distinguished him above all; the other bees are very fiery, and in comparison to their size, excessively combative, and they leave their stings in the wound; but the king himself has no sting. Nature did not wish him to be cruel, nor exercise a vengeance which might be dearly paid for, she deprived him of his sting and left his anger unarmed.[1]

It is strange to think that this was written about Nero in his youth, the tyrant who afterwards commanded Seneca to commit suicide! In one of his letters Seneca wrote:

It is our duty to copy the bees, who fly from flower to flower to gather honey. They carry home their harvest and place it in the combs. We are not, however, quite clear if the juice which they take from the flowers is ready-made honey, or whether by mixing some substance with it, or by means of some peculiarity of their breath, they change the material into honey. Some say the bees are only capable of collecting honey, not of preparing it; for in India honey is found on reeds, which is either made by the dew of that climate or by the rich and sweet juices of the reeds themselves.[2] It is said that our herbs possess this peculiarity also though in a less striking degree, and that the bees are born to collect this marvel for themselves. Others are of the opinion that the bees change what they take from the flowers into honey, and for this purpose use some sort of ferment which possesses the power of changing the different substances into one homogeneous mass."[3]

Seneca in this letter raised the interesting question as to the formation of honey. Vergil and many other writers describe it as coming down from heaven, but it is now known that the second of Seneca's alternatives is the right one, as the nectar gathered by the bees undergoes transformation in their bodies before becoming honey.[4]

---

[1] *De Clementia*, I. 19, 2. He is wrong in stating that the "king" has no sting.   [2] He is quoting Strabo, xv. 1, 20.   [3] Seneca, Epis. 84, 3.

[4] The bee is *A. mellifica* = preparer of honey, not *A. mellifera* = gatherer of honey.

In the first century of our era lived the great Greek physician and man of science, Dioscorides, whose chief work, *De Materia Medica*, was for nearly seventeen hundred years the chief authority for students on botany and the science of healing. He often mentions honey as a medicine, and also wax, propolis, and various honey wines. He differentiates between Sicilian, Sardinian, Pontic, and Cycladian honey, and places in order of merit, first Attic honey, of which that from Hymettos was the best; second Cycladic honey; third that from Hybla in Sicily; Corsican honey was regarded as poisonous.

The poet Ovid, too, speaks disparagingly of the bee of Corsica. He exclaims:

> Away from me, ill-natured tablets, funereal pieces of wood, and you, wax close writ with characters that will but say me nay, wax, which I think was gathered by the bee of Corsica and sent us under its ill-famed honey."[1]

Here, of course, Ovid alluded to the use of wooden writing tablets covered with a layer of wax; he also tells us that the Romans used to make waxen figures of people for the purpose of doing them injury,[2] a custom we found in Egypt and Babylonia.

From all the works mentioned above it can be gathered that beekeeping was practised in Imperial times in Italy on a large scale. The bees were kept in hives made of the bark of the cork oak, of fennel stems, of wicker-work, which was smeared inside with cowdung or, occasionally, of sawn pieces of wood. Pliny also mentions hives made from transparent lantern horn, used on the estate of a Consul near Rome,[3] and others made from mirror stones (*lapis specularis*), which served as observation hives.[4] Unfortunately we have no correct representation of a Roman hive. The straw skeps of the well-known "beehive" shape used for so many centuries in England and the Continent do not appear to have been used in the early Roman Empire, they are probably of Germanic origin.[5] The hives were either rectangular or cylindrical and about a yard long, and they perhaps may have resembled the

---

[1] *Amores*, I. 12, 7.   [2] *Heroides*, VI. 91.   [3] XI. 49.   [4] XXI. 80.

[5] For the origin and forms of primitive hives, see Armbruster, *Der Bienenstand als völkerkundliches Denkmal*, 1926, *Die alte Bienenzucht der Alpen*, 1928, and *Die alte Brenenzucht Italeins* (*Archiv für Bienenkunde*), 1929. See below, p. 151.

hive illustrated in Fig. 23, as it represents an Italian hive about the year 1000.

Dust or honey-water was thrown on the bees to quieten them if fighting,[1] and smoke was used when taking honey.[2] It was usually made by burning dried cowdung, the best material for it—as Pliny quaintly remarks—as it is related to the bees![3] He alludes to the belief that bees can be obtained from the dead bodies of cattle, which was very prevalent in classical times, and which spread over Europe and lasted to recent times. (See Chapter x.)

A great number of hives were kept in Italy—Varro mentions a friend of his who had let his hives for a yearly payment of 5,000 lb. (= 1,637 kg.)[4]—but the quantity of honey and wax required in Rome was so great that they were imported from different parts of the empire, especially from Spain, Sardinia, and Corsica. Diodorus Siculus also mentions that the Corsican honey was disagreeable, and tasted of absinthe or box, but it was produced in such quantities that the wax formed a large part of the revenue of the island. When Corsica was subdued by the Romans by the Praetor Pinarius in the year 181 B.C., he laid a tribute on it of 100,000 lb. of wax, which two years later he increased to 200,000 lb.[5] Sicilian and Pelignian wax was also highly valued, but the highest prices were obtained for the Punic and the yellow wax of Pontus, that of Crete was not so valuable.

Like the Greeks the Romans used honey largely in cooking. Martial writes: "The baker can deliver sweet foods to you in a thousand forms, for the bee works for him."[6] There were also several drinks either made of or mixed with honey. *Mulsum*, a wine sweetened with honey, was drunk at the beginning and ending of a meal.[7] Columella tells us that the proportion was four-fifths of wine to one-fifth of honey.[8] Vergil says that there are two kinds of bees, one of which makes the sweetest honey for making sour wine mild.[9] Another drink was *hydromel*, somewhat resembling our mead or metheglin; this was largely used in medicine, and Pliny

---

[1] Pliny, XI. 58; Varro, III. 30; Vergil, *Georg.*, IV. 87; Colum., IX. 6.

[2] Varro, III. 36; Pliny, XI. 45.

[3] Colum., XIV. 1, 2; Pliny, XXI. 80. [4] Varro, III. 10.

[5] R. Billiard, *Die Biene und die Bienenzucht im Altertum*, p. 68.

[6] Martial, XIV. 222. [7] Varro, III. 15.

[8] Colum., XII. 41. [9] *Geor.*, IV. 101.

gives it as remedy for several ailments.[1] A drink, apparently used more for medicine than enjoyment, was *aqua mulsa*, a honey-water; *oxymel*, a mixture of honey, vinegar, salt, and water, was used in preparing vegetables and as a remedy for throat and ear troubles; then there was *myritis*, made of myrtle-berries, old wine, and honey; *melomeli*, a mixture of honey and the juices of various fruits, and *clionomeli*, a compound of white of egg and honey.[2]

Under the "pax Romana" beekeeping probably reached its zenith, for when the empire gradually weakened under the continual eruptions of the barbarians who ravaged the once peaceful lands, men were no longer able to look after their bees, and it was not until the Middle Ages, when the Church began to use wax candles in large quantities, that the industry gradually revived.

[1] See Pliny, Chapters 51, 52, and 53.
[2] Billiard, *Der Biene und die Bienenzucht im Altertum*, p. 91.

CHAPTER IX

BEES AND HONEY IN GREEK AND ROMAN MYTHS

The Golden Age—Zeus fed in Crete on milk and honey—The Kuretes—The Melissae—Name applied to nymphs and priestesses of the Great-Mother—The "Delphic Bee"—The Thriae—Delphian temple of wax and feathers—Birds and bees—Doves bring ambrosia to Zeus—Dionysus and Aristaeus—The Muses—The "Birds of the Muses" bestow the gift of poetry—Bee-souls—Myth of Glaucus—Bees as prophets—Meaning given to swarms— Talisman to avert evil eye

As we have seen in the last two chapters, the Greeks and Romans practised beekeeping on a large scale. Their folklore contains many myths concerning bees and honey,[1] and they had many very ancient religious rites in which honey was used. These myths and rites are probably older than their knowledge of apiculture.

One of the early myths, alluded to by many classical writers, is that of the birth of Zeus, which seems to have originated in Crete. The myth carries us back to the Golden Age of the Greeks, an age of innocence and happiness, when, as Hesiod says:

The earth bore much substance, on the mountains the oak at its top yielded acorns and midway bees. (*Works and Days*, 233.)

Later many poets celebrated it as a time when all was spring, when flowers came up without seed, the rivers flowed with milk and nectar, the yellow honey was distilled from the green holm-oak, and the she-goat came unsummoned to the milk-pail.

This Golden Age occurred during the reign of Kronos, who had been warned that he would be dethroned by one of his children. In order to avert this fate, directly his wife, Rhea, had a child, he swallowed it. Five sons and daughters were thus bestowed inside him, but when the sixth child, Zeus, was born, Rhea determined to save him. A stone was carefully wrapped in swaddling clothes and Kronos unsuspiciously swallowed it. The infant Zeus was then

[1] These myths are practically all Greek in origin, and were taken over by the Romans.

concealed in a cave on Mount Dicte, which was full of sacred bees, who fed him on honey, and the goat Amaltheia gave him her milk. The cave was guarded by armed men, the Kuretes, who, when Zeus cried, clashed their armour and made a great noise so that Kronos should not hear him. Here in Crete the young god was reared, and he then fulfilled his destiny by dethroning his father and becoming himself the chief of the gods who lived on Olympus.

Another myth says that no one, god or man, might enter this cave where Zeus was hidden, and from which at certain seasons a light streamed forth. Four men, however, attracted by the honey, which they meant to steal, protected themselves with armour and managed to enter the cave. As they began to take the honey, they saw the cradle and swaddling clothes of Zeus, and at the sight the joints of their armour burst and it fell off. Thus unprotected they were attacked by the sacred bees and by Zeus, who thundered and would have slain the intruders, but was prevented by Themis and the Moirai (the Fates), who reminded him that the cave was a sanctuary and might not be defiled with blood. Zeus therefore contented himself with turning the men into birds.[1]

The scene where the angry bees are swarming round the four men after their armour has dropped off is depicted on a black-figured Athenian vase, dated about 550 B.C. (see Plate IX), now in the British Museum.

There are many variants of the birth myth, but two features appear in all: first, that there was a band of young men who guarded the infant Zeus, usually named the *Kuretes*, but sometimes the *Korybantes*; and secondly, that Zeus was fed either by bees or by nymphs, who fed him on honey. The former seems to have been the older form of the story; later the place of the bees was taken by nymphs or priestesses, who retained the name *bees*, and were known as *Melissae*, or bee-maidens.

The connection of the Kuretes with the Melissae is difficult to explain; before trying to give even a tentative explanation

---

[1] Antoninus Liberalis, XIX. See A. B. Cook, "The Bee in Greek Mythology," in *Jour. Hell. Studies*, vol. XV, p. 2; W. H. Roscher, *Lexikon der griech. und röm. Mythologie*, under headings "Keleus" and "Aigolis." The names given the four men in the myth are Greek names for birds: *Kerberos*, an unknown species; *Laios*, a blue thrush; *Keleos*, green woodpecker; and *Aigolios*, owl.

we give some of the passages where they are found mentioned together.

Vergil, alluding to the myth, says that Jupiter (Zeus) rewarded the bees for following the clanging noise made by the Kuretes to his cave on Dicte, where they fed him;[1] and in another passage when describing the noise made to attract bees when swarming, he writes: "They clash the cymbals of the Great-Mother."[2] This is the Mother-goddess, Cybele, an Eastern goddess who was early identified with Rhea, and whose attendants were called Korybantes, thus corresponding to the Kuretes of Rhea.

Other writers seem to use the names Kuretes and Korybantes interchangeably; in fact, Strabo states that "according to some the Kuretes were the same as the Korybantes";[3] and about two hundred years before him, Callimachus, the poet and chief librarian of the celebrated library of Alexandria, wrote:

> But, thee, O Jove, the associates of the Korybantes, the Dictean Meliae, took to their arms; thou suckest the full teat of the goat Amaltheia and moreover atest sweet honey. For on a sudden sprang the labours of the Pancrian bee on the mountains of Ida, which men call Panacra. Around thee vigorously the Kuretes dance, rattling their arms.[4]

Diodorus Siculus mentions an ancient tradition that the Kuretes taught the art of beekeeping;[5] and another story tells that the most ancient king of the Kuretes, named Gargoris, discovered how to collect honey.[6] Diodorus also relates that Zeus was placed in a sacred cave on Mount Ida in the care of the Kuretes, who lived on the mount, and that they took him to the nymphs, who fed him on a mixture of milk and honey, the milk being given by the nymph Amaltheia. He adds that Zeus wanted to reward his nurses, so he changed the colour of the bees to a bright, shining gold-bronze—the mountain being very high and exposed to cold winds, this change rendered them insensible to the rigours of the climate—the goat Amaltheia he placed in the sky as the star Capella.[7] Here we get a later version of the old story; the bees

---

[1] *Georg.*, IV. 150.   [2] Ibid., IV. 63.   [3] Strabo, III. 3.
[4] *Hymn to Jove*, 32.   [5] Diod., V. 63.
[6] See Dr. Rendel Harris, *Boanerges*, p. 352, who suggests that the name Gargoris may be connected with *gargara* = swarms.   [7] Diod., V. 70.

and goat of the older myth have become nymphs, but it is the original bees and goat who are rewarded.

Didymus, a celebrated Greek scholar, who lived about the same time as Diodorus—he was born about 63 B.C.—rationalized the myth still further. The following quotation is given by Lactantius:

> Didymus in his commentary on Pindar says that Melisseus, king of the Cretans, was the first who sacrificed to the gods and introduced new rites and ritual processions. He had two daughters, Amaltheia and Melissa, who nourished the youthful Zeus with goat's milk and honey. Hence the poetic fable derived its origin, that bees flew to the child and filled his mouth with honey. Moreover, he says that Melissa was appointed by her father as the first priestess of the Great-Mother, from which circumstance the priestesses of the same mother are still called *Melissae*.[1]

Another account says that the daughters of this king Melisseus were the nymphs Adrasteia and Ida, and that the Korybantes were their brothers.[2]

The title *Melissa*, the Bee, is a very ancient one; it constantly occurs in Greek myths, meaning sometimes a priestess, sometimes a nymph. The fact of its being used in this double meaning points to the original story as very old, for many of the later myths are evidently attempts to explain earlier ones. It is impossible to say when the title was first used, and we can only conjecture as to its origin. We have shown that beekeeping was a very ancient craft in Western Asia and Crete, both countries where the Mother-goddess was especially reverenced, and it is possible that her priestesses were named after the industrious, chaste, yet prolific creature whose honey was so prized by all. As we have seen, the bee was a symbol of the Ephesian Artemis, *Melissa* was possibly an early title for her priestesses, and certainly some of her priestly officials were called *Essenes*, the "King Bees"; but the latter were not the same as the Kuretes or Korybantes, whom we know in later times as the young men who clashed cymbals and danced in the ritual of the Great-Mother.

[1] Lact., *Div. Inst.*, I. 22. Translated in the Ante-Nicene Christian Library.
[2] One of the Kuretes is said to have been named Melisseus; and Diodorus (v. 61) mentions another Melisseus, king of the Chersonesos in Caria, who was regarded as the descendant of the Kuretes.

A ritual hymn of the Kuretes has been found at Palaikastro in Crete among the remains of a temple of the Dictean Zeus. The actual date of the stele on which it is inscribed is probably as late as the second or third century of our era, but the hymn itself is a survival of a ritual which must be very ancient. Part of the hymn runs:

Io, Kouros most Great, I give thee hail, Kronian, Lord of all that is wet and gleaming. . . . Thou art come to Dicte for the year, Oh, march and rejoice in the dance and song. . . . For here the shielded Nurturers took thee, a child immortal, from Rhea, and with the noise of beating feet hid thee away. [Here part of the hymn is missing.] And the Horai began to be fruitful year by year and Dike to possess mankind. . . . To us also leap for fleecy flocks, and leap for fields of fruit, and for hives to bring increase.[1]

Zeus was thus to come to Dicte, for it was there the "shielded Nurturers," the Kuretes, had hidden him with a noise of beating feet, and his coming was to ensure a plentiful harvest. In earlier times it would have been a fertility goddess, one of the Great-Mothers, who would have been invoked by the young men to come and prosper the flocks, herds, and hives. Here she is replaced by Zeus, for the worship of a god often surplanted the more ancient Great-Mother worship. In the myth related above, Rhea, the Mother-goddess, had her son, who was to become king of the gods, hidden in the cave where he was fed by the bees and guarded by the young men. A cave was a mysterious, sacred place to the ancients, a place often connected with the Netherworld, as were also the Mother-goddesses, and if bees hived in the cave, they also would be considered sacred to them. Perhaps the noise made by the Kuretes was originally a rude music meant to recall the swarming bees to the cave, the origin of the clashing of pots and pans, which is still done in some parts, when the bees swarm.[2] It cannot be proved, we can only point to the fact that beekeeping was a very early industry in Crete, and when the wild swarms issued from the cave the beekeepers would want to capture them, and might try to attract them into their hives with this rude music.

[1] Jane Harrison, *Themis*, trans. Sir Gilbert Murray, p. 7 et seq.
[2] See Dr. Rendel Harris, *Boanerges*, p. 350.

As was mentioned above the name *Melissa* was often applied to nymphs as well as to priestesses. Nymphs appear to have been closely associated with bees, perhaps partly because they were thought to inhabit hollow tree-trunks and caves where the wild bees lived—like the nymphs who lived in the bee-haunted cave on Ithaca[1]—or meadows, woods, and mountains, the haunts of the flowers which the bees loved.

One myth says that it was nymphs who dissuaded men from eating flesh and persuaded them to use fruits for food. One of these nymphs, Melissa by name, first discovered the use of the honey-comb and how to prepare mead by mixing honey with water, and she taught these arts to the other nymphs; it was from this Melissa, the myth says, that the bees got their name.

One of the titles of Zeus was *Melissaios*, the Bee-man. It is said that he had a son by a nymph, who, afraid of Hera's wrath, had the babe placed in a wood, where Zeus caused him to be fed by bees. The shepherd Phagros, son of Apollo and the same nymph, found the child and gave him the name Meliteus. He became a great hero, and founded a town which he called *Melita*, the honey-town. Another Melite, a town in Attica, is said to have owed its name to a nymph beloved by Heracles.

When the name *Melissae* is applied to priestesses, the goddesses whom they serve are either one of the Great-Mothers, as Rhea or Cybele, or goddesses of earth and nature like Demeter and Perse-phone. Porphyry says that the priestesses of Demeter, as initiated into the mysteries of the Earth-goddess, were called by the Ancients "Bees" (Melissae), that Persephone herself was named by them *Melitodes* (honeyed), and that the Moon (Selene, afterwards identified with Artemis) was called by them a Bee.[2] Calimachus mentions that the priestesses of Demeter were called Melissae.[3]

There is a myth of a Melissa, an elderly woman, a priestess of Demeter, who lived on the Isthmus of Corinth. She was said to have been intiated into the mysteries by the goddess herself. The women of the neighbourhood pressed her to tell them the secret, but she steadfastly refused, and they were so infuriated that they

---

[1] *Odyssey*, XIII. 104. The full-grown larva of bees just before they emerge from their cells are still called nymphs, a name for them which is mentioned by Pollux, 2. 147 (second century A.D.).

[2] *De ant. nym.*, 18.   [3] *Hymn to Apollo*, 99.

tore her to pieces. In wrath Demeter sent a plague to punish them, and she caused bees to come from Melissa's dead body.[1]

In view of the fact that the early priestesses of Artemis Ephesia were possibly called Melissae it is interesting to note that this title occurs in several Greek towns, like Corinth and Delphi, which were much influenced by Asia.

One of the most celebrated shrines in Greece was the Temple of Apollo at Delphi. Pindar (born *c.* 522 B.C.) says that the Pythia, the priestess who answered the inquiries of those who came there to consult the oracle, was known as the "Delphic Bee."[2] At Delphi, too, there were certain ancient maiden priestesses, called Thriae; they are not expressly called *Melissae*, but from the following quotation from the Homeric *Hymn to Hermes*, we gather that they must have been bee-priestesses. Apollo speaks:

> For there are sisters three, called Thriae, maiden things,
> Three are they and they joy in the glory of swift wings.
> Upon their head is sprinkled the flour of barley white,
> They dwell aloof in dwellings beneath Parnassos' height.
> They taught me love of soothsaying, whilst I my flocks did feed,
> Being yet a boy; of me and mine my father took no heed.
> And they flitted, now this way, now that, upon the wing,
> And of all things that were to be they uttered soothsaying;
> What time they fed on honey fresh, food of the gods divine,
> The holy madness made their hearts to speak the truth incline.
> But if from food of honeycomb they needs must keep aloof,
> Confused they buzz among themselves and speak no word of sooth.[3]

These Thriae were said to have been nymphs of Parnassos and nurses of Apollo.[4] They were endowed with prophetic power if they fed on honey, and Miss Jane Harrison aptly remarks: "The Delphic priestess in historic times chewed a laurel leaf, but when

[1] Serv. Verg., *Aen.*, I. 430. Pausanius says that the first priestesses of Demeter at Eleusis were daughters of King Keleos, which connects them with the Zeus myth. For an account and references for this and other Melissae, see Roscher's *Lexikon*, under heading "Melissa."

[2] *Pythian Ode*, IV. 62.

[3] Homeric Hymn in Mercur, 552-563. This translation is from Miss Jane Harrison's *Prolegomena*, p. 444. Shelley also translated the hymn.

[4] Philochoros frag. 125.

she was a Bee surely she must have sought her inspiration in the honeycomb."

That Delphi was originally connected with bees we can gather

FIG. 16.—COINS OR TOKENS

(i, vi) Delphi   (ii) Dyrrachium Obrimi   (iii) Dyrrachium Daminus
(iv) M. Plaetorius   (v) Boetium
Claudio Menetreio: *Symbolica Dianae Ephesiae*, Tabula IV, 1657)

from traditions concerning the ancient temple there. Pausanias writes:

They say that the most ancient temple of Apollo was made of laurel.
. . . The Delphians say that the second was made of wax and feathers,

and that it was sent to the Hyperboreans by Apollo. Another story is that the temple was built by a man of Delphi named Pteras, and that hence the temple got its name from its builder. They say that a city in Crete was named Apteroi after this Pteras, with the addition of a letter.[1]

Other writers have preserved this tradition. Philostratua says:

Apollo once inhabited a simple hut, and a small shanty was fashioned for him, to which the bees are said to have contributed their wax and birds their feathers;

And Plutarch quotes an ancient oracle:

Bring together feathers, ye birds, and wax, ye bees.[2]

Coins of Delphi with a bee type are illustrated in Fig. 16 (I, VI), and one of Aptera on Pl. VII, Fig. 18.

In these traditions there seems certainly to linger a faint trace of a prehistoric worship of, or perhaps reverence for, birds and bees, and the remembrance of the bees survived in the name *Melissae*. In Crete myths of birds and bees mingle in the birth cave of Zeus. In the *Odyssey* it is said that *doves* bring Zeus ambrosia from the bounds of Ocean,[3] a myth alluded to in the following lines of Moiro, a Byzantine poetess, who lived about 300 B.C.

The mighty Jove was nourished long in Crete,
. . . and him the trembling doves
Cherished, while hidden in the holy cave,
Bringing him from the distant streams of Ocean
Divine ambrosia; and a mighty eagle
Incessant drawing with his curved beak
Nectar from out the rock, triumphant brought
The son of Saturn, the necessary drink.[4]

---

[1] Paus., X. 5, 9. Commenting on this passage, Professor Middleton says: "With regard to the temple of wings and beeswax it should be noted that the priestesses of Apollo are sometimes called Melissae, a name given in other places to the priestesses of Artemis. It seems probable that this story is an unconscious survival of a bee-totem" ("Temple of Delphi," in *Jour. Hell. Stud.*, vol. ix).

[2] See Frazer, *Comment. on Paus.*, X. 5, 9. [3] *Odyssey*, XII. 68.

[4] Quoted by Athenaeus, XI. 80. In this story it is doves (Greek = *pelaides*) who bring ambrosia, which here denotes divine honey, to Zeus. They were considered as nymphs, and were placed in the sky as the Pleiades, the seven

If birds and bees, then, were reverenced as being connected with the sacred cave of Zeus in Crete, they may well have crossed the sea together to Delphi, hence the connection of birds' feathers and beeswax in the building of the old temple there. Crete had a much older civilization than Greece, and it is quite likely that many of the old beliefs accompanied the Mycenean culture to the mainland.

Besides the goddesses who had Melissae for their priestesses, two other divinities are frequently mentioned in connection with bees and honey—Aristaeus and Dionysus; the myths about them are inextricably mixed.

Aristaeus, the son of Apollo and the nymph Cyrene, was worshipped as the giver of good gifts to men and the protector of flocks and bees. In one of the odes of Pindar, Cheiron the Centaur, speaking to Apollo, says:

> There shall she [Cyrene] bear the son whom thou hast given,
> Whom glorious Hermes in his hour of birth
> Shall from his mother take, and bear to earth
> And to the Hours, the splendour-throned in Heaven.
> And while upon their knees the child is lying
> Soft-cradled, these between his lips shall pour
> Ambrosia and nectar; so undying
> Even as a god shall he be evermore,
> As Zeus and holy Apollo: sweetest, dearest
> To all his friends, to their heart ever nearest.
> Nomeus, "flock-warder," Agreus, these shall name
> Thy son, Aristaeus those acclaim.[1]

Aristaeus is here said to have been made immortal because fed by the Hours on nectar and ambrosia, the food of the gods, which we shall discuss in Chapter XII. Diodorus Siculus says that Aristaeus

doves. This constellation was of the greatest importance to the ancients, and it is noteworthy that all the old writers on bees, from Aristotle downwards, mention the Pleiades. Their rising was the signal of spring, bringing hopes of the earth's harvest; their setting was the beginning of winter. One of them was Electra, who bore Dardanos to Zeus, and Sir W. Mitchell Ramsey drew my attention to the fact that Hesychius, the lexicographer, says that another name for bee in Asia Minor was darda, so perhaps the old town of Dardanos, near the modern Dardanelles, was originally the Bee-town.

[1] Pythian, IX. 60, trans. A. S. Way.

was given by his father into the charge of nymphs, that it was they who gave him the three names of Nomeus, Agreus, and Aristaeus, and who taught him beekeeping, olive culture, and how to make curds from milk, and because he taught these arts to man he enjoyed divine honours like Dionysus.[1] Another story says that it was the Muses who taught him healing arts and prophecy, and who made him guardians of their herds. The connection of the Muses and bees will be discussed later.

In the fourth *Georgic* Vergil tells the story of Aristaeus and his bees, which all died because he had offended the nymphs; they, however, propitiated by sacrifices, taught him how to obtain new swarms from the carcases of dead oxen—a myth of which we shall speak in the next chapter. Aristaeus married a nymph, Autonoe, and they had several daughters, one of whom, Makris, lived in a sacred cave, and Dionysus as a babe was given into her charge by Hermes, and as she fed the child on honey, she may be termed a *Melissa*. Long afterwards, it is said that Medea was married to Jason in this cave of Makris, and of this myth Apollonius wrote:

And the self-same night for the maiden [Medea] prepared they the couch of the bride,
In a hallowed cave, where of old Makris wont to abide,
The child of the Honey-Lord, Aristaeus, whose wisdom discerned
The toils of the bees, and the wealth of the labour of olives learned.
And she was the first that received and in sheltering bosom bore
The child Nysaian of Zeus, on Euboea's Abantian shore,
And with honey she moistened his lips when the dew of life was dried
When Hermes bore him out of the fire.[2]

Here Dionysus is called by the title *Nysaian*. Diodorus says that as a babe he was carried to a cave on Mount Nysa and entrusted there to the nymph Nysa, another daughter of Aristaeus;[3] both these myths bring him into connection with the "Honey-Lord." Dionysus was usually regarded as the god of wine, but that was a later development; his worship is older than the cultivation of the vine. Wine superseded the honey-drink, yet honey was always sacred to him, and from the ivy-crowned wands of his followers,

[1] Diod., IV. 81. 2.
[2] IV. 1132. Apollonius lived in Egypt under the Ptolomies. A. S. Way's translation.   [3] Diod., III. 68.

the Maenads, flowed sweet honey.[1] Another of his titles was
Brisaios or *Briaeus*, a name which is said to be derived from the
word *blittein*, to take honey;[2] his temple stood on the slope of
Mount Brisa, and a myth tells of a nymph Brisa whom Dionysus
instructed in the art of beekeeping. Yet another myth relates that
Aristaeus was taught beekeeping by the Brisian nymphs.

Dionysus and Aristaeus are both credited with being the
originator of beekeeping. Oppian of Apamea, a Greek writer who
lived about A.D. 206, says in his *Cynegetica*, that Aristaeus was the
first to shut bees into hives, having first removed them from the oak-
tree, and that nymphs were the protectresses of bees. Ovid makes
Dionysus the discoverer of the first natural beehive, a hollow tree.
He tells the following story:

The attendants of Dionysus, the satyrs, were once making a continuous
clashing with their cymbals. Suddenly, attracted by the noise, swarms
of bees, which were until then unknown, appeared and followed the
clanging sound. Dionysus collected them and put them into a hollow tree,
in which he soon afterwards found honey. When the satyrs and their
leader, the old Silenus, had tasted the luscious food, they tried to discover
where it was to be found. Silenus heard the buzzing of the bees in the
hollow tree and espied the combs. He pretended, however, that he had
made no such discovery, but lazily lolling on his ass, he guided it to the
tree, meaning to help himself to the honey. The bees flew out and stung
him on his bald pate; he fell off his ass, which struck him with its hoof,
and he was forced to call for assistance. The satyrs came and laughed
at his plight; Dionysus also laughed, but showed Silenus how to apply
mud to the stings. Thus [adds Ovid], it is right that we should offer
honey-cakes to the discoverer of honey.[3]

The head of Aristaeus appears on the coins of many towns;[4]
on the one represented in Fig. 17, his head is on one side and a
bee on the other. A bronze figure of a young man, on whose
breast five large bees were symmetrically arranged, discovered in a
grave at Oliana in Sardinia, has been considered to be Aristaeus;

[1] Euripides, *Bacchae*, 108. On the great vase of Hieron Dionysus is adorned
with a necklace of honeycombs.

[2] It is also connected etymologically with Brito and Britomartis, Cretan
names for Artemis.   [3] Ovid., *Fasti*, III. 735.

[4] For example, at Carthaia, Coresia, Iulis in Ceos, Hybla, etc. See British
Museum Catalogue of Coins.

and the head of Dionysus surrounded by bees is engraved on a small plate of gold discovered in the Crimea. It is impossible here to attempt an explanation of these myths, but undoubtedly men believed that there was some connection, whose origin is lost in the mists of antiquity, between these two gods and bees.

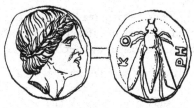

FIG. 17.—HEAD OF ARISTAEUS AND BEE. COIN OF IULIS IN CEOS

The Muses, originally nymphs of inspiring springs, afterwards regarded as the goddesses of poetry, arts, and sciences, were frequently connected in ancient times with bees, who were called "Birds of the Muses."[1] Fig. 18 represents a gem of a woman-headed bee, with a muse's lyre in the background.[2] According to one old myth the muses in the form of bees guided the ship of the Ionians from Athens to their new home on the banks of the River Melos, in Asia Minor.[3] It was, however, probably the sweetness of the muses' song which gave rise to the connection with bees. An anonymous verse in the *Greek Anthology*, addressed "To the Muses," says:

FIG. 18.—WOMAN-HEADED BEE WITH LYRE
(Southesk Coll., Pl. IX, H9)

> Euterpe shrills on perforated reeds,
> Forcing through them the spirit of the
> skilled bee.[4]

The muses conferred the gift of sweet speech, poetry, and eloquence, and often bestowed them on men by sending bees to their lips. Hesiod, one of the first writers to mention the Muses, calls them the daughters of Zeus and Mnemosyne, describes them as living on Olympus, and says that whomsoever they honoured and looked upon at his birth, on his tongue they shed a honeyed dew and from his lips would drop gentle words and he would speak counsel unerringly.[5] An old poem on Hesiod's death tells that—

[1] Varro, III. 16, 7.   [2] Now in the Southesk Coll. (Pl. IX, H9).
[3] The bee is often found on Ionian coins, perhaps in memory of this tradition.   [4] *Greek Anthology*, IX. 505.   [5] Hesiod, *Theog.*, 76.

The nymphs washed the body of Hesiod with water from their spring, and raised a tomb to him. And on it the goatherds poured libations of milk mixed with golden honey. For even such was the song the old man breathed who had tasted the pure fountain of the Nine Muses.[1]

We frequently read of poets and eloquent men whose lips had been touched in infancy or youth by the "Birds of the Muses." Pausanias visited the tomb of Pindar, and relates the following:

It chanced that the youthful Pindar was once journeying to Thespiae in the hot season at the hour of noon. Weariness and drowsiness overtook him and he lay down. While he slept bees flew to him and plastered honey on his lips. Such was the beginning of his career of song. When his fame was spread the Pythian priestess [the "Delphic Bee"] set him on a still higher pinnacle of renown by bidding the Delphians give to Pindar an equal share of all the first-fruits they offered to Apollo.[2]

Antipater of Sidon wrote of Pindar's tomb:

This earth holds Pindar, the Pierian trumpet . . . whose melody when thou hearest, thou wouldest exclaim that a swarm of bees from the Muses had fashioned it;[3]

and in another verse on Pindar's portrait:

It was not idly, Pindar, that the swarm of bees fashioned the honeycomb about thy tender lips.[4]

In Pindar's own odes are many allusions to the "Muses' Honey," by which he means the gift of song.

In the gymnasium of Zeuxippos at Byzantium were bronze statues of poets with inscriptions. Under Homer's was:

On Homer's cheeks sat innate modesty, the fellow of the Graces, and a Pierian bee wandered round his divine mouth, producing a dripping honeycomb;

and under that of Sappho:

The clear-toned Pierian bee sat at rest there, Sappho of Lesbos. She seemed to be weaving some lovely melody, with her mind devoted to the silent Muses;[5]

---

[1] *Greek Anthology*, XII. 55. The author was Alcaeus, third century B.C.
[2] Paus., IX. 23, 2.   [3] *Greek Anthology*, VII. 34.   [4] Ibid., XVI. 305.
[5] Ibid., Book II. These were written c. A.D. 552. Sappho lived in the seventh century B.C.

and there was a similar inscription under the statue of Sappho's friend, Erinna. On this Erinna, who died at the age of nineteen, there is another verse in the *Greek Anthology*:

> The lyric maid Erinna, the poet bee that drew
> The honey from the rarest flowers the Muses's garden grew,
> Hath Hades snatched to be his bride. Mark where the maiden saith,
> Prophetic in her wisdom, "How envious art thou, Death!"[1]

Sophocles, Plato, Vergil, and Lucan were all said to have been fed by bees, or had their lips touched by honey in their infancy.[2] Of Menander it was said:

> The bees culling the various flowers of the Muses bore off the honey to thy lips, the Graces themselves bestowed their gift on thee, Menander, endowing thy wit with fluent felicity.[3]

Theocritus, in one of his idylls, mentions a goatherd, Comatas, who devoutly served the Muses and used to offer them his master's goats. His master therefore shut him up in a cedar chest, but the bees came and fed him with honey, and when at the end of a year the master opened the chest, he found Comatas alive.[4]

Thus we constantly find that the Muses and the bees bring the gift of song to mankind, and when in a later chapter we speak of Germanic myths, we shall find that in northern countries the gifts of song and prophecy are connected with the honey-drink, mead. The expression "honey-sweet" is constantly used by all writers from Homer downwards; it denoted the pinnacle of the art of sweet speech, and is a totally different expression from the modern "sweet as sugar"; indeed, it is remarkable that in spite of the widespread use of sugar and other sweet materials in modern times, none of them has given us poetical phrases and similes like those from the pure product of the bee.

Like the Muses, who preferred to live on mountains as Helicon, Olympus, or Parnassus, so the bees loved to frequent the moun-

---

[1] *Greek Anthology*, VII. 13.

[2] The same was said later of many others—Ambrose, Isidore, Dominic, etc. St. Ambrose is represented in art with a beehive near him; on the back of the high altar of his church at Milan is a painting of him with bees swarming round his cradle.

[3] *Greek Anthology*, IX. 187. Menander lived about 342-291 B.C.

[4] *Idyll*, VII. 78.

tains covered with the sweet flowers from which they gathered the sweet nectar; like the Muses, too, who lived chastely and harmoniously together, so the bees became symbols of purity and chastity. This thought must have been in the mind of Euripides when he makes Hippolytus, stepping before the statue of Artemis, speak these beautiful words:

> To thee this wreathed garland, from a green
> And virgin meadow, bear I, O my Queen,
> Where never shepherd leads his grazing ewes,
> Nor scythe has touched. Only the river dews
> Gleam, and the spring bee sings, and in the glade
> Hath Solitude her mystic garden made.[1]

Bees, who lived in clefts of rocks or in caves, appear to have been considered as intimately connected with, if not actually embodying, the souls of the dead. These clefts in rocks or caves were thought to be entrances to the underground world of dead spirits. Vergil may have been thinking of the souls of the dead as bees when he describes Aeneas beside the waters of Lethe, and how he saw the unnumbered host of spirits who were drinking the waters, and compared them to the bees swarming in the meadows beneath the cloudless summer sun, so that the air was filled with the hum.[2]

Many references to "bee-souls" in the writings of the later Greek philosophers are connected with the belief in the transmigration of souls. The bees are emblematic of fresh incarnations. Porphyry says that the appellation Bee or *Melissa* was given to souls about to be born, but he adds:

All souls, however, proceeding into generation, are not simply called bees, but those who live justly, and who, having performed such things as are acceptable to the gods, will return whence they came. For this insect loves to return to the place whence it came, and is eminently just and sober.[3]

According to Porphyry also, honey, the embodiment of sweetness, is symbolic of the pleasure which draws souls down to be born, and it is a symbol specially suitable to aquatic nymphs:

[1] Sir Gilbert Murray's translation.
[2] *Aeneid*, VI. 703.
[3] *De ant. nym.*, 18.

Wells and streams are akin to Hybrid nymphs and still more to nymphs in the sense of souls, which our forefathers called by the special term *Melissas*, since they were producers of pleasure. So that Sophocles was not far wrong in saying of the souls, "The swarm of the dead hums and rises upwards.[1] Moreover, the ancients gave the name of *Melissae* to the priestesses of Demeter who were initiates of the chthonian goddess; the name *Melitodes* to Kore [Persephone] herself; the moon [Artemis] too, whose province it was to bring to the birth, they called *Melissa*, because the moon being a bull and its ascension the bull, bees are begotten of bulls. And souls that pass to the earth are bull-begotten.[2]

Porphyry thus states that the soul was conceived of as coming down from the Moon-goddess, Artemis, in the form of bees. He also adds that honey was considered a symbol of death, and for that reason it was usual to offer libations of honey to the chthonian— the underworld—divinities. It was only those souls who had lived a righteous life who were called *Melissae*, and afterwards they returned to heaven, just as the bee returned to her hive. There is a belief in Wales and other places, which we shall mention later, that the bee herself was the only animal who came direct from Paradise.

That the bee is a symbol of a fresh incarnation probably lies at the bottom of the old myth of Glaucus, the son of Minos and Pasiphae. Hyginus gives the following version of the tale:

Glaucus, while playing at ball, fell into a jar of honey. His parents sought for him and inquired of Apollo concerning the boy. Apollo made answer: "A mostrosity has been born to you; whoso can detect the meaning shall restore your son to you." On receiving this oracle Minos began to seek among his people for the monstrosity. They told him that a calf had been born, which thrice a day, once every four hours, changed its colour, being first white, then red, and lastly black. To get this portent interpreted Minos called together his augurs. They failed to find a solution, but Polyidus the son of Koiranus explained the portent by comparing the calf to a mulberry-tree, the fruit of which first is white, then red and when fully ripe, black. Then said Minos to him, " 'Tis thou who must restore my son." Hereupon Polyidus, while taking the auspices, saw an owl upon a wine-bin frightening away some bees. He welcomed the omen, and took up the lifeless lad from the jar. Minos then said to Polyidus, "Thou

---

[1] Fragment 795, Nauck.   [2] *De ant. nym.*, 18.

hast found the body, now restore the life." Polyidus protested that this was an impossibility, but Minos ordered him to be shut up in a tomb along with the boy, a sword being laid ready to his hand. When this had been done, suddenly a snake glided out towards the boy's body. Polyidus, thinking it intent on food, promptly struck with the sword and killed it. A second snake in search of its consort saw the dead beast, crept out with a certain herb, and by means of its touch, restored life to the snake. Polyidus followed this example with the like result. The boy helped him to shout inside the tomb and a passer-by told Minos of what had happened. He bade the tomb be opened, recovered his child safe and sound and sent Polyidus home laden with gifts.[1]

Fig. 19.—POLYIDUS AND GLAUCUS

(Furtwängler: *Antike Gemmen,* Pl. xxii, 16)

In the myth the bees, who were kept from entering the jar by the owl, apparently symbolize the soul endeavouring to regain the body within. The scarab represented in Fig. 19 perhaps illustrates this myth. Some scholars think that the figure bending over the pithos is Hermes invoking the dead from a burial-jar, while a soul in the form of a bee hovers over it; but Dr. Furtwängler thinks that it may represent an older, simpler form of the Glaucus myth, in which the boy died and was buried in a honey jar, but was restored to life by the seer Polyidus, the bee above the pithos being the symbol of the soul.[2]

As has already been mentioned, prophetic powers were ascribed to honey—the Thriae uttered true prophecies when they had

---

[1] Hyginus, fab. 136, trans. Dr. A. B. Cook. The story is also given by Apollodorus, 3, 3, 1. One of the lost dramas of Sophocles was *Polyidus the Seer;* a fragment which has been preserved says that Polyidus tried to discover Glaucus by means of divination. At the sacred rite—

> "Were present fleeces of sheep, and from the vine
> Drink offerings, and raisins well preserved;
> Fruits of all kinds, mingled with barley cakes,
> And olive oil, and that most intricate
> Wax-moulded fabric of the tawny bee."
>
> (Trans. Sir C. Young, "Everyman" edition.)

[2] *Antike Gemmen,* Pl. xxii, Fig. 16, and vol. iii, p. 253.

partaken of honey, if deprived of it, they were bereft of their powers. Pindar relates of the seer Iamus that, deserted by his mother Evadne when a babe, he was fed by two serpents on the "sweet dew of the bee," and that therefore his father, Apollo, declared that he should be a prophet excelling all others.[1]

The power of predicting rain was very generally attributed to bees—Aristotle, Varro, Vergil, Pliny, and others all say that bees were weather prophets.[2] This belief may perhaps be connected with the belief in "Bee-souls." Dr. O. Gruppe, the well-known mythologist, writes:

> Droughts especially appear to have accompanied the spirits of the dead in bee-form, and for this reason the honey offering was almost always customary in rain-magic, and the power of predicting rain was attributed to the bee.[3]

A story which seems to be connected with rain-magic is told by Pausanias of the oracle of Trophonius in Boeotia:

> This oracle was formerly unknown to the Boeotians, they discovered it on the following occasion. No rain had fallen for more than a year, so they dispatched envoys to Delphi from every city. When asked for a remedy for the drought, the Pythian priestess bade them go to Trophonius at Lebadea, and get the cure from him. But when they came to Lebadea, and could not find the oracle, Saon, the oldest of the envoys, saw a swarm of bees, and he advised them that they should follow the bees wherever they went. Straightway he observed the bees flying into the earth and followed them to the oracle.[4]

Pausanias also states that anyone consulting this oracle had to descend into a cleft in the rocks and take with him a barley-cake kneaded with honey.

In this story the "Delphic Bee" sent a swarm to conduct the men to the oracle; the appearance of a swarm was also considered as a sign that a stranger was to be expected. The Greeks had a proverb: "The siren heralds a friend, the bee a stranger"; in the *Aeneid* King Latinus saw a swarm on a sacred bay-tree near his

---

[1] *Pythian*, VI. 40–50.

[2] Arist., *Hist. Anim.*, 627b, 10; Varro. III. 16, 37; Vergil, *Geor.*, IV. 191; Pliny, *Nat. Hist.*, XI. 20.

[3] Gruppe, *Griech. Mythologie*, p. 801.   [4] Paus., IX. 40, I.

house, which he said denoted the arrival of a stranger (Aeneas).[1]
Later, especially among the Romans, swarms were supposed to
foretell misfortune. Livy relates that the Romans were alarmed,
for a wolf had entered the camp and a swarm of bees had settled
on the tent of the general, Scipio, who would not set out upon his
expedition until these prodigies had been expiated.[2] Another time
a swarm had been seen in the Forum, and so supplications had
to be made to all the deities who had shrines in Rome.[3] On another
occasion the consuls were detained by religious affairs, for various
prodigies had been seen, including a swarm of bees which had settled
in the Forum of Casinum, and so expiation had to be made.[4]
Tacitus also mentions that in A.D. 64 a succession of prodigies
kept the minds of men in constant dread, a swarm of bees had
settled on the Capitol.[5]

Pliny states that a swarm settled in the camp of Drusus just
before the decisive Battle of Arbalo, but he remarks that this was
contrary to the usual meaning given to a swarm by the augurs.[6]
The unlucky result of the Battle of Pharsalus was announced to
Pompey by a swarm settling on his standard, and the death of the
Emperor Claudius was foretold by a swarm settling in the camp.[7]

Swarms were also supposed to announce the attainment of
sovereignty. Cicero relates that before Dionysius of Syracuse
became king, he wanted one day to ride through a river, but his
horse sank in the mire and could not be extricated, so Dionysius
had to go on foot. Soon after he heard his horse neighing and
looking back saw it galloping towards him with a swarm clinging
to its mane. A few days afterwards he became tyrant of Syracuse.[8]

Among the finds in the ruins of the Artemisium of Ephesus were
some rosettes composed of bee-bodies and leaves alternately (see
p. 58). These headless bees were probably some sort of amulet connected with the worship of Artemis. They are illustrated on
Plate v. It seems strange that the bee should be one of the animals
considered to have the "evil eye," but the supposition that it was
so regarded is supported by the finding of a rosette in the Villa of
Cassius at Tivoli, which is depicted on Fig. 20, where a headless
bee is represented with a headless frog and lizard, both of which

---

[1] Aen., VII. 64.   [2] Livy, XXI. 46.   [3] Ibid., XXIV. 46.
[4] Ibid., XXVII. 23.   [5] Tacitus, *Annals*, XII. 64.   [6] Pliny, XI. 55.
[7] Dio. Cassius, 42.   [8] Cicero, *De divin.*, I. 33, 73.

animals are known to have been credited with the evil eye. We may therefore infer that the eyes of all three creatures were considered

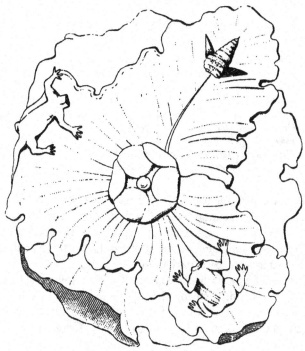

Fig. 20.—HEADLESS BEE, A TALISMAN TO AVERT THE EVIL EYE.
ROSETTE FROM TIVOLI
(G. Visconti: *Museo Pio Clementino*, Pl. A, vi, Num. 10)

baneful, and that this rosette and perhaps the headless bees of Ephesus were talismans for averting evil.[1]

[1] In the Caucasus, however, it was an ancient custom, which still lingers, to place the skull of a domestic animal, a horse or cow, on the top of the hives in order to avert the "evil eye" from the bees. L. Armbruster, *Der Bienenstand als völkerkundliches Denkmal*, 1926, p. 33.

CHAPTER X

THE "OX-BORN BEE"

*Belief in reproduction of bees from decayed carcases—The myth of
Aristaeus—Ovid—Vergil—Florentinus—Bulls must be cudgelled
to death—Best time for operation—Incubation period—Notices of
belief by Alexandrian and classical writers—Earliest, Antigonos of
Karystos—Bees and dead carcases—Samson and bees—Head of
Onesilus—Melissa of Corinth—Cleomenes—Lower Egypt possible
home of myth—Egyptian sacred bull—School of Euhemerus—
Herodotus on burial of sacred bulls—Possible origin of story—
Belief in it in the Middle Ages*

BEFORE we pass on to speak of honey used in Greek religious
rites, we must mention a belief which has already been alluded
to, the belief that bees could be reproduced from the decaying
flesh of oxen. This superstition persisted during the Middle Ages,
and indeed in some parts until quite recent times.

The belief appears to be connected with a myth of Aristaeus,
the "Honey-Lord," which, although evidently Greek in origin,
we know from the writings of the Latin poets, Ovid and Vergil.
We give a short account of the story as told by Ovid.

Aristaeus was weeping because all his bees had died, leaving the
unfinished combs. His mother, Cyrene, tried to console him, and told
him that Proteus would tell him how to obtain fresh swarms. So together
they went to seek Proteus, who usually lived in the sea, but at midday
used to come and rest on an island near the mouth of the Nile. Here
they found him, and Aristaeus bound him with fetters while asleep, for
Proteus had the power to change himself into any shape he liked. Thus
captured he was forced to speak and told Aristaeus that he must
bury the carcase of a slaughtered ox, and that from it he would obtain
what he wanted, for when the carcase decayed, swarms of bees would
issue from it. The death of one thus produced a thousand lives.[1]

Vergil devoted nearly half of the fourth *Georgic* to this story of
Aristaeus and his bees, which is too long to quote here. He relates
the method of obtaining these ox-born bees much more fully than

[1] Ovid, *Fasti*, I. 363 ff.

Ovid; the method which he says was always practised in Egypt was briefly as follows:

> Choose a small confined space, and erect in it a building with four windows, one facing each quarter, and with a tiled roof. Then take a bullock, whose second year's horns are just curling over its brow, stop up its nostrils and mouth and beat it to death without breaking the skin. Shut the bruised body up in the closed room, strewn with thyme and cassia, and after nine days the softened bones having fermented, wondrous creatures will appear, who with buzzing wings will fly into the air— a swarm of bees.

A very full account of obtaining a swarm, given by Florentinus in the *Geoponica*, is much the same as this of Vergil, only he says that the doors and windows of the place where the body is are to be plastered up with mud so as to exclude light and air, and it is not to be opened for three weeks, then only for a short time to air it, for it is to be closed again for another ten days. After that time clusters of bees will be found, while of the bullock nothing remains but horns, bones, and hair. Florentinus says that "king" bees come from the spinal marrow, or better still from the brain, ordinary bees from the flesh.[1]

The main idea of this singular superstition was that the *life of the bull passed into that of the bees*; from its decaying body men thought the larvae of the bees arose and developed; so, in order that the life power which lived in the animal should not be weakened, the bullocks which were to generate bees might not be killed in the usual way, but must be slowly cudgelled to death and all openings stopped up, for it was a common belief that the soul escaped by the natural openings of the body. The most appropriate time for this method of reproducing bees was said to be when the Sun entered the sign of the Bull (Taurus), because the idea of favourable weather and growing vegetation was bound up with it. The incubation period was reckoned at three weeks and ten days, that is a month (Vergil says nine days); and because moisture was regarded as an indispensable factor of life, it must be preserved and so precautions were taken to protect the body from the drying wind.

The problem which is still not solved is how and when did the belief in the *ox-born* bee arise. The earliest to mention it are the

[1] *Geoponica*, xv. 2, 21; quoted by A. B. Cook, *Zeus*, vol. i, p. 514.

Greek writers of Alexandria in the time of the Ptolomies—
Archelaos, Callimachus, Philetas, Nicander, all allude to it in their
poems and epigrams. We find no allusion to it in the earlier Greek
poets, although they often mention the bee, and it is singular, if the
belief is much older than the third century B.C., that Aristotle never
mentions it, although he evidently believed that some animals were
generated spontaneously, and in his *History of Animals* treats of the
reproduction of the bee at great length, as the subject puzzled and
yet interested him greatly. The later writers on apiculture who
mention it—some evidently believing in it, others somewhat
sceptical—are Mago the Carthaginian, Varro, Vergil, Columella,
Pliny, Celsus, Aelian, and Florentinus.

Varro says that bees are generated partly from bees and partly
from decayed oxen,[1] and he quotes an epigram of Archelaos, "The
bees are the streaming children of the decaying ox," and one
of Nicander, "The wasps are the offspring of horses as the bees are
of oxen."

Columella in the Calendar which he took from Hyginus says
that dried ox-dung is used for smoking bees, because the bees are
in some way related to oxen![2] He also remarks that Democritus,
Mago, and Vergil all state that bees can be generated from a dead
bullock, and that Mago had also asserted that this could be done
from the stomach of an ox, but adds that he agrees with Celsus, who
reasonably thought that bees did not die in such numbers as to
make it necessary to procure them in such a manner.[3] It certainly
would have hardly been worth while to kill an ox to procure a
swarm!

Pliny states that if the bees all die they can be renewed by covering
the carcase of an ox with dung, or according to Vergil, a bullock's
body; and he also mentions that wasps and hornets came from
horses' carcases and beetles from those of asses![4]

One of the earliest writers to mention the *ox-born* bee is Antigonos of Karystos, about 250 B.C., who states:

In Egypt if you bury the ox in certain places, so that only his horns

---

[1] *De re rust.*, III. 16, 4.   [2] Colum., IX. 14, 1.
[3] Ibid., IX. 14, 6. This Democritus is not the philosopher of Abdera.
Strabo (*Greek Anthology*, XII. 239) also alludes to the "ox-born bee."
[4] Pliny, XI. 70.

project above the ground and then saw them off, they say that bees fly out; for the ox putrefies and is resolved into bees.[1]

We have older references to bees being found in the skeletons of dead animals. There is the well-known story of Samson finding bees and honey in the carcase of the lion which he had killed,[2] and Herodotus gives us another example:

The people of Amathus because Onesilus had laid siege to their city, cut off the head of his corpse, and took it home with them to their city, where it was set up over the gate. Here it hung till it became hollow; whereupon a swarm of bees took possession of it and filled it with honeycomb. On seeing this the Amathusians consulted the oracle, and were commanded to take down the head and bury it, and henceforth to regard Onesilus as a hero, and offer sacrifices to him yearly; so it would go better with them.[3]

We mentioned above the case of Melissa, the priestess of Demeter, from whose body, torn to pieces by the infuriated women, the goddess caused bees to generate (see p. 96). Then there is also that of Cleomenes, the exiled king of Sparta, who had been killed by the king of Egypt, Ptolemy Philopater (222–205 B.C.), related by Plutarch:

A few days afterwards, the soldiers who watched the body of Cleomenes on the cross saw a great serpent winding about the head and covering all his face, so that no bird of prey durst touch it. This struck the king with superstitious terrors, for Ptolemy was now persuaded that he had caused the death of a person who was a favourite of heaven, and something more than mortal. The Alexandrians crowded to the place and called Cleomenes a hero, a son of the gods, till the philosophers put a stop to their devotions by assuring them that, as dead oxen breed bees, horses, wasps, and beetles rise out of the putrefaction of asses, so it is a common belief that human carcases when some of the marrow is evaporated and it comes to a thicker consistence, produce serpents.[4]

The cases mentioned do not help us much. Samson's lion and the head of Onesilus were inhabited by bees when dry and hollow, and that is quite possible; all beekeepers know that bees will never

[1] Antig., *Hist. mir.*, 19; quoted by A. B. Cook, *Zeus*, I, p. 514, and Gmelin, *Buch von Der Biene*, p. 11.   [2] Judges xiv.
[3] Herod., V. 114.   [4] Plutarch, *Cleomenes*, 34.

touch decaying flesh, but they might easily take possession of a hollow carcase, especially if, as would be the case in hot countries, the dried skin remained over the bones. The case of Melissa is possibly a myth to connect her with the Bee-maidens, the *Melissae* of Demeter, and the story also attributes the appearance of the bees from the body as due directly to the goddess. Plutarch's story tells the popular beliefs current at the time, but does not help to solve our problem.

All the evidence, however, which has so far been collected tends to point to Egypt or some neighbouring hot country as the home of the myth; the Alexandrian poets are the first to mention it, Antigonos of Karystos attributes the story to Egypt, Vergil definitely gives Lower Egypt near the Canopic mouth of the Nile as the place where the custom of producing the *ox-born* bees arose; Proteus, who, the myth says, was the first to tell Aristaeus to bury an ox in order to obtain new swarms, was connected by tradition with the island of Pharos close to Alexandria.

The bull was one of the most important of the Egyptian sacred animals, its fertilizing force was reverenced by all the ancients.[1] Hapi or Apis, the Egyptian sacred bull, was believed to have a miraculous birth. Herodotus says:

> Apis is the calf of a cow which is never afterwards able to bear young. The Egyptians say that fire comes down from heaven upon the cow, which thereupon bears Apis.[2]

The Apis was considered to embody the soul of Osiris, the god of resurrection and life in the next world. Attempts have been made to connect Apis with the Ox-born bee myth, but it presents difficulties, as the Apis was mummified and therefore would not decay. It is, however, true that in the third century B.C. there flourished in Egypt the philosophic school of Euhemerus, which taught that under the influence of the sun on the earth were generated not only the germs of plant life but also those of animals, and it was certainly believed that new animals developed not only

---

[1] Dionysus as the principle of life and generation was figured as a bull, and it was said by those initiated into his mysteries that, being torn in pieces as a bull, he was re-born as a bee. See De Gubernatis, *Zoological Mythology*, vol. ii, p. 217. Plutarch says that Dionysus was given the title *Bougenes*.

[2] Herod., III. 28.

out of the mud of the Nile but also out of animal carcases. That each animal can only have parents like itself was not generally recognized; on the contrary, the belief was widespread that an animal could change itself into another animal, certainly that a higher being like a god could easily assume many forms—for instance, the Homeric deities constantly appear as men. The ancient Egyptians also believed in the reincarnation of the soul, thus the belief may have arisen that the soul of the ox passed into that of the bees. That the "death of one should produce a thousand," as Ovid said, would present no difficulties to them.[1]

There is, however, one way in which possibly the sacred bull might be connected with the ox-born bee story, through a custom, mentioned by Herodotus, of burying certain of these animals. Before quoting what he says we must draw attention again to the passage of Antigonos of Karystos, which was given above:

In Egypt if you bury an ox in certain places, so that only the horns project above the ground, and then saw them off, they say that bees fly out, for the ox putrefies and is resolved into bees.[2]

Herodotus says that male kine were reckoned to belong to Apis,[3] but it was only black bulls with special marks—a white disc between the horns being one of the most important—who were really entitled to the name *Apis*;[4] others might be sacrificed if approved of by the priests, and they were disembowelled and the body filled with bread, raisins, honey, and aromatics, and thus filled the body was burnt; but he informs us, and this is important as it supports the statement of Antigonos, that when the kine die, the females, who are sacred to Isis, are thrown into the river, but

[1] See J. Ph. Glock, *Die Symbolik der Biene*, Heidelberg, p. 129–42. Some have even tried to connect the name with the Latin name for bee = *Apis*; but this has a short "a" and the bull *Apis* a long one, and the name *Hapi* probably means the Nile.

[2] In Dr. A. B. Cook's work on *Zeus* there is an interesting section (vol. i, para. 6 section g) about rituals connected with bulls' horns, which he traces in Crete and other ancient countries, showing how the horn was worshipped as the culminating point of its strength. There is no doubt that the rituals connected with bulls' horns are most ancient, but it seems doubtful if there were any definite religious rites connected with the belief in the production of bees from the bull's body, which is a reason for questioning if the belief in the ox-born bee is really primitive.　　　[3] Herod., II. 38.　　[4] Ibid., III. 28.

the males are buried in the suburbs of the towns with one or both of their horns appearing above the surface of the ground to mark the place. When the bodies are decayed a boat comes, at an appointed time, from the island called Prosopitis, which is a portion of the Delta, and calls at the various cities in turn to collect the bones of the oxen.[1]

Here we are told that the bulls are buried with the horns showing above the surface, the district mentioned is the Delta, near the Canopic mouth of the Nile, the very part where Vergil says the story originated. The bodies were allowed to decay, probably the horns would sometimes drop off before the boat came to collect the bones (or possibly might be sawn off by the people, as horns were used for many purposes), certainly insects would breed in the decaying carcases which were so near the surface, and would be noticed by the passers-by. The inhabitants were not naturalists, and what would be more natural than for the report to get abroad that bees, the royal symbol for the king of the Delta, were appearing from the bodies? So long as it was some insect resembling a bee,[2] it would be quite sufficient to set the tale going, and afterwards people were not likely to kill a valuable ox to obtain a swarm of bees, but the story that they could be so obtained would pass from one generation to another. A really marvellous thing about the myth is that it lasted for so many centuries, as we shall see in later chapters, right down to modern times; but in the Middle Ages the name of Vergil carried such weight that any story believed by him would be accepted unhesitatingly by the credulous and unscientific, especially as the myth seems to have had the support of such great Christian writers as St. Augustine and Origen.

---

[1] Herod., II. 41.

[2] The drone-fly, *Eristlais tenax*, has been suggested, but it presents difficulties, as it breeds in water. Osten-Sacken, *The Ox-born Bee of the Ancients*, Heidelberg, 1910, supports this theory.

CHAPTER XI

HONEY IN GREEK RELIGIOUS RITES

*Honey used in cults of the Spirits of the Dead, of the Underworld
Deities, and of Snakes—Honey-drink older than wine—Nephalia—
Offerings to the dead—To Demeter and Persephone—To other
Underworld divinities, Hecate, Eumenides—Fates and nymphs—
Honey-cakes given to Cerberus and other divinities in snake form
—Honey offering to some Upperworld gods, Helios, Pan, Priapus—
Eros and Aphrodite—Honey used at certain festivals*

In reviewing the rites in which honey figures, we are struck by
the fact that they belong to the earliest cults, those of the spirits of
the dead, of the underworld deities, and of snakes. Many of them
go back into the dim ages before there was any wine, when honey-
drinks were the only intoxicants known.

That there was a dim remembrance of a time when there was no
wine is proved by several myths, such as attributing its discovery
to Dionysus and others,[1] and another which describes how honey was
ousted by wine, under the form of a contest between Dionysus and
Aristaeus, the gods adjudging the victory to the former.[2] In the
Orphic myth alluded to by Porphyry, Zeus makes Kronos intoxicated by means of honey, for "wine was not"; and the goddess
Night also advised him to bind Kronos when he was lying under
the oaks, intoxicated by the honey produced by the bee.[3] Plato tells
that Porus in the Garden of Zeus was drunk, not with wine, but
with nectar, for "wine was not yet known."[4] Plutarch says that
mead was used as a libation before the cultivation of the vine, and
"even now those of the barbarians who do not drink wine have a
honey-drink."[5]

Porphyry, quoting Theophrastus, the successor of Aristotle, says:

Ancient sacrifices were for the most part performed with sobriety. But
those sacrifices are sober in which libations are made with water. After-

---

[1] See Karl Kirchner, *Die sakrale Bedeutung des Weines in Altertum*, Giessen,
1910, p. 3.
[2] Nonnos, *Dion.*, XIII. 258; quoted by A. B. Cook, *Jour. Hell. Stud.*,
vol. XV, p. 21.   [3] *De ant. nym.*, 7.
[4] Plato, *Sympos.*, 203.   [5] Plutarch, *Banquet*, 106.

wards, however, libations were made with honey, for we first received this liquid prepared for us by the bees; in the third place libations were made with oil; and in the fourth place with wine.[1]

Here, again, it is distinctly stated that honey libations are more ancient than those of wine.

These honey libations, the produce of the bee, who, as Porphyry puts it, was so eminently just and sober, were known as the "sober offerings," the *nephalia*, and such is the conservatism of religious ritual, that these *nephalia* were continued long after the introduction of wine. In some cases, indeed, as, for example, in the rites of the Bona Dea at Rome, the *wine* was not called by its name, but was spoken of as *milk*, and the jar in which it was carried was known as the *honey-pot*.[2]

The libations to the dead were generally threefold, and usually consisted of honey, oil, and wine; or honey and milk or water, oil, and wine; but whatever the constituents of the threefold libation were, honey was always one of them.[3] The inscription on a golden plaque, found in southern Italy, runs: "The dead is thrice offered a drink; a mixture [honey-mixture], milk and water."[4]

The offering of honey libations to the dead is a very ancient custom. It seems as if the primitive mind thought either that the spirits of the dead had to be propitiated and placated and that honey being the sweetest food known lent itself to that purpose, or that the spirits enjoyed the food that man himself enjoyed.

It is probably one of the oldest religious rites, and continued for thousands of years; it was still alive in the second century of our era; in the *Charon* of Lucian, Hermes is asked why men dig a trench and burn expensive feasts and pour wine and honey into

---

[1] Porph., *De Abstin.*, II. 20.

[2] Macrobius, I. 12, 25. Plutarch also (*Roman Questions*, xx) says: "When the women poured libations of wine to the Bona Dea, they called it by the name of milk."

[3] Sir A. Evans found in the Dictaean Cave in Crete the remains of a libation table with three cup-like depressions, which he thinks was probably used in such primitive worship as that to the shades of the dead. See *Jour. Hell. Stud.*, vol. xvii, p. 350. Cf. "Mycenaean Tree and Pillar Cult," in *Journ. Hell. Stud.*, vol. xxi, p. 113, and "Palace of Minos," vol. i, p. 629.

[4] See A. Dieterich, "Der Untergang der antiken Religion," in *Kleiner Schriften*, Leipzig, 1911, p. 472.

a trench. Hermes answered that he cannot think what good it can do them, but "anyhow, people believe that the dead are summoned up from below to the feast, and that they flutter round the smoke and drink the honey draught from the trench."[1]

In both *Iliad* and *Odyssey* are to be found survivals of a cult of souls. Achilles called on the spirit of Patrocles and poured out a wine libation, and placed jars of honey and oil by the pyre.[2] In the *Odyssey* the funeral of Achilles himself is described; he was "buried in the garments of the gods and in much unguents and in sweet honey."[3] Here the unguents and honey added to the pyre may have been a sacrifice, or, as was customary if the body was to be preserved some days before burial, have been used as preservatives; but in another passage there is a very full account of the rites customary when calling up the spirits of the dead.

Odysseus wants to call up the spirit of the seer Teiresias, and the enchantress, Circe, tells him first to dig a trench and make a libation to all the dead:

So, hero, draw nigh thereto, as I command thee, and dig a trench as it were a cubit in length and breadth, and about it pour a drink offering to all the dead; first with mead, and thereafter with sweet wine, and with the third time with water, and sprinkle white meal thereon; and entreat with many prayers the strengthless heads of the dead.[4]

When all this was done the spirit of Teiresias rose slowly in the trench. It seems to have been the belief that the spirits of the dead were invoked more easily with drinks than with foods.

In the *Persians* Aeschylus makes Atossa, the mother of Xerxes, invoke the spirit of her husband Darius. She offers him soothing drinks:

> A holy heifer's milk, white, fair to drink,
> Bright honey drops from flowers bee-distilled,
> With draughts of water from a virgin fount,
> And from the ancient vine its mother wild
> An unmixed draught.[5]

---

[1] Lucian, *Charon*, 22; quoted by Miss J. Harrison, *Prolegomena*, p. 75.

[2] *Iliad*, XXIII. 170. On this passage, see E. Rohde, *Psyche*, 4th ed., 1907, p. 15.   [3] *Odyssey*, XXIV. 68.

[4] Ibid., X. 519; XI. 27; trans. Butcher and Lang.

[5] *Persians*, 204; trans. Sir Gilbert Murray. Aeschylus was born 525 B.C.

Later, in Roman times, Silius Italicus tells how Scipio, wanting to call up his father's ghost, went to Apollo's priestess:

> And therefore to Autinoë (who then
> Under Apollo's name the sacred Den
> And tripod kept), he goes, and open lays
> The counsels of his troubled heart, and prays
> To see his father's face. Without delay,
> The Prophetess commands him straight to slay,
> To the shades below, the usual sacrifice,
> Two coal black lambs . . .
> . . . Likewise joyn
> To them choice Hony and purest Wine.

Scipio and the Priestess go together at night to sacrifice the animals, and

> On these they Milk infus'd
> Hony and Wine.[1]

As a rule these libations to the departed began at the funeral, but they were offered, as we gather from the instances given above, when the living called upon the spirits of the dead, or when they wanted to placate their ghosts. Euripides makes Helen send Hermione to the grave of Clytemnestra with offerings:

Take these offerings in thy hands. Soon as thou reachest Clytemnestra's tomb, pour mingled streams of honey, milk, and wine.[2]

Iphigenia makes the same offerings at her brother's tomb:

> O Spirit, thou unknown,
>   Who bearest on dark wings
> My brother, my one, my own,
>   I bear drink offerings,
> And the cup that bringest ease
>   Flowing through Earth's deep breast;
> Milk of the mountain kine,
> The hallowed gleam of wine,
> The toil of murmuring bees;
>   By these shall the dead have rest.[3]

---

[1] Silius Italicus, XIII. 415, trans. Thomas Ross, 1661. Silius lived about A.D. 25–102. Here the honey and wine were an offering to Pluto; the milk, honey, and wine to Persephone.   [2] Eurip., *Orestes*, 114.

[3] *Iphigenia in Tauris*, 159–65, trans. Gilbert Murray.

The libations to the dead—of which honey always formed a part—thus varied at different times, because the conception of the continued existence of the state of souls in Hades developed and changed, but there was one cult in which men were very chary of altering the sacrifice, the cult of the underworld divinities, their sacrifice remained unaltered, and was usually wineless. The reason for this seems to have been that men were afraid to offend these ancient and important deities, and also the causes which led to changes of sacrifice in other cults—the changes in the daily diet of men themselves, which caused them to offer their own food to the gods—did not apply here, for there was no food offering in the sacrifices to the underworld gods, the sacrificer ate and drank nothing himself.[1]

We have seen in Chapter IX how the bee, often found in clefts in the rock and in caves—places which were considered as leading to the habitation of the chthonian gods—was connected with the worship of such divinities as Rhea, the Cretan Zeus, Demeter, and others. We mentioned that the priestesses of Demeter were called *Melissae*, and that Persephone, as queen of the Netherworld, was called *Melitodes*, so it was quite appropriate that honey should be offered to them. Pausanias tells that he visited the shrine of Black Demeter at Phigalia in Arcadia, but that he

sacrificed no victim to the goddess, such being the custom of the natives; instead they bring the fruit of the vine and other cultivated trees, and also honeycombs.[2]

Demeter (Ceres) as Corn-Mother was also offered honey; and Vergil sings

> Let all rural labourers adore Ceres; for her
> dilute honeycombs and soft wine.[3]

Jason was told by Medea to propitiate Hecate, "pouring from a goblet the hive-stored labour of bees";[4] and on another occasion he pours into the river libations of honey and pure oil to earth,

---

[1] See Paul Stengel in *Hermes*, vol. 29, p. 286.   [2] Paus., VIII. 42, 11.
[3] *Geor.*, I. 344. Ovid (*Fasti*, IV. 458) says Ceres had honey offered her when in the house of Triptolemus' parents.
[4] Apollonis Rhodius, *Argonautica*, III. 1036; cf. Ovid, *Met.*, VII. 24.

and to the gods of the country, and to the souls of heroes, beseeching them to aid him.[1]

Dionysus had the *nephalia* offered to him in Athens, probably when his netherworld character was to be emphasized, a survival possibly of his early days before he was regarded as god of wine.[2]

The *nephalia* were offered to the Eumenides. Sophocles gives a vivid picture of the expiation made by the unhappy Oedipus to them. He is told by the Chorus:

> An expiation instant thou must make
> To the offended powers whose sacred seat
> Thou hast profaned.

Oedipus.   But how must it be done?

Chorus.   Take thou a cup wrought by some skilful hands,
> Bind it with wreaths around . . . Then turning to the sun
> Make thy libations . . .
> The water from three fountains drawn; and last,
> Remember, none be left. . . . Water with honey mixed,
> No wine; this pour upon the earth.[3]

In the *Eumenides* of Aeschylus the ghost of Clytemnestra exclaims:

Oh, and yet plenty of my provisions have ye lapped, wineless drink offerings, sober, soothing draughts. Give ear, because my plea is for my very life."[4]

Pausanias also mentions the honey offering to the Eumenides. Of his visit to Corinth he writes:

We come to a grove of evergreen oaks and a temple of the goddesses whom the Athenians name the Venerable, and the Sicyonians name Eumenides [the Kindly]. On one day every year they celebrate a festival in their honour, pour libations of honey mixed with water and use flowers instead of wreaths. They perform similar ceremonies at the Altar of the Fates.[5]

---

[1] Ap. Rh., II. 1271.

[2] Philoch. on Sophocles' *Oed.*, Col. 100; Plutarch, *De tuenda Sanit.*, XX, quoted by T. Wächter, *Reinheitsvorschriften in griechischen Kult*, Giessen, 1910, p. 110, who gives other examples.   [3] *Oed.*, Col. 468.

[4] Aeschylus, *Eumenides*, 104, trans. Headlam.   [5] Paus., II. 11, 4.

As Pausanias remarks in this passage, the Moirae or Fates had also these same "sober offerings," and this custom has continued down to the present day. In his visit to Greece early in the nineteenth century, Dodwell visited a cavern opposite the Acropolis, the so-called prison of Socrates; outside he saw two Turkish women, who warned him at his peril not to go into the cave, as they had something of importance to do there, and the Greek who was with him said they were performing some magical ceremonies as the cavern was haunted by the Moirae. The Greek refused to enter the cave, but Dodwell went in and found:

In the inner chamber a small feast, consisting of a cup of honey, white almonds, a cake on a little napkin, and a vase of aromatic herbs burning. This votive offering was placed upon a rock which was flat at the top and was probably originally an altar or table.

Dodwell goes on to relate that he took the things away with him and gave the cake to his ass, to the horror of the Greek, who was certain something evil would befall him for his impiety in destroying the hopes and happiness of the two women by removing the offerings they had made to the Fates in order to render them propitious to their conjugal aspirations. On the way home the ass ran away and broke Dodwell's camera obscura to pieces![1]

In *Modern Greek Folklore and Ancient Greek Religion*, Mr. Lawson writes that Spartan women will make a wearisome journey to Tatgetus to lay a honey-cake in a certain cave there, and he mentions several districts where the same custom exists, and adds, "everywhere honey in some form or other is an essential part of the offering by which the Fates' favour is to be won."[2] He also states that it is believed that the Fates are always present, even though invisible, on the third or fifth night after the birth of a child. The house door is left open or unlatched, and on a table are set such dainties as the Fates love, always including honey; in Athens formerly the offerings were a dish of honey, three white almonds, a loaf of bread, and a glass of water.[3]

Offerings of honey were made to nymphs, especially the water

---

[1] E. Dodwell, *Tour in Greece*, London, 1819, p. 396.
[2] *Modern Greek Folklore and Ancient Greek Religion*, Cambridge, 1910, p. 21.   [3] Ibid., p. 125.

nymphs. Pausanias says that in Elis the inhabitants once a month sacrificed to the gods:

> They sacrifice after an ancient fashion; for they burn on the altars frankincense together with the wheat which has been kneaded with honey. They place sprays of olive also on the altars and pour libations of wine. Only to the Nymphs and the Mistresses do they not pour out libations of wine, nor do they pour them on the common altars of all the gods.[1]

The association of the nymphs with bees and honey is a very ancient one. In the cave on Ithaca, sacred to the Naiad nymphs, there are "mixing-bowls and jars of stone, and there, moreover, bees do hive."[2] The Nereid nymphs were fickle creatures and often malicious towards women, so that at marriages and childbirth great care had to be taken to guard against their envy, and to appease them offerings of food in which honey was the essential ingredient were set out for them. This custom has also continued to the present day. In Athens whirlwinds are said to occur most frequently near the old Hill of the Nymphs; and women of the lower class when they see the cloud of dust approach fall to crossing themselves and repeating "Honey and milk be in your path!"[3] In Corfu a few decades ago the peasantry used to make actual offerings of both honey and milk to the Nereids. Mr. Lawson writes:

> The gift of honey is of special significance. In every recorded case which I know of offerings to Nereids in modern Greece, honey is expressly mentioned and seems indeed to be essential; it is probably from their known preference for this food that at Kastoria in Macedonia they have received the name of the "honeyed ones."[4]

Honey-cakes were a special feature of many rites, especially in the cults of snakes or creatures guarding the entrances to the Netherworld. Cerberus, the three-headed dog who guarded the entrance to Hades, had honey-cakes thrown to him by those going there. In the Aeneid a cake of honey and wheat is given him by the Sibyl in order to propitiate him; hence the phrase, "A sop to Cerberus."[5]

[1] Paus., v. 15, 10. The *Mistresses* were Demeter and Persephone. Hestia (Vesta) had not many temples of her own, but had offerings at the public altars; honey, milk, and bread were offered to her before food. See Gruppe, *Griech. Mythologie*, p. 1405.   [2] *Odyssey*, XIII. 106.

[3] J. C. Lawson, *Modern Greek Folklore and Ancient Greek Religion*, p. 140.

[4] Ibid., p. 150.   [5] *Aeneid*, VI. 420.

The dragon who guarded the sacred tree in the garden of the Hesperides was tended by a priestess, who sprinkled its food with "dewy honey and sleepy poppy."[1]

The serpent was the familiar animal, sometimes the actual embodiment of the earth deity, and was regarded as the incarnation of the departed spirit and as a sacred and mystic animal in Greek religion.[2] Serpents were sacred to Trophonius, and when anyone wanted to consult his oracle, he had to descend into a hole and take with him barley-cakes kneaded with honey. There was a legend that the man who first descended into the cave found there two serpents, which he appeased with honey-cakes, but it was said that the persons who visited this oracle never laughed again, because of the fright which the serpent had given them.[3] The finding of this oracle and its connection with bees was mentioned above (p. 109).

On the hill of Kronos at Olympia there was a cave where Eileithyia and Sosipolis were worshipped. Eileithyia is only another name for the Mother-goddess; Sosipolis was associated with a serpent. Legend said that when the Arcadians invaded Elis, the baby Sosipolis (the Saviour of the City) was set naked before the Elean army, and that he changed into a snake and the Arcadians ran away. The snake vanished into a crevice in the earth, probably on the spot where his cave sanctuary was afterwards built. Here at his shrine Pausanias says was an old woman who was bound by custom to live chastely. She brought water to the god for washing, and placed for him barley-cakes kneaded with honey. Pausanias adds:

They burn all sorts of incense to Sosipolis, but they do not pour out libations of wine.[4]

In the sanctuary of Ge-Olympia at Athens there was a cleft in the rock and Pausanias writes:

It is said that after the deluge which happened in Deucalion's time, the water ran away down this cleft. Every year they throw into it wheaten cakes kneaded with honey.[5]

---

[1] *Aeneid*, IV. 484. Gruppe says that on a bowl of Assteas one of the Hesperides is named Melisa, that is, Melissa (*Griech. Mythologie*, p. 32).

[2] See Farnell, *Cults of the Greek States*, vol. iii, p. 10.

[3] Paus., IX. 39, 11; and Sir J. Frazer's commentary on the passage.

[4] Ibid., VI. 20, 2.   [5] Ibid., I. 18, 7.

This sanctuary was possibly connected with the Snake Child, Erichthonius, who Hesychius says dwelt "in the sanctuary of Erechtheus," of which Pausanias writes:

There is also a building on the Acropolis called the Erechtheum. Before the entrance there is an altar of Supreme Zeus, where they sacrifice no living thing, but they lay cakes on it, and having done so they are forbidden by custom to make use of wine.[1]

On the Acropolis, too, there was a sacred serpent, which Herodotus says was fed monthly with a honey-cake, and he relates that when the Persians were threatening Athens and those in authority wished the people to leave the city, they were told by

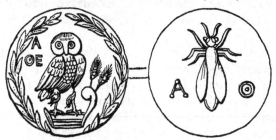

FIG. 21.—COIN OF ATHENS: OWL (SYMBOL OF ATHENA) AND BEE
(F. Creuzer: *Symbolik*, Pl. 94, Fig. 341cc)

the priestess that the honey-cakes which up to this time had always been consumed, now remained untouched, and so the people readily consented to go, as they believed that the deity had abandoned the city.[2] The bee was also associated with Athens. Fig. 21 represents a coin of that city.

Aelian describes the snake cult of the people of Epiros, which they believed was derived from Delphi:

The people of Epiros sacrifice in general to Apollo. There is a grove dedicated to the god and it has a circular enclosure and within are snakes, playthings surely for the god. Now only the maiden priestess approaches them, and she is naked and brings the snakes their food. Now if they take their food kindly, that is taken to mean that there will be a plentiful year and free from disease; but if they frighten her and do not take the honey-cakes which she offers them, they portend the reverse.[3]

[1] Paus., I. 26, 5.   [2] Herod., VIII. 41.
[3] Aelian, *De Nat. Anim.*, XI. 2, quoted in *Themis*, p. 429.

Certain manifestations of Zeus, like Zeus-Ktesios, had a snake form. Clement of Alexandria has preserved a fragment of Euripides, which is addressed to him thus:

> Ruler of all, to thee I bring libation
> And honey-cake, by whatso appellation
> Thou wouldst be called, or Hades, thou, or Zeus,
> Fireless the sacrifice. . . .[1]

There was a great snake, Meilichios, later worshipped as Zeus Meilichios, who was not originally Zeus himself, but an underground being addressed by the title *Meilichios*, the Gracious or Kindly One.[2] Asclepios also had a snake form, and both he and Amphiaros had the honey offering.[3] The snake seems to have been regarded as a symbol and vehicle, not of mortality, but of immortality; it was thus sacred, and therefore it appeared suitable to offer it the food given to all the underworld deities—honey.

There were, however, some upperworld divinities to whom honey was offered. The chief of these were Helios, Mnemosyne, the Muses, and the Nymphs (whom we have already mentioned), Pan, Priapus, Eos, Selene, and Aphrodite Urania.[4]

As a reason for giving honey and not wine to Helios, Athenaeus writes:

> Among the Greeks those who sacrifice to the Sun, as Phylarchus tells us in the twelfth book of his history, make their libations of honey, as they never bring wine to the altar of this god; saying that it is proper that the god who keeps the whole universe in order and regulates everything, and is always going round and superintending the whole, should be in no respect connected with drunkenness.[5]

Pan and Priapus, often mentioned in the Latin books on bee-keeping, were regarded as the special protectors of gardens and bees. On a statue of Pan was written:

> Having left the slopes of Maenalus I abide here to guard the hives, on the watch for him who steals the bees.[6]

---

[1] Eur. frag., 904.

[2] See Roscher, *Lex.*, under heading "Meliuchios"; and Gruppe, *Griech. Mythologie*, p. 136, who says that *Melichios* stands for *Melissos*, the comforter with honey. According to Hesychius, one of the by-names of Zeus was *Melissos*.

[3] E. Rohde, *Psyche*, I, p. 121.

[4] For authorities, see T. Wächter, *Reinheitsvorschriften in griech. Kult*, pp. 109–14.   [5] Athen., XV. 48.   [6] *Greek Anthol.*, XVI. 189; cf. XVI. 12.

Vergil prays that Priapus, the protector against birds and thieves, may take the bees under his care;[1] and Calpurnius, a poet who lived in the reign of Nero, and wrote eclogues somewhat in imitation of Vergil, wrote:

We offer to the Lares of the fruit-planted garden, and consecrate to thee, Priapus, combs full of clear dripping honey.[2]

In the *Greek Anthology* a poem of Crinagoras tells that Philoxenides offers a modest feast to Pan and Priapus which includes the "bees' ambrosia";[3] and an epigram of Zonas of Sardis says:

Hie ye, ye tawny hive bees to feed on thyme. . . . Take a pick at all and mould your waxen vessels so that Pan, the Saviour of the Bees and Keeper of the Hives, may have a taste himself, and the bee-man, smoking you with his skilled hands, may leave a little portion for you also.[4]

In an idyll of Theocritus a shepherd says he will set eight bowls of milk and eight full of the richest honeycombs for Pan.[5] Pausanias, too, mentions a statue of Priapus on Helicon:

This god is worshipped where there are pastures of goats and sheep or swarms of bees, and the people of Lampsacus esteem him more than all the gods.[6]

Hermes, too, had honey offerings:

Hermes, ye shepherds, is easily contented, rejoicing in libations of milk and honey.[7]

Cakes made of flour mixed with olive oil and honey and into which flowers had been kneaded were offered to Adonis.[8] In Rome among the offerings to Fortuna Virilis was a poppy bruised with snow-white milk and honey from the squeezed combs;[9] and Janus was also given honey in a snow-white jar, in order that the year might be sweet during all its course.[10] The honey libation to Aphrodite Urania is mentioned in a fragment of Empedocles preserved by Porphyry:

And with libation poured upon the ground
Of yellow honey, Venus is propitious made.[11]

---

[1] *Geor.*, IV. 110.   [2] Calpurn., II. 64.   [3] *Greek Anthol.*, VI. 232.
[4] Ibid., IX. 226.   [5] *Idyll*, V. 58.   [6] Paus., IX. 31, 2.
[7] Antipater, *Greek Anth.*, IX. 72.   [8] Theocritus, XV. 94.
[9] Ovid, *Fasti*, IV. 152.   [10] Ibid., I. 189.   [11] Porph., *De Abst.*, II. 21.

Of Aphrodite's son and companion, Eros, we are not told that he had any honey offerings, but there are many stories of him and bees. In the *Greek Anthology* a verse attributed to Plato tells:

He [Eros] lay among the rose blooms smiling, bound fast by sleep, and above him the tawny bees were sprinkling on his dainty lips honey dripping from the comb.[1]

An unknown imitator of Theocritus, in a pretty little poem known as "The Robber of Honeycombs," tells another story:

The thievish Love—a cruel bee once stung him as he was rifling honey from the hives, and pricked his finger-tips all; then he was in pain, and blew upon his hand and leaped and stamped upon the ground. And he showed his hurt to Aphrodite and made much complaint, how the bee is a little creature and yet what wounds it deals! And his mother laughed and said, "Art thou not even such a creature as the bees, for tiny thou art, but what wounds thou dealest!"[2]

Another version, attributed to Anacreon, but really written much later, runs as follows:

> Once Eros found a little bee
> Sleeping upon a rose,
> And was stung by it.
> Hardly had he felt the finger
> Of his little hand wounded,
> He ran, he flew, sobbing
> To the beautiful Kypris.
> "Alas! alas! I am dying,
> I have been bitten
> By a little serpent
> Who has however wings,
> The country people call them bees."
> Then she spake, "If the sting
> Of the bee causes such pain,
> Dost thou not think that it hurts
> When thou, my son, woundest?"[3]

A small piece of jewellery, about the fourth century B.C., now in the British Museum, representing Eros carrying a small plaque on which is a bee, is shown on Plate V; another gem on

---

[1] Plato, *Greek Anth.*, XVI. 210.   [2] Theoc., XIX, Lang's translation.
[3] *Anacreontea*, 33 (40), Bergck.

Plate xii, and an old engraving illustrating the above story in
Fig. 25, c.

Honey was used in certain festivals. Plutarch in his *Life of
Theseus* gives an account of the ritual of the *Oschophoria*, or Feast
of Boughs, a sort of harvest festival or offerings of first fruits. A
branch laden with all sorts of fruits, called the *Eiresione*, was
carried round and a hymn sung over it:

> Eiresione brings
> Figs and fat cakes,
> Soft oil and honey sweet,
> And a wine cup strong and deep.

There was a procession and races for youths in connection with
the festival; the prize was a *kykeon* or drink, made of oil, wine,
honey, cheese, and meal![1]

At the Thesmorphoria, a women's autumnal festival, honey-
cakes were used; Athenaeus says that:

At this festival cakes of a peculiar shape are made of sesame and honey,
which are called *melloi* throughout all Sicily and are carried about as
offerings to the goddesses;[2]

and he also mentions other cakes made of wheat flour, honey,
and sesame which were used at the festival of the Elaphebolia.[3]

In Rome, at the Terminalia, a man carried a basket, out of
which he threw the products of the earth three times into the
midst of the flames, and his little daughter offered sliced honeycombs.[4] In one of his poems Tibullus says a man who had prayed
to the Lares of his fathers and had gained his prayer, would with
his own hand bring the honey-cake, his daughter following with
the honeycomb in hers.[5] At the Liberalia old women crowned
with ivy sold cakes of oil and honey in the streets. These old women
were called *sacerdotes Liberi*—Liber was identified with Dionysus—
and carried with them a small altar. From every cake they sold
a small piece was taken and offered on the altar to Liber in the name
of the buyer.[6]

We have briefly reviewed the Greek myths about bees, and the
use of honey in their religious rites; we will now discuss honey as
the "Food of the Gods."

[1] Plut., *Theseus*, 22.   [2] Athen., xiv. 56.   [3] Ibid., 55.
[4] Ovid, *Fasti*, ii. 650.   [5] Tib., i. x. 20.   [6] Ovid, *Fasti*, iii. 725 and 741.

CHAPTER XII

THE FOOD OF THE GODS

Divine food which conferred immortality—Mead—Honey from the skies—Myths of birds carrying off divine drink—Allusions to ambrosia and nectar in Homer—Two traditions regarding the food and drink of the gods, probably originated in various uses of honey—Honey as food of divine and human children—Honey conferred prophetic powers—Mead, the drink of the Indo-Europeans, supplanted by the Soma of the Indo-Iranians in India—Soma and Madhu in the Vedic Hymns—Note: Amrita

IF it is asked why the gods needed food if they were immortal, the reply is that they were not believed to be immortal unless they feasted on heavenly fare—the *nectar* and *ambrosia* of the Greeks, the *mead* of Teutonic mythology, the *soma* of India, another name for which was *amrita*. This word is related to the word *ambrotos*, which again is connected with *ambrosia*, both words containing a reference to the food by partaking of which the gods kept up their immortality.

This divine food also conferred immortality on men. Pindar sings of Tantalus,

> Who from the feast of the gods could dare
> To steal the ambrosia and nectar whereby
> They had given him immortality?[1]

and a hymn of the Rig-Veda says: "We have drunk *soma*, we have become immortal"; and another verse of the same hymn:

> I have partaken wisely of the sweet food
> That stirs good thoughts, best banisher of trouble,
> The food round which all deities and mortals,
> Calling it honey-mead, collect together.[2]

In the chapter on Greek ritual we found that the Greeks had a tradition of a time when "wine was not." The idea of the immortal drink was older than wine, much older than the Homeric times

---

[1] *Olym. Ode*, I. 63.   [2] Rig-Veda, VIII. 48, trans. A. Macdonell.

when wine was in common use, and therefore must probably go back to the undated period before the Indo-European stem divided, when the only intoxicating drink was *mead*, the Sanscrit *madhu*, the Greek *methu*, the Avestan *madu*, the Lithuanian *medus*, and similar names in kindred languages.

The belief that honey came down from the skies and was collected by the bees from plants was very general. We find it in Hesiod, Aristotle, in Vergil, and other classical writers, and in the Vedas of India where the Asvins, Lords of the Kingdom of the Clouds, bring honey to the bee, and *madhu* is said to stream from the clouds. The Germanic peoples believed that it fell from the skies on to the World ash-tree, Yggdrasil (see Chapter XIV), and much the same belief occurs among the Finns. The manna of the Bible has also been compared with honey-dew, as it fell during the night (Exod. xvi. 14), and "the taste of it was like wafers made with honey" (Exod. xvi. 31); in the Psalms it is called heavenly food (Psa. lxxviii. 25; cv. 40).

The idea that the sky was the proper place for the dwelling of the gods and for the home of the divine food seems to go back to the Indo-European period; there are various myths relating to the stealing of this divine drink from its place in the sky, where it was guarded by some vigilant demon, by the bird of the god, or by the god himself in bird-form—the eagle of Indra,[1] the nectar-bearing eagle of Zeus, Odin in the form of an eagle carrying off the mead.[2]

The belief that there was a heavenly drink and these myths connected with the carrying off of the drink, can hardly be regarded as Nature myths, nothing happening in the sky could have given rise to them. Its origin must have been an earthly intoxicating drink, whose mysterious properties were the reason for regarding it as the drink of the gods; and it seems almost certain that it was a honey-mead with which the Indo-Europeans intoxicated themselves, and which was raised to the rank of the drink of the gods.[3] It therefore appears likely that the widespread belief in the heavenly origin of honey and honey-dew was connected with the myths of the heavenly drink. It may perhaps also be granted that the belief of

[1] Rig-Veda, IV. 26. 1–7; V. 45, 9; IX. 68, 6.   [2] See under, Chapter XIV.
[3] "The primitive Indo-European intoxicant was a honey product" (H. D. Griswold, *The Religion of the Rig-Vedas*, 1923, p. 8).

the divine immortality being dependent on some drink—amrita, ambrosia, mead—arose in the Indo-European period.[1]

We will now consider how the Greeks regarded the divine food, which they called nectar and ambrosia. Athenaeus remarks that Homer "allots to the gods a very simple way of life and plain food, namely nectar and ambrosia."[2] In the Homeric poems the two, nectar and ambrosia, are usually mentioned together, but ambrosia has also the meaning of a healing ointment or salve. In the *Iliad* Hera cleansed every stain from her winsome body with ambrosia, the sweet savour of which went forth to earth and heaven.[3] Ambrosia is rubbed over the corpse of Sarpedon, probably to preserve it from decay;[4] and both nectar and ambrosia are used as materials for embalming. Thetis

shed on Patrocles ambrosia and red nectar through his nostrils, that his flesh might abide the same continually;[5]

and while Achilles is mourning his dead friend, refusing all food, Athena, sent by Zeus, "distils into his breast nectar and pleasant ambrosia so that no pains of hunger come upon him."[6] The extremely pleasant odour of this nectar and ambrosia, their sweetness and agreeableness, are often praised.

In the Homeric poems and in Hesiod ambrosia usually denoted the *food*, nectar the *drink* of the gods. In the *Odyssey* Calypso spread a table with ambrosia for Hermes, and mixed the ruddy nectar, so that he might eat and drink;[7] and then her maidens placed ambrosia and nectar for her, but for Odysseus "all manner of food to eat and drink, such as is meet for man."[8]

It is remarkable, however, that side by side with this tradition there runs another, evidently very ancient, in which the meaning is reversed. Athenaeus, after observing that Homer was acquainted with nectar as the drink of the gods, writes that others held a different opinion, and he quotes Anaxandrides, who says:

Nectar I eat, Ambrosia drink;

---

[1] See Professor H. Oldenberg, *Die Religion des Vedas*, 2nd ed., 1917, pp. 169–71; Griswold, *The Religion of the Rig-Vedas*, p. 217; Macdonell, *Vedic Mythology*, p. 114.   [2] Athen., I. 16; cf. Hesiod, *Theog.*, 639.

[3] *Iliad*, XIV. 170. In the *Aeneid* the wounds of Aeneas are healed by this ambrosial salve (*Aen.*, XII. 419).

[4] *Iliad*, XVI. 665.   [5] Ibid., XIX. 40.   [6] Ibid., XIX. 345.

[7] *Odyssey*, V. 93.   [8] Ibid., V. 199.

and Alcman, "Nectar they eat at will"; and a poem of Sappho,

> The goblets rich were with ambrosia crown'd,
> Which Hermes bore to all the gods around.[1]

This remarkable interchange of the two meanings can be simply explained if nectar and ambrosia were originally different forms of some substance like that of the heavenly honey, which was enjoyed as a food, and when fermented, as a drink. Many ancient writers say honey was also used as a salve, as a preservative for dead bodies, and in embalming. We have already mentioned several cases of this latter use, such as the Babylonian custom of covering the body with wax and then placing it in honey. Porphyry states that:

Some persons have thought that the nectar and ambrosia which the poet pours into the nostrils of the dead for the purpose of preventing putrefaction, is honey; *since honey is the food of the gods.*[2]

Human children were fed with honey immediately after birth among the Greeks, Indians, Germans, and Hebrews, and there are many cases in which divine children were said to be fed with it. We have already mentioned several, such as that of Dionysus—who perhaps was originally not the god of wine but the god of mead; and there are two traditions about the birth of Zeus: the one says he was fed by the sacred bees on honey, and the other, already known in Homeric times, says he was fed on ambrosia brought by the Peleiades, the seven doves, from the extreme western confines of the ocean.[3] This agrees wonderfully with the Indian, Persian, Germanic, and Finnish belief, according to which the bees or birds bring the honey from the sky or from Paradise, which the ancients always located in the extreme west. Both myths apparently refer to the same idea, for the old writers on apiculture all agree that the bees only collect honey between the rise and setting of the Pleiades.

The origin of the use of honey in offerings to the dead may have been either that the dead man was a hero or demi-god, and that therefore he must receive the same offerings as the gods, or that the dead were thought to require the same food as they enjoyed in life—a belief held by many primitive peoples.

---

[1] Athen., II. 8; Euripides, in *Hippolytus,* mentions a *spring* of ambrosia.
[2] Porph., *De ant. nym.,* 16.   [3] See above, Chapter IX.

The conception of nectar and ambrosia and of honey both included the ideas of sweetness,[1] loveliness, pleasant odour, of healing and life-giving qualities, of the gift of sweet speech and prophetic power—the Thriae, the nymphs of Parnassos, could prophesy only when they had partaken of the honeycombs (see p. 97)—and it seems, therefore, as if the Greeks, at any rate, formed their conception of the food of the gods on the many uses of the sky-sent honey.[2] Can we in any way also connect the soma of India with honey?

As we have said above, *mead* was the intoxicating drink of the Indo-Europeans, but as the family broke up, some members, the Indo-Iranians, went towards India, and as they changed their habitat they seem to have made a change in their drink. Their honey-mead was replaced by *soma*, which played a very important rôle in Vedic ritual, and was finally personified as a god. Soma was a plant, which has not yet been definitely identified. From the description of it in the Vedas we learn that it was a mountain plant, with long tendrils, that it grew on rocks and apparently also on trees, that it was crushed and the juice pressed out between stones, that it was yellow in colour, that it was placed in tubs and then mixed with milk, also often with barley meal and honey, and that it then fermented.[3]

In many of the Vedic hymns soma is called *madhu*, which leads us to suppose that the old Indo-European name of the honey-drink may have been transferred to the newer drink, just as the Greeks kept the old name when they changed their sacrificial honey-drink to wine. Professor Oldenberg also suggests that soma might be called *madhu*, because the words "honey," "dripping-with-honey," "rich-in-honey," and similar expressions were often

[1] Athenaeus says (II. 8) that ambrosia was considered to be nine times sweeter than honey.

[2] The identification of nectar and ambrosia with honey is well advocated by W. H. Roscher, *Nektar und Ambrosia, Studien zur griechischen Mythologie*, Leipzig, 1883.

[3] For description of making soma, see H. Grassmann's translation of the Rig-Veda, vol. ii, p. 184. Book IX of the Rig-Veda consists of hymns addressed to Soma. Dr. Rendel Harris identifies the soma plant with some species of ivy; he thinks "the equation between soma and nectar appears to be established"; see *Origin and Meaning of Apple Cults*, Manchester University Press, 1919, pp. 39, 40.

used by the Vedic poets when they wished to denote anything sweet and pleasant—they imagined all sorts of things, as butter, milk, the waves of water or of the air, to be like honey, which was to them the chief bearer of sweetness—and also specially because soma was really mixed with the sweet substances, milk and honey.[1]

In his *Vedic Mythology* Mr. Macdonell states that soma was mixed with honey, and that mythologically *madhu* is the equivalent of soma when the latter means celestial ambrosia; that figuratively soma is called the "juice of honey" (R.-V. v. 43, 4), and its juice is intoxicating and honeyed (*madhumat*). This latter expression he remarks simply means sweet, but as applied to honey originally seems to have meant "sweetened with honey," some passages pointing to the admixture, and the honey-mead "may have survived into the Vedic period by amalgamating with soma."[2]

It is impossible from the evidence we possess to prove that the soma, which was offered to the Vedic deities, was equivalent to the nectar and ambrosia of the Greeks, but it is clear that the conception of honey entered into both, and we may be allowed to state that, owing to its many useful qualities, honey thus became the substratum for the mythical representation of the Food and Drink of the Gods.

NOTE TO CHAPTER XII

Besides the Vedic *amrita*, the immortal essence of soma, we read in the Avesta of a drink, *Haoma*, which also seems to have been an elixir of immortality. In *La Vie Future d'après le Mazdeisme*, Dr. Söderblom remarks that because of its beneficent efficacy Haoma became the drink attributed to the gods. Through this liquid the faithful united himself to the god and participated in his immortality. He writes:

The name "eau de vie" is a remembrance of the importance attached to the pagan intoxicating drink. What would one not sacrifice to obtain a drink which gave life ? A Chinese emperor in the third century before Christ sent an expedition to fetch the life-giving drink from the golden

---

[1] *Religion des Vedas*, p. 365.
[2] A. A. Macdonell, *Vedic Mythology*, pp. 105 and 114.

isles. Among the Indo-European people the sacred drink was mead [hydromel], among the Hindus the juice of the Soma-Haoma. . . . [This Soma-Haoma], the extract of the Indo-Aryan plants, has its counterpart among the Greeks and Germans in *honey*, which by many peoples, especially by the Babylonians and Finns, was regarded as a remedy against all illnesses and a preservative against corruption.[1]

Professor Hillebrandt, however, remarks that *madhu* is seldom mentioned in the Avesta, and therefore he does not think it is another name for Haoma. It is mentioned twice, and in both places simply means honey.[2] Professor Oldenberg writes:

It must be noted that the Avesta, which otherwise agrees so well with the terminology of Soma with the Vedas, does not know of Soma = madhu.[3]

On the other hand, Professor Meyer says that soma, which was drunk by the Indians in such quantities in the Vedic period, appears according to the testimony of the Avesta to have been used also by the Iranians.[4] The evidence, therefore, that Haoma might have been a drink compounded with honey is slight, though of course it is possible that in bygone ages it might have replaced a honey-drink.

[1] *La Vie d'après le Mazdeisme*, pp. 331 and 334.
[2] *Vedische Mythologie*, I, p. 238.   [3] *Religion des Vedas*, p. 365.
[4] *Geschichte des Altertums*, 2nd ed., 1909, paragraph 576.

CHAPTER XIII

BEES AND HONEY AMONG THE GERMANIC AND SLAVONIC PEOPLES IN CENTRAL EUROPE

PART I—HISTORICAL

Bees in primeval forests of Europe—Beginnings of beekeeping— Mead mentioned by Pytheas—Mead older than beer—Made in enormous quantities—Mixture of beer and honey—Place names— Thomas of Cantimpré—Life of bees compared with that of man —Need of Church for wax candles—Large apiaries kept by monks —Roman formula for blessing the Easter tapers given in "The Beehive of the Romishe Churche"—Wax used by kings and nobles —Bees plentiful in Poland—Honey and wax levied by feudal lords—Bees used in warfare—Belief in ox-born bees—Swammerdam

THE honey bee is indigenous in the greater part of Europe, and among the huge forests and heath lands of Northern and Central Europe our own ancestors learnt a primitive beekeeping. As the ground was gradually cleared and cultivated, every occupier had his allotted portion of the forest, and in it he marked those trees in which the wild bees had made their nests, in order to show his right to the honey in them.

The next step towards beekeeping proper was taken when the men hollowed out holes in trees for the bees, often quite high up in the highest and straightest fir-trees, so that they had to climb up in order to take the honey. From this custom comes an old Russian word for a bee-man, which means "tree-climber" (*drevolazecu*), and a Lithuanian one meaning "bee-climber" (*bitkopis*). Later hollowed-out logs were hung in the trees; then these logs were placed, either horizontally or perpendicularly, on the ground in the clearings in the forest, and lastly they were put near dwellings.[1] These hollowed-out tree-trunks, known as *Klotzbeute*, are still used as hives in parts of Germany, Poland, Lettland, and Russia (Fig. 22). Pliny mentions a huge honeycomb, 8 feet long,

[1] See O. Schrader, *Real-lexikon der Indo-germanischen Altertumskunde,* under heading "Bienenzucht."

which had been found in Germany;[1] probably this comb came from one of these hollow tree-trunks. The words *Beute* (old High German, *biutta*), meaning that which holds the bees, and *Bienenstock*, meaning a tree-stump for bees, words now used in German for hives, are both reminders of the old primitive beekeeping of Central Germany.[2]

The inhabitants of Germany, being mostly of Indo-European stock, must have derived their knowledge of a honey-drink from

FIG. 22.—HOLLOW TREE-TRUNKS, USED AS HIVES
(*a*) Without Door   (*b*) With Doors

their remote ancestors, but the oldest historical authority for it is that of the traveller Pytheas, a contemporary of Alexander the Great, who in 334 B.C. sailed with a fleet from Cantium into the North Sea to visit the amber lands. He notes that the people near Ems put honey on their bread and made a drink from honey and corn.[3] This drink was the mead of our forefathers, which, as we shall see in the next chapter, the old myths say was enjoyed by gods and men.

There is no doubt that mead is an older drink than beer in the

[1] *Nat. Hist.*, XI. 33.

[2] Schrader, *Real-lexikon der Indo-germanischen Altertumskunde*, p. 141; V. Hehn, *Kulturpflanzen und Haustieree*, 7th ed., 1912, p. 582. In English a bee colony is also a *stock*.   [3] Strabo, IV. 5, 5.

North, and it was made in enormous quantities. Even as late as the ninth century Wulfstan the traveller related to King Alfred that among the Esthonians there was so much honey that the king and his nobles drank mares' milk and left the mead for the poor and servants, for beer was unknown among them.[1] We can gauge the quantity of mead made in the Upper Elbe district, when we read that in 1015 a fire in Meissen, which had been caused by some enemy, was extinguished by mead, as the inhabitants were short of water![2]

When beer was first made, honey was mixed with it to sweeten it, so that this beer may be considered a connecting link between mead and real beer made from hops and malt. This sweetening of beer with honey is constantly mentioned in Lettic and Finnish folksongs. The use of the hop plant was known to the Saxons of Britain and one of their names for it was *hymele*. It has been suggested that this word is connected with *ymbe*, an old Germanic word which in the form *imb* is still used for a swarm of bees,[3] and it may thus hint to us that the older drink was composed of honey. The Latin *mulsum* (wine and honey), *hydromeli* (water and honey), and *mel* (honey) are always translated into Anglo-Saxon by the word *beor*, whilst *cerevisia* and *celia* are translated by *ealu* (ale). Possibly, therefore, the word *beer* (German = *Bier*) was originally the name for the old German mead-beer. There is a close connection between *biuza*, an old word for beer, and the Saxon word for bee, *beo*. Perhaps these may both have meant honey, for there is an old northern word for bee, *byfluga*, whose original meaning cannot have been "bee-flies," but "honey-flies" (compare the Egyptian *âfa-bat* = flies from honey), and *biuza* may be a composite word for *bi-wesa* or *bi-wis-a*, which really denoted honey or bee-juice.[4]

The mixture of mead and beer does not seem to have met with the approval of the Church, who in the Councils of Aachen (817), Worms (868), and Tribur (895) spoke strongly against the custom; the reason why is not apparent.[5]

---

[1] Hehn, *Kulturpflanzen und Haustierce*, p. 150.

[2] J. G. Bessler, *Geschichte der Bienenzucht*, Stuttgart, 1886, p. 96.

[3] See Cockayne, *Leechdoms, Wortcunning and Starcraft of Early England*, 1864, vol. ii, p. ix.   [4] Schrader, *Real-lex.*, under "Bier," p. 145.

[5] Bessler, *Geschichte der Bienenzucht*, p. 92.

In the district round Eger in Bohemia (Czechoslovakia) there was a very flourishing mead industry. In the town itself in 1460 there were thirteen mead breweries, which produced yearly three hundred and eighty-four barrels, which shows what a quantity of bees and honey there must have been in that neighbourhood. After the Reformation and the Thirty Years War the industry gradually decreased, and in 1684 there was only one mead brewery left in Eger.[1]

München and South Germany, now the centre of the beer industry, made in former times great quantities of mead. Ulm, on the Danube, at the beginning of the twelfth century had huge mead breweries which were very celebrated. Honey fairs were held there and at other towns of Württemberg. In other districts also large quantities of mead were brewed, especially on the Baltic coasts of Livland and Prussia, and at Dantzig and Riga. The Emperor Rudolf of Habsburg and several others of his line granted privileges to the mead brewers. On the Rhine an old document says that the judges at the assizes had a jug of mead placed before them, so full that a fly could drink from the top edge![2] A very ancient proverb says, "Bienen kommen eben so weit als Baren," which means that a mead-drinker had the power to perform just as much as a meat eater.[3]

Many places in Central Europe owe their names to the bees, which shows how widespread the industry was in former times. These names are mostly formed from two words meaning bees, *Bienen* and *Immen*, and from *zeideln*, to collect honey. In Bohemia we find Biendorf, Bienenhof, Imigau, Immichen, Zeidler, Zeidel-wald, Bienenthal, Wcelaken, and Wcelnitz (from Czech *vcela* = bee); in Hungary, Meli-Mejorek (= Bee-garden) and Zeiden. Place names with *Immen* generally show where formerly bees were kept in the forest trees; examples are, Immnitz in Saxony, Immen-rode in Thuringen, Immenstadt in Bavaria, Immenhausen in Württemberg, Immendingen in Baden, Immendorf near Cologne, Immbach and Immigrath near Düsseldorf.[4] In Switzerland are Immensee, a village in Canton Schwyz; Immenfeld, a castle and

[1] Bessler, *Geschichte der Bienenzucht*, p. 199.   [2] Ibid., p. 96.
[3] Ibid., p. 67. Bessler and Glock both give a number of proverbs about bees and honey.   [4] Ibid., p. 96.

chapel in the same Canton; Immenberg, a hill in Canton Thurgau; and Bienburg in Canton Baselland.[1]

On the Lower Rhine is the Immenkappel, and the name is explained thus. One night thieves broke into the Abbey Church of Altenburg, and amongst other sacred vessels stole the ciborium in which the Host was kept. The thieves placed this under a thorn bush in the Sulztal; a swarm of bees flying past stopped, and built their combs over the Host, which was found later when the honeycombs were removed. In memory of this a chapel was built and called Immenkappel (= Bienenkapelle).[2]

Beyenburg in Rhenish Prussia is also said to owe its name to the bees. Two stories are told of it. One states that a number of nobles who disapproved of the nunnery there banded together to destroy it. They surrounded the house and the nuns in their peril held a consultation as to what to do. They decided to place their hives round the nunnery, and when the nobles tried to take the place by storm the nuns overturned the hives and the bees forced the men to retreat; since then the place was called Beyenburg. The other tradition says that the soldiers came to the town in which the nunnery was, hoping for rich booty. They took all the cattle from the village and then went to the nunnery, but were driven away by the nuns setting their bees on them.[3]

Beekeeping in Europe increased enormously with the spread of Christianity. Bees were held to be models of industry, order, purity, economy, courage, prudence, and co-operation. The purity of the bee is illustrated in an old Italian manuscript, known as the "Exultet Roll," now in the John Rylands Library in Manchester, and dated about A.D. 1000. The text praises the bees, "who produce posterity, rejoice in offspring, yet retain their virginity," and is illustrated by the three drawings, reproduced in Fig. 23. The first is of bees on a green plant; the second a hive, the form of which is interesting, as it probably shows the type of hive used by the Romans; the third depicts the interior of the hive, showing the combs and bees at work.

[1] The names of the Swiss places were sent to the writer by Professor O. Schneider-Orelli of Zürich.

[2] Karl Knortz, *Die Insekten in Saga, Sitte und Literatur*, Annaberg, Sachsen, 1910, p. 30.

[3] Fr. Berger, *Von Biene, Honig und Wachs*, Zürich, 1916, p. 36; Knortz, Ibid.

About 1259 a Dominican monk, Thomas of Cantimpré, wrote a work called *Bonum universale de apibus*,[1] in which he compares

FIG. 23.—PART OF THE "EXULTET ROLL"
(From the Manuscript in the John Rylands Library, Manchester)

the life of the bees with the life and duties of the Christian, especially of the clergy and monks. As there is but one king bee in the hive, that proves, says Thomas, that there should only be one king,

[1] Afterwards entitled, *Miraculorum et exemplorum memorabilium.* See Karl Meyer, *Der Aberglaube des Mittelalters*, Basel, 1884, p. 154.

one pope. As the king does not use his sting, so bishops must be mild. He compares the lay brothers of the monastic orders to the drones—not a very complimentary comparison—and the slaughter of the drones to the scourging of the lay brothers, which took place occasionally. In the evening sudden stillness falls upon the hives, even so should it be in a convent. The unity among the bees should serve as an example for the monks, who should also be encouraged by their virgin purity. The seven, or at most ten years of life which are granted to bees, correspond to the sevenfold gifts of the Holy Spirit and to the Ten Commandments. The whole work proceeds thus, some real or imagined episode of bee life is seized upon and applied to the clergy.

Many others used the same comparison between bee life and that of men. Abbot Sturm, founder of the great monastery of Fulda, taught that the virgin bees showed an example of an ordered cloistered community. Ambrose, Augustine, Jerome, Basil, Tertullian all drew comparisons between bee life and the life of Christ. Peter of Padua called Christ *apis aetherea*; as the bee flies up into the air, she is a symbol of the soul who enters the kingdom of heaven.[1]

The Church needed huge quantities of wax for candles, for all candles for the services on Easter Day, as well as all candles used on the altar at every mass, had to be made of bees' wax.[2] In a quaint book, *De roomsche Byen-korf*, written in Flemish in 1569 by Filips van Marnix, Heer van St. Aldegonde, under the pseudonym of Isaac Rabbotenu, there is given the Latin formula from the Roman Mass Book used on Easter Eve when blessing the Easter tapers.[3] The book was translated into English by George Gilpin the Elder in 1580 and dedicated to Sir Philip Sydney under the title of

[1] Glock, *Die Symbolik der Bienen*, p. 233.

[2] In one church on great feast days sixty candles burnt on the high altar; in Einsiedeln day and night sixteen huge candles, each weighing 30 lb., burnt in the chapel at the expense of the Swiss Cantons; Roger, Count of Shrewsbury, gave the monks of Ouche every year before Lent 100 livres for lights to be burnt before the picture of Christ on the cross. See Gmelin, *Buch von der Biene*, p. 48.

[3] In June 1933 the Pope issued an order that the public burning of candles before images of saints must cease, but that the faithful who wished to offer them at the Mass "should procure candles of regulation beeswax and leave them in the sacristy to be burned on the altar in accordance with the Liturgy."

THE BEEHIVE OF THE ROMISHE CHURCHE

A work of all good Catholikes; wherein both the Catholike
Religion is substantially confirmed, and the Heretikes
finely fetcht over the coales.

The following is Gilpin's translation of the Latin formula:

Forsomuch as wee doo marvelouslye wonder, in considering the first
beginning of this substance, too witte, waxe tapers, then must we of
necessitie commend the originall of Bees; for they are sober in diet and
exceeding chaste in ingendering. They make closets and found them on
the souple wax. They gather of the flowers with their fete, and yet the
flowers are not endamaged by it; they bring forth their younge swarmes
through their mouths, like as Christe (for a wonderful example) proceeded
from his Father's mouth; they have a fertile chastitie without bearing,
which example Christe hath thought good to followe and ordayned to
have a carnal mother, for love of Chastitie. Therefore, O Lorde, are such
worthy giftes offered and presented upon thine altar, wherein the Christian
Religion is assured, that thou delightest exceedingly, through our Lord
Jesus Christe. Amen.

That the chief church of Wittenburg before the Reformation
used thirty-five thousand pounds of wax shows what an amount was
wanted. Every monastery and abbey, therefore, had apiaries; for
instance, at Kloster Neustadt alone was a bee-house with three
hundred stocks of these "industrious creatures of God." Many
peasants had hives of their own; those who held land under a
monastery often had to pay a yearly rent in the form of wax; for
example, ten peasants had to deliver sixty-seven pounds of wax to
the monastery of Corvey.[1] Presents or legacies of wax were very
common. There is mention of such a gift in Württemberg as early
as 783, and in 843 another monastery received a present of honey
and that of Fulda forty stocks of bees.[2]

In the foundation deeds of the Collegiate Church of Alt-Bunzlau
in Bohemia, dated 1039, it is stated that of the honey which was
collected in the Dominican estates of Saaz and Alt-Bunzlau, a
tithe must be paid; for this reason a monastery had its bee-master,
who received the tithe and prepared the necessary candles and
seals. At the monastery of Trebnitz in Silesia in 1204 the chief of

[1] They were called *ceroceuruales*, and eventually formed a sort of guild.
See Bessler, *Geschichte der Bienenzucht*, p. 93.   [2] Bessler, ibid., p. 164.

the bee-masters (which implies that there were several) as long as he kept bees had to pay a *garniec* of honey yearly.[1]

Beekeeping was largely practised in Serbia, chiefly by the monks. King Stefan Nemenja (1159–1195) presented the monastery of Xilander with four large apiaries; King Miluton (1275–1321) gave the same monastery several villages in which were many bee-gardens, and King Duszan (1336–1355) granted it a number more. Duszan, in the foundation charter of the Church of St. Michael, marked the boundaries of the huge apiary of Statina, which he presented to it. There were several thousand hives in it, and Duszan appointed ten of the most capable bee-masters of the time to look after them.[2]

The wax candles used in the churches were considered the symbol of the Saviour and of the virgin body of Christ, because the bees carried the wax from the best and sweetest-smelling flowers. The wick denoted the soul and mortality of Christ, the light the divine person of the Saviour. The author of the *Beehive of the Romishe Churche* (see p. 146) alludes to some of these beliefs when, defending the title of his book, he writes:

> Our dear and loving mother, the holie church of Rome, ought not to scorn or disdaine that we do compare her customs and orders to a *Bee-Hive*, considering that shee herself doth compare the incomprehensible generation of the Sonne of God from his Father, together with his birth out of the pure and undefiled Virgine Marie unto the *Bees*; which were in verie deede a great blasphemie, if the bees were not of so great vertue, that by them wee might liken and compare the holie church of Rome. And, seeing, she saith, that God is delighted with the giftes and presentes of the bees, why should not shee herself exceedingly rejoyce with our Bee-Hive.[3]

From this quotation and from the title of the book it would be difficult to gather that it is really a satire on the life and practices of the Church of Rome, an answer to a defence of the Roman Church written by Maister Gentian Harvet. In the English edition, however, this purpose is explained in a Preface:

> Good Christian Reader, thinke it not lost labour to reade this little booke, which as it beareth the name of a Bee-Hive, so it containeth good

---

[1] Bessler, *Geschichte der Bienenzucht*, p. 152.   [2] Ibid., p. 210–11.
[3] This is also quoted by W. Hone, *Ancient Mysteries*, 1823, p. 283.

store of wholesome hony. . . . Gentle Reader, thou hast such a book as will make thee privie to all the practices of the Babylonicall Beast (Rome, I mean), the denne of Dragons and Devils, which if it were translated into other tongues by the industrie of the learned, it would increase choler abundantly in the Pope, the College of Cardinalls, Monasteries of Monkes, Fraternities of Friars, Nests of Nonnes and the rest of the Pharisaical Frie. . . .[1]

This quotation also explains a woodcut which appeared in the original edition, and also in the German translation of 1581, and which is reproduced in Fig. 24. In the centre is the Papal tiara as a hive, on which rests the Pope as the King Bee, surveying the other bees, who with shorn heads, mitres, and cardinals' hats are flying round him, engaged in shriving, burying, and saying Mass.

Wax candles were also largely used at funerals. There is an old Flemish folksong which alludes to this custom, and which speaks very highly of the bees:

T's een angenaeme beeste,	It is an agreeable creature,
Die getrouw is aen den mensch,	Who is faithful to man,
Verdrieft van uns de höllsche gesten,	Drives from him the evil spirit
As het geat ten laesten end.[2]	When his last end comes.

Wax was employed in the houses of kings and nobles. Charles the Great was much interested in apiculture; at his estate of Stefansworth the Emperor had seventeen, and at Geisenweiler fifty hives, and he ordered that on each of his estates there must be a special bee-master, an *Imker* or *Zeidler*. The woods round Nürnberg were made into his *Pingarten* (Bee-garden);[3] later only fifty bee-masters were allowed to keep bees in these woods; no one else might capture a swarm or take honey there. Charles was not only interested in beekeeping on his own estates, but his laws also allude to it. In his celebrated Capitulary all branches of agriculture are treated, and there is a section about the care of bees.[4] Charles gave the Church the right to collect a honey tax from the peasants, and he himself imposed a wax tax on the Saxons.[5]

---

[1] This Preface was written by John Still in the English edition of 1580.

[2] Bessler, *Geschichte der Bienenzucht*, p. 53; Glock, *Die Symbolik der Bienen*, p. 240.   [3] Bessler, ibid., p. 94.

[4] *Leges Caroli* I. 181; see Gmelin, *Buch von der Biene*, p. 49, and Glock, *Die Symbolik der Bienen*, p. 225.   [5] Gmelin, ibid., p. 49.

FIG. 24.—THE BEE-HIVE OF THE ROMISHE CHURCHE

(From the title-page of the German (1581) edition of *De roomiche byen-korf*, by Filipe van Marnix, Herr van St. Aldegonde; John Rylands Library, Manchester)

Beekeeping is mentioned in several codes of laws before Charles's time. In an old Slavonic code of the fifth century allusion is made to "bee-houses," which held five or more stocks, and another Germanic code not much later refers to hives made of bark or wood which were hung in the forest trees in order to entice the wild swarms to enter them, and which were then brought to the bee-houses. A West Gothic code, dating from 466, says that anyone who finds a swarm in the fields or woods can claim it, only he must make three signs near to show his right to it; whoever damaged these signs had to pay the man double the value, and received twenty stripes as well. The Salic Law (486–496) has regulations about the theft of bees; the Bajuvarian Code (744–748) states that the owner of a swarm, which had flown on to another man's land, may drive it back by smoke or three blows with a reversed axe; if this did not succeed the bees became the property of the man on whose land they had settled. In the same code three kinds of hives are mentioned, of wood, of bark, and of plaited twigs or wands.[1]

This is one, if not the earliest, notice of plaited hives. The straw "skep" also originated in Germany at least as early as Carolingian times. In various forms it is found in all the countries which formed the Carolingian empire.[2] Plate x, which is taken from a drawing of Pieter Bruegel, dated 1565, shows one of these forms. It also shows how "Wanderbienenzucht" was practised in Germany in the sixteenth century, for the beekeepers, who have protected themselves by wearing quaint masks, are preparing the hives for removal to other quarters.

Beekeeping was very flourishing in Poland, and even wealthy men occupied themselves with it. In the year 900 the Polish prince Piast kept an apiary near Keuschwitz and worked in it himself; he made mead from his honey, and it was always offered to his guests. Taxes of honey and wax were levied by princes all over Poland, and there were special tribunals to decide on cases con-

---

[1] Gmelin, *Buch von der Biene*, p. 47. This is one of the earliest notices of plaited "skeps." Armbruster, *Der Bienenstand abs völkerkundliches Denkmal*, 1926, p. 89.

[2] For the antiquity of straw skeps, see Armbruster, ibid., Chapter IV. The Germanic tribes who settled in Britain probably introduced the straw hive there.

cerning bees, and from the documents that remain it can be gathered what an important industry beekeeping was. Gallus, a traveller in the eleventh century, wrote, "There is a plentiful supply of bread, meat, and honey," and he adds that the woods were rich in honey.[1] Russia, too, must have had a plentiful supply of honey, for Marco Polo relates that a tribute of wax was made to the king of Western Tartary, and that much wax was collected.

The feudal lords of Germany demanded honey and wax from their peasants. In Austria the lords of the manors in whose hands lay the rights of hunting and beekeeping did not carry on the latter themselves, but allowed the peasants to do it on payment of certain amounts of honey and wax. Usually the payment for every two hives was two small barrels or jars of honey.[2]

There are many stories told of bees used in warfare, some go back to classical times, and it is said that in the Great War of 1914–18 the German troops in East Africa used bees against the British.[3] A thousand years before this, Immo, the general of the Emperor Henry I, besieged by Geiselbert, Duke of Lorraine, threw bees on the attacking force, which made the horses so wild that the siege was raised. The inhabitants of Gussing in Hungary, besieged by Duke Albert of Austria in 1289, defended themselves with hot water, fire, and bees! It is related that when the Turks besieged Stuhlweissenberg under the Sultan Murat, the inhabitants, when their need was greatest, threw hives on to the attackers and the bees accomplished what they could not do.

In the *Kissingen Parish Chronicle* it is stated that in 1642, when the Swedish general, Reichwald, attacked the town, on the advice of a man named Peter Heil the besieged threw all the hives which they had in the town at the Swedes, which caused such disorder that they rode away. In memory of this deliverance a procession was formed yearly from the parish church to St. Mary's Chapel, which lay outside the town. A Thuringian parish record relates that in 1637 on his route to Erfurt, Colonel Gotze passed through the Instrutt Valley, and some of his men fell on the village of Riethgen and were on the point of plundering the house where Pastor Seidenschwanz lived. The pastor and his family had fled, and only the maid remained. Just as the men were entering

[1] Bessler, *Geschichte der Bienenzucht*, pp. 215–18.
[2] Ibid., p. 164.   [3] Berger, *Von Biene, Honig und Wachs*, p. 37.

PLATE X.—DIE BIENENZÜCHTER. PIETER BRUEGEL, 1565

(Reproduced by permission from Professor Ludwig Armbruster: *Der Bienenstand als völkerliches Denkmal*)

PLATE XI.—ST. SOSSIMA AND ST. SAWATIJ, PATRON SAINTS OF
BEEKEEPING IN THE UKRAINE

(From Professor Ludwig Armbruster: *Die alte Bienenzücht der Alpen*)

the house, the resolute maiden ran to the bee-house in the garden and threw several skeps on the floor of the house. She then prudently crept into a haystack, and the soldiers, attacked by the enraged bees, stopped their work and ran away.[1] It is strange that though beekeeping was practised on such a large scale during the Middle Ages in Central Europe, no advance in bee-knowledge was made beyond that possessed by the classical writers Varro, Vergil, Columella, and Palladius, and the belief that bees could be reproduced from decaying carcases was almost universal.

Except for the section on bees in the *Capitulary of Charlemagne*, there was no work on bees until Peter de Cresentiis, who lived at Bologna at the end of the thirteenth century, wrote a work which was printed at Augsburg in 1474. This book taught that bees were partly produced from bees, partly from decayed oxen.

In the middle of the fourteenth century Konrad von Megenberg, Canon of Regensburg Cathedral, the author of the first German book on Natural History, taught that bees came from the bellies of oxen:

Es werdet pienen (Bienen) aus frischen Waldrinderbäuchen, die man Urochsen nennet, so man zu Latein *bubuli* heisst;

these, he said, must be covered with cow dung. He also stated that bees came from the skins of oxen, which were buried in the ground.

Magister Michael Herren, in his *Verdolmetschten Veltbau*, printed in 1563, gives very full directions for producing bees from oxen, which he had taken from the *Geoponica* of Constantine Porphorygenitus, which we quoted on p. 113.[2] Even the reformer, Melanchthon, believed in this method. Johannes Colerus, whose work on bees, *Nützlichen Bericht von denen Bienen oder Immen*, published in 1611, and which was the standard work on the

---

[1] For these and other examples, see Bessler, *Geschichte der Bienenzucht*, pp. 88–9. In the *Naturalist's Library*, vol. 38, p. 195, a story tells of a small ship attacked by a Turkish corvette. Happily the small ship had some earthenware hives of bees on board, which were thrown on the Turkish ship with such good effect that the small ship escaped.

[2] Part of the section on bees in the *Geoponica* of Constantine (911–959) was written by Florentinus (third century).

subject for many generations, held the same belief. It had also been upheld by the French writers, Carolus Stephanus and Johannes Libaltus, in their work which was translated into German in 1533.[1] Fig. 25 (*d*), page 201, shows a quaint print of the "King" Bee issuing from the hive followed by the bees, taken from a French work on the *Hieroglyphiques des Aegyptiens* of Horapollo, published in 1543, to illustrate "how the people obey their King."[2]

It was not until 1702 that Florinus in his book on bees wrote:

I will not discuss if the bees come from carcases, I say shortly that they reproduce like other animals, but on account of the modesty of the creatures, the copulation has never been seen.[3]

Finally Swammerdam, the celebrated Dutchman, in his work which was translated into German in 1752, proved the true sex and functions of the queen bee, the drones, and workers.[4]

[1] Glock, *Die Symbolik der Bienen*, pp. 134–6.
[2] *Orus Opollo de Aegypte de la signification des notes Hieroglyphiques des Aegyptiens*, Paris, 1543.
[3] Bessler, *Geschichte der Bienenzucht*, p. 130.
[4] Swammerdam died in 1685, but his work on bees, written in Dutch, was not published till 1740, when it appeared in Dutch and a Latin translation by Boerhaave. See Réaumur, *Mémoires pour l'Histoire des Insectes*, Amsterdam, 1741.

CHAPTER XIV

BEES AND HONEY AMONG THE GERMANIC AND SLAVONIC PEOPLES IN CENTRAL EUROPE

PART II—MYTHS AND FOLKLORE

Bee the only creature who came unchanged from Paradise—Bee divinities—Mead offered to Swantovit—Mead drunk by gods and heroes—Odin and Othrörir, the magic mead—Balder and Loki—World tree Yggdrasil—Mimir's spring—Unborn children—New-born children fed with honey—Bee-souls—Honey offered to the dead—Bees and honey in wedding customs—Blessing the fields—Bee charms—Votive and other images made of wax—Unlucky to buy bees—Charms used against thieves—Telling the bees of a death—Church festivals connected with bees—Meanings of swarms—Tanging a swarm

IN heathen and Christian times alike bees have been revered as specially gifted animals, and everywhere we find myths and folk beliefs about them. In Germany in the district of the Lech it is said that "The *Imb* [the bee] is the only creature which has come to us unchanged from Paradise, therefore she gathers the wax for the sacred services," and that all animals except the bees perish (*crepiren*), the bees like men die (*sterben*).[1]

Bees were thus regarded as sacred creatures, and in many places traces are found of bee-divinities. The Romans had a goddess of bees, Mellona or Mellonia;[2] then there was a Roman-Germanic goddess named Nantosvelta, whose altar has been found near Sarrebourg, where she is represented as carrying a staff on the top of which is a beehive.[3] The heathen Poles, Livlanders, and Silesians had their own Bee-god, Babilos (or Bybulus), and a Bee-goddess,

---

[1] Karl, Freiherr v. Leoprechting, *Aus der Lechrain, zur deutschen Sitten und Sagenkunde*, München, 1855, p. 80. As the bee is the only creature to have come pure from Paradise, the opposite is said of the louse; it was not even created there, but appeared on Adam and Eve after they were driven out. In other parts of Germany the bees eat (*essen*) food like men; they do not devour (*fressen*) like animals.　　[2] St. Augustine, *De civ. Dei.*, 4. 34.

[3] F. J. M. de Waele, *The Magic Staff or Rod in Graeco-Italian Antiquity*, Ghent, 1927, p. 149; cf. S. Reinach, *Cultes, Mythes et Religions*, I, Paris, 1922, p. 219, Figs. 1 and 2.

Austeia; the Russians had a bee-god, Zosim, who was said to be the discoverer of apiculture, and his image, as protector of bee-keeping, was placed by the hives.[1]

In later times, in the Ukraine (south-west Russia) the patron saints of beekeeping were St. Sossima and St. Sawatij. It would be interesting to know if the old Russian Bee-god, Zosim, had been transformed into the Christian saint, Sossima. Plate xi, reproduced from an old picture, shows these two saints taking a swarm. St. Sawatij is shaking the branch on which the bees have settled, and St. Sossima is sprinkling the swarm with water. Below is depicted a very primitive hive made of a tree-trunk with a cover which has a ring of some sort round it, either to keep it together or to weight it.[2]

There is a remarkable Circassian story in which the Thunder-god, usually a protector of bees, was angry with them and destroyed them. His mother, Merime, tried in vain to protect them, but they all perished except one, which she had hidden under her garments. From this bee descended a new race of bees, and Merime was considered their patroness. The Ossetens in the Caucasus also worshipped a Bee-goddess, Meritta, or Merissa.[3]

In Russia, between the Volga and the Oka, is a tribe, connected with the Finns, called the Mordvins, who were heathen as late as 1813. The eldest son of their Mother-goddess, Ange Patyai, was Nishki Pas, the sun of the sky, of the sun, of fire, and light. He was the chief protector of bees. At this place in the sky there were many habitations where the souls of good men lived. As bees cluster round their queen, so the souls surrounded Nishki Pas, and hence he obtained the name of the Beehive-god. Ange Patyai's second son, Sviet-Ver-Nishki-Velen Pas (God of the world forest beehive community), was ruler of the earth; her eldest daughter, Nishkende Tevtyar, had a beehive on the earth, where real bees lived. She protected beekeeping, which was a favourite occupation of the Mordvins from remote ages.[4]

[1] Glock, Symbolik der Bienen, p. 247; J. Grimm, Teutonic Mythology, London, 1880, p. 697.

[2] Armbruster, Die alte Bienenzucht der Alpen, 1928, p. 136. See below, p. 258.

[3] Wolfgang Menzel, Die vorchristlichee Unsterblichkeiten, Leipzig, 1870, p. 128; Glock, Die Symbolik der Bienen, p. 248.

[4] Hon. J. Abercromby, "Religious Beliefs of the Mordvins," Folklore Journal, vol. vii, 1889, pp. 70–1.

Among some of the Slavonic tribes the sun was worshipped under the name of Swantovit. An account of his worship at Arkona in the island of Rugen, which was Slavonic until the fifteenth century, is given by the old writer, Saxo Grammaticus, about 1215. Swantovit's idol was set up in a shrine on the island, and taxes were paid by the people to support it. Great ceremonies were held in connection with the harvest. The priest took a cup from the hand of the idol and brought it to the crowd who stood outside the temple. In the cup was mead, and from the quantity it contained he prophesied the fortunes of the coming year. If the mead had decreased since last poured in, scarcity was to be feared; if it had increased there would be abundance. The mead in the cup was poured at the feet of the idol and the priest filled the cup again, praying for prosperity in peace and war. Then at a draught he drank the mead which had been dedicated and refilled the horn, which was placed in the hands of the idol and remained undisturbed till the next annual festival. At this ceremony honey-cakes, "round in shape and great, almost up to the height of a man's stature," were offered to the god.[1]

Mead is mentioned in many myths. In the so-called *Zeidel-moos* near Wunsiedel tradition says that the Veneti and the dwarfs lived together and caroused at night on the sweet mead.[2]

Constant allusion is made to mead in the northern sagas, and gods and heroes drank quantities of it; on one occasion Thor is said to have consumed three tuns!

In the mythology of the Germanic peoples this mead assumes magic properties, for it bestowed the gifts of wisdom and poetry and imparted immortality. When the Asa-gods and the Vana-gods made peace, they mixed their spittle in a vat and out of this they made Kvasir, who was so wise that he could answer any question. Kvasir was killed by the dwarfs, and his blood mixed with honey was put into a cauldron. This cauldron, and sometimes the mead which it contained, was called *Othrörir*. It was given into the charge of the giant Suttung and guarded by his daughter Gunnloth in a mountain. Odin was most anxious to obtain this magic mead,

---

[1] Saxo Grammaticus, Book XIV, trans. Elton and Powell, 1894. In later times Swantovit was christianized under the name of St. Vitus.

[2] Bessler, *Geschichte der Bienenzucht*, p. 157. *Zeideln* = to take honey, *moos* = moss or moor.

but he could only get into the mountain by guile. He disguised himself, entered into the service of Suttung's brother, the giant Baugi, did the work of nine men, and as a reward claimed a drink of the magic mead. This Baugi could not give, but he bored a hole through the mountain with a gimlet, and Odin in the form of a serpent crept through and so reached Gunnloth. He made love to her, and by her connivance drank up the mead in three draughts; he then deserted her, and in the form of an eagle flew away to Valhalla.[1]

Odin thus gained the gift of tongues and poetry; the Ynglinga-saga tells that he spoke in rhyme, and that therefore poetry was called "Odin's gift," or "Odin's drink," and poets the "mead-bearers of Odin.[2]

Odin had no intention of giving this magic mead to men, but when he was flying away with it pursued by Suttung, who had discovered that Gunnloth had given him the drink, he spilt some out of his mouth on to the earth, and so man obtained the gift of poetry. Later Othrörir became almost identified with the poetic art. An old poem, the "Runahal," says:

> A drink I took of the magic mead,
> Taken out of Othrörir.
> Then began I to know and to be wise,
> To grow and to weave poems.[3]

Heimdal, Odin's son, the watchman of the gods, drank mead; in the *Poetic Edda*[4] we read:

> Heimdal there
> O'er men holds sway, it is said;
> In his well-built house does the warder of heaven
> The good mead gladly drink.[5]

---

[1] For an account of Odin obtaining the mead, see the *Poetic Edda*, the "Havamal," trans. H. A. Bellows, New York, 1923, p. 50.

[2] J. Grimm, *Teutonic Mythology*, writes: "Othrörir contained the sweet drink of divine poetry, which imparted immortality, and from the exertion made by Odin to regain possession of it when it had fallen into the hands of the dwarfs and giants follows its identity with amrita, nectar, and ambrosia."

[3] Quoted by Glock, *Die Symbolik der Beinen*, p. 230.

[4] There is the *Elder* or *Poetic Edda*, date and authorship uncertain, and the prose *Edda* of Snorri Sturluson, who died 1241.

[5] *Poetic Edda*, "Grimnismol," v. 13, p. 90.

Mead is constantly drunk in Valhalla, the abode of dead heroes; it is presented to them by the Valkyries, the Fate Maidens. Balder drinks it there; in *Balder's Dream* the wise woman says:

> Here for Baldr the mead is brewed,
> The shining drink.[1]

On one occasion the gods were assembled for a feast when Loki, the black sheep of the gods, who was responsible for Balder's death, entered and wanted to drink with them, but no one would speak to him, so Loki said:

> Thirsty I came into this thine hall
> I, Lopt, from a journey long
> To ask of the gods that one should give
> Fair mead for a drink for me.[2]

Then he taunted the gods, but none would give him the magic mead, until at last Sif, Thor's wife, came forward, poured some mead into a crystal cup, and said:

> Hail to thee, Loki, and take thou here
> The crystal cup of old mead;
> For me at least of all the gods,
> Blameless thou knowest to be;

and Loki took the cup and drank the magic mead.

The honey of which this divine drink was composed seems to have been regarded as a dew from heaven or from the world-tree, Yggdrasil. The Eddas tell of this great ash-tree, Yggdrasil, a symbol of air, sky, clouds, and perhaps of the growing power of Nature; its branches cover the whole earth, and it had three roots spreading into the Underworld. At one of its roots was the Urthar spring, whose water was so sacred that anything put into it became as white as the skin inside an eggshell. This spring was guarded by the Fates, the Norns, and they sprinkled the sacred water daily over the tree in order to protect it from decay. This dew, which fell from the tree on to the earth, was called the "honey-fall" (*hunangfall*), and on it, as the old writer, Snorri, says, the bees fed. In Teutonic heathendom it seems to have been generally believed that all arts and culture came from the Underworld; swans and

---

[1] *Poetic Edda*, "Baldr's Draumar," v. 7, p. 197.
[2] Ibid., "Lokasenna," v. 6, p. 154. Lopt = Loki.

bees, too, came from a paradise somewhere underground, where the Fates lived.[1]

Another well connected with Yggdrasil was Mimir's well. Mimir was one of the guardians of the world-tree, and a maternal uncle of Odin. Out of this spring he drank mead every morning, and Odin went to him whenever he wanted good advice; for this mead was as Othrörir, and bestowed wisdom on those that drank it.

According to an old myth children were dipped into Holde's well; Frau Holde or Helle was the leader of the underground spirits. An Alsatian myth represents her spring as a beautiful stone well lying in a meadow; out of it flowed milk instead of water, and round it bloomed great flowers which were full of honey, and with which the unborn children were quietened.[2] The souls of the unborn are also connected with crickets (*Heimchen*). Originally the name *Heimchen* was not used for crickets but for bees, and the unborn souls were conducted by Mother Perchta from her heavenly home to the earthly world of the body. This was done on the *Perchtennacht* (January 6th), the New Year.[3]

The newborn child was regarded as a "soul" or "spirit" until it had received food; if a child's mouth had once been smeared with honey, it might not be killed.[4] There was an old Friesian law which allowed the father to kill or expose his child, but if the babe had had milk and honey its life must be spared.[5] The divine food, honey, thus secured life for the child, and in early Christian times it was used immediately after baptism (see Chapter XXI). This custom of smearing the child's lips with honey we have noticed already in connection with India.

In a dirge sung by the skald Egill Skalla-grimason, who lived from 902 to 980, over his drowned son, the air, sky, or clouds are represented as a beehive (*býskip*), the abode of the dead spirits. The hive the poet had in his mind would be the old-fashioned straw skep, or the beehive shape of the family barrow, and perhaps he may also refer to the belief that the soul became a bee.[6]

[1] F. York Powell, *Religious Systems of the World*, p. 281.

[2] Mannhardt, *Germanische Mythen*, p. 424.

[3] W. Menzel, *Die Vorchristliche Unsterblichkeiten*, p. 127.

[4] Mannhardt, *Germanische Mythen*, p 424   [5] Knortz, *Die Insekten*, p. 2.

[6] "Burr's býskips í bae kominn
Kvanar son kynnis leita."

See Mannhardt, *Germanische Mythen*, p. 371.

In several German folktales the soul comes out of the body of a sleeping person in the form of a bee (we shall find the same belief in Scotland), and in the Engadine it is believed that the souls of men leave the world in the form of bees, therefore when the head of the house dies the eldest male member of the family goes to the hive stand, knocks three times, and says:

> Ime, dîn här est dot,
> Verlatt mi nit in meiner not.

(Little bee, thy master is dead, leave me not in my sorrow).[1]

It is for this reason that no one likes to buy the bees of a dead man, for it is feared that they will fly away to seek their master.

Sometimes the bee-soul comes back to the body, which is then re-animated. In the parish of Klein-Fetten in the Lower Engadine some young fellows on their way home saw an old woman lying on the path with her face to the ground. They thought she was dead, and carried her into the nearest house. Soon after a bee flew into the room humming, and then went into the open mouth of the woman. Those present were not a little astonished when they saw the woman get up, and in a very grumbling tone told them that when anyone found her lying on the ground again, they might leave her alone.[2]

There are many customs which originated in heathen times, and which were later overlaid with a veneer of Christianity; among these is the custom of offering food to the dead. In Russia it was an ancient custom to place a cup of honey by the corpse at a funeral; in White Russia a portion of food at a feast was put aside for the dead, and after the guests had eaten, the remains of the mixture (honey and cakes) was placed by the windows, presumably for the spirits. This mixture was called *syta*, and it has been compared with the Sanscrit *suta*, soma-juice, or soma sacrifice.[3] At the Russian commemorative feast a dish called *kanuna*, which consisted of *syta* and crushed barley or wheat, was offered at the beginning of the feast; each guest took three spoonfuls, two he ate, the other he poured on the table for the dead.[4]

---

[1] Glock, *Die Symbolik der Bienen*, p. 252.

[2] From the *Schweizer Mercur*, 1858, quoted by Knortz, *Die Insekten*, p. 36.

[3] The Indian food for the dead consisted of honey and rice.

[4] Schrader, *Real-Lex.*, under heading "Ahnenkultus"; Glock, *Die Symbolik der Bienen*, p. 248. In South Russia it was considered a deadly sin to kill a bee.

Bees and honey play a part in many wedding customs. In Bavaria and Bohemia the beehives were adorned with a red cloth at a wedding, so that bees and men could rejoice together. In Westphalia the following verse was recited before the newly married couple:

Imen in, imen ut,	Bees in, bees out,
Hir es de junge brut.	Here is the young bride.
Imen um, imen an,	Bees around, bees about,
Hir es de junge mann.	Here is the young man.
Imekles, verlatt se nitt,	Little bees, desert them not
Wann se nu mal Kinner kritt.	When in time they have children.[1]

In Croatia when a wedding procession arrived before the bridegroom's house, his parents stood on the threshold with a cup, which must not be of glass. The sponsors wanted to lead the bride into the house, but the bridegroom addressed his mother, "Mother, what is in this cup?" "Son, my honey and thy goodwill." As the bride entered, the doorstep and the posts of the doors were smeared with honey, and the mother-in-law handed the bride as she crossed the threshold a spoonful of honey. In some places the bride received milk and honey to drink, in order that she might live peaceably with her husband. When the bride entered the house, a jar of honey and a bunch of flowers were handed to her, and she used the honey to smear the post of every door through which she passed. The people say this is done so that her new housemates may meet the bride as kindly as she meets them.[2]

In the Bocca of Cattaro in Dalmatia the bridegroom's mother handed the bride on her arrival a spoonful of honey; but directly the bride opened her lips she drew back the spoon several times, and then suddenly put the spoon into the bride's mouth. When the bride entered the house, the following verse was sung:

The bride comes in a happy hour,
She has brought a blessing with her,
Round her head there gleams the sunlight,
In her hand there sits a falcon,
Peace and concord brings she with her,
In her mouth the honey's sweetness.[3]

[1] Bessler, *Geschichte der Bienenzucht*, p. 57; Glock, *Die Symbolik der Bienen*, p. 253.   [2] Bessler, ibid., p. 214.   [3] Bessler, ibid., p. 215.

Among the Poles, while drink was handed round to the guests at a wedding a song was sung:

> Industrious as a bee's life is the life on the land,
> And sweet as honey is the marriage state.[1]

There was an old Germanic custom of blessing the fields. If a field had not yielded well, it was believed to be bewitched and an exorcism had to be performed. The following is an ancient example:

From the four corners of the field pieces of sod were cut, oil, meal and honey laid upon them, then they were sprinkled with holy water. The sods were then carried to church, placed with the green side facing the altar, four masses were said over them, and they were taken back to the field before sunset. Charms were recited there and the ploughing of the bewitched field begun. At the beginning of the first furrow meal from all kinds of corn was laid and when the ploughman reached the end of the furrow he ought to find buried there a pot of honey.[2]

There were many charms to use when bees were swarming, some of which certainly originated in heathen times. A charm for catching a swarm is given here; though taken from an old English manuscript, it was probably used by our ancestors before they came to Britain.

Take some earth, throw it with thy right hand under thy right foot and say:

> "I take under foot, I found it,
> Lo! Earth is powerful
> Against everything in the world,
> Against spite and against forgetfulness."

Throw over them some gravel (or earth) where they swarm and say:

> "Sit ye, Victory Women, sink to the earth,
> Do not fly wildly to the woods,
> Be ye as mindful of my good
> As every man is of food and country."[3]

[1] W. Mannhardt, *Mythologische Forschungen und Sammlungen*, Stuttgart, 1844, p. 194; Knortz, *Die Insekten*, p. 38.

[2] Quoted by Glock, *Die Symbolik der Bienen*, p. 232, from *Cod. exon.*, 5214; see Cockayne, *Leechdoms, Wortcunning and Starcraft of Early England*, vol. i, p. 399.

[3] The MS. is in the Library of Corpus Christi College, Cambridge, No. 41, p. 202. A translation is given by Cockayne, *Leechdoms, Wortcunning and Starcraft of Early England*, p. 385. Cf. Julius Zupitza, "Bienensegen," in *Anglia*, vol. i, pp. 189-95.

In this charm the swarm is called *ymbe*, by which name it is still known in parts of Germany. The sudden emergence of a swarm was regarded by warriors going to battle as a favourable omen, and from this arose the name *Sigewif*, *Siegweiber*, that is "Victory Women" as applied to bees. The title is also given to the Valkyries or Fate Maidens who dispensed mead in Valhalla to warriors fallen in battle, but there is no doubt that in this charm the name applies to the bees.

One of the oldest Christian bee charms is that of Lorsch in the Grand Duchy of Hesse. Lorsch was one of the places where bees were kept by Charles the Great; this charm dates from the ninth century. It was discovered in the Vatican in 1865, and runs:

Kirst, imbi is hûze!	Kirst, the swarm is here!
Nû fliuc dû, vihu mînaz,	Now fly, my dear one, here,
Hera fridu frône in Godes munt,	Under the care of the Lord God,
Heim zi commonne giount.	Safely home.
Sizi, sizi, bina,	Settle, settle, bee,
In bot dir sancte Maria.	Holy Mary commands thee.
Urolob ni hatês dû,	No leave hast thou to fly
Zi holce ni flûc dû,	Away to the woods,
Noh dû mir nindrinnês,	Thou must not escape me,
Noh dû mir nintuninnês,	Thou must not flee from me,
Sizı vilu stillo unirki,	Settle quietly here,
Godes unillon.	It is God's will.[1]

A Latin charm to prevent swarming bees from flying away addresses them as "handmaidens of the Lord"; it is entitled "Ad Apes Conformandas:

> Vos estis ancillae Domini,
> Vos faciatis opera Domini,
> Adjuro vos per nomen Domini,
> Ne fugiatis a filiis hominum.[2]

Another Latin charm of the ninth century was discovered on a gilded book cover in the Royal Library of Vienna; it ends with the words:

> Sanctus Lucas, Sanctus
> Marcus, Sanctus Mathaeus,
> Sanctus Johannes vos custodiunt.[3]

[1] Bessler, *Geschichte der Bienenzucht*, p. 53; Glock, *Die Symbolik der Bienen*, p. 253. "Kirst" may mean "Christ" or some personal name. See Armbruster, *Archiv für Bienenkunde*, 1934, p. 83.

[2] Bessler, ibid., p. 54; Glock, ibid., p. 237.   [3] Bessler, ibid., p. 54.

Here the bees are under the protection of the four evangelists, who were regarded as the guardians of the four quarters of the world, so probably this charm was recited to prevent the bees from flying away in any direction.

A remarkable charm of the fourteenth century also found on the cover of a book in the Schassburg School Library connects the bees with Mary and Joseph. It runs:

Maria stund auf eim sehr hohen berg. Sie sach einen swarm bienen kommen phliegen. Sie hub auf ihre gebenedeyte hand, sie verbot in da zu hant, versprach im alle hilen und die beim verslozzen; sie sazt im dar ein fass, das Sanct Joseph hat gemacht, in das sollt er phliegen und sich seines lebens da genugen. In nomine p.f.sp.s. Amen.[1]

(Maria stood on a very high hill, she saw a swarm of bees flying towards her. She lifted her blessed hand, she forbade it to fly away, promised it health and prosperity. She placed for it a vessel [hive] which St. Joseph had made, into it it should fly and enjoy its life. In the name of the Holy Trinity. Amen.)

In the ninth century in Upper Swabia, a district then under the monastery of St. Gall, a charm to prevent swarming was already used; it is noteworthy that it calls the large bee the "mother" of the bees, for in the Middle Ages it was nearly always called the "king."

Adjuro te, mater aviorum	I adjure thee, mother of the bees,
Per Deum regem coelorum	By God, the King of Heaven,
Et per illum redemptorem	And by the Redeemer,
Filium Dei te adjuro	The Son of God, I adjure thee,
Ut non te in altum levare	That thou rise not in the air,
Nec longe volare,	Nor fly far from here,
Sed quam plus cito potest	But as quickly as thou canst
Ad arborem venire, ibi te collocas	Settle in the tree
Cum omni tuo genere vel	With thy whole swarm,
Cum socia tua	With thy companion (?)
Ibi habeo bona vasa parata	I have prepared thee here a good hive
Ut vos Dei nomine laboretis.	So that ye work in the name of God.
In nomine p.f.Sp.s. Amen.[2]	In the name of the Holy Trinity. Amen.

[1] Glock, *Die Symbolik der Beinen.* p. 237; Bessler, *Geschichte der Bienenzucht*, p. 55.

[2] Bessler, ibid., pp. 55 and 164; Glock, ibid., p. 237; *Notes and Queries*, 1st Series, vol. x, 1854, p. 321.

In Transylvania (Siebenburgen) the following charm was recited in early spring when the bees were beginning to fly:

> In nomine Patris, filii und aller Sanctorum!
> Maria gen Aufgang hebt die rechte Hand,
> Maria gen Sonnenuntergang hebt die linke Hand,
> Damit ihr, teure Bienen, sollet fliegen,
> Damit ihr viel Honig sollet kriegen,
> Honig fürs Jesuskindlein,
> Wachs für den heiligen Altar.
> Deshalb beschützt euch die heiligen Margaret.
> In Namen Gottes, des Vaters, Amen.[1]

(In the name of the Father, Son and all Saints. Maria at sunrise raises her right hand, Maria at sunset raises her left hand, so that you, dear bees, may fly about, so that you may get much honey. Honey for the Christ child, wax for the holy altar. Therefore St. Margaret protects you. In the name of God the Father. Amen.)

In other parts of Transylvania the villagers in spring place the house key where the bees can fly over it, they then become more industrious, and also no strange bees can rob the hive of its honey. When the first bee appears at the entrance of the hive they say:

God spake and there was light; God spake, there were the bees; God spake, there was wax; God speaks, blessed be your flight: God will speak, blessed be your return.

Or sometimes they use this verse:

> Bienchen, Bienchen, Bienchen,
> Reise ins grüne Land,
> Speise von Blumen und Gras,
> Fulle mir Korb und Fass.[2]

(Little bee, fly into the meadows, feed on flowers and grass, fill hive and jars for me.)

In Westphalia when the bees swarm, they say:

> Ime, der maut mi nit verlaten
> Ich maut bruken dine raten.

(Bee, thou must not leave me, I may need thy advice.)

---

[1] H. v. Wlislocki, *Volksglaube und Volksbrauch der Siebenburger Sachsen*, Berlin, 1893, pp. 121-2; quoted by Knortz, *Die Insekten*, p. 34.   [2] Ibid.

If the bees are flying away, they call out:

Ime kuem heraf	Bee, go up
Un brenk uns huonich und vass!	And bring us honey and wax!
Et-wass for de hillgen	Some wax for the saints
Un et huonich for use kinner!	And some honey for our children![1]

In Holstein, in the Luneburger Haide, in Brunswick and Westphalia the following charms are used:

Kün, Kün, Kün,	Kun, Kun, Kun,
Imenwiser, set di	Bee-leader, settle
Up min gebêt,	At my request
Up min lôf un gras	On my tree and grass,
Un drey mi flitich	And bring me busily
Honig und wass,	Honey and wax,
Kün, Kün, Kün.	Kun, Kun, Kun.

And:

Im, du sast di setten	Bee, thou must settle
An ênem groenen twich,	On a green twig,
Un dregen honnig un wass!	And gather honey and wax.

Or

Immenwiser, sett di nidder	Bee-leader, settle down
Up Laub und Gras,	On tree and grass,
Bring mir honig und wachs!	Bring me honey and wax.[2]

In Bavaria they sing:

Little bee, little bee,
Stay with me in the green grass,
Where once Jesus, Mary and Joseph sat.[3]

Somewhat similar to these is an old Belgian charm:

O koning der bien,	O King of the bees,
Daalt hier in't gras,	Stay here in the grass,
Om te vereeren	In order to honour
Het altar des heeren	The altar of the Lord
Met zoeten honinc ende was!	With sweet honey and wax![4]

---

[1] Glock, *Die Symbolik der Bienen*, p. 254.
[2] Bessler, *Geschichte der Bienenzucht*, p. 59; Glock, *Die Symbolik der Bienen*, p. 251. [3] Glock, ibid., p. 251. [4] Glock, ibid., p. 254.

It will be noted that several of these charms allude to the beeswax used for the church candles. Wax had also been used in heathen times to make votive images in temples. These offerings were largely made by the Greeks and Romans, but with this difference. They offered them as a sort of thankoffering when the evil which had threatened them had been averted; the Germanic peoples placed the waxen figures of a part or a whole of the body in their temples, and in early times also at cross-roads, in order to cure the evil—childless parents, for instance, would bring a waxen image of a child. These offerings, which originated in heathen times, were given a Christian interpretation and countenanced by the Church, and to this day they will be found at well-known pilgrim resorts. At Kevelaar in Rhenish Prussia, as Heine says:

> Wer eine Wachshand opfert,
> Dem heilt an die Hand die Wund,
> Und wer einen Wachsfuss opfert,
> Dem wird sein Fuss gesund.[1]

Magic figures might be made out of dough or metal, but wax made by the sacred bees was considered the most appropriate substance. Over the wax figure, known as the *Atzmann*, secret words were uttered and were supposed to take effect on absent persons. The *Atzmann* was either hung up in the air, plunged in water, placed before the fire, or stabbed with needles and buried under the doorstep; the person aimed at felt all the ills inflicted on the figure. In the eleventh century such a use of magical figures led to a horrible persecution of Jews at Trier.

The wax from young bees (that is, from new combs) was supposed to be much the most efficacious for these figures, and it was important to imitate as much as possible the features of the person who was to be bewitched. Regular baptismal services of the images were held, and they were anointed with holy water; the wax from which they were made was sometimes stolen from the churches. Naturally the clergy tried to stop the practice; in a Bull of Pope

---

[1] "He who offers a wax hand, the wound on his hand is healed; he who offers a wax foot, his foot becomes sound." When this poem, *Die Wallfahrt nach Kevelaar*, was published in 1810, Heine wrote a note to it saying that the belief existed then; a friend of his had offered a wax foot and been healed, and he believed that later the same man, who was unhappy in love, had offered a wax heart. He did not say if this was also effective.

Gregory IX in 1233 every magician who made these wax figures was threatened with eternal damnation, and in 1219 Archbishop Gerhard of Bremen excommunicated the people of Stedding for making them.[1]

The custom was also common among the Slavs. The priests of the chief god of the heathen Lithuanians and Semagites, Potrimpos, told fortunes from the forms which melted wax made in water. A woman who had expected the return of her son consulted the high priest of Potrimpos, and he told her that her son had been shipwrecked, because the wax poured into the water had formed into the image of a ship and of a man swimming near it.[2]

The ancient title for a bee-master, *Bienenvater* or *Immenvater*, shows the intimate relationship between the bees and their caretaker; those who tend other animals, such as cattle, sheep, horses, pigs, or dogs, never receive on that account the name of *father*.[3] Formerly people made contracts with their bees and gave them written assurances that they would love them and take good care of them, and they used to go and wish them a "Happy New Year."[4]

A true *Bienenvater* when he takes honey gives some to his neighbours, because the bees have taken the nectar from their flowers; if he does not give any away, in the next season he will have a bad harvest. He who refuses honey to the sick will also next season have sick bees and empty combs. And he who will not give honey to children sins against Mary and Joseph, the parents of the Christ-child.[5]

If anyone is buying bees they must not be paid for in money only. In buying a hive it should not be handled or examined too closely; in selling one it should not be overhauled or you will lose the blessing. In the Upper Palatinate and in Austria it is believed that when bees are inherited or received as a gift, they thrive the best.[6]

In Lower Austria if a hive is bought, the buyer should have a

[1] See Glock, *Die Symbolik der Bienen*, pp. 245-7.
[2] Schwenck, *Mythologie der Slawen*, cited by Glock, ibid., p. 247.
[3] In the Lechrain every village had its *Immenvater*, who kept bees because their neighbourhood is good for man. v. Leoprechting, *Aus der Lechrain, zur deutschen Sitten und Sagenkunde*, p. 80.
[4] Bessler, *Geschichte der Bienenzucht*, p. 57.
[5] Glock, *Die Symbolik der Bienen*, p. 255.   [6] Ibid.

mass read, give alms or do some other good work, and also every swarm taken should be greeted with the words "Gruss Gott," and the day of its arrival written on the hive with consecrated chalk. In Bavaria and other Roman Catholic countries it is said that bees bought or moved on a Friday will not thrive.[1]

Anyone starting beekeeping should begin with three hives, the sacred number; and he has the most luck with them who buys the first swarm, receives the second as a gift, and finds the third.[2]

Bees will not thrive in a quarrelsome family or if one member deceives another; if their owners are miserly, the bees will refuse to work and so perish.[3]

In the Wetterau anyone who is carrying a beehive over the road must not look behind him, or speak a word, he must not even reply to a greeting. If he does the bees will fly away.[4]

In Oldenburg the witches carry beehives on their heads; these can be seen if you walk backward in church as far as the altar.[5] This seems a strange superstition; there does not seem to be any special reason why the witches should carry hives, for it is said that they hate the chaste bees because they provide wax for the Church,[6] but perhaps they are using magic means to prevent the bees from making the wax!

In Westphalia it is believed that stolen bees will die. The people also think that there are means of keeping thieves away from the hives, of getting back hives which have been stolen, and of punishing the thief. The following is one of the charms which keeps away thieves; you must go three times round the hive and say:

Steh' Stock fest	Stay, stock, fast
In deinen Bienkäst,	In thy hive,
Dass dich keine Diebeshand berühre,	That no thief's hand may touch thee,
Und dich von hinnen führe.	And take thee from hence.
In namen, u.s.w.	In the name of the Father, etc.[7]

[1] Bessler, *Geschichte der Bienenzucht*, p. 60.
[2] Glock, *Die Symbolik der Bienen*, p. 255; Knortz, *Die Insekten*, p. 39.
[3] Bessler, *Geschichte der Bienenzucht*, p. 60.
[4] Knortz, *Die Insekten*, p. 39; Wuttke, *Die deutschen Volksaberglaube der Gegenwart*, 2nd ed., p. 401.   [5] Knortz, ibid., p. 39; Wuttke, ibid., p. 240.
[6] J. Klek, *Bienenkunde des Altertums*, IV, 1926, p. 38.
[7] Bessler, *Geschichte der Bienenzucht*, p. 61.

In the Neumark on St. Peter's Day the following charm against thieves must be spoken over the hives:

> Ich binde dich durch Gottes Hand,
> Damit sollst du stehn in Teufels Band;
> Bei Leiden und Jesu Christi Blut
> Mache du Schelm, du Dieb, mit deinen Ende gut.[1]

It was also believed that the stolen hive could be recovered if a piece of an altar-cloth and some wax were put into a bag and hung on a mill wheel; for the conscience of the thief would prick him as long as the wheel revolved, unless he restored the hive. Another belief was that if dead bees and a piece of refuse were put into a cloth without touching them with the bare hand and it was buried after sunset at the place where the stolen hive had stood, the thief would get consumption.[2]

In Pomerania it was thought that robbing by bees could be prevented or encouraged by the magical use of a gimlet. If this tool was turned forwards, while repeating the three most sacred names, in the straw or wood of the hive, the owner's bees could go and successfully rob other peoples' hives; if it were turned backward the bees of others would come and rob his hives. It was also believed that the bees could be encouraged to rob (the hives of others, of course) if a piece of the windpipe of a wild animal, like a fox or marten, was placed at the entrance hole, so that the bees flying in and out must creep through.[3] This must be contagious magic, for we must suppose that the courage of the fox or marten would pass to the bees, and so make them valiant in attack.

Another Pomeranian belief was that if a so-called toad-stone was put under the hives, the bees would prosper;[4] we presume by banishing bee-devouring toads and frogs.

In Lower Austria hives are painted with bright colours, decorated with stars, crosses, or the name of Jesus; in Franconia, on the contrary, bees are thought to do better if they are in a neglected hive.

If the bees are lazy in Westphalia, the next spring the *Bienenvater*

---

[1] Bessler, *Geschichte der Bienenzucht*, p. 61.   [2] Ibid.
[3] Glock, *Die Symbolik der Bienen*, p. 254; Bessler, *Geschichte der Bienen-zucht*, p. 60.   [4] Ibid.

will earnestly admonish them, remind them that the Church needs
wax and the children honey, and beg them to lay this to heart and
do better this year.[1]

All these superstitions show how highly bees were regarded,
and so it can be understood how the custom arose of telling the bees
of important events connected with the family, and specially of the
death of their owner. It may be that the custom of telling the bees
of a death originated in the idea that the bees were "souls," or
that they were creatures who could fly up into the heavens from
whence they had come. The custom is very widely spread; we
find it all over Central Europe, in the British Isles, in America,
where the settlers from Europe carried it, and the first allusion to
it can be traced to classical times; for in the *Greek Anthology* we
find the bees are to be told of a death, though here the purport of
the "telling" is not the same as that attributed to it later:

Naiads and chill cattle-pastures, tell the bees when they come on their
springtide way, that old Leucippus perished on a winter's night, setting
snares for scampering hares, and no longer is he tending the hives dear
to him.[2]

In the Middle Ages it was believed that the bees, if they were
not informed of the death of their master, flew up into the sky in
order to seek him there. This is still a belief in some parts of
Germany, England, and America.[3]

Among the Wends a beekeeper before his death decides to
whom his hives, either all or in part, shall belong, and when he is
dead his heir knocks on the earth three times by the hives left to
him and says:

Pcolka, votar jo tod,   Little bees, Father is dead,
Net som ja gospodar.   I am your master now.[4]

In Westphalia after the master's death, the friends or members
of the family go to the hives and say:

Ime, dinn haer es dout,   Bee, thy master is dead,
Du sass hewen kaine nout.   Thou shalt suffer no loss;[5]

[1] Bessler, *Geschichte der Bienenzucht*, p. 60.
[2] Book VII. 717, author unknown.   [3] Knortz, *Die Insekten*, p. 38.
[4] Ibid., p. 38.   [5] Bessler, *Geschichte der Bienenzucht*, p. 57.

Or:

| Bienchen, unser Herr is tot, | Little bees, our master is dead, |
| Verlasst mich nicht in meiner Not. | Do not leave me in my sorrow. |

It is said that when a *Bienenvater* dies, if the heir does not go up to the hives and tell them he is master now the bees will follow their master and die. In Altenburg and Württemberg when a *Bienenvater* dies the hives are moved a little. If they are left in the same place the bees will die. In other districts when the funeral passes the hives they are turned round, so that the entrances face the other way. In Masuren, directly the corpse leaves the house the covers are lifted from the hives so that the dead man may bless them once more; and in Bohemia the hives are draped with black.[1] We shall find similar customs in Britain.

There are certain festivals of the Church which are of importance to bees. On the night before St. Thomas's Day (December 21st) and on the eves before Christmas and Epiphany the beehives in Lower Austria as well as the dwellings and barns are sprinkled with holy water and smoked with incense. In Moravia it is believed that the bees will have much honey, but will not swarm if the hives are moved on Christmas Eve; in Masuren there will be abundant swarms if it snows on New Year's Day. If the weather is fine on St. Peter's Day, the people in Mecklenburg say that the hives must be cleaned, that is, the rubbish swept from the floor with a feather broom. At Candlemas (February 2nd) a *Bienenvater* may not travel or visit anyone outside his house; if he does, say the people in Waldeck, in the next spring the young swarms will fly away. Of the same festival there is a saying in Mecklenburg:

| Lichtmas hell und klar | If Candlemas is bright and clear, |
| Macht de Immen schwar. | The bees will swarm. |

In the Lower Rhine district a good season was foretold if the procession of lights which went round the church at Candlemas was not extinguished by the wind.[2]

[1] Bessler, *Geschichte der Bienenzucht*, p. 58.
[2] Ibid., pp. 57–8; Wuttke, *Die deutschen Volksaberglaube der Gegenwart*, pp. 401–2.

It is a common custom in Germany to take the hives into bee-houses in the winter; the people in Swabia place the bees out in the open on Gertrudistag (March 17th), and before their removal they sprinkle the hives with water and salt consecrated at Epiphany.[1] In Oldenburg it is said that no bee will fly away the whole year, and that they will settle low down when they swarm, if they are fed on Maundy Thursday before sunrise and the food is mixed with some earth thrown up by a mole the previous night. On Good Friday in Masuren the people feed the bees before sunrise with meal and bless the hives, going round them scattering the meal and saying:

Ihr Bienen und Königinnen, setzt euch auf eures Herrn Acker und Wiesen, wie es der Herr Christus geboten, zum Sameln von Wachs und Honig, in Namen Gottes des Vaters, u.s.w.

(You bees and queens, settle on your master's fields and pastures, as the Lord Christ commanded, in the name of the Father, etc.)[2]

A piece of wood cut from the entrance of a hive on St. Andrew's Eve is believed to bring good luck in the Voigtland and in Oldenburg. Bees and love are closely connected, for it is a common folk-belief that bees will not sting a chaste maiden or youth. In Mecklenburg if a girl is frightened of bees she is jeered at; and in Posen maids test their lovers by taking them past a hive.[3]

There are various meanings attached to where a swarm settles. In Switzerland if one settles on a dry twig in the garden, it means that the sick man in the house will die; and it is also believed that if a swarm flies away and is not found within three days the children will lose their parents. In Lower Austria it is considered lucky if a swarm settles on the house, but war is to be feared if the bees fight one another or want to go back to their hive. Once when the crown of Poland was vacant, one of the candidates, Michael Wiscionsky, was chosen because a swarm of bees settled on him during the election.[4]

[1] Bessler, *Geschichte der Bienenzucht*, pp. 57–8; Wuttke, *Die deutschen Volksaberglaube der Gegenwort*, pp. 401–2.

[2] Bessler, ibid., p. 63; Wuttke, ibid., p. 193; Knortz, *Die Insekten*, p. 39.

[3] Wuttke, ibid., p. 331; Knortz, ibid., p. 30.

[4] Bessler, *Geschichte der Bienenzucht*, p. 218. His reign, however, was not a very prosperous one. In the crown of the kings of Poland was a diamond bee, to remind them that all virtues are to be found in the bee-state.

Magic power is possessed by the wood on which a swarm settles. In the Voigtland if a girl wants partners at a dance she carries a piece of a twig on which a swarm had settled; and if a man going to market strikes his cow with a bough cut like a cross on which bees had settled on a Good Friday, he will have many buyers for his cattle.[1]

In Westphalia they say that bees can talk and also understand the speech of men.[2] Bees are said to love music and song; church bells are said to make them swarm,[3] and the custom, so common in England, of making a noise on pots and pans in order to attract the swarm, is very frequently met with in Germany. An old German writer on bees, Johann Colerus, in his *Nützlichen Bericht von den Bienen oder Immen*, said that the bee was a "Musicum Animal." In Switzerland sickles and scythes are struck when there is a swarm and a bunch of fresh flowers put in the hive prepared for it.

In the Upper Palatinate if the bees take no notice of the noise, the bread on the dresser is turned round in order to cause them to settle. Whether the bees attend to this cannot be stated! In Westphalia the branch on which they wish to swarm is shaken, and the following verse recited three times:

Bimour, sette dick,	Bee folk, settle here,
Tüh van düesem plattse nitt.	Do not go from this place.
Ick giäwe di hëus un platts,	I give thee house and place,
Dëu sass driän hunaich un wass!	Thou must bring me honey and wax.[4]

Many similar superstitions will be found in our own land, but before we pass to the British Isles we must mention some old folk-beliefs and stories of Finland.

[1] Knortz, *Die Insekten*, p. 30; Wuttke, *Die deutsche Volksaberglaube der Gegenwart* p. 342.   [2] Wuttke, ibid., p. 109.

[3] Certainly Sunday is a favourite day for swarming.

[4] Bessler, *Geschichte der Bienenzucht*, p. 62.

CHAPTER XV

FINLAND. THE *KALEVALA*

The Finns and allied peoples—Mordvins heathen till 1813—
Believers in magic—Finnish folk-tales of mead and beer from
the "Kalevala"—Honey needed to harden iron—Honey obtained
from the storehouse of the Almighty brought Lemminkainen back
to life—Prayers and charms for making salves—Allusions to honey
in the "Magic Songs"—Honey in marriage customs in various lands

THE Finns are one of a group of peoples, the Finnish-Ugrian, to which belong the Livlanders on the Baltic, the Esthonians, several tribes in Russia—the Mordvins, Votiaks, Ostiaks, and others—the Magyars of Hungary, and more distantly, the Turks.

Most of these peoples were Christianized late; indeed, the Mordvins were heathen as late as 1813, and some of the other tribes are still hardly affected by Christianity. It is therefore not surprising to find a number of primitive beliefs among them, and fortunately the Finns, the most civilized of the group, have had much of their folklore compiled in the epic poem known as the *Kalevala*, and in other collections of magic songs and charms.

The Finns were great believers in magic, and the ancient belief was that if a man knew and could recite a poem describing the "origin" of anything, he had power over that object and could thus avert evil. These songs and charms were a very early expedient for defence against the dangers of the unseen world.

Finland is a country of huge forests and heathlands, and here from time immemorial there must have been bees in abundance, and they are frequently mentioned in the poems.

As was mentioned in the last chapter, among the Esthonians in the ninth century *mead* was the drink of the people, as beer was then unknown, and its use had probably been learnt centuries before when these tribes were still in the district of the Ural Mountains, where they must have had some connection with the Iranian peoples, as is shown by the similarity of the words for *honey* and *bee* in the different languages. The following table gives some of the forms.[1]

[1] From Hon. J. Abercromby, *Pre- and Proto-Finns*, vol. i, p. 230.

	Finnish	Mordvin	Ceremic	Votiak	Zirian	Ostiak
Honey	mesi	med	mü	ma	mu	mavi
Bee	mehilainen	mäks	müks	mus	mos	———

	Magyar	Zend	North Persian	Osetan
Honey	méz	madhu	mai	müd
Bee	méh			
Fly (of honey)		makhsi	magas	

Connected with these forms are the Greek *Me-lissa*, and the German *i-me*, modern *imme*.

We know very little of the beekeeping of these remote ages, but the traders from the East probably carried the knowledge of the craft westward and taught the natives how best to take their honey and wax. We know from Marco Polo that honey and wax were abundant in Russia in his day, and that tribute was partly paid in wax to the Tartar kings. Beekeeping would start in the trees in which the wild bees lived, and then when agriculture was more developed artificial hives would be introduced in which better honeycombs could be produced.

In the last chapter it was mentioned that the Mordvins, a tribe which practised beekeeping very early, had a Beehive-god and a goddess, Nishkende Tevtyar, who protected beekeeping, but no such beings are mentioned in the Finnish songs. In one of the "Magic Songs," however, on the "Origin of Ale," the lovely maiden Kalevatar creates a bee.[1]

The story tells how a girl, Osmotar, made some ale of barley and hops, but she could not get it to ferment, and said:

> What must now be added to it,
> What is needful to provide for,
> That the ale may be fermented,
> ·And the beer be brought to foaming?

She tried several methods, but none was successful, until at last Kalevatar, the lovely maiden, brought a mustard pod to Osmotar, who rubbed it with her hands and with both her thighs, and thus a bee was born! She then addressed the bee:

> O thou bee, thou bird so nimble,
> King of all the flowery meadows,

[1] "Origin" in Finnish = "Birth."

and told him to fly to an island in the ocean where he would find
honey-dripping swards on the edge of a field. Then she said:

> Bring thou honey on thy clothing,
> From the fairest of the herbage.

The bee flew off, a short time elapsed and he came buzzing back.
He arrived in a mighty fuss, brought virgin honey on his wing, and
placed it in the woman's hands, and Osmotar put it in her ale,

> And the beer at length fermented.

The heroes heard of this beer and soon flocked to drink it; chief
among them was Lemminkainen (about whom we shall hear some
more presently), and

> Drunken was the ruddy rascal
> With the beer of Kalevatar.[1]

From this story we glimpse a time when there was no beer, and
then of a time when a mixed drink, a honey-beer, was made, and
which was apparently a powerful intoxicant. A charm has been
preserved which also shows this connection between beer and
mead. It begins: "O bee, the nimble bird, the king of the meadow
flowers, fly thither where I bid," and then the bee is told to fly
to the isle and bring honey from the luscious grass, and from the
cup of the golden flower, "as ferment for the ale, as balm for the
new-made drink."[2] Even after the introduction of ale, mead was
still a favourite drink, and one used on important occasions.

Two of the chief heroes of the *Kalevala* are Vainamoinen, the
Son of the Wind and the Virgin of the Air, always spoken of as a
great singer and as "old and steadfast"; and Ilmarinen, the great
primeval smith, a young, vigorous man. Both are suitors for the
hand of the Maiden of Pohjola. Her mother, "Pohjola's old mistress," one day sees both men approaching her house and wonders
what they are coming for. So she and her daughter perform certain

[1] *Kalevala*, Runo xx; Abercromby, *Pre- and Proto Finns*, vol. ii, p. 330.
All the quotations from the *Kalevala* are from Kirkby's translation in "Everyman" edition.

[2] Abercromby, ibid., p. 246. In this charm the bee is called the nimble
bird, and king of the meadow flowers; other names for it are honey-wing,
blue-wing, the lively bird, the active fellow.

magic rites with a rowan log which was on the fire. If the log exuded blood it would mean that they came for war; if clear water, it would denote peace. But neither water nor blood came from the log:

> From the log there oozed forth honey,
> From the log dripped down the nectar;

and an old crone in the chimney-corner muttered:

> From the log if oozes honey,
> From the log if drips the nectar,
> Then the strangers who are coming
> May be ranked as noble suitors.

Then Pohjola's old mistress told her daughter to prepare a tankard of mead and to place the tankard in the hand of the man whom she chose as a husband. Vainamoinen entered first, but the maid rejected him as too old:

> For an old man is a nuisance,
> And an aged man would vex me.

Ilmarinen then came in, and on seeing him

> Brought the maid of mead a beaker,
> Placed a can of drink of honey
> In the hands of Ilmarinen,

thus choosing him for her husband.[1]

In this story *honey* dripping from the log was an omen of the arrival of lovers, and *mead* was the drink chosen to be offered to the favoured lover. When the marriage of Ilmarinen was celebrated later, ale and mead were provided for the guests:

> Honey from the taps was oozing,
> Ale around the lips was foaming,
> Mead the mood of all enlivened.[2]

Another story in the *Kalevala* tells of the Origin of Iron, how it was made from the milk of the three fair daughters of Creation from the black, white, and red milk which flowed from them. Ilmarinen, the primeval craftsman, had found the iron and had taken the ore to his home, but he could not make it harden. He

---

[1] Runo XVIII. 560 to end, and Runo XIX. 1–6. [2] Runo XXV. 402.

pondered what to do, tried various methods, but the results did not please him. Then

> From without a bee came flying,
> Blue-winged from the grassy hillock,

and the smith addressed it as follows:

> O thou bee, my nimble comrade,
> Honey on thy wings convey me,
> On thy tongue from out the forest.

The bee hastened off on his journey to fetch the honey. Now the hornet, "bird of Hiisi" (the Evil Power), had listened to Ilmarinen's request, and when the bee had gone brought hissing of serpents and acid of ants, and hidden poison of toads, that the steel might be poisoned, and Ilmarinen,

> He the greatest of the craftsmen,
> Was deluded and imagined
> That the bee returned already,
> And had brought the honey needed,
> Brought the honey that he wanted,

and so he put the things the hornet had brought into the iron, which was furious, and struck at people and so caused wounds.[1]

In this story the bee was too late for its honey to be of use to Ilmarinen, but in the following tale it plays a more important part.

Lemminkainen, a handsome, jovial, reckless fellow, went to Pohjola, the North Country, to demand the hand of the fairest maiden there. His mother had warned him to expect disaster if he persisted in his request, and so it happened. An old cowherd, whom Lemminkainen had offended, lay in wait for him by a river, killed him, and after cutting his body into eight pieces, cast it into the deep river Tuonela.

When his mother heard of his tragic death, she made a magic rake, and with infinite trouble she raked out of the torrent the pieces of her son's body:

> And her son she pieced together,
> Shaped the lively Lemminkainen.

---

[1] Runo IX. This story is told as a spell to heal the wound of Vainamoinen which had been caused by iron.

This she did with the help of her magic art, but he was speechless and helpless, and she herself could do no more. But she knew something was still wanted to restore her son, and she spoke to herself:

> Whence shall we obtain an ointment,
> Whence obtain the drops of honey,
> That I may anoint the patient?

She then addressed the bee:

> O thou bee, thou bird of honey,
> King of all the woodland flowerets,
> Go thou forth to seek for honey,
> Back from Metsola's fair meadows,
> Tapiola, for ever cheerful,
> From the cup of many a flower,
> And the plumes of grasses many,
> As an ointment for the patient,
> And to quite restore the sick one.

So the bee flew off to Metsola's fair meadows, collected honey from six bright flowers and from a hundred grasses and came back,

> With his wings all steeped in honey,
> And his plumage steeped in nectar.

Lemminkainen's mother took this magic ointment and anointed her son with it, but, alas! he was still speechless and helpless. Again she addressed the bee:

> O thou bee, my own dear birdling,
> Fly thou in a new direction,
> Over nine lakes fly thou quickly,
> Till thou reach a lovely island,
> Where the land abounds in honey,
> There is honey in profusion,
> There is ointment in perfection.

The bee, the active hero, flew off again on his journey over nine lakes to the island, found the honey, made the ointment, put it into cups, and brought back seven on his back. Lemminkainen was anointed with it, but,

> Even yet there came no healing,
> Still her toil was unavailing.

For the third time she addressed the bee:

> O thou bee, thou bird aerial,
> Fly thou forth again a third time,
> Fly thou up aloft to heaven,
> And through nine heavens fly thou swiftly.

She then gave him directions for his journey past the stars to the bright dwelling of Jumala the Creator. But the bee, the "bird of wisdom," felt unequal to the task, and asked:

> How can I perform thy bidding,
> I a man so small and helpless?

The woman said he was quite able to do it, so

> From the earth the bee rose swiftly,
> On his honeyed wings rose whirring,
> And he soared on rapid pinions,
> Swiftly past the moon he hurried,
> Past the borders of the sunlight,
> Rose upon the Great Bear's shoulders,
> O'er the Seven Stars' backs rose upwards,
> Flew to the Creator's cellars,
> To the halls of the Almighty;
> There the drugs were well concocted,
> And the ointment duly tempered
> In the pots composed of silver,
> Or within the golden kettles.

From this store the bee gathered honey in abundance, and he flew back with hundreds of little vessels full of honey and the best of all the ointment. Lemminkainen's mother tasted it, and then said emphatically:

> Tis the ointment that I needed,
> And the salve of the Almighty,
> Used when Jumala the Highest,
> The Creator heals all suffering.

With this she anointed her son, and he rose up completely cured.[1]

[1] The story is from Runo xv; Lemminkainen's Recovery.

This story is a very interesting one, for it reminds us of the belief found among the Greeks, Romans, Germanic peoples, and in India that honey came from the sky, from heaven, and was brought to man by the sacred bee. Here the best honey was far out of man's reach, past the moon, past the sun, past the stars, right in the store-room of the Almighty; other honey was good, but this was the real heavenly food.

There are many charms or prayers to be recited when using salves, in which honey and the places where it may be obtained are alluded to. One prayer, addressed to Ukko,[1] the God who dwells in the sky, asks him to rain honey from the sky to make a goodly salve, the best of magic remedies. Another asks the bees to fetch honey from the flowers in Metsola (the Woodlands), a third asks the bee to go over nine seas to get the honey from an island, and a fourth tells him to go past the moon, past the sun, and the backs of the Seven Stars (The Great Bear), to the chambers of the Almighty.[2] These are the three different places the bee is told to visit in the above story.

These prayers or charms which originated in heathen times were used after the Finns were converted to Christianity. In one of these there is an echo of the belief of the heavenly origin of honey:

O Virgin Mary, Mother dear, descend from above, bring water from far away, fetch honey in a little stoup from the sky above, from beyond the courtyard of the stars as ointment for the hurts. . . . Milk honeyed milk from thy honeyed breasts into a golden-handled cup.[3]

There are several magic songs which give the "origin" of salves; they seem to have been in great request among the Finns as remedies against many evils. One charm tells us that Vuotar, maker of salves, all summer concocted salves in delightful Metsola on the edge of the steadfast hill. Delightful honey was there, strong water was there, from which she prepared a salve.[4]

More interesting is the following story of the "Origin of Salves":

---

[1] Another name for Jumala; Ukko was also Thunder-god.
[2] Abercromby, *Pre- and Proto Finns.*, vol. ii, pp. 301-3.
[3] Ibid., p. 299.   [4] Ibid., p. 388.

A field boy living very far to the north started off to prepare a salve. He encountered a fir-tree, questioned and addressed it: "Is there any honey beneath thy bark to serve as a salve for hurts, as embrocations for sores?" The fir-tree hastily replied, "There is no honey on my boughs, no virgin honey beneath my bark; thrice in summer, during this wretched summer season, a raven croaked upon my crown, a snake lay at my roots, a wind blew past me, the sun shone through me." The boy goes on his way, keeps stepping forward, finds an oak on a trampled plain, makes an inquiry of the oak, "Is there any honey on thy boughs, any virgin honey beneath thy bark, to serve as salve for hurts, as embrocation for sores?" The oak made answer intelligently: "There is honey in my boughs, virgin honey beneath my bark. Upon a previous day, indeed, honey trickled on my crown from gentle drizzling clouds, from fleecy clouds, then from my boughs it fell upon my leafy twigs and in under my bark."[1]

Another song of the origin of salves asks where are honeyed unguents rightly confected to serve as remedy for hurts, and the answer is given:

Behind the stars in the sky, near the moon, in a crack in the sun, on the shoulder of the Great Bear. Thence may the ointment trickle down, may a drop of honey drip from under the mouth of the gracious God, from under the head of the Blessed; it is an efficacious salve for every kind of injury.[2]

Yet another tells of a blue cloud and a rainbow and a maiden in the cloud, upon the rainbow's edge:

From her the milk appears, from her breast it overflows. It flowed down upon the ground upon a honey-dripping mead, upon the headland of a honeyed field. From it salves are obtained to serve as ointment for sores, as embrocations for wounds.[3]

Honey was thus largely used in ointments, to mix with beer, and as a drink; it was also used to sweeten cakes. The following charm shows it used to form a honey-cake to propitiate the forest spirits and to give good spoil to the hunter.

[1] *Folklore*, vol. iv, "Magic Songs of the Finns," p. 43 f.; Abercromby, *Pre- and Proto Finns*, vol. ii, p. 385; *Kalevala*, Runo IX. 428 ff.

[2] *Folklore*, vol. iv., p. 44.   [3] Ibid., pp. 44-45.

O Kuutar![1] bake a suet cake,
A honeyed bannock, Fäivätar,[2]
With which I'll make the Forest kind,
Will make the Backwoods well disposed
Upon my hunting days,
During the time I seek for game.[3]

The divine powers were often called upon to give honey for various needs. Ukko is implored to send rain from heaven, to distil honey from the clouds, so that the corn may sprout;[4] to let honey drizzle down on to the newly sown corn.[5] Here it is the rain which is called *honey*, and it is often used in a figurative sense in other passages. Vainamoinen, when pestilence overwhelmed his people, raised a "warmth like honey," a "heat sweet as honey" in the bathroom (the bathroom is a great feature in the home life of the Finns), and prayed to Jumala to change the water into honey to avert the sickness;[6] and he begs Ukko, "Thou of Gods the Highest," to send honey that their sores might be anointed and healed.[7]

The wife or daughter of Nature[8] is called Suvetar or Etelätär, and she is often called upon to help the farmers. In a charm to benefit cattle she is thus addressed:

Distinguished woman, Suvetar, Nature's old wife, Etelätär, pray bring thy horn from the centre of the sky, from the sky a honeyed horn, a honeyed horn from the depths of the earth. Then blow thy horn that lakes of milk may issue forth . . . into liquid honey turn the swamps . . . feed my kine with honeyed food . . . water my cattle with honeyed drinks.[9]

Etelätär is also "the youthful maid," the "boisterous, the jolly girl," who is asked to cause a honeyed cloud to arrive in the honey sky and to rain liquid honey on to the growing shoots of corn.[10] Among the *Magic Songs* there is one of the "origin" of the dog. It describes how the dog originated from the chilly wind,

---

[1] The Moon's daughter.   [2] The Sun's daughter.
[3] *Folklore*, vol. i, "Magic Songs of the Finns," p. 17.
[4] *Kalevala*, Runo II. 328.   [5] *Pre- and Proto-Finns*, II, p. 222.
[6] Runo XLV. 220 ff.   [7] Runo XLV. 327.   [8] Also Goddess of Summer.
[9] *Pre- and Proto-Finns*, vol. ii., p. 212; *Kalevala*, Runo XXXII. 116 ff.
[10] *Pre- and Proto-Finns*, vol. ii., p. 223.

and then comes the following amusing story, apparently of the domestication of the dog, in which honey plays a unique part.

> The best maiden of Pohjola
> Was standing near a well, was underneath a window front,
> Engaged in melting virgin honey.
> The honey hardened on her finger-tips, with it she smeared its teeth.
> A useful dog was the result, a neat white-collared dog was got
> That does not eat me up, that does not bite in the very least.[1]

We see, then, what an important place is given to honey in these old folk-tales of the Finns. It had also a place among the wedding customs of the Mordvins. At the bride's house a wax candle was placed on a table and prayers made to the Goddess of the Dwelling and to the Goddess of the Homestead; at the bridegroom's home his parents made offerings to the same goddesses, consisting of dough figures of domestic animals. The father cut off a corner of a loaf placed on the table, and at the same time when the offerings were made scooped out the inside of the loaf and filled it with honey. At midnight he drove to the bride's home, placed the honey-bread on the gatepost, struck the windows with his whip, and called on the girl's father to let her marry his son, and cried out, "Take the honeyed bread from the gatepost and pray."[2]

Honey occurs in the marriage customs of many nations, some have already been mentioned; we give some more examples here to show how many different peoples possess similar customs, which may possibly have had their origin in the early times before the Indo-European family had split up into its various groups.

Among the Albanian gipsies the bride smears some honey on the doorposts of her new home and is given three loaves to take in with her. At Vlach weddings in Turkey the bride was given honey and butter with which she smeared the doorposts.[3] Among the gipsies of Croatia and Turkey a cup of honey is handed to the bride, and in some parts her face is smeared with honey.[4]

This custom of smearing face and doorposts with honey is probably a very ancient one; it is still found in modern Greece,

---

[1] *Folklore*, vol. i, p. 31. The dog was the earliest domesticated animal among the Finns.　　[2] Ibid., "Marriage Customs of the Mordvins," p. 423.
[3] *Jour. Gypsy Lore Soc.*, vol. ii, p. 353.　　　　　[4] Ibid., p. 351.

where so many primitive customs survive. In the *Customs and Lore of Modern Greece* Sir Rennell Rodd writes:

> At the close of the ceremony the priest and the newly married couple join hands and solemnly walk three times round the altar through the incense fumes, while the wedding guests pelt them with sweetmeats, a symbolism which has its roots in antiquity and which among the peasantry takes the form of smearing honey on the lintel of the young bride's house.[1]

He also notes that:

> Upon the arrival of the bridal pair at the bridegroom's cottage, his mother stands waiting there with a glass of honey and water in her hand. From this glass the bride must drink that the words of her lips may become sweet as honey, while the lintel of the door is smeared with the remainder, that strife may never enter in.[2]

A somewhat similar custom is recorded in a report of the superstitions of the Sudans, a Lettish-Prussian people in West Samland, in the year 1526, where it is stated that the eyes of the bride are covered, her mouth smeared with honey, and she is led to all the doors of the house.[3]

In Rhodes the husband on arrival at the new dwelling dips his finger in a cup of honey and traces a cross with it on the door, while those present cry out, "Be good and sweet as the honey is!" After the wedding it is usual to send all the guests a cake made of honey and sesame.[4]

In Serbia the bride is received into the bridegroom's house by his mother, who gives the bride a spoonful of honey three times, and hands her a small child whom she must kiss three times, a key, and wheat grains, which she must scatter on all sides.[5]

Among the Serbian gipsies in the course of the marriage ceremonies, which last some days, the bridegroom sends the bride skeins of yellow silk, and the next day these are stuck over her face with honey and purple stain. She then leaves her father's house; on her arrival the mother-in-law hands her a sieve of oats and some honey.

[1] *Jour. Gypsy Lore Soc.*, vol. ii, p. 91.   [2] Ibid., p. 95.
[3] Mannhardt, *Myth. Forschungen*, p. 358.
[4] Rennell Rodd, *Customs and Lore of Modern Greece*, p. 99.
[5] Mannhardt, *Myth. Forschungen*, p. 357.

She scatters the oats from the sieve and smears the honey on the doorpost.[1]

In Rumania the priest gave the newly married pair a honey-cake or a piece of bread spread with honey; in Sicily, on leaving the church the bride was handed a spoonful of honey.[2] In Poland the young bride, having been blessed by the Church, was led three times round the hearth in her husband's house, her feet washed, the bridal bed sprinkled with honey and her mouth smeared with it, her eyes were then bound with a veil, and she was led to every door in the house.[3]

Such widespread customs must have had an early and perhaps a common origin; they were evidently intended as precautions against evil spirits, whose influence was specially dreaded at weddings, as charms to ensure happiness, or they had some other meaning now lost in the obscurity of ages.

[1] Hastings, *Encyclo. Religion and Ethics*, under "Honey."
[2] Mannhardt, *Myth. Forschungen*, p. 362.					[3] Ibid., p. 356.

CHAPTER XVI

THE BRITISH ISLES

PART I—CHIEFLY HISTORICAL

Beekeeping one of the oldest crafts—Mead, the "drink of the gods"—References to mead in old British and Irish poems—Place-names on England and Ireland—Irish Brehon Laws—Laws of Hywel the Good—Origin of bees in Paradise—English Bee Laws, King Alfred—Domesday Book—Forest Laws regarding honey—Value of wax—Wax profiteers—Importation of wax in fourteenth century—Queen Elizabeth's "Acte for the true melting, making and working of Waxe"—Her recipe for metheglin—Early books on bees—G. Whitney—E. Southern—J. Gerarde—C. Butler's "Feminine Monarchie"—W. Lawson—S. Hartlib's "Reformed Commonwealth of Bees"—Belief in ox-born bees—S. Purchas's "A Theatre of Politicall Flying Insects"—J. Howell—Moses Rusden—Daniel Wildman—Thomas Wildman—John Daye—Bernhard de Mandeville's "Fable of the Bees"—Shakespeare

THE honey bee is indigenous in the British Isles, and beekeeping is one of our oldest crafts. The earliest inhabitants must have enjoyed the honey from the wild bees' nests in the forests, which in ancient times covered a large part of the country. Frequent mention is made of mead in the old British and Celtic legends, which shows that the people knew how to make an intoxicating drink from honey, and when mead is made in any quantity it usually denotes that bees are domesticated and their honey used as well as that of wild bees.

As among the Germanic peoples mead was the drink of the gods. When the gods and heroes sat down to meat, they devoured whole oxen and drank their mead from vats. In the Celtic Paradise there are rivers of mead. The Irish gods when they were sent to exile sought a paradise, situate in some unknown isle of the west; the chief of the gods who went there was Manannan, son of Lêr,[1] and he sang a song extolling this land of the gods:

> Rivers pour forth a stream of honey
> In the land of Manannan, son of Lêr.

[1] He gave his name to the Isle of Man. Note that the fairies come from the west; Fairyland, the underground paradise, is in the west.

His golden-haired daughter, Niamh, who chose Ossian from among the sons of men to be her lover, carried him off there on her fairy horse, and as they went she described to him this country of the gods:

> Abundant there are honey and wine . . .
> Death and decay thou wilt not see.[1]

In some of these songs there is mention of a hazel-mead. A poem of the seventh century, "King and Hermit," tells of Marvan, the king's brother, who became a hermit and who rejoiced in the honey, the cup of "mead of the hazel-nut," and the swarms of bees, the "little musicians of the world," which God had given him;[2] and in the story of the four children of Lêr who had been changed into swans, but retained their human mind, the daughter, Finola, remembering their former happy life, sang:

> Yet oft have we feasted in days of old,
> And hazel-mead drank from cups of gold.[3]

Dr. Joyce, in his *Social History of Ancient Ireland*, infers from these poems that "hazel nuts were sometimes used as an ingredient in making mead, probably to give it a flavour." In the Highlands of Scotland, however, an elixir is still remembered by the people made of "Comb of the honey and milk of the nut" (*cìr na meala 'is bainne nan cnò*). The Highlanders regard the hazel as a "milk" tree, the "milk" being the white juice of the green nut.[4] In many countries the "Mother-Goddess" is connected with trees whose fruit produces "milk"; it was, as we have seen, an ancient custom to feed newborn infants on milk and honey, and this hazel-mead may be a remembrance of this custom.

Mead is often extolled in the old Welsh and Irish poems. Taliesin, the famous Welsh bard of the sixth century, is represented as singing:

---

[1] C. Squire, *Celtic Myth and Legend*, p. 346.
[2] *Ancient Irish Poetry*, trans. Kuno Mayo, p. 48.
[3] P. J. Joyce, *Old Celtic Romances*, p. 24.
[4] Mr. D. A. Mackensie, to whom I am indebted for this information, also told me that he had recently heard of this elixir of milk and honey as a tonic for children in the Western Highlands. For an account of "Milk-goddesses," see Mr. Mackensie's *Myths of Pre-Columbian America*, p. 166.

May abundance of mead be given to Maelgyn of Anglesey, who
supplies us
From his foaming mead horns, with the choicest pure liquor.
Since his bees collect and do not enjoy,
We have sparkling mead, which is universally praised.[1]

Finn Mac Cumall, the Irish hero, was offered a cup of white
silver by a princess, who told him that the drink it contained was
"mead, delectable and intoxicate."[2] Fergus of the honeyed words
was bard of the Fenians, and Esirt the bard sang of him: "His eye
is bland, as it were a stream of mead"; and in a lay on the death of
Fergus, we find these poetical words:

The noble willow burn not; within its bloom bees are a-sucking, all
love the little cage.[3]

In an old Welsh story, that of Killhwch and Olwen, one of
the tasks Killhwch has to perform before he can gain Olwen is to
get honey, "honey that is nine times sweeter than the honey of
the virgin swarm, without scum or bees, to make bragget for the
feast."[4] This honey must have resembled the ambrosia of the
Greeks, which was said to be nine times sweeter than ordinary
honey.

All these stories show that there was plenty of honey to make
mead; indeed, in one old poem entitled "Cadair Teyrn On,"
Britain is called "The Honey Isle";[5] and an Irish story recalls the
Golden Age, for in the time of Cormac, son of Art:

It was with the fingers' tips that men might gather honey as they
walked, seeing that it was for the righteousness of Cormac's governance
it rained down from Heaven. In his time it was that vessels could not
be had for the milk, for the kine shed their milk without cessation.[6]

Truly a "Land of Milk and Honey!"

[1] *The Mabinogion*, trans. Lady C. Guest, "Everyman" edition, p. 278.
Maelgen began to reign about 517.
[2] Standish O'Grady, *Silva Gadelica*, p. 221.   [3] Ibid., p. 278.
[4] *Mabinogion*, p. 114. Bragget was a mixture of ale and honey fermented
with yeast.
[5] Edward Davies, *The Mythology and Rites of the British Druids*, 1809, p. 121.
Mead figures largely in the old English poem of Beowulf (= Bee-wolf). The
mead-bench and the mead-hall are often mentioned.
[6] *Silva Gadelica*, p. 97.

We now turn to more definite historical notices of bees and their products.[1] In Britain beekeeping, if not already practised, would certainly be introduced by the Romans during their long and peaceful occupation, and it was continued by the Anglo-Saxons when they settled there.

This is shown by the various old English place-names in districts where bees and honey were abundant. In old English charters we get some place-names no longer in existence, as *Hunigbroc*, *Honigburne*, *Honighyrst*, but we still have in Suffolk *Honington* (called in Domesday Book *Hunegtuna*), which means honey-farm or a farm where bees are kept; *Honeydon* in Bedfordshire, meaning "Honeytown"; *Honnington* (in Domesday, *Hunitone*), and *Honiley*, the honey-lea, both in Warwickshire; *Honeybourne*, near Evesham in Worcestershire, and in the same county, *Honeybrook*, which was in 866 *Honigbroc*.

Of bee place-names there is *Beausale*, in Warwickshire, mentioned in Domesday Book as *Becshelle*, which means "Hill of the Bees"; *Beoley*, near Redditch in Worcestershire (in 972 *Beoleahe*, in Domesday *Beolege*), the Bee-lea or meadow; *Beobridge* in Shropshire, and *Beley* in Gloucestershire, which was in 992 *Beoleahe*. There are several places called *Beeston*, whose old English form would be *Beostun*,[2] where *Bees* is used as a personal name, hence they mean bees' farm. There are also places as *Bickerstaffe*, *Bickerton*, *Bycardyke*, which probably owe their name to the bees. In the Cockersand Chartulary (Lancashire) an Adam *le Byker* is mentioned, a name which has been connected with a North English word *byke*, a beehive, or nest, or swarm of bees, and who was probably the man who looked after the bees' nests in the woods. In old English charters are found two place-names,

---

[1] Old English form of bee was *beo*, which is related to the old High German *bi* or *bie*; in Welsh bee = *gwenynen*, which form is also found in Brittany. The modern Gaelic is *be-ach* (*ch* gutteral, *ach* is diminutive); an old form is *earc*. Modern Irish is also *beach* (pro. *bah*); there are older forms, *bech*, *earc*, and *arc*. The word *honey*, with its allied forms *hunig*, *honning*, *honig*, is only found in Germanic languages; the Celtic form for honey—Gaelic, Irish, and Welsh—is *mil*, which is connected with the Greek and Latin words for honey, *meli* and *mel*.

[2] For these place-names, see W. W. Skeet, *Place-names of Suffolk and Bedfordshire*; W. H. Duignan, *Warwickshire and Worcestershire*; J. B. Johnston, *Place-names of England and Wales*.

Bycera-feld and *Beocera-gent*, which are derived from old English *bycera*, *beocera*, bee-farmer, and the above names are probably derivatives from these.[1]

There are several surnames, as Beeman or Beaman, Beman, and many in which honey forms a part, as Honeybill, etc. The surname Honeyman appears in an old roll of 1183 in a Latinized form as *Custosapium*.[2]

In Ireland, *Clonmel* in Tipperary, or *Cluainmela* as it is called at the present day, is so named from the abundance of wild bees' nests (*clon* = meadow); and two other *Clonmels* and *Clonmelsh* or *Cluainmilis* have the same derivation. Near Dublin was a place called *Lannbeachaire*, the "Church of the Bee-man," so named because St. Molaga kept bees there, and which appears in the records of the See of Dublin as *Lambeecher*. There are several names ending in *namagh*, that is, *nambeach*, "of the bees," as *Cornamagh* in Cavan, *Rathnamagh* in Mayo, and *Coolnamagh* in Cork.[3]

The Latin writer, Solinus, who lived in the third century, states that there were no bees in Ireland:

> No bees have been brought thither, and if anyone scatters dust or pebbles brought from thence among the hives in other countries, the swarms will desert their combs.[4]

This is certainly a libel on the soil of Ireland and Solinus was misinformed, though it is possible that he may have meant domesticated bees, which a legend says were introduced by a Welsh saint (see below, p. 212). The truth is that great attention was paid in Ireland to the care of bees, which is proved by numerous mention of them in various early codes of laws.

The Brehon Laws, which are transcripts made from the eighth to the thirteenth centuries from earlier copies, have a whole section on "Bee-Judgements," which give very full directions as to the ownership of swarms, and what amount of honey had to be paid

---

[1] See article by R. E. Zachrisson of Uppsala in *Zeitschrift für Ortsnamen-Forschung*, Band IV, Heft 3, p. 247, who refers to Miss Gilchrist's article in *The Times Litt. Supplement*, November 1922.

[2] C. H. Bardsley, *Our English Surnames*.

[3] P. W. Joyce, *Irish Place-names*, 1910.

[4] Solinus, 22. 4 (Mommsen, p. 112, 1).

to the chief of the tribe. They state that as the bees belonging to a man gathered honey from the surrounding lands, the owners of the adjacent farms were entitled to a small proportion of the honey. It is also mentioned that a sheet was sometimes spread out so that a swarm might alight on it, and that at the time of getting honey the bees were smothered.[1] This is one of the earliest notices of the practice of smothering bees, a custom which certainly did not prevail in Greece and Rome, but was customary in England and parts of Europe, especially Germany, until quite recent times. The custom probably originated when taking honey from the wild bees' nests in the forests of Central Europe, was known there to our forefathers, and was continued after bees were domesticated.

Another early Irish code of laws, the Book of Aichill, gives a long list of injuries caused by bee stings to man and beast, and also fines for wantonly killing bees.[2]

We can gauge what abundance of honey there was by the size of the vessels in which it was measured. The Brehon Laws mention four sizes of vessels used when measuring honey in large quantities. A *milch-cow* measure was one which, when full, an ordinary person could lift as far as his knee; a *heifer*, one he could lift to his waist; a smaller *heifer* to his shoulder; and a *dairt* or still smaller heifer vessel which he could raise over his head. It was a quaint way of measuring!

The standard measure of capacity, another curious measure, was the full of a hen-eggshell (12 of them = 1 pint); and a *sellann*, equal to four eggshellfuls, was often used in measuring honey.[3] This measure frequently occurs in the Rule of the Culdee Monks,[4] who were allowed to drink thick milk mixed with honey on the eves of Christmas and Easter.

The monks who followed the Rule of St. Ailbe, a contemporary of St. Patrick, were allowed to have for dinner,

on clean dishes herbs or roots washed in water, likewise apples and mead from the hive to the depth of a thumb.[5]

[1] *Ancient Laws of Ireland*, vol. iv, Brehon Law Tracts, 1879, Bee-Judgements, pp. 163–203. Summary of Laws given by Joyce, *Social Hist. of Ancient Ireland*, 1902, vol. ii, Chap. XXI.

[2] *Ancient Laws of Ireland*, vol. iii, p. 433; see also Joyce, *Irish Place-names*, p. 146. This code is said to date from the third century, but such an early date is not likely. [3] Joyce, *Social Hist. of Ancient Ireland*, p. 376.
[4] Ibid., p. 147. [5] Ibid., p. 120.

Mead was a drink in great request, and was called the "Dainty Drink of the Nobles." The great banqueting-hall of Tara was called "Tech Mid churada,"[1] the mead-circling house. It is probable that more honey was used for making mead than for other purposes. Large quantities of mead were paid as rent, and hives stocked with bees were given as part of a tribute paid to a king. The mass of the people used honey with their porridge or stirabout, and meat and fish were often basted with it. In an old manuscript we read that Ailill and Maive, king and queen of Connaught, had a salmon basted with honey and broiled for the young chief Fraech; the dish "was well made by their daughter, Findabair."[2]

In Wales Hywel the Good (died 950) drew up a code of laws, which contained many of a much earlier period. The laws show that the Welsh princes had certain privileged officials at their Courts, and among them were the mead-brewer and the butler. We read that, "The protection of the mead-brewer is from the time he shall begin to prepare the mead vat until he shall cover it," and that of the butler "is from the time he shall begin to empty the mead vat until he shall finish."

The mead-brewer was an important personage: "he had his land free, his horse in attendance, and his linen clothing from the queen and his woollen clothing from the king, and that at the three principal festivals." His lodging was in the hall with the steward, and when he was making the mead he was allowed part and a third of the wax. It is noted that "the worth of a vat of mead which is paid to the king is six score pence, and it is to be divided thus: the third to the king, the second third to him who makes it, and the third third to him who gives the mead," and the size of the vat "is nine hand-breadths when measured diagonally, that is, from the farthest bottom groove to the hither rim."

The worth of an old stock is given as 24d., of a first swarm 16d., of a second, called a "bull" or "stag" swarm, 12d., of a

---

[1] Eugene O'Curry, *Manners and Customs of the Ancient Irish*, vol. i, p. ccclxxvii.

[2] Joyce, *Social Hist. of Ancient Ireland*, p. 147. In Irish myths the salmon is the source of knowledge; its red spots came from the rowan berries or red hazel nuts that fell into the pool.

third swarm 8d.[1] If a hive swarm after August, it is 4d. in value, and is called a "wing" swarm, which does not become an old stock until the calends of May, and its value is then 24d.; other swarms become a mother hive worth 24d. the ninth day before August. The worth of a beehive was 24d., and a wild stock in the woods was the same value. If one of these wild stocks was stolen and the tree cut in which it was, the worth of the tree and the worth of the hive had to be paid to the owner of the land. If a man found a wild hive not before marked and showed it to the owner of the land, he was to have 4d. and his dinner, or all the wax.

No swarm was of more value than 4d. until it had been three days settled, and at all times in serene weather; a day to find a place, a day to remove, and a day to rest.

The Welsh are very fond of *Triads*, and one of the "Triads of Law" was: "Three things which the law suffers not to be appraised: meal and bees and silver, because their like is procurable."[2]

These laws about bees are of interest to all beekeepers, but for the mythologist the most interesting part of the code is the following remarkable statement of their origin, which introduces the section on bees:

The origin of Bees is from Paradise, and on account of the sin of man they came hence, and God conferred his blessing upon them, and therefore the mass cannot be said without the wax.[3]

Why this clause was inserted in the code we do not know, but here is found the direct statement that the bee was regarded as a sacred creature; it came from Paradise innocent, and therefore its wax was the only substance worthy to make the candles for the sacred mass. The belief that bees came from Paradise was held

---

[1] The first issue of bees from a stock is usually called a *swarm* and the others *casts*. In Surrey the second swarm is called a *cast* and the third a *cote*; in the Midland counties the third swarm is a *spindle*. It would be interesting to know the origin of these names.

[2] An old Welsh story relates that Henwen, the sow of Dallwyn Dallben, the chief of mystics, came from Gwent to Cornwall, where she deposited three grains of wheat and three bees; hence Gwent is famous for producing the best wheat and honey (E. Davies, *Myth and Rites of Brit. Druids*, p. 426).

[3] *Dull Gwent Code*, Book II, Chap. XXVII. 1. For the above laws, see *Ancient Laws of Wales*, published by Commissioners of Public Records, 1841, and *Welsh Medieval Laws*, trans. A. W. Wade-Evans, 1910.

in the district of the Lech in Germany (see p. 155), it appears as we shall see later in many folk stories, and seems vaguely to have been the belief held by Vergil, when he wrote that bees possess a share of the divine reason and of the breath of life which originated in the ether which is pervaded by God (*Geor.*, IV. 220). With Vergil, as with philosophers like Porphyry, it was probably connected with the belief in the reincarnation of the soul, and this statement that bees came from Paradise must undoubtedly be connected with the belief in "bee-souls," found in the British Isles as elsewhere.

An echo of the belief in bees from Paradise is found in a poem of Dafydd ap Gwilym, a contemporary of Chaucer, an ode to the snow, in which the snowflakes as they fall from the sky are likened to bees from heaven:

Gwenyn	o	Nef	Gwynion	ynt.
Bees	from	Heaven	white	are they.[1]

The early English laws do not mention bees and honey so often as the Welsh and Irish codes. In Wales and the English counties on its borders food rents (*gwestva*) were often paid, and in the laws of King Ina of Sussex (688) a *gwestva* is recorded in which 10 *dolia* of honey were included—a *dolium* was a large earthenware vessel used for storing wine and other liquids.[2] King Alfred made a law that every beekeeper must announce the issue of a swarm by ringing bells or clashing metals, so that it might be followed and captured. As his code contains many laws earlier than his reign, this regulation may go back to the times when the English were still on the Continent and were using such bee charms as the one mentioned on p. 163. By King Alfred's time beekeeping was becoming an important occupation as the Church required so much wax for candles, and the king also used them for measuring time.

In Domesday Book the statistics for the Eastern Counties frequently mention hives of bees. Honey was measured by the *sextary* (nearly a pint), and was valued at 12d. or 13d., but there was also a larger sextary, "cum majori mensura," which was worth 13s. 4d. Wild honey found in the woods had to be accounted for; from the

---

[1] For this quotation I am indebted to Mr. Williams of the National Library, Aberystwyth.

[2] F. Seebohm, *The English Village Community*, 1905, pp. 210-13.

large wood at Eling, 3 sextars of honey were given to the lord. It is also recorded that the Bishop of Worcester in the time of Edward the Confessor had rights of hunting and honey in the wood at Malvern. In Wiltshire the sheriff had as part of his rents 16 sextars of honey or 16s. in lieu thereof. In King Edward's time the shire of Warwick, with the borough and the royal manors, rendered £65 and 36 sextars of honey, or £24 6s. in lieu of the honey; in 1086 the royal manors and pleas of the shire produced £145 of weighed money and 24 sextars of honey; in these cases the larger sextary was used.[1]

Later we have such notices as that in 1258 "Roger Wiskard paid rent for one toft [dwelling-house] half a stone of wax";[2] and about the same date in the Isle of Wight Thomas Biseyt's rent was a pound of wax and a pound of cummin, paid at Michaelmas.[3] In Cumberland in 1300 Thomas de Luscy held the wood of Allerdale within the Forest of Engilwode (modern Inglewood) and had rights to the honey there.[4]

Besides the rights of certain nobles to the honey in the forests, the first charter of Henry III, in 1217, only two years after Magna Charta, declared that "Every freeman . . . shall likewise have the honey which shall be found in his woods."[5] At that period this privilege was a real boon to those allowed to exercise it; sugar was not brought to England before the fifteenth century, so honey was the only sweetening material, and besides being used in food and medicine many beverages were made of it, bragget, metheglin, piment, and morat, as well as the universal mead. The wax was of great value, since candles of tallow are first said to have been used in 1290; those of wax were a luxury, and were used only by the rich. Wax candles were used to measure time, and in the laws of Hywel the Good of Wales there is noted the right of the king's chamberlain to as much wax as he could bite from the end of a taper![6]

In the reign of Henry VI there were profiteers in wax. The wax-chandlers sold wax candles and wax for images, figures, and other objects made for offerings, at a much higher rate than the

---

[1] For references to Domesday, see A. Ballard, *The Domesday Inquest.*
[2] *Calendar of Inquisitions,* 1916, vol. i, p. 85.　　　　　[3] Ibid., p. 215.
[4] Ibid., p. 500.　　　　　[5] *Statutes of the Realm,* vol. i, p. 12L
[6] Richard Thomson, *Historical Essay on Magna Carta,* 1829, p. 353.

6d. which was their proper value, "By which means divers of the People be defrauded of their good Intent and Devotion"; so in 1433 the king ordered that they might only charge 3d. on the pound of wax beyond the value of the plain wax, and the justices of the peace were to punish offenders. The only exception was for funeral lights, "to be made for Nobles that do die!"[1] Apparently the wax-chandlers were allowed to make an extra profit on these occasions. This Act was repealed by James I in 1623.

There was not sufficient honey to supply the demand in England in the reign of Richard II, so some was imported, and a statute of 1380 states that all vessels of honey which were imported had to be lawfully gauged by the king's gaugers and a tax paid on them.[2]

Just two hundred years after, in 1580, Queen Elizabeth passed an "Acte for the true melting, making and working of Waxe." Honey and wax were more plentiful then, and much was exported, but it was often adulterated and so the queen promulgated this Act.

Whereas by the goodness of God this Land doth yield great plentie of Honye and Waxe, as not onlye dothe suffice the necessarye uses of the Queenes Majestie and her Subjects to be spent within this Realme, but also a great quantitie to be spared to be transported unto other Realmes and Countreys beyonde the Seas by waye of Merchaundize, to the great Benefite of her Majestie and the Realme; yet nevertheless a greate part of the waxe made and melted hathe byn founde to bee of late verye corrupt;

therefore the Queen ordained a penalty of 2s. a pound for mixed wax, half to be paid to the Queen and the other half to the person defrauded. Makers of wax cakes were to mark them with their initials, and all wares must be made with "good holsome pur and convenient stuffe." Corrupt wax was to be forfeited. A proviso was added for private persons selling their own wax in small pieces in the open market.[3]

Queen Elizabeth's Commissioners made repeated inquests into the state of the forests and their reports show that wild bees were very abundant there, the old hollow oaks being very storehouses of honey. The Queen was very fond of the honey-drink, metheglin.

[1] *Statutes of the Realm*, vol. ii, p. 286.
[2] Ibid., p. 16.
[3] Ibid., vol. iv, p. 670.

In *England's Interests*, written by Sir John More in 1707, directions are given for making it:

We find by history that it was the approved and common drink of our ancestors, even of kings and queens who in former ages preferred the liquors of the product of this island before those imported from foreign countries, as did the famous and renowned Queen Elizabeth, who every year had a vessel of metheglin made for her own drinking. A recipe of this queen's metheglin coming to my hands, I shall oblige the reader therewith as follows: Take a bushel of sweet briar leaves, as much of thyme, and a peck of bay leaves; and having well washed, boil them in a copper of fair water; let them boil the space of half an hour or better, and then pour out all the water and herbs into a fat [vat], and let it stand till it but be milk warm; then strain the water from the herbs and take to every gallon of water, one gallon of the finest honey, and beat it together for the space of an hour; then let it stand for two days, stirring it well twice or thrice a day; then take the liquor and boil it again, and skim as long as there remains any scum; when it clears put it into a fat as before and let it stand to cool. You must then have in readiness a kive of new ale or beer, which as soon as you have emptied suddenly, presently put in the metheglin, and let it stand three days a-working and then tun it up in barrels, tying at every tap hole, by a pack-thread, a little bag of beaten cloves and mace to the value of an ounce. It must then stand half a year before it be drunk.[1]

The books on the management of bees in modern times are innumerable, but the earliest English books on the subject were written in the sixteenth century. Before that time the writings of Varro, Vergil, Columella, Pliny, Aelian, and Palladius were known to classical scholars. There was, indeed, an English translation of Palladius, but it was probably very little known, as, though it was written about 1420, it was not printed until 1873.[2]

We will mention here some of the earlier English writers on bees, though we do not propose to say anything about their methods of beekeeping.

---

[1] Sir J. More probably got this from C. Butler, who gives it in his *Feminine Monarchie*, published 1609. Butler says metheglin = "meth of the vallie," and that it is meth compounded with herbs; he remarks that *meth* is incorrectly called *mede* (mead). The story is quoted by W. C. Cotton, *My Bee Book*, 1842, p. 134.

[2] Printed by the Early English Text Society from an MS. in Colchester Castle Library.

Geffray Whitney, although not the author of any book on apiculture, was acquainted with the classical writers on the subject, and in his *Choice of Emblemes*, published in 1586, has several

(a) (b)

(c) (d)

FIG. 25.—(a), (b), and (c) from Geffray Whitney: *A Choice of Emblemes,*
Leyden, 1586.

(d) "King Bee" and Hives, from Horapollo: *Hieroglyphiques des Aegyptiens,* Paris, 1543.

illustrations of bees and hives, three of which are reproduced on Fig. 25. Under Fig. 25(a), dedicated to Richard Cotton, he wrote:

> The maister bee, within the midst dothe liue,
> In fairest roome, and most of stature is.
> And euerie one to him dothe reuerence giue,
> And in the hiue with him doe liue in blisse.

The next figure (*b*), dedicated to Hughe Cholmeley, is headed "Ex Bello Pax," and this verse below:

> The helmet stronge, that did the head defende,
> Beholde for hiue, the bees in quiet serv'd
> And when that warres, with bloodie bloes, had ende,
> They hony wroughte, where souldiour was preserv'd;
> Which dothe declare, the blessed fruites of peace,
> How sweet she is, when mortal warres doe cease.

The story of Eros, stung by the bees and complaining to his mother, which was given on p. 131, is represented in Fig. 25(*c*)

In 1593 Edmund Southern wrote a treatise on "*Bees*," in which occurs the following story:

A parson came to a gentleman who kept bees and demanded tithe. The gentleman said it was not customary to pay tithe on bees, but he would pay it on honey and wax, "Bees cannot be told," he said, "therefore how shall I pay them?" The parson, however, demanded the tenth swarm, which was to be brought to his house. It fortuned within two days that the gentleman had a great swarm, the which he put into a hive, and towards night he carried it to the parson's house; the parson and his wife and family he found in a fair hall; the gentleman saluted them and told the parson he had brought some bees. "I mary," quoth the parson, "this is neighbourly done, I pray you carry them into my garden." "Nay, by troth," quoth the gentleman, "I will leave them even here." With that he gave the hive a knock against the ground, and all the bees fell out. Some stung the parson, some his wife, and some his children and familie, and out they ran as fast as they could into a chamber, and well was he who could shift for himself, leaving their meate on the table in the halle. The gentleman went home carrying the empty hive.

Four days after he was summoned before the magistrate and asked why he had misused the parson. He replied that the parson would have a swarm of bees, and he had left them in the hall. "Why did you not leave them in the hive?" asked the magistrate. He replied, "I would if they had been in my garden." "Why did you not let the parson have the hive?" "I could not spare it, for I bought the hive in the market, and I am sure, covetous as the parson is, he can have no tythe of that. I buy in the market according to the English laws, but I did by the bees as he willed me, and as I have ever done by all his other tythes, which I have ever left in his hall, and so I did these; yet there was no bees ever demanded in tythe in our parish until now; but honey and wax he shall have with good will." The magistrate agreed this was fair, and so they were contented and afterwards became friends.[1]

This story is interesting, as it shows that tithes on honey and wax were paid in the reign of Queen Elizabeth.

In 1597 in his *Herball* John Gerarde mentions that "the countrie people use to kill or smoother Bees with Fusseballs [puffballs], being set on fire, for the which purpose it fitly serveth"; and he also says that the leaves of mallows, mint, and the bay-tree are good against the stinging of bees.

In 1609 Charles Butler, Rector of Wooton, published in Oxford his books on bees, *The Feminine Monarchie*; as he states in his Preface, "We must not call the Queen 'Rex,' the Bee-state is an Amazonian or feminine kingdom." It is a quaint book, and repays reading by the curious. There were several editions; the most interesting is the third, published in 1634, as it gave new matter, including some stories which are given in the next chapter. One sentence would be very acceptable to Charles I, and his Queen to whom the work was dedicated:

Bees abhor as well poliarchy as anarchy, God having showed in them unto men an express pattern of a perfect monarchie, the most natural and absolute form of government.

The charming little poem prefixed to this work is taken from this book. Butler had a high opinion of the musical capacity of the bees, and he gives some staves reproducing the Bees' Song, and adds: "In this *Melissomelos* or Bees-madrigall, Musicians may see the grounds of their art."

Butler's knowledge of bees was no more than that of the Latin writers, with whose works he was acquainted. Of the bee's sting he writes:

If thou wilt have the favour of the bees that they sting thee not, thou must avoid such things as offend them; thou must not be unchaste and uncleanly; for inpuritie and sluttishness (themselves being most chaste and neat) they utterly abhor.

The bees gather honey of two sorts: "the one pure and liquid, which is called Nectar; the other grosse and solid, which we may by the like reason tearme Ambrosia." "As skilled astronomers the

[1] Quoted by C. Cotton, *My Bee Book*, p. 102.

bees have foreknowledge of the weather"; and they have such intelligence that Butler concludes with Vergil:

That the Bees doe participate divine wisdom and celestial influence. Which big conceipt is confirmed by their propheticall pressages of many extraordinary events and specially of the sweet concurrence of man's sweetest ornaments.

This is an allusion to the belief that bees give men wisdom and the gift of poetry, and Butler, after mentioning that bees alighted on the lips of famous men like Plato, Pindar, and Ambrose, remarks, "But none of these are more memorable than the Bees of Vives, in the College of Bees"—this college is Corpus Christi College, Oxford, so called by the founder Bishop Fons in the original charter—and he continues:

When Vives was sent by Cardinal Wolsey to Oxford there to be the public professor of rhetoric, being placed in the College of Bees, he was welcomed thither by a swarm of bees; which sweet creatures, to signify the incomparable sweetness of his eloquence, settled themselves over his head, under the leads of his study, where they have continued above 100 years. . . . How sweetly do all things thus accord, when in this "mousaion," newly consecrated to the Muses, the Muses' sweetest favourite was thus honoured by the Muses' Birds. The truth of the story has the special testimony of a worthy antiquary of our time, who had heard his master, Dr. Benefield, call these Bees, Vives' Bees.[1]

In 1631 William Lawson published *The Country House-wifes Garden*. He writes: "I have learnt by experience, being a Bee-maister meselfe"; and he thinks that women may profitably take care of bees, so he gives them practical directions. Unlike Butler, whose hive was a "Feminine Monarchie," Lawson calls the queen the "Master Bee," and makes some quaint statements, among which is:

Snayles spoile them [the hives] by night like thieves, they come so quietly and are so fast, that the Bees feare them not.

In 1655 appeared Samuel Hartlib's *Reformed Commonwealth of Bees*. In it there is an interesting account of an "Experiment of the

---

[1] This story does not give the reason why the College was called the College of Bees. Erasmus inscribed a letter to the first president thus: "Eras. Rot. Joanni Claymunde Apum Praesidi. "

Generation of Bees, practised by that great husbandman, old Mr. Carew of Anthony in Cornwall."

Take a calf, or rather a sturk [steer] of a year old, about the latter end of Aprill, bury it eight or ten days, till it begins to putrifie and corrupt; then take it forth of the earth, and opening it, lay it under some hedge or wall, where it may be most subject to the sun, by the heat whereof it will (a great part of it) turn into maggots, which (without any other care) will live upon the remainder of the corruption. After a while, when they begin to have wings, the whole putrified carcase should be carried to a place prepared where the hives stand ready, to which, being perfumed with honey and sweet herbs, the maggots after they have received their wings, will resort. The gentleman in Cornwall, that practised this experiment, uses hogsheads, or bigger wine casks, instead of Hives, and the practice of the Bee being to fill the upper part of the cask in the first part of the summer, and so still to work downwards, the gentleman's usuall custome was (through a door in the upper part of the cask) to take out what honey he wanted, without disturbance to the Bees, whose work and abode was thus in the lower part of the cask.

Then follows a Dr. Arnold Boate's observation on this experiment:

"I did ever think that the generation of Bees out of the carcase of a dead calf, given us by divers of the Ancients, but most amply and elegantly by Virgil, in the fourth book of his Georgicks, had been a fiction, but am glad to find the contrary by your [Hartlib's] letter, which confirmed the same out of modern and English experience. And I would have as little thought that Bees would have wrought in such vast hives as hogsheads, whereas some of the Ancients give us a caveat, even of the ordinary hives, not to make them too large, lest the Bees should be discouraged out of a despair to fill them.[1]

We see here how late the "ox-born bee" myth lasted in England; in 1610 Ben Jonson had written in the *Alchemist*:

> Beside, who doth not see, in daily practice,
> Art can beget bees, hornets, beetles, wasps,
> Out of the carcases and dung of creatures;
> Yea, scorpions, of a herbe, being rightly placed;[2]

---

[1] This passage is quoted by C. Cotton in *My Bee Book*, 1842, p. 354. Cotton in his Preface says he wanted when a boy to try Vergil's method and tried to procure a dead cow; his parents heard of his wish and gave him a swarm instead!　　　　　　　　　　　　　　　　　　　[2] Act II, Scene 3, 381.

and a few years after Hartlib's book, in 1678, Samuel Butler wrote
in *Hudibras*:

> The learned write, an Insect Breeze
> Is but a Mungrel Prince of Bees,
> That falls before a Storm on Cows,
> And stings the Foundress of his House;
> From whose corrupted Flesh that Breed
> Of Vermine did at first proceed.[1]

Two years after Hartlib's *Reformed Commonwealth* appeared,

A Theatre of Politicall Flying Insects, wherein especially the Nature,
Worth, Wonder of the manner of Right Ordering of the Bee is discovered
and described, by Samuel Purchas, M.A. Pastor of Sutton in Essex.
London 1657.

Space unfortunately forbids a long account of this interesting
book. Purchas had studied the classical writers; he gives many
stories from various parts of the world, and is always careful to
give his authority. About the generation of bees, he writes:

It hath been an ancient tradition that Bees have a twofold production;
by generation and putrifaction. . . . I am somewhat dubious because
it [the latter] was never authentically proved to bee performed by any.
But they tell us that the best sort is procreated of a corrupted Lion.
And therefore say it is no wonder, that being so small creatures, they
fear not any, nay prevail over the greatest with a lion-like courage assaulting
them. Some say they are bred of bulls, cows or calves; . . . but more
absurd is the opinion of others, that if the ashes of Bees are bedewed
with sweet wine, and exposed to the sun in a warm place, there will
bee a present resurrection of the former burnt Bees.

Purchas knew of the Egyptian Bee hieroglyph, for he writes:

The Egyptians perhaps by the Hieroglyphick of a Bee signified a King,
because it becomes a commander of a people to mingle with the sting
of justice the honey of clemency. Memorable to this purpose was the
practice of a certain King of France, who having conquered the Insubrians
and entered their city, by a symbol or type thus expressed his clemency
wearing a coatfull of Images on pictures of Bees, and this motto written
upon it: *Rex mucrone caret*, the King wants or useth not his sting.

Honey is more plentiful in Russia, he remarks, than in any part
of the world; the Russians use a great quantity of it in their ordinary

[1] Part III, Canto 2.

drink, "which is meade of all sorts," and yet much is exported, also a large quantity of wax, amounting to "1,000 tun hath been shipped yearly, and yet the great men use but little tallow, but much wax for their lights." He also notes the use of honey and wax candles in many Russian wedding customs.

Purchas relates that

A certain Countryman stole a wax candle from the Altar and found it turned to a stony hardness, whereby melting, he acknowledged his guilt before many that stood by, and the wax candle recovered its former softness.

He says he could relate many such stories, but has given enough. We wish we had space to quote more of his quaint tales, which are given in the first part of his book; in Part II he moralizes on the nature of the "Politicall Flying Insect"; we give one quotation:

The Queen Bee [for it is an Amazonian Commonwealth], transcends in greatness and beauty of body, but which is more praiseworthy in a commander, in mildness and gentleness—therefore though they have stings, they never use them. The laws by which the Commonwealth is ordered are natural, not written, but graven in their manners; and so studious are they of peace, that neither willingly nor unwillingly do they offer injury to any of their subjects.

In the *Parley of Beasts* (1660) James Howell also lauds the bee. He makes her say: "Know, sir, that we also have a religion as well as so exact a government among us here; our hummings you speak of are so many hymns to the Great God of Nature." He describes the illness and death of bees in a hive thus:

> If bees be sick, (for all that live must die),
> That may be known by signes most certainly;
> Their bodies are discoloured, and their face
> Looks wan, which shows that death comes on apace.
> They carry forth their dead and do lament,
> Hanging o' th' dore, or in their hives are pent.

Another writer in the reign of Charles II was the king's own bee-master, Moses Rusden, who published in 1679 the *Further Discovery of Bees*. In the royal Bee-house at St. James's there were glass-windowed hives, and Rusden evidently knew a great deal about bees, but as his aim was to uphold the divine right of kings, he will not admit the female sex of the Royal Bee, but writes of the king with his generals, soldiers, and all the errors of the classical writers as if he believed them. He recognizes, however, that the worker bees are female, but is very puzzled about the drones. He *cannot* admit them to be males, so contents himself with saying that their only use is to keep the brood warm while the worker bees are away gathering honey.

The reign of Charles II might be termed a connecting link with the old and modern beekeeping; for the great Dutch naturalist, Jan Swammerdamm, was born in 1637 and died in 1685, the same year as Charles. It was he who definitely proved the female sex of the one large bee in the hive and the sex and functions of the drones.[1] One English writer, Daniel Wildman, who published in 1775 *A Complete Guide for the Management of Bees*, however, wrote: "I am fully convinced that the modern received opinion that the Queen Bee is the general Parent of their whole stock, is absolutely without foundation." His opinion was that the young bees were produced by the worker-bees and drones, so he may be classed among the ancient writers![2]

Before turning to the legends and superstitions about bees and honey found in the British Isles, we must mention shortly two books in which bee-life is treated symbolically. The first is *The Parliament of Bees*, by John Daye, the earliest extant edition of which is dated 1641, but it was written earlier, possibly about 1607. Charles Lamb, alluding to this book in *Extracts from the Garrick Plays*, writes: "The very air seems replete with humming and buzzing melodies. Surely bees were never so berhymed before." The sub-title of the 1641 edition is "A Beehive furnisht with twelve Honycombes as Pleasant as Profitable, being an Allegoricall Description of the Actions of Good and Bad Men in these our daies." The controversy as to whether the large bee in the hive was a "king" or "queen" was still undecided in Daye's time, and he calls it

[1] His work (see above, p. 154) was not published till 1740.

[2] Thomas Wildman, who in 1768 had written *A Treatise on the Management of Bees*, was a more advanced beekeeper and acquainted with the works of Swammerdamm and Réaumur. Other early books include: John Gedde, *A New Method of Beehouses and Colonies*, 1675; Joseph Warder, *The True Amazons or the Monarchy of Bees*, 1713; John Thorley, *Mellisselogia, or the Female Monarchy*, 1744; John Keys, *The Practical Beemaster*, 1780. All these men are forerunners of modern beekeeping.

"Mr. Bee." This "Mr. Bee" acts as *Pro-rex* in the Parliament under Oberon, and an illustration of the Parliament is given in Fig. 26.

The second book is a satire on the life of the people and their

THe Parliament is held, Bils and Complaints
Heard and reform'd, with feverall reftraints
Of ufurpt freedome ; inftituted Law
To keepe the Common-Wealth of Bees in awe.

FIG. 26.—THE PARLIAMENT OF THE BEES, WITH "MISTER BEE" AS PRO-REX

(John Daye: *The Parliament of Bees*, London, 1641)

rulers in the time of Queen Anne, and was written by Bernhard de Mandeville, a doctor of French extraction who had settled in London. It appeared first anonymously in 1705, under the title of *The Grumbling Hive or Knaves turn'd Honest*, but it is much better known by the title given to it in the 1714 and all later

editions, *The Fable of the Bees, or Private Vices, Publick Benefits.*
It is, as the sub-title shows, a professedly paradoxical work, and
Mandeville did not deserve all the abuse poured on him, not only
in England, but also on the Continent. It is really a serious economic
work, and contains much that is true of public life in every age,
and has to a great extent become a classic. Lovers of bees will be
gratified to think that the wonderful bee-state furnished the ground-
work for Mandeville's book.[1]

That the bee-state should be compared with human kingdoms
and communities was inevitable, and the well-known lines of
Shakespeare will occur to many:

> So work the honey bees,
> Creatures that by a rule in nature teach
> The art of order to a peopled kingdom;
> They have a king and officers of sorts;
> Where some like magistrates, remain at home,
> Others like merchants venture trade abroad;
> Others like soldiers armed in their stings,
> Make boot upon the summer's velvet buds;
> Which pillage they with merry march bring home
> To the royal tent of their emperor:
> Who, busied in his majesty, surveys
> The singing masons building roofs of gold,
> The civil citizens kneading up the honey,
> The poor mechanic porters crowding in
> Their heavy burdens at his narrow gate,
> The sad-eyed justice, with his surly hum,
> Delivering o'er to executor pale
> The lazy yawning drones.[2]

[1] The last edition, edited by F. B. Kaye, in two volumes, was published
in 1925. In his *Symbolik der Bienen* Glock gives the original English version
side by side with a German translation.   [2] *Henry V*, Act 1, Scene 2.

CHAPTER XVII

THE BRITISH ISLES

PART II—LEGENDS AND SUPERSTITIONS

Stories of saints and bees: St. Medard, David, Modomnoc, Patrick, Finian, Brigit, Gobnat—Piety of the bees, honour of the Host— Telling the bees of a death, etc., a widely spread belief—Stories of "Bee-souls"—Witches as bees—Tanging a swarm—Unlucky to buy bees—Meanings given to swarms—Bees sing at Christmastide —"A swarm of bees in May"—French versions of the rhyme— Use of wax figures

THERE are several stories told of saints which connect them with bees and honey. Most of them come from Wales or Ireland, but the following, told by Charles Butler, is of a French saint.

The holy St. Medard kept bees, which a thief stole by night. They, in their master's quarrel, left their hives, and set upon the malefactor, and eagerly pursuing him whichever way he ran, would not cease stinging of him, until they made him (whether he would or no) to go back again to their master's house, and then falling prostrate at his feet, submissively to cry for mercy for the crime committed. Which being done, so soon as the Saint extended to him the hand of benediction, the Bees, like obedient servants, did forthwith stay from persecuting him, and evidently yielded themselves to the ancient possession and custody of their master.[1]

The birth of St. David of Wales was foretold to his father by an angel thirty years before the event. He was told:

On the morrow thou shalt find a stag, a fish and a honeycomb. Thou shalt part of these to thy son, who shall be born 30 years hence. The honeycomb proclaims his honeyed wisdom.[2]

David is said to have founded twelve monasteries and then settled down in one of them. Here he and the other monks kept bees, so that they might have plenty of honey to give to the poor. One of these monks, St. Domnoc or Modomnoc,[3] went to Ireland

[1] *Feminine Monarchie*, p. 138. St. Medard was a weather saint like St. Swithin.　　　[2] S. Baring-Gould, *Lives of the Saints*, 1897, vol. iii, p. 14.
[3] Also called Dominicus.

(some say he was an Irishman); he was very fond of bees, and a large swarm followed him and settled on the prow of the ship where he sat. He returned with them to the monastery, and then tried to leave the place unobserved, but in vain, the bees again followed. Three times this happened, so at last he went to David and asked his leave to take the bees with him; and David blessed him and the bees and bade them depart in peace, saying that henceforth bees should prosper in Ireland, and should no longer increase in Glyn Rosyn. "This," says the old chronicler, "was found to be the fact; swarms forthwith decreased at David's, but Ireland, in which up to that time bees could never thrive, is now enriched with plenty of honey. It is manifested that they could not live there before; for if you threw Irish earth or stone into the midst of the bees, they disperse, and, flying, they will shun it."[1]

After St. Modomnoc had settled with his bees in Ireland it is said that they were carried off by a monk named Molaga to his own monastery, which received the name of *Lannbeachaire*, the Church of the Bees.[2] It is also said that St. Aidan, another disciple of St. David, took a hive of bees with him, as he had been told they were scarce in Ireland. Some have suggested that under the figure of a swarm of bees is signified a number of monks;[3] we prefer the literal interpretation of the story!

The *Book of Lismore* relates a story of St. Patrick's boyhood. The children of the place in which Patrick lived used to bring their mothers honey from the comb:

So his nurse said to him, "Thou bringst no honey to me, my boy, even as the boys bring it to their mothers." Then Patrick taking a vessel goes to the water, and sained the water, so that it became honey, and relics were made of that honey and it used to heal every disease.[4]

Another story tells how once when Patrick was at sea and all the provisions were finished, the sailors asked him for food, and "God gave them a fresh-cooked swine and wild honey was brought to Patrick like John the Baptist."[5]

[1] Baring-Gould, *Lives of the Saints*, p. 14; J. Ceredig Davies, *Folklore of West and Mid Wales*, 1911, p. 227.
[2] Baring-Gould and Fisher, *Lives of the British Saints*, 1908, vol. iii, p. 300; *Ancient Laws of Ireland*, vol. iv, Introduction.
[3] Gould and Fisher, ibid., vol. i, p. 121.
[4] *Anecdota Oxeniensia, Lives of the Saints from the Book of Lismore*, p. 152.
[5] Ibid., p. 155.

St. Findian fed six days of the week on bread and water, but on Sunday was allowed salmon and "the full of a cup of clear mead."[1] The well-known St. Brigit is also connected with mead. Once a certain man of Brigit's household made mead for the king of Leinster. When they came to drink it, not a drop was to be found. Brigit rose to save the wretched man and she blessed the vessels, and the mead was found in fullness and that was a wonderful miracle.[2]

In the annals from the *Book of Leinster* it is related that Niall the Showery, son of Fergal, reigned seven years and died as a pilgrim in Iona. He got his name from the fact that there were three showers in his reign, "to wit, a shower of white silver, a shower of honey, and a shower of wheat."[3]

But perhaps the most interesting saint connected with bees is a woman, St. Gobnat of Ballyvourney, Co. Cork. She was probably born early in the sixth century, and was a patroness of bees. St. Abban, son of the king of Leinster, installed her as abbess of Boirnech, afterwards known as Baile Muirne or Ballyvourney. There are several legends about St. Gobnat, and three versions of one which connects her with bees.[4] The first is told by Crofton Croker in *Fairy Legends and Traditions of the South of Ireland*:

Over eight hundred years ago, a powerful chief on the point of waging war against the head of another clan, seeing the inferiority of his troops, prayed to St. Gobnat for assistance, in a field adjoining the scene of the approaching battle. In this field was a beehive, and the good saint granted his request by turning the bees into armed men, who issued from the hive with every appearance of military discipline, arranged themselves in ranks and followed their leader to the contest where they were victorious. After the battle gratitude instigated the conquering chief to visit the spot from whence he had obtained such miraculous aid, when he found that the hive had also been transformed from the straw or rushes, of which it was composed, into brass, and that it had become not unlike a helmet in shape. This relic is in the possession of the O'Hierley family and is held by the

---

[1] *Anecdota Oxeniensia, Lives of the Saints from the Book of Lismore*, p. 229.

[2] Ibid., p. 197. In another story water in vats is turned into mead by Brigit.

[3] Whitney Stokes, *Tripartite Life of Patrick*, 1887, p. 521.

[4] See *Lives of the Irish Saints*, trans. from original MSS. by Charles Plumer, Oxford, 1922, p. 7; W. G. Wood-Martin, *Elder Faiths of Ireland*, London, 1902, p. 226. St. Gobnat's Day is February 11th. There is a church dedicated to her at Kilgobnet near Dungarven.

Irish peasantry in such veneration that they will travel several miles to procure a drop of water from it, which, they imagine, if given to a dying relative or friend, will secure their ready admission into heaven. Not long since water from this brazen beehive was administered to a dying priest by his coadjutor, in compliance with the popular superstition.[1]

Two other versions of the story were sent the writer by Dr. P. C. Lee, of Cork. One runs:

St. Gobnat was held in great estimation by the neighbouring princes, who were engaged in feud with other chieftains. She was one day in the convent garden, where she cultivated herbs and kept bees. While engaged in her occupation she was interrupted by O'Hierley, the *Flath-an-l' orthar* (western chieftain), who humbly asked her if she could in any way assist him to recover his cattle, which were all stolen by O'Donoghue of the Glens during his absence on a hunting expedition in Kerry. St. Gobnat listened with sympathy to the tale, knowing that the loss of the cattle meant starvation and ruin to those who depended on their kine for means of subsistence. She told the chief she might be able to help him if he would promise to become a Christian. O'Hierley agreed, whereupon St. Gobnat said a little prayer and made the sign of the cross upon the nearest *biachra* or beehive, which was changed into a brass helmet, while the small winged inmates disappearing, O'Hierley to his astonishment saw outside the garden a goodly band of soldiers able to do battle for him anywhere. St. Gobnat presented him with the helmet, which was long preserved by his descendants and considered very efficacious in warding off fevers and epidemics.

It is also said that the beehive was turned into a bell, and there is still in existence an old bronze bell said to have been the property of St. Gobnat, and the two holes at the top where the clappers were fastened were said to be those by which the bees escaped to sting the marauders; for the third and perhaps the most probable version of the story relates that St. Gobnat saw from her garden a great number of men sweeping down from Ballyvourney to drive away the cattle in the absence of their owners, who were engaged upon a similar errand! Seizing one of her hives, she ran towards the enemy shaking out the bees, who soon routed the raiders completely.[2]

[1] Crofton Croker, *Fairy Legends*, London, 1825, pp. 273-4.

[2] Dr. Lee also informed the writer that Gobnat's English name is Abigail, and that she is known as Gobnait, Gobnit, Gobinet, or Gobeneta, and in Co. Limerick as Deborah or Judith.

We now give some stories illustrating the alleged piety of the bees, which are medieval in origin and were written in Latin. Two are given by Butler in the *Feminine Monarchie*, and all four in a book written by Father Toussain Bridoul and published in 1672, and translated into English in 1687, and called: "School of the Eucharist Establishment upon the Miraculous Respects and Acknowledgements which Beasts and Birds and Insects upon several Occasions have rendered to the Holy Sacraments of the Altar." It consists of extracts given in alphabetical order, and begins with Bees.[1]

1. Bees honour the Holy Host in divers ways, by lifting it from the earth and carrying it to their hives as it were in procession. A certain peasant of Auvergne perceiving that his bees were likely to die, to prevent this misfortune, was advised after he had received the Communion to reserve the Host, and to blow it into one of his hives. As he tried to do it, the Host fell on the ground. Behold now a wonder! On a sudden all the bees came forth from their hive, ranged themselves in good order, lifted the Host from the ground and carrying it upon their wings, placed it amongst the combs. After this the man went about his business, and on his return found that the advice had succeeded ill, for his bees were all dead.

2. A certain woman having some stalls of bees which yielded not unto her the desired profit, but did consume and die of the murrain, made her moan to another woman, who gave her counsell to get a Consecrated Host and put it among them. According to whose advice she went to the priest to receive the Host; which when she had done she kept it in her mouth, and being come home again she took it and put it into one of her hives; whereupon the murrain ceased, and the honey abounded. The woman therefore lifting up the hive in due time to get the honey, saw there (most strange to be seen) a Chappel built by the Bees with an Altar in it, the walls adorned by marvellous skill of architecture, with windows set in their places, also a door and a steeple with bells. And the Host being laid on the Altar, the Bees making a sweet noyse flew round about it.[2]

[1] These four stories are given in *Notes and Queries*, 1st Series, vol. x, 1854.
[2] This story is from Caesaris of Heisterbach who died *c.* 1240. A legend of the same character is given by Mr. Hawker from Cornwall (see *Notes and Queries*, 1854, vol. ix, p. 167).

3. Certain wicked men in order to get the silver box in which the Holy Host was hidden, stole it and took it away with them, and then they threw the most sacred body of Christ under a beehive. Several days after the owner of the hive saw that often at certain times when the work of carrying food had been neglected, the Bees were sounding forth a most mellifluous harmony. When, by chance, he arose in the middle of the night, he saw a very bright light over the beehive, and the Bees were humming more sweetly than any music. He was immediately struck by this unusual sight, and moved by the secret guidance of God, he laid the matter before the Bishop. The latter, with many others besides, betook himself thither, and when the hive had been opened he saw near the foot of the hive a most beautiful vessel made out of the whitest wax in which the Eucharist had been placed. Around it a choir of Bees was humming and keeping watch. The Bishop accordingly took the Sacrament and carried it back to the Church with very great honour; and many who approached it were healed of innumerable diseases.[1]

4. A peasant swayed by a covetous mind, being communicated on Easter Day, received the Host in his mouth and afterwards laid it among his Bees, believing that all the Bees of the neighbourhood would come thither to work their wax and honey. This covetous, impious wretch was not wholly disappointed of his hopes; for all his neighbours' Bees came indeed to his hives, not to make honey, but to render there the honours due to their Creator. The issue of their arrival was that they melodiously sang to Him songs of praise as they were able; after that they built a little church with their wax, from the foundations to the roof, divided into three rooms, sustained by pillars with their bases and chapiters. There they also had an Altar, upon which they had laid the precious body of our Lord, and flew about it, continuing their musick. The peasant coming nigh to the hive where he had put the Holy Sacrament, the Bees issued out furiously by troops, and surrounding him on all sides, revenged the irreverence done to the Creator, and stung him so severely that they left him in a sad case. The punishment made the miserable wretch come to himself, who, acknowledging his error, went to find the priest and confessed his fault to him.

[1] From Thomas of Cantimpré, about 1233.

We get in these stories, which were firmly believed, a picture of how the bee was reverenced in the Middle Ages. Even Butler does not quite know whether to believe in them or not. Before giving the stories he writes:

I have heard of bees so wise and skilful, as not only to descry a certain little God Almighty though he come to them in the likeness of a wafer cake, but also to build him an artificial chapel. If I should relate the story, all men, I know, would not believe it; notwithstanding, because every man may make some use of it, you shall have it.

Many must have believed in them even in the seventeenth century, for strange to say the belief was taken over to America, though in rather a different form. Mrs. Panton, in *Within Four Walls*, writes:

I wonder whether any of my readers recollect that it used to be a custom in the Roman Catholic villages in America to place in the centre of a hive of bees, which was found in every cottage garden, a wee morsel of the consecrated wafer, kept back from the Celebration? Well it used to be the case, and this atom was called "The Little God Almighty," and was supposed to ensure the bees from all harm, and that the crops of honey in such a protected hive would be far above the average. It was placed there by the priest, and it was supposed to be the centre around which all that went on in the hive moved.[1]

The following story, this time from Ireland, is told by Lady Gregory, and is called "The Priest and the Bees."[2]

There was a good honourable well-born priest, God's darling he was, a man holding the yoke of Christ; and it happened he went one day to attend a sick man. And as he was going a swarm of bees came towards him, and he having the Blessed Body of Christ with him there. And when he saw the bees he laid the Blessed Body on the ground and gathered the swarm into his bosom, and went on in that way upon his journey, and forgot the Blessed Body where he had laid it. And after a while the bees went back from him again, and they found the Blessed Body and carried it away with them to their own dwelling-place, and they gave honour to it kindly and made a good chapel of wax for it, and an Altar and a chalice and a pair of priests, shaping them well out of wax to stand before Christ's Body. But as for the priest, when he

[1] *Within Four Walls*, p. 274. Quoted in *Notes and Queries*, Series 8, vol. vii, 1895, p. 46.   [2] *A Book of Saints and Wonders*, London, 1907, p. 136.

remembered, he went looking for it carefully, penitently, but he could not find it in any place. And it went badly with him, and he went to confession, and with the weight of the trouble that took hold of him he was fretting through the length of a year. And then an angel came to him at the end of a year, and told the way the Body of Christ was sheltered and honoured. And the angel bade him bring all the people to see the wonder; they went there and when they saw it a great many of them believed.[1]

If anyone were asked, "Do you know any superstitions about bees?" a few might reply in the negative, but the majority would answer, "Oh yes, you must tell them of a death."

Examples of this belief in Germany have already been given in Chapter XIV; the belief also prevails in France, and was taken over to America by European settlers. In the British Isles it is very general in England, Wales, Scotland, and the Isle of Man, but does not appear to be prevalent in Ireland.[2]

The form in which this belief now appears is that the bees must be told of the death of their owner; if not, they will be offended, dwindle, and die. Sometimes other deaths in the family are told to them, also marriages and other important events. In the case of death in many districts the hives are decorated with crape and portions of the funeral feast placed before them. All news must be whispered gently and politely to the bees. In some places the hives are either removed to another place or turned as the funeral procession passes them.

This custom of "telling the bees" of a death is difficult to trace to its origin. Possibly it arose in the belief of a mysterious connection between the bees and the souls of the dead. The germ of this belief was found in ancient Egypt, then among the Greeks, later in Central Europe, where we gave examples of the soul taking a bee form, and now we come across it in the British Isles.

Sir Laurence Gomme, in *Ethnology in Folklore*, writes:

[1] This is the only story which says that human figures were made.

[2] Cases are reported from Berkshire, Buckinghamshire, Cheshire, Cornwall, Cumberland, Derbyshire, Devon, Essex, Gloucestershire, Hampshire, Kent, Lincoln, Lancashire, Monmouth, Northampton, Northumberland, Oxford, Rutland, Shropshire, Somerset, Sussex, Suffolk, Wiltshire, many parts of Wales, the Isle of Man, and Scotland.

This message to the bees is clearly best explained, I think, as being given to the winged messengers of the gods, so that they may carry the news to spirit land of the speedy arrival of a newcomer;[1]

and he reminds us that the bees supplied the sacred mead and were therefore in direct contact with the gods. It may, however, be that the bee was not regarded so much as a messenger between man and the gods, but as a form of the soul itself.

It is, of course, a widespread belief that the soul can leave the body and that it can assume various forms. From the remotest ages bees have been regarded as mysterious creatures, and therefore it would not be surprising if they were looked upon as a symbol of the soul, or as the soul itself. The following anecdote, written in 1854, shows how bees can be regarded by a child, who is nearer to the primitive mind than grown-up people:

A gentleman was staying at a friend's house and in the garden was a large beehive on the model of a house. One day his friend's niece (a child of nine years) was standing by him watching the busy throng in the hive; at last she said to him, "What are these?" He answered her with some surprise, "Bees." "No," she replied, "we only call them so, they are fairies, or rather they are *souls*. If you had watched them as I have, you would not say that were mere insects."[2]

The cases of "telling the bees," which have been collected, are so numerous that space forbids to tell of all, so only the most representative are told here. One of the earliest notices occurs in Camerarius's *Historical Meditations*:

Who would believe without superstition (if experience did not make it credible) that most commonly all the bees die in their hives, if the master or mistress of the house chance to die, except the hives be moved to some other place.[3]

William Ellis, in *Modern Husbandmen*, published in 1750, relates:

Immediately the woman was dead, I was requested by the person in attendance to go with them into the garden to awake the bees, saying

[1] *Ethnology in Folklore*, p. 127.
[2] *Notes and Queries*, vol. x, 1854, p. 500. The writer signs himself "Eirionnach."
[3] 1500–1574. English translation 1621, quoted in *Notes and Queries*, Series 7, vol. x, p. 321.

it was a thing which ought to be done when a person died after sunset. I reasoned with them, but it was in vain, for they actually went out at midnight and did awake them.[1]

This is the only case we have come across in which the bees were to be told if the death took place after sunset, usually the time of death is immaterial. In the following case, besides being told of the death, the bees were also fed:

My mother, who passed much of her youth in the village of Bakewell in Northamptonshire, tells me that the belief in the necessity of telling the bees everything was very strong there. At the death of a sister of hers, some of the cake and wine which was served to the mourners at the funeral was placed inside each hive, in addition to the crape put upon each. At her own wedding in 1849 a small piece of wedding-cake was put into each hive.[2]

At Stallingborough, in Lincolnshire, about 1840, a few days after the death of a cottager, a woman staying with the bereaved family asked the widow, "Have the bees been told?" The reply being in the negative, she at once took some spice cake and some sugar in a dish and placed the sweets before the hives, then rattling a bunch of keys repeated this formula:

> Honey bees, honey bees, hear what I say!
> Your Master J. A. has passed away.
> But his wife now begs you will freely stay,
> And still gather honey for many a day.
> Bonny bees, bonny bees, hear what I say![3]

In 1892 a woman in Staffordshire, who had forgotten to tell the bees of her husband's death, some time after found all the hives deserted except one, so in order to save this she gave the hive to her little boy, and then told the bees they had a new master and must work for him. A Shropshire woman was more thoughtful; after the death she went to the bees and said: "Bees, bees, the poor master's dead, so you mun work for me."[4]

In Cornwall they announce the death by tapping on the hive and saying: "Brownie, brownie, brownie, your master is dead"; in

[1] *Folklore Record*, III, 1880, p. 136.   [2] *Folklore*, III, 1892, p. 138.
[3] *County Folklore*, vol. v, Lincolnshire, 1908, p. 29.
[4] *Folklore*, XXII, 1911, p. 24.

Buckinghamshire they tap the hives three times and say: "Little brownies, your master is dead," and when the bees begin to hum, it shows that they consent to remain.[1] In Devonshire an apprentice boy was once sent back from the funeral procession by the nurse to tell the bees of the death, as it had been forgotten. It was usually the custom to put some honey and wine before the hives on the day of the burial.[2]

A gentleman was once speaking of the superstitions about bees and the maid said to him, "Why, master, don't you remember as our Lizzie put crape on the hives when poor Dick died? An' when our Jim's bees swarmed into Mary Owen's garden, an' her said they were hern, an' Jim said they wasna, and he got 'em back again and our Lizzie says, 'Aye,' he says, 'it's all very well but they'll be sure to die,' and die they did, everyone on 'em. Theer mun never be no fuss nor quarrels over bees; they're curus creatures, and they wunna stand it."[3]

This story reminds us of another belief about bees, that they will not thrive in a quarrelsome family. This, though not so common as that of "telling the bees," is found in many parts. A quaint superstition prevalent to this day in Northumberland is the belief that a dead man's bees will not thrive. They are said there to be unable to find pasturage for themselves even among the luxuriant heather, and hives that have belonged to anyone recently dead, rarely find a purchaser.[4] Bees must also be treated politely. One old writer said: "No creature is more wreakful, nor more fervent to take wreak, than is the Bee, when he is wroth !"[5] and so all news must be politely given in a whisper; if harshly spoken they will desert. Bees abhor all bad language, as a Northumbrian once remarked: "It wouldn't do to swear before the bees. They'd pretty soon leave the place."

The superstition of "telling the bees" still lingers; a friend told the writer that a woman in Sussex lately told her that her baby girl had died because she had forgotten to tell the bees of her birth; and in Oxfordshire the bees are believed to die if not told of a death. Miss Angeline Parker wrote in *Folklore* in 1923:

[1] *Notes and Queries*, vol. iv, p. 308.　　　　[2] Ibid., vol. v, p. 148.
[3] Ibid., Series 7, vol. x, p. 234.
[4] A. H. and A. Cooper, *Northumberland*, 1923, p. 103.
[5] *Notes and Queries*, Series 10, vol. ix, 1908, p. 434.

Indeed this is so firmly believed in at the present time, that when someone asked an old man whether he intended to tell the bees of the death of his brother, he answered, shortly, "I shall if I dunt want 'em all to die."[1]

We will now give some stories of "Bee-souls." In many the soul leaves the body while it is asleep or in a trance. The old Norse had a special name, *hamfarir*, for these wanderings of the soul of a living person.

Our first example comes from Lincolnshire. It relates that two travellers lay down side by side to rest, and one fell asleep. The other, seeing a bee settle on a neighbouring wall and go into a little hole, put his staff into the hole and so imprisoned the bee. Wishing to pursue his journey, he endeavoured to awake his companion, but was unable to do so till, resuming his staff, the bee flew to the sleeping man, and went into his ear. His companion then awoke him, remarking how soundly he had been sleeping, and asked him what he had been dreaming of. "Oh," said he, "I dreamt you shut me up in a dark cave, and I could not wake till you let me out." The narrator of this story firmly believed that the man's soul was in the bee.[2]

In *My Schools and Schoolmasters*,[3] Hugh Miller relates this story:

Two young men had been spending the early portion of a warm summer day in exactly such a scene in which he (a Sutherland cousin) communicated the anecdote. There was an ancient ruin beside them, separated, however, from the mossy bank on which they sat by a slender runnel, across which there lay, immediately over a miniature cascade, a few withered grass stalks. Overcome by the heat of the day, one of the young men fell asleep; his companion watched drowsily beside him, when all at once the watcher was aroused to attention by seeing a little indistinct form, scarcely larger than a bumble bee, issue from the mouth of the sleeping man, and, leaping upon the moss, move downward to the runnel, which it crossed along the withered grass stalks and then disappeared amid the interstices of the ruin. Alarmed by what he saw, the watcher hastily shook the sleeper by the shoulder, and awoke him, though with all his haste the little creature, still more rapid in its movements, issued from the interstice into which it had gone

---

[1] For many other instances of "telling the bees," see the volumes of *Folklore* and *Notes and Queries*.

[2] *Notes and Queries*, 1851, vol. iii, p. 205.   [3] Chapter VI.

and flying across the runnel instead of creeping along the grass stalk and over the swarm as before, it re-entered into the mouth of the sleeper, just as he was in the act of awakening. "What is the matter with you?" said the watcher, greatly alarmed, "What ails you?" "Nothing ails me," replied the other, "but you have robbed me of a most delightful dream. I dreamt that I was walking through a rich and fair country and came at length to the shores of a noble river; and just where the clear water went thundering over a precipice, there was a bridge of silver, which I crossed; and then entering a noble palace on the opposite side, I saw great heaps of gold and jewels, and I was just going to load myself with treasures, when you rudely awoke me and I lost all."

Our next story also comes from Sutherlandshire:

Two men were travelling along Speyside on foot, the elder of the two men was weary and they sat down to rest under a tree. The wearied man fell into a troubled sleep and his fellow-traveller saw an insect like a bee, only without wings, creep out of his mouth. This bee crawled along the man's clothes and down to the sod and to a little stream near, where it could neither fly nor swim over. It turned back again and again, till the man who was watching let it creep on his sword and helped it to cross. It then went on for two hundred yards or more and disappeared into a cairn. Presently the sleeper awoke and told his friend that he had had a strange dream; a wee, wee crayterie no bigger than a bee had told him of a hidden treasure and promised to show it to him. It had seemed as if the bee had come out of his mouth and had gone out of sight into a cairn. The watcher, who had seen the bee go into the cairn, laughed at the story, but the elder said it must be true and he would go and look for the cairn. So they quarrelled and the younger man killed the other, who with his last breath took the tree under which he had slept to be witness that he was foully murdered. The murderer went to the cairn, found the treasure, and became a rich man, but aye where he went men saw a tree above him and behind him, aye walking where he walked, and staying where he stayed, and so he was always unhappy, had no wife nor friend and weary of it all, confessed to the priest.[1]

These stories relate that the soul left and returned to the body of a living person. The Rev. Alexander Macgregor writes:

There was a superstition in Rossshire whereby it was believed that the soul did not finally and completely leave the body until the corpse had

[1] Rev. W. Forsyth, "Dornoch," in *Folklore Journal*, vol. vi, 1888, p. 17; quoted by G. Henderson in *Survivals in Belief among the Celts*, Glasgow, 1911, pp. 82-5.

been laid in the grave. There was a similar superstition in Perthshire, whereby it was believed that at the moment of dissolution, whether by a natural death or by an accident, the soul or spirit was visibly seen leaving the body in the shape of a little creature like a bee.[1]

In his *Scenes and Legends* Hugh Miller tells the story of William Fiddler and a companion, both of Cromarty, who were seized by consumption at the same time. The companion died, and Fiddler attended the funeral. That night in a dream he heard the voice of his dead companion asking him to meet him on the hillside to the east of Cromarty. He dreamt that he went to the place indicated and sat on a bank. He wept as he thought of his dead companion. At this moment a large bee came humming from the west[2] and began to fly round his head. It hummed ceaselessly round and round him, until at length its murmurings seemed to be fashioned into words, articulated in the voice of his dead friend. "Dig, Willie, and drink," it said. "Dig, Willie, and drink." He accordingly set himself to dig and no sooner had he turned a sod out of the bank than a spring of clear water gushed from the hollow; and the bee, taking a wide circuit, and humming in a voice of triumph, flew away. He looked after it, but as he looked the images of his dream began to mingle with those of the waking world, the scenery of the hill seemed to be obscured by a dark cloud, in the centre of which there glimmered a faint light; the rocks, the sea, the long declivity faded into the cloud, and turning round he saw only a dark apartment and the first beams of the morning sun coming in at the window. He rose and after digging the well, drank of the waters and recovered.

Mr. Donald Mackensie, who sent the writer this story, added: "I know this well. It is still called 'Fiddler's Well,' and is supposed to cure consumption."

In Scots witch trials there are references to bee-souls. Here it is the witch who assumes the form of a bee. A child was poisoned by its grandmother and another woman "in the shape of brown bees"; these witch-soul bees carried poison "in cleuchs, wings, and mouths."[3] A woman, Janet Watson, in 1661 was visited by

---

[1] From "Highland Superstitions," in vol. ii of *Celtic Magazine*, Inverness. I owe this and the next story to Mr. Donald Mackensie.

[2] The Underworld Paradise is in the west.

[3] J. G. Dalyell, *The Darker Superstitions of Scotland*, 1834, p. 563.

a big bee, which rested on the mark which Satan gave her. Other witches flew about as bees or wasps.[1] In the trial of Elspeth Cursetter for witchcraft, she acknowledged that she was "on the buird in the likeness of a bee."[2]

It is also related that when the Archbishop of St. Andrews was cruelly murdered in 1679, "upon the opening of his tobacco box, a living, humming bee flew out," which was regarded to be a familiar spirit or a devil.[3]

In Lincolnshire we have also the bumble bee figuring as a devil or familiar. A woman went to Louth to consult the wise man. He put his head into a cupboard mumbling some incantations to his familiar spirit. On reopening the door of the cupboard a large bumble bee flew out and settled upon the open book. The wise man noted the part of the page on which the bee alighted and gave his advice accordingly.[4]

It is noteworthy that all the examples of "bee-souls" given above come from districts where the custom of "telling the bees" and putting crape on the hives still exists.

Of late years the convenient word "tang" has been used to denote the custom of beating pans, kettles, and other metal articles when the bees are swarming. It is an old word formerly used locally, and meaning to emit a sharp and loud ringing or clanging noise; and was used in Wiltshire and Shropshire when making this noise for a swarm. In Shropshire they would say: "Mak 'aste and fetch th' warmin'-pan an' the key o' th' 'ouse to tang the bees."

This custom of tanging a swarm was as universal in the British Isles as in the Roman Empire, and it may be that the custom was introduced into Britain by the Romans, but it is certain that the English were acquainted with it before they came to England. The antiquity of the custom was discussed on p. 95.

It has often been disputed whether or no the bees heard this tanging (the villagers had no doubt at all on the subject), and if they did, whether the bees were frightened or pleased with the noise. Many scientists of last century denied the sense of hearing to the bees, but of late years it has been established that they do

[1] Communicated by Mr. Mackensie.
[2] Dalyell, *The Darker Superstitions of Scotland*, p. 564.
[3] Ibid., p. 563. [4] *Folklore*, XI, 1900, p. 438.

hear, though their hearing is not very acute. In King Alfred's time, as we have seen, this tanging was necessary for a man to establish his right to a swarm, and it is possible that this custom was practised among the Hittites and other ancient peoples for the same reason; for when a swarm had once left its hive, without some such indication, it was very difficult for the owner to prove his right to it. That it really causes the bees to settle is very improbable, though the following story of the author's bees may amuse readers.

One day she was away from home and came back in the evening to learn that a large swarm had come out, and instead of settling in the trees near had flown away over a small lake near the bee-garden. A friend and some girls had made a great noise with tins and cans, and when the swarm was nearly over the lake it returned quite suddenly and settled in a hollow tree close to them!

Charles Cotton tells us that

Bees in Siberia are called by the master of the hives; by a blast of his whistle he can call all the bees of the village after him, conducting them by this signal sometimes to one field of flowers, sometimes to another. With another blast of his whistle he leads them back to their hives, whenever impending rains or approaching night gives warning to sound a retreat.[1]

He gives no authority for this statement, but says it was a very common practice in the East (see above, p. 40).

Cotton also writes:

In France they put their hives into a boat, some hundreds together, which float down the stream by night and stop by day. I have heard that the bees come home by the ringing of a bell, but I believe they would come home just the same whether the bell rings or no;[2]

which they certainly would!

To return to the superstitions regarding bees, it is often considered unlucky to *buy* bees. From Hampshire a gentleman writes:

There is not one peasant, I believe, in the village, man or woman, who would *sell* you a swarm of bees. To be guilty of selling bees is a grievous omen indeed, than which nothing can be more dreadful. To

[1] *My Bee Book*, p. 338.   [2] Ibid., p. 89.

barter bees is quite a different matter. If you want a hive, you may easily obtain it in lieu of a small pig or some other equivalent. There may seem little difference in the eyes of an enlightened person between selling and bartering, but the superstitious beekeeper sees a great distinction and it is not his fault if you do not see it too![1]

In another district "it is commonly regarded a fortunate omen to buy a hive of bees by exchanging a commodity for it of equal value, or to give gold for it, if change is to be returned."[2]

In the north-east of Scotland the first swarm of bees of one who intends to be a beekeeper must be got in some other way than by purchase, a bought swarm was thought to lead to disaster in beekeeping.[3]

In Warwickshire they believe that no one will have luck with bought bees;[4] the Welsh say that a hive given to any person will give good luck to the household, but a hive of bought bees will not thrive so well.[5] A cottager in Denbighshire said a friend had given her a hive and that consequently she had had good luck with it.[6] It was also a belief in Wales (as well as in other parts) that stolen bees would make no honey, and that the bees would die.[7] In Wexford (Ireland) people beginning beekeeping are particular that they only invest hard and honestly earned money in the purchase of a swarm.[8] As a Shropshire woman once said: "They're coorus craiturs, bees. There's a luck about 'em for sartain."

There are a good many other omens connected with bees. In many parts it is said that if a swarm alights on dead wood it foretells death. This belief has been traced in Sussex, Wiltshire, Lincolnshire, and the northern counties of England. The poet Gay mentions this among his rustic omens:

> Swarmed on a rotten stick the bees I spied,
> Which last I saw when Goody Dobson died.[9]

[1] *Notes and Queries*, Series 1, vol. ix, p. 446.
[2] *Folklore Record*, III, p. 82.
[3] Rev. W. Gregor, *Folklore of North-East Scotland*, p. 147.
[4] *Folklore*, XXIV (1913), p. 240.
[5] M. Trevelyan, *Folklore and Folk-stories of Wales*, p. 85.
[6] Elias Owen, *Welsh Folklore*, p. 338.   [7] Ibid., p. 340.
[8] *Folklore Record*, v, p. 82.
[9] *Shepherd's Week*, Part V, 108–9.

A doctor in Sussex (Mr. Martin, of Pulborough) told the following:

> A woman one day when she was near her confinement saw a swarm of bees on a dead hedge stake, and turning to her husband said, "That's a token of death and it's sent to me." From that time, much to the surprise of the doctor, her husband and the nurse both thought she would die. At the end of ten days the woman actually died. When the doctor called the husband he knew how it was to end, as they had had a token when they saw the bees on the dead hedge stake.[1]

In Lincolnshire it is said that if a swarm alights on a dead tree or the dead bough of a living tree, there will be a death in the family of the owner during the year.[2] In Wiltshire they foretell death when a swarm alights on dead wood.[3] A writer in *Notes and Queries* remarks:

> The myths connected with bees alighting on dead or living wood may perhaps find a parallel in Polynesia, where the dead assemble on a huge tree with dead and living branches, and only those who tread on the living branches come back to life. In both the dead or living wood had a significance connected with life and death.[4]

In Anglesey the belief takes rather a different form, as they say there that the branch or twig on which the swarm settles will wither.[5]

In Durham it is lucky for bees to be kept in partnership,[6] and in Northumberland it is never considered lucky to be the sole owner of bees. A man and woman, not man and wife, should be partners. If either should die, someone should go to the hive at midnight, tap each hive three times, and tell the bees to work for their new master or mistress as the case may be.[7]

Other beliefs, found in Wales, are that a strange swarm settling on a house or entering a garden, is a sign of prosperity; it is also lucky when they make their home in the roof or any part of the house, and unlucky when they fly away from their home.[8] The Welsh bees are very clever, as they understand Welsh! A woman

1 *Folklore Record*, I, p. 58.   2 *County Folklore*, vol. v, p. 28.
3 *Notes and Queries*, Series X, vol. ix, 1908, p. 433.   4 Ibid.
5 *Folklore*, XIX, p. 339.   6 Ibid., XX, p. 73.
7 *County Folklore*, vol. iv, p. 12.
8 Trevelyan, *Folklore and Folkstories of Wales*, p. 85; Elias Owen, *Welsh Folklore*, p. 338.

on the borders of Cardigan and Carmarthenshire said that they had a queen, who leads, and that the bees follow her when she bids them come in these words: *dewch, dewch, dewch,* that is, come, come, come![1]

In many parts of England and Scotland the bees are said to emit a buzzing sound exactly at midnight on Christmas Eve. The districts in which this belief have been found are Northumberland, Cumberland, Yorkshire, Wiltshire, and in Fife and North-East Scotland.[2] Whether this belief arose on account of the dissatisfaction when the alteration of the calendar took place in 1752 or earlier we have not been able to discover, but in Yorkshire the custom was to go and watch by the beehives on the old and new Christmas Eves in order to determine which was the right one, for the people said that the bees would make a humming noise when the birth of the Saviour took place; and as the bees dislike innovations they affirm that this humming takes place on the old Christmas Eve.[3]

G. Henderson, in *Folklore of the Northern Counties*,[4] states:

Bees are said at Christmas-time to hum a Christmas hymn. Thus the Rev. Hugh Taylor writes: "A man of the name of Murray died at the age of ninety, in the parish of Earsdon, Northumberland. He told a sister of mine that on Christmas Eve the bees assemble to hum a Christmas hymn and that his mother had distinctly heard them do this on one occasion when she had gone out to listen for her husband's return. Murray was a shrewd man, yet he seemed to believe this implicitly!" It is mentioned by Hutchinson (*History of Cumberland*, vol. i, p. 555) that in the parish of Whitbeck, in Cumberland, bees are said to sing at midnight as soon as the day of the Nativity begins, and that the oxen also kneel in their stalls on the same day and hour.

In Wiltshire this belief has been noted as recently as 1908.[5]

Good Friday is a lucky day to remove bees in Devonshire, and in Cornwall they add that any other day will be fatal to them.[6]

Swarming is one of the last things a modern beekeeper desires, and he does his best to prevent it, but in the olden days the earlier the

---

[1] J. C. Davies, *Folklore of West and Mid Wales*, p. 226.
[2] W. Gregor, *Folklore of North-East Scotland*, p. 147.
[3] *County Folklore*, vol. ii, p. 274.　　　　　　　　[4] 1879, p. 311.
[5] *Notes and Queries*, Series X, vol. ix, p. 433 (1908).
[6] *Folklore*, XXVIII (1916), p. 73.

bees swarmed the better, as may be gathered from the old rhyme, which is known all over the country:

> A swarm of bees in May,
> Is worth a load of hay;
> A swarm of bees in June,
> Is worth a silver spoon;
> A swarm in July,
> Is not worth a fly.

We have not been able to discover how old this rhyme is, but it is very general, and there are several variants. For instance, in Sussex we get the value of a July swarm as a butterfly,[1] and in Wexford (Ireland) the rhyme takes the following form:

> A swarm of bees in May,
> Is worth a cow and calf that day;
> A swarm of bees in June,
> Is worth a silver spoon;
> A swarm of bees in July
> Is not worth a butterfly.[2]

Here the May swarm is rated very high, and in another version we even get it valued at "a cow and a calf and a load of hay!"[3] In Cornwall it was not considered quite so valuable:

> A swarm of bees in May,
> Is worth a yow [ewe] and lamb same day.[4]

In Cornwall also it was the custom that the inside of the hives should be rubbed with "scawnsey buds" (elder flowers) to prevent a new swarm from leaving them; and another belief in that county, one which we have not found elsewhere, is that honey should always be taken on St. Bartholomew's Day, he being the *patron saint* of bees.[5] Why should St. Bartholomew have taken bees under his protection?

We find several versions of the "swarm in May" rhyme in France; one of the oldest forms seems to be: "*Un essaim de may, Vaut une vache à laict*"; and in Normandy we find:

> Un essaim du mois de mai,
> Vaut une vache du pays de Bray;

[1] *Folklore*, XXV, p. 369.   [2] *Folklore Record*, V (1882), p. 82.
[3] Ibid., III, p. 82.   [4] *Folklore Journal*, V, p. 192.   [5] Ibid.

in other districts:

> Un essaim de mai,
> Vaut un veau de l'année.

Another French version introduces an *April* swarm, which was considered too early, as it is only worth a sheep, the May swarm being valued at a milking cow, and the June swarm at a bushel of corn, the July one is not worth mentioning.

> Jeton d'avril,
> Vaut une brebis;
> Jeton de mai,
> Vaut une vache à lait;
> Jeton de juin,
> Vaut un boisseau de grain.[1]

There are not many proverbs connected with bees in English, though there are many in German. The best known is to "have a bee in your bonnet." In his *Scottish Proverbs* Kelly gives this with the additional word, "There's a bee in your bonnet-case," equivalent to the English, "There a maggot in your head." In Herrick's "Mad Maid's Song" occurs the verse:

> Ah! woe is me, woe, woe is me,
> Alack and well a-day!
> For pitty, Sir, find out that Bee
> Which bore my love away.
> I'le seek him in your bonnet brave,
> I'le seek him in your eyes;
> Nay, now I think th'ave made his grave,
> I' th' bed of strawberries.[2]

In Lincolnshire they have a saying: "He's set th' beä-skep [beehive] in a buzz," meaning a person has stirred up anger or raked up a scandal.[3]

We have already noted the custom, which dates back to Ancient Egypt, of making a waxen image of a person in order to do him some injury. This was common in the Middle Ages, both in England and Scotland, and was a practice largely carried on by

---

[1] Eugene Rolland, *Abeilles, Guêpes, et Frelons*, Paris, 1911, p. 26.
[2] *Notes and Queries*, Series 3, vol. 9, p. 325.
[3] *County Folklore*, vol. v, p. 413.

reputed witches. The story goes that one of the old Scots kings was suffering from consumption, and he imagined that he was bewitched; so he ordered a search to be made for the originator of his illness. At last a woman was discovered who was roasting a wax figure of the king before her fire. She confessed it was her intention to kill the king, so she and her wax image were both burnt and the king recovered![1] We cannot vouch for the truth of this story.

In *Hall's Chronicle* it is recorded that Prior John, a French naval captain, raided Helmston, in Sussex. The French were pursued by English archers, and Prior John was shot in the face with an arrow. "Thereupon he offered his image of wax before Our Lady at Bolleye [Boulogne] with the English arrow in the face for a miracle."[2] We may presume this was done for the purpose of obtaining a cure for his wound.

These numerous superstitions which occur all over the British Isles show what an important rôle our little insect has played in the life of the people; we shall find many of the same superstitions in France.

[1] Professor Knortz, *Die Insekten in Saga, Sitte und Literatur*, 1910, p. 28.

[2] Hall, *Sixth Year of Henry VIII*, p. 568; quoted in *Folklore*, vol. xxvi, p. 92.

CHAPTER XVIII

CUSTOMS AND SUPERSTITIONS IN FRANCE

*Place-names—Napoleon's coronation robes—Mottoes—Order of the
Bee—Telling the bees of a death; examples in France and Switzerland—Hives put into mourning at funerals and decorated for
weddings—Unlucky to sell bees—Hives must not be counted—Bees
dislike bad language and uncleanness—Omens and dreams—Tanging a swarm—Charms—Pilgrimages for success with bees—Bees
sing at Christmastide—Other festivals: Candlemas, Rogation Days,
Good Friday, Corpus Christi—Bees in Paradise*

THAT beekeeping was a widespread industry in France we learn
from the number of place-names which occur in all parts. The
usual name for a bee is *abeille*, but it is also known as *avette*,[1] *mouche-
a-miel* (honey-fly). or simply *mouche*, *achate*, and *boûrde*; a hive is
a *ruche*, which had many older forms. From these words we get
place-names such as L'Abeil, L'Abeille, L'Abelliers, La Roche-
Abeille, L'Apier, Achères, Acherolles, Les Ruches, Les Mouches;
in an old document of 1213, Torum Abeillerium; in one of 1549
Malles Abeilles; in districts near the Pyrenees, Abeilhan, Abelha,
Bournac; in the tenth century Villa Rucharia, and many
others.[2]

It has been suggested that the French *fleur-de-lis* was originally
a bee and not a lily; this is not a very probable suggestion, but it
is true that Napoleon, wishing to have some older royal emblem
than the *fleur-de-lis*, had his coronation robes made of green, the
Merovingian colour, and covered with golden bees, and he constantly used the bee as armorial bearings. He is said to have got
the idea of the golden bees from the three hundred golden bees
which were found in the tomb of the Frankish king, Childeric I
(died 481), when it was opened at Tournai in 1653. These ornaments are mentioned by Sir Thomas Browne in his essay on

---

[1] The words *abeille* and *avette* derive from the Latin:

　　　apis—ape—apicula—abelha—abeille.
　　　apis—ape—apette—avette.

[2] For these and other place-names, see Eugene Rolland, *Abeilles, Guêpes, et
Frelons; Extrait du tome* 13 *de la Faune Populaire de France*, Paris, 1911.

Urn Burial, written only three years after the tomb was opened, as "three hundred golden bees," but M. Thierry maintained that they were *fleurons* attached to the war harness of Childeric's war horse; two of them are represented in Fig. 27.[1]

There are several old French families which have a bee in their coat of arms, and this device appears on that of the Estates of Burgundy in 1485 with the motto, *Plebis amor, regis custodia.* A history of Orleans written in 1648 mentions a portrait of Joan of

FIG. 27.—"GOLDEN BEES" FROM THE TOMB OF CHILDERIC I
(F. Dahn: *Urgeschichte der Germanischen Völker,* III, Pl. 42, No. 15)

Arc accompanied by a hive with a bee on it, and the words: *Virgo regnum mucrone tuetur,* that is, a virgin defends the kingdom at the point of her sword.[2]

There was for a short time an "Order of the Bee," founded by Louise Bénédicte, wife of Louis Auguste de Bourbon, Duc du Maine, in 1703. The token of the Order was a gold medal which showed on one side a hive and on the other a bee with the inscription, from Tasso's *Aminta:*

Piccola si, ma fa puo gravi le ferite.[3]

In France are many of the same superstitions regarding bees as in Britain; for instance, that of telling the bees of a death occurs in all parts, and also in Switzerland.[4] The usual formula is, *"Belles, votre maître est mort,"* or sometimes, *"Abeilles, petites abeilles, je viens vous avertir que votre maître est mort."* The bees must always be addressed politely, if called by any opprobrious name they will resent it and attack you with their stings. In Picardy, Artois, and the North of France the person who informs the bees taps the hive thrice; in Guernsey this is done with the key of the house, and if the bees answer with a hum, it is understood that

[1] See William Jones, *Crowns and Coronations,* London, 1883, p. 365.

[2] Le Maire, *Hist. d'Orleans,* 1648, p. 203, quoted by Rolland, *Abeilles, Guêpes, et Frelons,* p. 39.

[3] "I am small, but my sting can make deep wounds." The Princess was a very small woman.

[4] For these and the following superstitions, see Rolland, *Abeilles, Guêpes, et Frelons,* pp. 21–39, and Paul Sebillot, *Le Folklore de France,* vol. iii, pp. 300–21, Paris, 1906.

they will remain and work for their new master. In Normandy the death of any member of the family is announced thus: your father, mother, brother, sister, uncle, and so on, is dead. It is noteworthy that the dead person is always referred to as a relative of the bees. The hives were usually draped in black, but in La Vendée a black ribbon was only put on for the master or mistress.

In some parts one of the dead man's garments is buried in front of the hives before the funeral takes place. In Mayenne a piece of his linen, the dirtiest which can be found, is fastened to each hive, the bees will then think he is there and so will not be tempted to follow him. In the Val d'Ajol, in order to prevent the bees from following their late master, the people put a piece of consecrated wax in each hive. In the Côtes-du-Nord the hives wear mourning for six months, and during that time the bees are said not to hum. In other parts the black remains on the hives for three weeks or forty days. In the Basse Pyrenees they uncover the hives when the person dies, and leave them so until after the funeral—not very pleasant for the bees if the weather is bad! As in Britain the bees often have a part of the funeral fare given them.

In Vienne there is a curious custom of hunting and dispersing the bees with a handkerchief when the master dies; if they do not want to fly about it is considered unlucky. This is an unusual custom, generally the bees are requested to remain in the hives.

Bees are also informed of a baptism or marriage. In these cases the hives are decorated with red or other bright-coloured cloths, and in some parts with a piece of the wedding dress and in Normandy and Guernsey with a piece of white linen. In parts of Brittany at any great rejoicing or when there was a specially good harvest a red ribbon was placed on each hive.

In France as in Britain it is considered unlucky to sell bees, but they may be bartered for some article of equal value. In Guernsey there is no objection to selling them provided they are paid for in gold; in other parts they exchange them for a measure of corn. If bees are by any chance bought you must not bargain for them—if you do they would die during the year—and if anyone is buying a hive from you, do not let him choose his hive; the bees are very sensitive, those that were not bought would soon perish, therefore the buyer must take the hive at random.

If too much is paid for bees the people in the Vosges say they do not prosper. In Bigorre (Pyrenees) they say that sold bees will not live and that the hives of the seller will not thrive, also that stolen bees die during the year. In the Jura, if hives are bought you must not go in front of the hive to remove them, you must go to the back; the bees must be in front of you.

The belief is very general that you must not count your hives; if you do it will bring you bad luck or will give the hives disease or they will stop working. In the Côtes-du-Nord they arrange the hives in such a way that they are very difficult to count, and in Limousin they always leave some empty. In the Pays d'Albret if you count the hives it makes the badgers come! And in the Côtes-du-Nord you may count your *bees* but only two by two!

It will bring you luck to give away wax; if you sell it the bees will not do well. An old book says that if a man found a swarm in his garden, he ought to give away a piece of money; if not the bees would sting him and do no good.[1]

In Corrèze, when starting beekeeping they say you succeed best if one swarm is stolen, one found, and one bought. This seems to contradict other superstitions.

It is a very general belief that you must not swear at bees; they will either die or sting those who use bad language. If you quarrel about them they will die, and in Lorraine they say they will not live unless the owners are good and intelligent. In fact, the peasants in many districts attribute to the bees the gift of being able to distinguish any people who do not do their duty, for they will pursue and sting them. They will also sting any girl who has lost her chastity (a belief also found in Germany), and any ill-living man.

In many districts it is said that if the bees leave their hive or die, it is a sign of a death in the family, and in others that if the queen settles on a person, it foretells his death. In Vienne they say that if anyone is stung by a bee, it is an announcement that one of his relatives in Purgatory is asking for his prayers. Here we have a belief that the bees are in touch with the next world.

[1] *Les Evangiles des Quenoilles*: "Quant un homme trouve en son pourpris (garden) un vaisseau d'eeps (swarm of bees) attachies en un corbe, s'il ne l'estrine d'une pièce d'argent, c'est mauvaise signe." Gloss on this passage: "Baudinon Georgette dist que cellui qui approprie a soy les eeps sans les estriner (etrenner) comme dit est ou (au) texte, elles ne feront que picquier cellui, et jamais ne l'aimeront ne lui feront prouffit." Quoted in *Notes and Queries*, Series 8, vol. x, p. 475.

There are other omens connected with bees. If the first swarm of the year is seen and taken by a young girl, it is a sign that she will marry that year. In Belgium they say that he who can catch the first butterfly which he sees in spring will find a swarm during the year.

That dreaming of bees foretells gain and profit is a belief found in many parts, though in an old collection of dreams, the *Songes de Daniel*, published about 1600, it is said that to dream of a quantity of bees signifies that someone is speaking against the dreamer. In Allier if a person in the service of another dreams of a swarm, it is a sign that he will be dismissed during the year.

Tanging a swarm is a very general custom, and there are various charms which are recited in order to cause a swarm to settle. Sometimes it is only a short one as, "*Bas, Bas! assis, petites, assis*"; or "*Sié, sié! mes avettes!*" or "*Belles, à pied, à pied!*" Sometimes it is an invocation or prayer. In the Eure district they recite:

Jesus Christ with St. John being in the country of bees, said to them, "Where are you going?" "To the valley of Josaphat." "No, no, little bees, stay where you are."[1]

In the Ardennes they say, "Bee, whom God has made to illuminate the church, I adjure thee by the Holy Trinity to stop!" This resembles several of the German charms given in Chapter XIV.

In the Vosges if you wish a swarm which had just left a hive to return to it, make the sign of the cross and throw two handfuls of earth in the direction of the deserters and they will go back to their hive immediately. This charm reminds us of the old Anglo-Saxon one quoted on p. 163.

In Seine-et-Marne they kneel before the hive and pushing a finger into the earth recite, "Bee, God has created thee in this place, and God prays thee to stay in this place," then, rising, they cross themselves.

Another charm is, "Bee, stop! thy wax is for the Virgin, thy honey for me, come down, *belle, belle, belle*," but while saying this you must be careful to extend your arms to prevent them coming on your head.

In Belgium this charm is used:

[1] Rolland, *Abeilles, Guêpes, et Frelons*, p. 31, who gives other examples.

In the name of the Father who has created you, of the Son who has redeemed you, of the Holy Spirit who has sanctified you, settle in this tree.

Another French charm must be repeated three times, but first you must collect three stones, place them to form a cross, then say:

Our Saviour went to the Jordan to wash his hands, drops of water fell from them, bees were formed from the drops. They wanted to fly away, but our Saviour said to them, *"Belles,* you must stay here in the name of the Father, Son, and Holy Spirit."[1]

In France there are several places to which pilgrimages are made to pray for success with bees. At Maxerolles in Poitou the pilgrims hang a big piece of wax on the neck of the statue of the Virgin. In the neighbourhood of Loirent they carry wax to the chapels dedicated to St. Peter, as he is favourably disposed towards bees. At a well dedicated to St. Martin at La Grand-Verrière the pilgrims make offerings for the well-being of their hives.[2]

The belief that bees sing in their hives on Christmas Eve, which was noted in Britain, is found in many parts of France, in Belgium, Switzerland, and Germany. In Mecklenburg they add that the devout listener hears them sing, "Glory to God in the Highest." In Switzerland, in the Jura district, every hive intones a choral chant at midnight, and in many places it was the custom for someone from the house to listen by the hives at that hour.

Several other festivals are connected with bees in France. On the eve of Candlemas (February 2nd) there was a custom of decking the hives with ribbons and singing, "Bee, awake, work for God and me!" In other parts on Candlemas Day the people went round the countryside with a wax candle blessed that day, making a circuit at some distance from the hives, and they believed that the swarms that year would not go beyond that circle. In the Aisne the folk say that every good beekeeper ought to make, or have made, candles from the wax of his own bees and have them blessed at Candlemas—they will serve him for the day of his funeral.

On Rogation Days in Saone-et-Loire you must burn a candle

[1] Coisy, *Médecine myster.,* 1830, p. 7, quoted by Rolland, *Abeilles, Guêpes, et Frelons* p. 32. Other stories of creation of bees are given in the next chapter.
[2] St. Valentine is also a patron of beekeeping in France.

blessed at the altar of the Virgin so that the bees will give much honey and prosper.

In the Vosges on Good Friday the people clean up and tidy the place where the hives stand, and place on each hive a small wax cross or a branch of box blessed on Palm Sunday; this is done to ensure the prosperity of the hives and prevent the bees from straying when swarming. In Orleanais a branch of box blessed on Palm Sunday was placed in each hive. The person who put them there had to bring them home from church without speaking a word, then he had the power of making the bees swarm when he wished. In Limoisin these consecrated branches were credited with preserving the bees from misfortune and from thunder; and in Wallonia if one is planted near the hives, the swarms will not stray far.

On Corpus Christi Day in the Vosges the hives have a consecrated crown placed on them, in order to protect the bees from disease and accident. In Picardy and in Belgium the peasants say that if a swarm settles in a hive on the eve of this festival, it will make a waxen cake in the form of a monstrance. In parts of Brittany, if the bees swarm on St. Anne's Day they say a wax taper will be found in one of the straw hives which is then named the hive of the King; if they swarm on a day consecrated to the Virgin, a comb is formed in the shape of a cross, that is then called the hive of the Queen. In Meurthe-et-Moselle if the bees swarm on Good Friday, they are said to make their cells in the form of a cross; if on Corpus Christi in the form of a wafer.

We noted that in Germany the bee was considered so much superior to other animals, that when one dies they use the same word used when a man dies, and not that used for other animals, and in France the same distinction is made; one must say, "l'abeille *meurt*," not "l'abeille *creve*." In several parts, too, the near connection between man and the bees is shown in the belief that the prosperity of the hives depends on the health of their master; in the Gironde they say that the number of bees diminishes as their master grows old; if he dies they leave the hive and go away.

There are several old sayings connected with bees. We noted the "swarm in May" rhyme in the last chapter. Another saying states that "If Christmas is mild and muddy every swarm is worth a cow," and "On St. Simon's Day (October 28th) the bee is worth a pigeon"; a third, "If the spring is fine, the bees make more honey and less brood." One which comes from the Basse Pyrenees reminds us of the belief that bees came from Paradise, with the addition that they have someone to look after them there: *"Qu'a dit aco? L'abélhè de Pardies,"* which means, "Who has said that? The beekeeper of Paradise."[1]

Thus in France as elsewhere the bee has endeared herself to many, and so all these superstitions have arisen about her. We now give some folk-stories from many lands, which also show the interest which she has aroused in different peoples.

[1] Rolland, *Abeilles, Guêpes, et Frelons*, p. 33.

CHAPTER XIX

FOLK-STORIES FROM VARIOUS LANDS

Pride of bees—Golden and silver hives—Roumanian story of origin of bees—Obedience of bees—Stories of bees and their stings —Bees and snakes—Creation of bees by God and of wasps by the Devil—Creation of bees from hole in Christ's forehead—Bees sent as messenger to the Devil—White bees in Paradise—Why the colour was changed—Why the bee is black and has a narrow waist—Stories why bees do not visit the red clover—Miscellaneous stories

THERE are so many folk-stories about the bee that it is very difficult to make a selection. As a rule the bee is regarded as a model of every virtue, but there is a series of tales, connected with the sting of the bee, which represent her as a proud, self-satisfied creature. Our first story comes from Nièvre, France.

When the good God was distributing his gifts to the animals which he had just created, the bees demanded to be housed in a silver hive, and, in order that they might be respected, they asked that their sting might be fatal. The Lord was wroth at their malice and presumption, and said to them, "You shall inhabit hives of straw or of osier covered with cowdung, and every bee that stings shall die."[1]

A variant from Basse Bretagne says that the bees asked for a golden hive; in Morbihan that they were put into a golden hive and whoever dared to touch it was wounded by their stings and died; but seeing that the bees were becoming proud and revengeful, God punished them by forcing them to live in little straw hives and by saying that they themselves should die if they used their stings.[2]

In Haute-Bretagne a story says that there were no bees in the world until the coming of Jesus Christ; they were then created and were just going to disperse over the world when one of them said, "Everyone whom I pierce with my sting shall die." "Nay," answered our Lord, "everyone whom thou stingest shall recover, but after having stung, thou shalt die."[3]

[1] E. Rolland, *Abeilles, Guêpes, et Frelons*, p. 36.
[2] P. Sébillot, *Le Folklore de France*, vol. iii, p. 301.   [3] Ibid.

A Pyrenean story relates: God was once walking on the earth, and said to the grasshopper, "What art thou doing?" "I am singing." "That does no good." He said to the spider, "What art thou doing?" "I am spinning." "That is no use." He said to the ant, "What art thou doing?" "I am working in order to live." "That is very good." He said to the bee, "What art thou doing?" "I am kneading together everything that is good." "Do not be so proud, thou makest honey, but thou stingest, and that does not bring thee happiness, for thou diest of it."[1]

In the neighbouring district of the Landes a story shows the bee in a better light: The grasshopper was singing and his mother was dying. God said to it, "Thou wilt certainly go to the funeral?" "Oh, no, it is so hot, I cannot do anything but sing." "Good, thou shalt always sing till thou art dry." In the same circumstances the spider answered, "I shall not go to the funeral, it is so fine, I must spin." "Well, thou shalt always spin, and thy work shall have no value." When the bee was asked the same question, she answered, "It is beautifully fine for collecting honey, but I shall leave all and go and bury my mother." "That is well; all that thou henceforth makest, honey and wax, shall benefit everyone."[2]

In a tale from Poitou the bee, ant, and spider were sisters. Their mother was ill; the ant said she had no time to look after her, the spider said she had begun some work and must finish it, the bee said she had much work to do, but work could remain work, she would go and look after her mother. God rewarded her by allowing her to live in a house. She wanted a golden one and that all whom she should sting should die. God said she should have a wooden house covered with cowdung, and so it is, and she herself dies if she stings.[3] Here we have the filial piety but also the pride of the bee.

From Rumania, where there are many folk-tales of animals, we give the following story, one of many, of the *origin* of the bee.

WHY IS THE BEE BUSY AND THE SPIDER SULLEN?

A very poor woman had two children, a son and a daughter. When they were grown up, seeing their mother could not provide for them,

[1] Rolland, *Abeilles, Guêpes, et Frelons*, p. 36.   [2] Ibid.
[3] Oskar Dähnhardt, *Natursagen*, Leipzig and Berlin, 1907 (= *N.S.*), vol. iv, p. 269.

they went to find work. The girl went to a place where they were building houses, and there she worked, day and night, carrying bricks and mortar to the builders; the son went to a weaver and learnt there to weave clothes. Not long after their mother fell ill, and knowing that her end was approaching, she sent for her children. When the message reached the daughter, she was carrying a heavy load of bricks in her apron. She dropped them and ran home as fast as she could and she found her mother at the point of death.

When the message reached the son he was weaving. He said, "Let her die, I cannot give up my work." And there he stayed quite alone, working away, surly and grumbling, all the time. When the mother heard what the son had said, she cursed him and said, "As thou hast said, so shall it go with thee. Day and night thou shalt weave incessantly and never see the joy of it, what thou dost others shall destroy; in a corner shalt thou sit hated by everybody." To her daughter she said, "Daughter, thou hast been sweet to me and a joy in my last hours; mayst thou always be sweet to all." And with these words she died and her blessing and her curse came true. The girl was changed into the active busy bee, whose honey sweetens everything and whose wax candles are made to be lit before the icons of the saints and in the churches, and to be put by the head of the dying and the dead. The brother was turned into a spider, who sits alone, sullen and spiteful in the corner and weaves his webs never finishing; whoever sees a web brushes it away, and whoever can kills the spider.[1]

In this and the next two stories the obedience of the bee is emphasized. One comes from Rumania; the other is a folk-tale of the Votiaks, a Finnish tribe in Russia.

When God had created all the animals, he gathered them together in order to bless them and to give them rules for their lives. The bee came also, tired and wounded by her long journey. As a reward for her obedience God ordained that her blood and sweat should become honey, and that her wax should burn in the churches.[2]

As the good God was walking one day on the earth he met a wasp and asked it for some honey. The wasp answered, "I will not give thee any; I have hardly enough for myself." Then God said: "As thou wilt give me no honey, then thou shalt only have a little for thyself and a very little for others." Then God met the bee and asked her for honey. The bee replied, "I have honey for thee as

[1] Dr. M. Gaster, *Rumanian Bird and Beast Stories*, London, 1915, pp. 68–70.
[2] Dähnhardt, *N.S.*, vol. iii, p. 189.

much as thou wilt." God said: "As thou art not miserly, thou shalt always have much honey for others and wax for me."[1]

Quite a number of tales are connected with the *sting* of the bee. The first given here comes from Lithuania.

1. When the Lord God had created the animals he gave each a weapon with which to defend itself. He asked the bee what kind of a weapon she would like to have, and she begged for a sting which should be so poisonous that it should kill anyone whom she stung. But God would not grant her request; he gave her, indeed, a sting, but it was not the man whom she stung who should die, but she herself.[2]

2. Here is a Rumanian version. When God assembled the animals to tell them of their work, the bees said they did not like preparing so much wax and honey for men, so they begged for a sting to protect themselves and their honey, and that anyone whom they stung should die. However, God did not fulfil this arrogant request, but ordained that they should go on working for men; they should have a sting, but only to terrify, not to hurt. If they used it in spite of this command, they should die themselves.[3]

3. This tale from Lithuania attributes the origin of the sting to the devil. At the time when the animals were fighting as to whom should be their king, the birds were angry with the insects, because they only appeared when the battle was over. Since then birds have always pursued insects because of their dilatoriness. They also pursue the bee because they think that she did not do her duty in the right way. As the bee, however, was not guilty of the laziness of the other insects, the devil, at her request, gave her a sting, so that she could defend herself against the birds.[4]

4. One of the oldest versions is that attributed to Aesop, who said that the bees asked Zeus for the privilege of killing men with their sting, but Zeus decreed that they should die if they used it.

5. Another variant, found both in Sicily and Malta, relates that when God created the bee, he made her able to collect a little honey daily. The bee obeyed, but when man had tasted the honey, he wanted to have it at any cost, and to prevent that the bees began to sting everyone. When the Lord heard that he punished

[1] Dähnhardt, *N.S.*, vol. iii, p. 250. [2] Karl Knortz, *Die Insekten*, p. 30.
[3] Dähnhardt, *N.S.*, vol. iv, p. 266. [4] Ibid., p. 203.

them by commanding that they should only make a few drops daily, and that they should die immediately if they used their sting.[1]

6. A Rumanian version says the bees begged for a sting and God granted their request, but on condition they would only use it when they had collected 12 *oken* of honey. That is the reason why the bee is so industrious. However, she is never able to collect so much, and therefore she must die if she uses it.[2]

7. This and the next story are from Caucasia, and connect snakes with bees. Snakes and bees asked the Prophet about their fate. He said that serpents should kill anyone whom they stung; they themselves should live but they should have headaches. The bee, on the contrary, should not have headaches, but she should die if she used her sting.[3]

8. Formerly the bee was better than she is now. Once she said to Christ that he whom she stung should die. He replied, "Then thou shalt die!" And since then the bee dies. The serpent also said: "Whom I sting dies." Christ said: "Good, if thou stingest anyone he shall die, but the earth shall not receive thee." The earth does not, indeed, receive it when its time comes.[4]

9. The shortest story is from Russia. The bee asked God that man should die of her sting. God replied, "Who, then, will keep thee?"[5]

Another set of folk-tales are concerned with the creation of the bee.

A beautiful legend of Morbihan in Brittany tells that bees were created from the tears which Jesus shed on the cross. Not one fell on the ground, but they all became these winged creatures, which flew away with the Saviour's blessing to take sweetness to men.[6]

The story that bees were created by God and flies or wasps by the devil or by St. Peter, is found in various parts. Our first examples come from Hungary.

(*a*) When the Lord God created bees, the devil tried to make some, but his became wasps.

---

[1] Dähnhardt, *N.S.*, vol. iv, p. 267.   [2] Ibid.
[3] Ibid., p. 268.   [4] Ibid.   [5] Ibid.
[6] Sébillot, *Le Folklore de France*, vol. iii, p. 301. In several Slavonic tribes the bee is said to come from Christ's navel when on the cross; in Moravia, bees originated from His blood.

(*b*) The Lord God went to the devil to see how his bees were and to ask what they had collected and carried. The devil showed him the bees; they were in a hive, but there was nothing that they had gathered; they had been put there in a heap and so they were still. "Come, now, and look at mine," said God. They went and, behold, the bees had gathered something already; there were several lovely combs, honey, and wax. Then the devil was furious and knocked his own hive over, because his bees had gathered nothing. Then they flew apart, turned to flies, some came here, too, and since then there have always been flies.

(*c*) Other variants make use of the double meaning of the Hungarian name for flies, *legy*, which also means "be" or "become." The devil was called by God when he was also trying to make bees, and the word *legy* turned the devil's creation to flies.

(*d*) The creation of flies is also attributed to St. Peter, as the result of an unfortunate attempt to make bees. Christ gave Peter a handful of dust, because Peter wanted to create something. The tale ends in the same way. Christ tells Peter to open his hand and say *legy*, and flies are the result.[1]

A Polish version is that God created bees, but when the devil tried to make a creature like them, he could not, but only made wasps.[2]

A French version from the Vannes, where there are several kinds of flies whose creation is attributed to the devil, is fuller. One day the Saviour, St. Peter, and St. John were resting after their work in the shade by the side of the road. Jesus amused himself by creating various kinds of flies. The devil was passing by, and stopped to see what Jesus was doing; he said he could make just as good creatures. Jesus accepted the challenge, so the devil tried for some time, repeatedly remade his work, and at last succeeded in making wasps. Jesus immediately made bees, and said that in order to prove which was the better they must be examined in every possible way. After a thorough examination it was agreed that in form and colour the wasps certainly surpassed the bees, but as regarded their character and usefulness, it was unanimously agreed that the bee deserved the palm.[3]

An Austrian variant attributes the wasps to St. Peter. The

[1] Dähnhardt, *N.S.*, vol. i, p. 167.   [2] Ibid.

[3] Ibid., and Sébillot, *Le Folklore de France*, vol. iii, p. 300.

Lord Jesus made the bees; He created them by throwing little bits of wood into a basket. Peter wanted to make some too, so he did the same, but wasps were the result.[1]

Another series of the "Creation of Bees" tales relates that they were produced out of maggots from the Lord's head, or from a maggot taken out of a hole in His head and placed in a hollow tree. These stories often introduce an old woman who is baking and from whom Jesus asks bread, and who, refusing, or treating Him rudely, is turned into a woodpecker or an owl. These tales are found in Russia and many parts of Central Europe. Here is a version told by the South Slavs.

Christ and St. Peter were once wandering through the world, and came to a woman who was making little flat cakes. Christ spoke to her and asked her if she would bake one for Him. The woman was a kindly soul; no beggar left her house without a gift, and she did not want this man to go away empty-handed. "Yes," she said, "I will make one also for Thee," and she thought she would give Him the smallest cake on the oven shelf. Just as she was shutting the oven door, Christ took hold of her hand. "Wait a moment, I want to mark it, so that I shall not take any other when they are baked." He stepped nearer and pressed His finger on the dough and then the woman put the cakes to bake.

The two unknown men lay down in the shade to rest. Now Jesus' cake rose enormously; in a short time His cake was larger than all the others. The woman was astonished, and regretted that she had promised Him that one. "Must I really give Him that one?" she said to herself. "I'll bake Him another; it would really be a pity to give Him that one." So she hastily made another, pressed it with her finger, and put it into the oven. When all were baked the woman called the strangers and gave Jesus the cake which she had made for Him. He, however, refused to take it, looked sharply at the woman and said: "Woman, that is not My cake; give Me the one which thou hast promised Me." The woman pretended not to understand, tried to press Jesus to take the other cake, and asserted stoutly that it was the right one. But as she could not persuade Him, she became angry and threw the cake at His forehead. Then Jesus took it and went away.

After a short time He said to Peter, "Look at Me. What is the

[1] Dähnhardt, N.S., vol. i, p. 167.

matter with My forehead where the woman struck Me?" Peter
looked and saw a wound, and in the wound a beautiful little grub.
They went on; again Christ spoke and asked Peter to look at the
wound. "It hurts me horribly," He said. Peter looked, and what
did he see? A little creature resembling a fly, which immediately
flew away. "Look, Peter," said the Lord. "That little creature is
the bee; she will prepare wax for all time, without which no holy
mass can be read." And that is the origin of the bee.[1]

Another version is told in Little Russia. Christ and St. Peter
came to a baker and wanted to buy bread, but it was not ready;
there was only the dough, which had been divided into equal
parts. Then Christ chose one of the parts and said, "This piece is
Mine." The baker's wife promised Him this, but she was astonished
when she saw how the piece which Christ had chosen grew
immense. As she took the bread from the oven, Christ wished to
take His piece, but she said, "Thou shalt take such a piece; it tastes
just the same as the other." They disputed about it, and it came
to such a pass that the woman struck Christ on the head with
the poker, so He and Peter went away. As they came to the wood,
Christ said His head hurt, and there in the wound was a little worm;
and Peter found it and showed it to Christ, who said, "Put it into
the hole in that tree." And they went on. Some time after, when
they passed the tree again, they found a quantity of honey there.
The bees had come from the Lord's head.[2]

A Polish variant relates that Jesus was travelling with Peter
and Paul, and asked an old woman for a night's hospitality. She
refused and threw stones at them, one of which struck Paul on the
head. As the weather was hot the wound putrefied, and little
maggots appeared in it, which Jesus removed and placed in a
hollow tree. Some time after they passed the tree again, and Paul
was told to look in the tree and found to his surprise that bees had
come from the maggots and had made honey.[3]

A similar story but without the old woman is told in Bohemia.
Jesus and Peter were walking through the woods together and came
to a hollow tree. Peter said, "Whatever is the use of this tree?"
The Lord stopped and told Peter to look at His forehead, as some-

[1] From Krauss, *Sagen und Märchen der Sudslaven*, vol. ii, p. 421, quoted
by Dähnhardt, *Naturgeschichtliche Volksmärchen* (= *N.V.*), p. 88, and *N.S.*,
vol. ii, p. 129.   [2] Dähnhardt, *N.S.*, vol. ii, p. 130.   [3] Ibid.

thing itched there. As he looked a little grub came out of the forehead, and Jesus put it into the hollow tree. When they passed that way again they found that the grub had become a hive of bees.

Our last version is from Russia. When Jesus Christ was on earth with His disciples they did not understand Him; they were simple people. St. Peter kept saying, "Lord, I am hungry." As Jesus Christ had eaten nothing Himself, he merely smiled. Later, however, when Peter was asleep, Christ took his guts and hung them on a pear-tree. When Peter awoke he was surprised to find that he was not hungry. As the hours passed they went by the pear-tree again, and on it was a great swarm of bees. Peter said, "Lord, what is that?" Jesus replied, "Peter, dost thou not recognize thy guts? Thou art better without them, and the bees will be of use to men and will honour God."[1]

Many of the following tales show a distinct dualistic conception of the world; in its foundation the devil takes a large, almost an equal part, though in the end the stories always make him fooled and cheated by some animal, which in our examples is the bee. She is represented as playing about in Paradise, which reminds us of the belief in her divine origin, found in Wales and other places.[2]

Why is the Bee Black, and why is it making Honey?
How did the Bee outwit the Devil?

In the beginning only water and God and the devil existed. These two were all the time moving about upon the face of the waters. After some time God, feeling rather tired of this flitting about without rest or peace, said to the devil, "Go down to the bottom of the sea and bring up in My name a handful of the seed of the earth." The devil did as he was bid, but whilst he was plunging to the depths he said to himself, "Why should I bring up the seed in His name? I will take it in my own." And so he did.

---

[1] Dähnhardt, *N.S.*, vol. ii, p. 130. Dr. Rendel Harris suggests that this cycle of stories may be derived from old myths of the hollow oak and the sacred bees of the Thunder God, which were found there. See *Ascent of Olympus*, p. 2.

[2] For a very interesting account of the probable origin of these and many other animal stories, see Dr. Gaster's Introduction to his *Rumanian Bird and Beast Stories* (1915).

When he came up God asked him, "Hast thou brought the seed?"
The devil replied, "Here it is." But when he opened his hand to
show the seed it was quite empty; the water had washed the seed
away.

Then God sent him again, but the devil did the same. For a third
time God sent him to the bottom of the sea to bring up the seed.
This time the devil bethought himself, and instead of taking the
seed in his own name as he had determined, he took it now in God's
name and his own; he would not do it in God's name alone. When
he came up the waters had washed all away, except a few grains
under the nails of his fingers. God asked whether he had brought
the seed. He replied "To be sure," but when he opened his hand
it was empty; still there were the few grains under the nails. God
rejoiced greatly at these few, which He collected carefully and made
a small cake of them which He put upon the waters, where it
floated, and God sat upon it to rest. Being very tired, God fell
asleep. What did the unclean one think? "What a lucky thing for
me," he said to himself. "Now I can drown Him." And he tried
to turn the cake over so that God should fall into the water. But
what happened? In whichever direction God rolled the cake of
earth expanded and stretched under Him. The devil kept turning
and the earth got bigger and bigger, and became larger than the
waters, and God awoke and the devil ran away and hid himself
in one of the clefts. God then decided to ask the devil what to do
with the earth which had become so big.

Now of all the beasts and creatures which God had made, none
were more pleasing in His sight than the bee, which was then
playing in Paradise. The bee was white and not black as she is
now, and I will tell you how she changed her colour.

God sent the bee to ask the devil what He was to do and what
good advice he could give Him. The bee went at once as she was
commanded, and came to the place where the devil lived. "Good
morning, uncle," said the bee. "Good morning, sister," said the
devil. "What has brought you to me?" "Well, you see, God has
sent me to ask you what He is to do with this huge earth." But the
devil grumpily and sneeringly replied, "If He is God, He ought
to know better than ask a poor devil for advice. I am not going
to tell Him; let Him find out for Himself."

The bee, who was a clever little thing—it was not for nothing that God's choice had fallen upon her—pretended to fly away; but she soon crept back stealthily and settled noiselessly upon the beams of the door. She knew that the devil could not keep any secret, and that he would surely speak out. So, indeed, it happened. No sooner did he think himself alone than he started chuckling and muttering to himself.

"A clever man that God really is. He asks me what to do. Why does He not think of mountains and valleys?" (You must know that the earth when first made was flat like a pancake.) "Let Him take the earth in His arms and squeeze it a bit, then it will soon fit all right."

The bee overheard what he said, and rejoicing that she had got the answer spread out her wings and started flying away. The buzzing of her wings betrayed her, and the devil, hearing the noise, rushed out of his cave with his whip in his hand, and said, "O, thou thief! So that is the way thou hast cheated me. Mayst thou feed on what comes out of thy body!" And he struck at her with his whip. This changed the bee's body black; moreover, he hit her so badly that he nearly cut her in two. That is why the bee has such a narrow waist, so that she looks as if she were cut in two and barely hanging together by a thread.

Limping and sore the bee came back to God, and told Him what she had overheard; God was greatly pleased, and, squeezing the earth in His arms, He made hills and valleys, and the earth grew smaller. Then turning to the bee He said, "Out of thy body henceforth shall come only honey to sweeten the life of man, and he shall bless thee for thy gift; also thou shalt bring forth wax for candles for the altar." Then God went on to ask the bee what reward she would claim for the errand she had so well fulfilled. The bee, impudent and greedy, replied, "Why should man share my gift and have my honey? Give me the power to kill with my sting."

And God was angry with the impudence of the bee, and replied: "All the honey shall be thine alone if thou art able to make a gallon of it during the summer; if not, man may share it with thee. And because thou hast asked for the power of killing with thy sting, meaning to kill men with it, thine own death shall be in thy sting."

This is the reason why the bee works so industriously and

indefatigably during the summer. Each hopes to make a gallon of honey and never succeeds, and this is the reason why the bee dies if it stings anyone.[1]

* * * * *

In another version of the story the place of the devil is taken by the mole, who is outwitted in the same way by the bee. There are also some few variants among the Bulgarians and Letts, but none are so full as the Rumanian story. We give the Bulgarian version.

Making the Earth Smaller

When God had made the sky and earth, He made the earth a little too big, the sky was not large enough to cover it. God noticed that the devil and the hedgehog were talking together, and sent the bee to listen to what they said. "God does not know," said the devil, "that He must take a stick and strike the earth with it as hard as He can to make valleys and mountains on it, then the sky will fit it quite well." When the bee heard that she flew to God and told Him. Then God created mountains and valleys on the earth, and the sky was quite sufficient to cover it. Then He blessed the bee and commanded that her produce should serve to lighten marriages and baptisms and that her honey should heal the sick.[2]

A Rumanian story telling how God wanted to know if it were better to have one sun or several is called:

Why is the Bee Black, and why has it a Narrow Waist?

When God created the bee she was white of colour, hence her name *albina*, the white one. One day, however, God sent the bee to the Evil One to ask him for his advice, as to whether He should make one sun or several. The bee went off to the Evil One and told him God's message. Then she slyly hid herself in his bushy hair, for the bee knew he would talk to himself aloud, and she would be able to find out his true thoughts. And so it happened, for no sooner did he think the bee was not within earshot than he started talking to himself and said, "One sun is better than a number of suns, for if there were a number of suns the heat would be much

[1] Gaster, *Rumanian Bird and Beast Stories*, pp. 60–4.
[2] Dähnhardt, *N.S.*, vol. i, p. 127.

greater than my fire, and I should not be able to torture and to burn. Then, too, if there were several suns, they would shine all day and all night, and the people would not fall into my power. One sun would be best."

When the bee heard his reasoning and the conclusion to which he had come, she started flying off to God. As the Evil One heard her buzz, filled with anger at the trick which the bee had played him, he struck at her with his whip across the body. The white colour was thus turned black, and the body of the bee cut nearly in twain, the waist became as thin as a thread. It is due to the merit of the bee that there is only one sun now in the heavens and not several.[1]

There is a somewhat similar story in Bulgaria, only in this it is the question whether the sun should marry, not whether more should be created. The story runs:

When God grew old He wanted to marry the Sun. He invited all the creatures, among them also the devil, but he saddled his ass and rode away angrily. Then God sent the bee to find out the thought of the devil. The bee settled on his head and heard him mutter: "Oh, yes, it is a long time since God remembered me who helped Him in making the world, but He does not know what He is doing now. If He marries the Sun He will destroy mankind and burn up the world."

The bee heard this and flew off to tell God. The devil noticed her and tried to kill her. He ran after her and shot at her. The bee hid herself in a hollow tree, but at last he hit her and cut her in two. With difficulty she reached God and told Him what had happened. The Lord blessed her and said, "Thy lower part shall be thy best and the upper part may remain as it is"; and He joined the two parts together. God thereupon stopped the wedding, and the sun has remained an unmarried maiden to this very day, whilst the bee is making honey even now.[2]

According to yet another version the bee got its form and colour from the fiery sky-whip, the lightning, with which St. Peter struck her, because, as a disobedient child, she had striven with her parents.[3]

As beekeepers well know, one of the flowers which contains

[1] Gaster, *Rumanian Bird and Beast Stories*, p. 71.
[2] Ibid, p. 72; Dähnhardt, *N.S.*, vol. i, p. 129.   [3] Dähnhardt, *N.V.*, p. 90.

the most nectar is the red clover, which, however, the bee cannot reach because the corolla tube is too narrow and her proboscis too short. This fact was not generally known until modern times, and there are a number of folk-tales which tell that the bees do not visit the red clover, because they desecrated the Sabbath. There is one version in Pomerania that the bees' tongue was made short as a punishment for working on Sunday, but the following, which come from all parts of Europe, are the more common versions.

Why the Bees Avoid Red Clover

1. This comes from Austria, East Prussia, Pomerania, and Silesia.

When the good God created the bees, He said to them, "Six days shall ye fly from flower to flower to gather what ye require, but ye shall rest the seventh day." Then the bees flew from flower to flower, worked to their hearts' content, and prepared wax and honey day after day without rest. In particular they visited the red clover, from which they gathered the best honey. Now when the Lord's day came they did not trouble about His commandment, but they flew busily about, working and labouring in the hive without stopping as they had done on the weekdays. Then God punished the disobedient creatures and said, "From this time ye shall never find honey in the red clover!"[1]

2. From the Vogtland, Saxony, Suabia, and Prussia.

In the olden days when animals could speak, Sunday was bright and golden, all put away their work according to God's command and rested from their labours. The men went early to church, sang proudly and devoutly, and in the afternoons they went about singing in the beautiful world. The birds kept their rest and sang glorious songs, even the least important creatures would enjoy the day; the spiders would play in the sunshine, the gnats danced over the waters. Only the bees remained at home in their dark abode. They were not allowed to work that day, and therefore could not fly over the flowers and gather honey.

Then the bees consulted how they might change this, and they sent messengers to the Lord to say to Him, "Dear Father, Thou art so good and givest every creature a beautiful Sunday for enjoyment. Now we are without a Sunday festival. We have, indeed, rest, but no light, no colour, no air, no song. Let us also go out with the others. We will lay on ourselves a hard condition; we will not in future disturb the red clover." God smiled as the messengers said this right solemnly and modestly, and he spoke in friendly earnest, "Keep Sunday according to your desire, but keep your word and for all time avoid red clover." The bees flew back happily to announce this decision. From that day no bee has ever drunk from red clover.[1]

3. From East Prussia.

The bee is a desecrater of the Sabbath. The good God said, "Six days shalt thou work." The bee retorted, "Why hast Thou, then, dear God, arranged that we have to eat on the seventh day? Because we have to eat on the seventh day, therefore we must also work on that day." "Thou mayst work," said God, "but as a punishment for thy impious thought I forbid thee to go to the flower which gives the most honey, the red clover." Therefore the bee never visits red clover.

4. From Pomerania.

Just at the height of the honey flow there was a dreadful storm, so that no bee could leave the hive. For eight days there was storm and rain, and as the sun came out on the ninth day it was Sunday and work was forbidden. But the bee said, "What does Sunday matter to me? I have been obliged to rest eight days, and I am not going to be lazy on Sunday." Then God exhorted her to desist from her intention, but it was no use, the whole day the bee worked with all her might. Then God spoke, "As a punishment for breaking the Sabbath, the flowers which bear the most honey shall be closed to thee for ever." From that time the neck of the red clover became so long and narrow that no bee can suck honey out of it.

5. From East Prussia.

God went one day to visit the earth to look at everything, and it was Sunday, and He noticed that the bee was gathering honey. "Have I not commanded thee to rest on Sunday?" called out God. "Oh," said the bee, "I cannot rest on Sunday, for it rains in the week." Then God was angry and said, "Thou shalt be punished

[1] Dähnhardt, N.V., p. 92.

for that." And since then the bee dare not go to the red clover, although it has the most sweetness in it.

6. A Mecklenburg version relates that the Lord Christ came to earth one Sunday, and told the bees they must rest. "No," said they. "The red clover is so sweet." "Then from now ye shall never gather a drop from the flowers which carry the most honey." And so it is.

7. Our last example is from White Russia.

God once met a bee and asked her: "Where dost thou find the most food?" At that time the meadows yielded the best, and the bee thought, "God will certainly take the honey from us. No, I am not so stupid," so she replied, "From the lime trees." God said: "Well, if from the lime trees, never go to the meadows. I know better than thou where the most honey is." Therefore there is no honey to-day in the cornfields.[1]

We will end this chapter with a few miscellaneous stories from various parts. The first is from Rumania.

Why is the Wasp the Gipsies' Bee?

In the beginning the wasp belonged to the Rumanian and the bee to the gipsies. When the former saw how useless and dangerous the wasps were and how useful the bees, they cheated the gipsies into exchanging them.

Those of aforetime tell us that when God made the living creatures which move with the sun, He made the bee first. The Gipsy stole the bee from the hand of God, saying, "Give it to me, O Lord, that I may eat of its honey, I and my little ones. And of the wax I will make candles to light them for Thee in the church." God did not say anything, but kept silence and looked angrily at the Gipsy and made up His mind to punish him. He therefore made at once the big wasp, and gave it to the Rumanian, saying, "Take this, for the bee has been ordained for the Gipsy, and he has taken his share." The Rumanian took the wasp and thanked God. Some time afterwards the Gipsy met the Rumanian and asked him if his bee had brought in much honey. The Rumanian, smart as ever, replied, "My bee has filled many barrels, for this bee carries the honey in bagfuls, as it is so big and strong."

[1] Nos. 3–7 are from Dähnhardt, *N.S.*, vol. iii, pp. 306–8.

The Gipsy said his bee had not filled a cup with honey. "Let us exchange our bees, my little Rumanian." So they agreed to do so, and the Gipsy went with the Rumanian to his hut and gave him the hive of bees and the Rumanian took it home, and when they reached the forest the Rumanian showed the Gipsy a big tree as thick as a barrel and as high as the heavens, where he had already put the wasps, and where they had grown to a very large number.

"Here, you Gipsy, are my bees in this hollow tree. It is full of honey, enough to satisfy your whole nation of gipsies and some to remain over." "Thank you, may God bless you," said the Gipsy.

The Rumanian went home to look after the bees. The Gipsy and his friends brought ladders and pots and pans. They climbed the ladder, but the wasps came out and stung them so much that they ran away, and they have had enough of wasps' honey to last them to the end of their days. Since then the bee has belonged to the Rumanian.[1]

A Mongolian Story.

The King of the Birds, Garuda, sent two birds and the bee to dine upon the earth and to find out whose flesh was best eating. On their return they met Bur-khan (King of the Storm). He asked them whose flesh was best to eat. They replied, "Human flesh." Bur-khan, to save man, persuaded them not to tell this to Khan Garuda. The birds agreed, but, not believing that the bee would keep silence, they cut out her tongue. When they flew up the birds reached Khan Garuda first, and told him that the most delicious flesh was the snakes; for so Bur-khan had advised them to say. Then the bee arrived, but to the question of Garuda she could only answer with an unintelligible buzzing.[2]

Bees from Egypt.

This tale tells how bees were obtained from Egypt when they were unobtainable elsewhere.

"There were bees in Egypt. Now when the New Covenant had been established, a new offering, wax, was needed. For this it was

---

[1] Gaster, *Rumanian Bird and Beast Stories*, p. 135.
[2] *Folklore Journal*, vol. iv, p. 18; Dähnhardt, *N.S.*, vol. i, p. 333.

necessary to have bees, and the people said, 'There are bees in Egypt, but we cannot get them from there; there is no way of getting permission.' Then Nicholas, the wonder-worker, said he would bring them, and he went to Egypt, but in vain. He could not get any bees. Then St. Sossim said he would try, and he was sent. He made a hive out of a reed and went to Egypt, where he caught ten bees and a queen, and he put them inside the reed. In the early morning he fled. The Egyptians followed him, caught him, and examined him, shaking him three times, but they found no bees, as they were in the reed. So Sossim brought the bees, and out of them came the swarms which we have."[1]

St. Sossim is regarded as patron saint of beekeeping in the Ukraine.[2]

A Lithuanian Folk-tale.

In olden times there lived on the peninsula of Schmorbe on Oesel a great many sorcerers. When Christianity was brought to Oesel the devil wanted to prevent the people of Schmorbe from becoming Christian by making the river divide Schmorbe from Oesel. He dug out quite a large piece, and when the sun became hot he took off his stockings and worked with naked legs. Suddenly a bee flew and stung the Evil One on the shin. This caused him so much pain that he had to stop digging and ran away, calling out: "Thou wretched bee, thy race shall never prosper in Schmorbe as long as my eye watches over little children there." Here the bee is the protectress of Christianity, and therefore is not favourably regarded by the devil.[3]

Our last tale comes from Hungary. Once Jesus and Peter were walking together. "It must be a fine thing to be God," said Peter, "to help the widows and orphans, to reward good works, to punish the wicked. If I could do that, there would be no wicked people in the whole world."

Jesus turned round and saw a swarm of bees on a young tree, and said to Peter, "Take that swarm in thy cap; we may perhaps need them." Peter put the swarm in his cap; there were so many

[1] From Dobrovolski, I, 286, No. 55, quoted by Dähnhardt, *N.S.*, vol. i, p. 128, note.　　　　　　　　　　　　　　[2] See above, p. 156.

[3] From *Bienemanns Livländischen Sagebuch*, quoted by Knortz, *Die Insekten*, p. 28.

bees that a cluster settled on his hand. Suddenly a bee stung him, and crying out he threw them all on the ground. "What is the matter, Peter?" asked Jesus Christ. "May the devil take this swarm away! A bee has stung my hand." "Why dost thou not look for the one who stung thee?" "Yes, if I could only do that, but they are as alike as two peas." "Thou seest, Peter," said Christ, "if thou wast God, thou wouldst act just like this. If one man among many sinned, thou wouldst be ready to punish all the innocent for his sake."[1]

[1] From *Ungarischen Volksmärchen*, *übersetzt von Elisabeth Sklarek*, quoted by Knortz, *Die Insekten*, p. 35.

CHAPTER XX

THE BEE IN AMERICA

"Apis mellifica" not introduced till seventeenth century—"Meli-
ponas" and "Trigonae indigenous"—Maya hieroglyphs—Maya
beekeeping—Honey paid as tribute to Spaniards—Yucatan hives—
Mexican hives—Bees used in warfare by Quiche—Maya and Aztecs
levy honey tribute—Maya festivals connected with beekeeping—
Bee illustrations from Codex Troana—Aztec hieroglyph for bee—
Maya glyphs "caban" and "cauac"—Acan, the god of mead—
Bee-souls—European superstitions found in America—Telling the
bees—Whittier's poem—Beekeeping among North American Indians
—Honey a cure for illness; drives away evil spirits—Honytree
described by Thevet

In the New World we know little of the bee in ancient times,
indeed, we may say that the story of our honey bee, *Apis mellifica*,
only began in recent times, for it is not indigenous, and was introduced by European settlers; into New England probably about
1638, into New York about 1780, into Kentucky about 1793,
and west of the Mississippi in 1797. It was introduced into British
North America at the end of the seventeenth century; its history
in South America does not begin till the nineteenth century.

There are, however, other families of honey bees which are
indigenous in America, the *Meliponae* and *Trigonae*, and when
the Spaniards conquered Mexico and Central America they found
that beekeeping was an industry among the natives, and it is these
bees which chiefly concern us in this chapter.

In pre-Columbian times, the Maya in Central America, and
later the Aztecs in Mexico, had a civilization which included a
system of hieroglyphic writing, and some of their manuscripts,
known as the American Codices, have been preserved. Unfortunately these hieroglyphs have not all been definitely deciphered,
though much has been done in that direction. On some of these
codices, and especially on the Maya Codex Troana (also known
as Tro-Cortesianus) a number of insects are depicted which have
been usually identified with some species of bees, and although
scholars are not quite unanimous as to what insect they represent,
still, as we shall hope to show, the majority are in favour of their

being bees, probably either *Melipona fulvipes* or *Trigona cupira*, both of which are stingless varieties.

The Maya of Yucatan went in largely for beekeeping, though they obtained even more honey from wild bees than from those kept in hives. Bishop Diego de Landa, who was Bishop of Merido, the capital of Yucatan, from 1573 to 1579, records that every Indian at that time must deliver, as tribute to the Spaniards, a pound of wax, which was collected out of hollow trees and crevices in the rocks, as not enough could be got from the beehives.[1] Dr. Stempel, from whose article we quote this, is a professor of zoology, and writes:

We can certainly infer from this statement of Landa, that the greater part of the honey and wax was obtained chiefly from wild bees, and that could only have been from *Meliponae* and *Trigonae*, whose nests even to-day are sought for and robbed just in the same way by the people in the forests, as these stingless bees do not allow themselves to be cared for and cultivated in such a convenient way as does our *Apis mellifica*.

Professor Stempel adds, however, that *Melipona fulvipes* and *Trigona cupira* are frequently kept by the natives in Yucatan, and that therefore we can assume that they were taken as models for the representations in the manuscripts; a more exact recognition is impossible.[2]

These bees, when domesticated, were probably kept in wooden hives or hollow logs. The comb they make is not so regular as that of our honey bee, and though the cells are sometimes six-sided, yet, as Darwin noted in his *Origin of Species*, they vary from three to six sides, and he considered them as intermediate between the bumble bee (*Bombus*) and the honey bee of Europe (*Apis mellifica*).

The following is an account of a Mexican beehive, written by a naval captain, Basil Hall, in 1820,[3] and it is interesting as giving a description of a native hive, which was probably very similar to those used by the Maya in pre-Columbian times.

[1] Quoted by W. Stempel, "Die Tierbilder der Mayahandschriften," in *Zeitschrift für Ethnologie*, vol. 40, Berlin, 1908, p. 736.   [2] Ibid.
[3] Captain Basil Hall, R.N., F.R.S., *A Journal Written on the Coasts of Chili, Peru, and Mexico in the Years* 1820, 1821, *and* 1822, Constable & Co., 1826, vol. ii, p. 80 ff.

From the Plaza we went to a house where a beehive of the country
was opened in our presence. The bees, the honeycomb and hive, differ
essentially from those of Europe. The hive is generally made out of a
log of wood, from 2 to 3 feet long and 8 or 10 inches in diameter, hollowed
out and closed at the end by circular doors, cemented closely to the wood,
but capable of being removed at pleasure. Some persons use cylindrical
hives made of earthenware, instead of the clumsy apparatus of wood;
these are relieved by raised figures and circular rings, so as to form rather
handsome ornaments in the verandah of a house, where they are suspended
by cords from the roof, in the same manner that the wooden ones in the
villages are hung to the eaves of the cottages. On one side of the hive,
halfway between the ends there is a small hole made, just large enough
for a loaded bee to enter, and shaded by a projection to prevent the rain
from trickling in. In this hole, generally representing the mouth of a
man or some monster, the head of which is moulded in the clay of the
hive, a bee is constantly stationed, whose office is no sinecure, for the
hole is so small he has to draw back every time a bee wishes to leave
or enter the hive. A gentleman told me the experiment had been made
by marking the sentinal, when it was observed that the same bee remained
at his post the whole day.

When it is ascertained by the weight that the hive is full, the end pieces
are removed and the honey withdrawn. The hive we saw opened was
only partially filled, which enabled us to see the economy of the interior
to more advantage. The honey is not contained in the elegant hexagonal
cells of our hives, but in wax bags not quite as large as an egg. These bags
or bladders are hung round the sides of the hive, and appear about half
full, the quantity being probably just as great as the strength of the wax
will bear without tearing. Those nearest the bottom being better supported are more filled than the upper ones. In the centre or the lower
part of the hive we observed an irregular-shaped mass of comb, furnished
with cells like those of our bees, all containing young ones in such an
advanced state that when we broke the combs and let them out they flew
merrily away; but they never stung us, though our faces and hands were
covered with them. It is said, however, that there is a bee in the country
that does sting, but the kind we saw seems neither to have the power nor
the inclination, for they certainly did not hurt us; and our friends said
they were always *muy manso*, very tame, and never stung anyone. The
honey gave out a rich aromatic perfume and tasted differently from ours,
but possessed an agreeable flavour.

We have a confirmation of the statement that the Maya
practised beekeeping from the *Popol Vuh*, the sacred book of the

Quiche, one of the Maya tribes. It is related there that when the heroes conquer their enemies, the only occupations which they allow them to retain are the making of pots and beekeeping;[1] which shows how important the craft was.

In another story of the *Popol Vuh*, the Quiche relate. that the ancestors of their tribe, whose town lay on a mountain, were once besieged by a neighbouring tribe, so they entrenched themselves as well as possible. Then they made wooden figures which looked like men, placed them on the ramparts, hung shields and bows on them, and put gold and silver crowns on their heads. Then they hunted for hornets, wasps, and bees, and brought them to the camp. They put the little creatures into four great calabashes and placed these round the town; they were to help in defeating the enemy. Now the enemy sent spies to the town, who reported that they had seen a few men—the wooden figures—but not many; so they came in great numbers to attack the town and had nearly got in, when suddenly the covers of the calabashes were taken off and the insects flew out like smoke, flew in the eyes, noses, and mouths of the enemy, hung on their legs and arms, which they stung and so obliged the men to throw down their weapons, when they were attacked and killed by the men of the town.[2] This story shows that some of the bees were not stingless!

The Maya imposed a tribute of honey upon conquered tribes, as did also the Aztecs. In the Codex Mendoza (Mexican) is a list of tributes sent to Montezuma by towns situated in the *tierra calante*, the "hot lands"; one hundred towns sent two hundred jars of honey annually, fourteen towns sent two hundred jars, and others three hundred jars, so that altogether Montezuma received seven hundred jars from these "hot lands." The jars were pottery, covered with a network of cord to facilitate suspension during transportation (see Fig. 28 (*h*)). Mrs. Zelia Nuttall, who sent the writer this information, added that she thought this honey would be collected from wild bees, as bees were not domesticated in Mexico. This is, however, a mistake, as Las Casas, one of the earliest bishops in Mexico, mentions hives of bees there.

Some of the honey may have been artificial honey made from the *maguey* (agave) plant; it was carried in large jars, and is ex-

[1] T. A. Joyce, *Mexican Archaeology*, London, 1914, p. 243.
[2] Felix Liebrecht, *Zur Volkskunde*, Heilbronn, 1879, p. 75.

plained in the Mendoza Codex as "thickened maguey honey"
(*miel de maguey espesa*), but there is also mention of small jars of
bees' honey (*cantarillo de miel de abeja*).[1]

FIG. 28.—MAYA AND AZTEC HIEROGLYPHS AND FIGURES

(*a*) Maya Glyph *Kan*   (*b*) Maya Glyph *Cib*   (*c*) Maya Glyph *Caban*
(*d, e*) Glyphs of the Bee from Codex Tro-Cortesianus, 9A
(*f*) Maya Glyphs denoting "Honey" and "Honey-wine"
(*g*) Maya "Mead Jar"   (*h*) Aztec "Honey Jar." (Codex Mendoza)
(*i*) Aztec Glyph, Place-name, Pipiyoltepec = Mountain of the Bee. (Codex
    Mendoza, 15, 3)
(*j*) Men Carrying Tribute. (Humbolt MS., Frag. XI)
(*k*) Conventionalized Insect showing Antennae. (Nuttall Codex 3)

A tribute of honey was also collected from the Mexicans by
the Spaniards after the Conquest, and in the Humbolt MSS. the
two men carrying small jars on their backs are probably delivering
the "bees'" honey demanded (Fig. 28 (*j*)).

[1] Eduard Seler, "Mexican Picture Writings," in *Bulletin* 28 *of Bureau of
American Ethnology*, p. 211.

Bishop Landa records that the Maya had certain ceremonies connected with beekeeping, during which much honey wine was consumed and also offered to the *Bacabs*, deities of agriculture. In the month *Zotz* beekeepers prepared for their festival, which took place in the next month *Tzec*; besides this, in the month *Mol* the beekeepers held another festival in order that the gods might send abundance of flowers for the bees.[1]

We mentioned above that there is a remarkable series of pictures in the *Codex Troana*, which we will now consider. This manuscript, the original of which is in Madrid, was reproduced by Brasseur de Bourbourg in 1869.[2] On several of the pages are depicted insect figures, which he identified as bees, and the little group of cubes on the *cauac* sign (Fig. 29 (8)) as a honeycomb. Professor Cyrus Thomas, in his studies of the *Codex Troana*, named the whole section in which these insects appear as a "Calendar for Beekeepers," and explained them as relating to the above-mentioned festivals of beekeepers. Professor Brinton calls the insect the "Bee God," and suggests that it is connected with the planet Venus.[3] Dr. W. Stempel is of opinion that the insects depicted are bees (four forms of these are shown in Fig. 30 (*a*)). He writes:

It must indeed be admitted that it is difficult for a zoologist to recognize in this insect, which apparently had a chewing jaw, two wings and two peculiar continuations of the hinder part of the body, as a bee, let alone a distinct species of *Melipona* or *Trigona*; but on the other hand, some much more distinctly shown characteristics are indicated, such as the head with the eyes, the upper lip and the altogether characteristic feelers, which distinctly indicate that a bee is intended. Many other things also agree with this view.

The one great authority to deny that the bee is intended is Professor Seler, of Berlin. In his earlier works on the subject, he called the insects bees; but in his articles on the "Animal Figures

[1] Joyce, *Mexican Archaeology*, p. 267, and A. M. Tozzer and G. A. Allen, *Animal Figures in the Maya Codices*, Cambridge, Mass., 1910, p. 300 (*Papers of Peabody Museum*, IV, No. 3).

[2] *Manuscrit Troana, Etudes sur le système graphique et la langue des Mayas,* 1869.

[3] Daniel G. Brinton, *A Primer of Mayan Hieroglyphics*, University of Pennsylvania Series in Philology, Literature, and Archaeology, vol. iii, No. 2, p. 59.

[4] Stempel, *Zeitschrift für Ethnologie*, 1908, p. 736.

of the Maya Manuscripts," he writes: "I cannot regard these insects, as Stempel does, as bees."[1] His opinion is that they represent some kind of beetle.

That they do not resemble bees is hardly an argument against them, for the Maya and Aztecs conventionalized their animal figures to such a degree, that the only undisputed figure of a bee, which appears in the *Mendoza Codex*, might also be repudiated, for it is even less like a bee than these. It is shown in Fig. 28 (*i*), and is undoubtedly intended for a bee, as it is the hieroglyph of the town *Pipiyoltepec*, a name which means the mountain of the bee (Mexican, *pipiyoli* = bee, *tepec* = mountain).[2]

In their *Animal Figures of the Maya Codices*, published in the same year as Dr. Seler's articles, Dr. Tozzer and Dr. Allen write:

A portion of the Tro-Cortesianus appears to treat of apiculture, or, at all events, contains numerous figures of bees, some of which are shown in Plate 2.

This plate is reproduced here as Fig. 29.[3]

Fig. 28 (*c*) represents the Maya glyph *caban*, which seems to have a connection with bees and honey. Dr. Seler says it means "that which is brought down" or descending, and that the root *cab* may also denote honey or beehive.[4] Drs. Tozzer and Allen write:

The *caban* form in connection with the hive in Plate 11, Fig. 10, may have some phonetic significance, as *kab* is honey in Maya. This sign occurs very frequently in the pages devoted to apiculture. The figures of the bees in the Codex show a number of interesting variations. In Figs. 1–3, 5, and 11, the insect is less conventionalized than in Figs. 4 and 6. The hairy feet are well indicated as well as the segmented body and a single pair of wings. All the figures show an anterodorsal view so that, on account of the size of the first pair of legs, only the tops of the second pair appear in Figs. 1, 3, and 5. In Fig. 2, however, two pairs are seen, and in Figs. 4 and 6 the anthropomorphic tendency is further shown by providing the insect with two pairs of limbs, each with four or five digits and a conventionalized face, eyes, and mouth. In Fig. 1, the bee is represented without mouth parts, but antennae only. This may

[1] E. Seler, "Die Tierbilder der mexicanischen und der Maya Handschriften," in *Zeitschrift für Ethnologie*, 1910, p. 262.   [2] Ibid., p. 260.

[3] By kind permission of Dr. Tozzer.

[4] "Mexican Chronology," in *Bulletin* 28 *of American Ethnology*, p. 50.

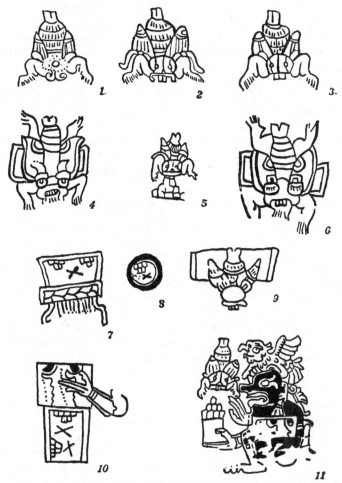

FIG. 29.—HONEY BEES (MELIPONAE) (CODEX TRO-CORTESIANUS)

1. Possibly a Drone
2, 3. Bees
4, 6. Bees more Conventionalized
5. Bee and Honeycomb
7. Honeycombs apparently in a Hive
8. Maya Day-sign *Cauac*, possibly representing a honeycomb
9. Bee
10. Honeycombs in a Hive
11. Bee and Honeycomb and War-god (M.)

(Reproduced by permission from Plate II in *Animal Figures in the Maya Codices*, by A. M. Tozzer and G. M. Allen (Cambridge, Mass., 1910). *Papers of the Peabody Museum of American Archaeology and Ethnology*, vol. iv, No. 3)

indicate a drone or a queen bee that takes no active part in the work of
gathering honey or making comb. Fig. 2 is perhaps the least reduced
of all the figures and shows the worker bee with antennae and mouthparts.
The so-called "cloud balls" of the day sign *Cauac* (Fig. 8) may represent
the honeycomb. *Cauac* is usually supposed to have some connection with
lightning and thunder, although Valentini agrees with the authors in
associating *Cauac* with the bees and honey. The *Cauac*-like forms in
Figs. 7 and 10 have been described above as hives.[1] The representation
of legs in the full drawing of a bee as four large limbs, coupled with the
method of drawing the insect as seen from above and in front, may have
led to its final expression by an X-shaped mark shown in connection with
the hives (Figs. 7, 10). This X is also seen in the day sign *Cauac*.[2]

After alluding to the beekeeper's festivals, Dr. Tozzer adds:

It seems clear therefore that we have represented in the pages of the
Tro-Cortesianus Codex the rites carried out in this connection. The more
or less realistic drawings of the bees (Figs. 1–6, 9) represent the god of
the bees and to him offerings of food and incense are being made. Fig. 11
shows the war god (M) with his eagle headdress offering a mass of honey
in the comb to the God of the Bees.[3]

Thus, in spite of the unlikeness to bees, it may fairly be con-
ceded that the verdict is in favour of these insects representing
bees. Mrs. Zelia Nuttall, another great authority on the American
Codices, writes: "There is no doubt that the *Codex Tro* contains
representations of bees, and that Cyrus Thomas and Tozzer were
correct in their identifications."[4] Dr. Tozzer also wrote to the
author, "There is no doubt they are bees."[5]

The Maya knew how to prepare a mead from honey, to which
an infusion of the root of a plant was added. Fig. 28 (*a*) represents
the glyph *kan*, which denotes the colour yellow, and in conjunction
with the element for *tree* is used to denote honey or honey wine
(Fig. 28 (*f*)). On another glyph, *cib* (Fig. 28 (*b*)) is a figure used

---

[1] "What appear to be improvised hives are shown in Figs. 7, 10, where
the combs are noted depending from the ceiling or walls. These combs are
composed of cells roughly four-sided, though in Fig. 11 several hexagonal
cells are present in the mass of comb held by the black god, M."

[2] Tozzer and Allen, *Animal Figures of Maya Codices*, p. 299 f.

[3] Ibid., p. 301.

[4] In letter to author dated April 1925.   [5] In letter August 1925,

on the jugs from which the intoxicating drink mead foams (Fig. 28 (g)). Dr. Seler thinks that *cib* has some connection with the "pulque god,"

for *ci* is the maguey plant and is also used to denote the *pulque* made from it as well as other intoxicating drinks. *Cib* therefore might mean "that which is used for making wine," either the honey or perhaps more correctly the narcotic root which was added to the fermented drink.[1]

Acan was the god of the intoxicating mead. The four *Bacabs*, the gods of the cardinal points, who were especially gods of the harvests and of the food supply generally, are also called *Acantum* in Landa's work; he does not explain the meaning,[2] but Professor Brinton writes:

The word *acan* meant mead, the intoxicating hydromel which the natives manufactured. The god of this drink also bore the name *Acan*. Thus it would be appropriate for the Bacabs to be gods of wine.[3]

This honey drink of the Maya cannot be compared with the nectar and ambrosia of the Greeks or the soma of India, as it did not confer immortality, although it was health-giving and intoxicating. Some later writers say that the mead which Quetxalcoatl quaffed did make him immortal, but that is not in the earliest form of the myth.

There are many more bee figures in the *Codex Tro;* the only ones we have space to mention are depicted in Fig. 30. Fig. 30 (c) shows the Rain God Chac, with the hive below and the Bee God descending on to the offering; in Fig. 30 (d) it is descending towards an armadillo, which animal is twice associated with the bee in this codex. Here it is probably the symbol of the god or hero, Itzamma, and is seated beneath an overhanging roof. Fig. 30 (b) shows two bee figures descending on various objects, perhaps offerings.[4] It is much to be hoped that further discoveries in Central America may give us some more clues for the elucidation of these interesting ceremonies connected with the bee, depicted in the *Codex Troana.* We should then be able to grasp more of the beliefs of these remarkable people. Professor Waser of Zürich

---

[1] *Mexican Chronology*, p. 49.
[2] D. G. Brinton, *American Hero Myths*, p. 156.   [3] Ibid.
[4] Tozzer and Allen, *Animal Figures in Maya Codices*, p. 347.

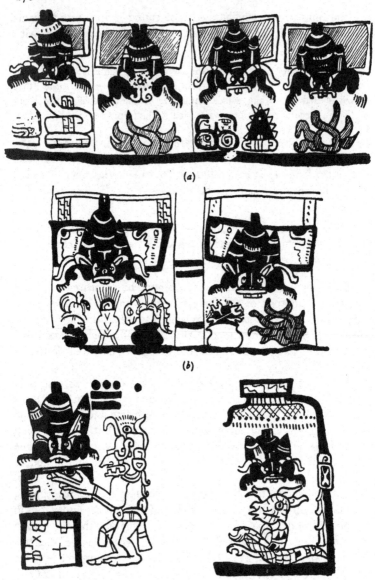

FIG. 30.—FROM THE CODEX TRO-CORTESIANUS

(a) Four Bee Forms   (c) Rain God, Chac, Bee descending on Hive
(b) Bee Forms descending on Offerings   (d) Bee descending on Armadillo

notes that the Toltecs, who preceded the Aztecs in Mexico, held that the soul becomes an insect; he does not specify which, although he is writing of the bee-soul—which seems as if the "Bee God" might possibly be a form of the soul.[1]

We have noted in former chapters that many of the superstitions regarding bees were taken across the Atlantic by the early European settlers. Among these that of telling the bees of a death was common in the country districts of New England. Whittier's well-known poem, *Telling the Bees*, written in 1858, commemorates this custom. The scene described is minutely that of the Whittier homestead. We quote part of the poem.

> There are the beehives ranged in the sun,
>   And down by the brink
> Of the brook are her poor flowers, weed o'ergrown,
>   Pansy and daffodil, rose and pink.
>
> .   .   .   .   .
>
> Just the same as a month before,
>   The house and the trees,
> The barn's brown gable, the vine by the door,
>   Nothing changed but the hive of bees.
>
> Before them, under the garden wall,
>   Forward and back
> Went drearily singing the chore-girl small,
>   Draping each hive with a shred of black.
>
> Trembling I listened, the summer sun
>   Had the chill of snow;
> For I knew she was telling the bees of one
>   Gone on the journey we all must go!
>
> Then I said to myself, "My Mary weeps
>   For the dead to-day;
> Haply her blind old granddad sleeps
>   The fret and the pain of his age away!"

[1] O. Waser, "Über die äussere Erscheinung der Seele in den Vorstellungen der Völker," in *Archiv für Religions-Wissenschaft*, Band XVI, 1913, p. 353.

But her dog whined low; on the doorway sill
   With his cane to his chin
The old man sat; and the chore-girl still
   Sang to the bees, stealing out and in.

And the song she was singing ever since
   In my ear sounds on:
"Stay at home, pretty bees, fly not hence!
   Mistress Mary is dead and gone!"

This custom is mentioned by Mark Twain in *Huckleberry Finn*. The negro says to Huck:

If a man owned a beehive, and the man died, the bees must be told about it before sun-up next morning or else the bees would all weaken down and quit work and die. Jim said bees wouldn't sting idiots, but I didn't believe that, because I had tried them lots of times myself and they wouldn't sting me!

These superstitions refer, of course, to our honey bee, *Apis mellifica*, which the North American Indians called "the white man's fly." These Indians rarely occupy themselves in beekeeping, but they are clever in taking the honey of the wild bees; for soon after the European bee was introduced, it increased very quickly, and numerous swarms took possession of the hollow trees in the forests. The Indians find these nests by capturing a few bees, which after a while they release and then observe the direction in which they fly, for they will go direct to their home; hence arose the expression, "in a bee-line."

The Cherokee Indians, however, did practise beekeeping. Mr. Mooney, in his book on *The Myths of the Cherokee*, writes:

Bees are kept by many of the Cherokee, in addition to the wild bees, which are hunted in the woods. Although they are said to have come originally from the whites, the Cherokee have no tradition of a time when they did not know them, there seems, however, to be no folklore connected with them.

In 1706 the Cherokee had bees and honey, and did a considerable trade in beeswax; and as early as 1540 the de Soto narrative mentions a pot of honey in an Indian village in Georgia.[1] This

---

[1] *Bureau of American Ethnology*, vol. xix, Part I, pp. 82, 214, 309.

cannot have been from *Apis mellifica*, if the statement that they were not introduced there till 1638 is correct.

In New England if you do not wish to be stung by a bee, they say you must hold your breath when near them, and then they will not attack you.[1]

The following story, told by an old Irishwoman, is related in the *Journal of American Folklore*, and shows a belief in honey as a *heal-all*.

Mark Flaherty was once riding in the meadows after sunset. Suddenly he heard a voice close behind him, but could see no one. Returning home, he again heard the voice, but could not discern the cause. When he reached home he went to bed, but could not sleep, as it seemed as if some one was sitting on his breast. The next morning he found that his hair had become white during the night. In the evening he again heard a mysterious voice and saw a man creeping after him, but who withdrew directly he tried to approach him. So after that Flaherty did not go out after sunset; he became ill and was soon nothing but skin and bones. One day a beggar came to him and said, "You must go to the bees and fetch so much honey that you can rub yourself all over with it from head to foot. But you must fetch the honey yourself, if anyone does it for you, it won't do you any good. The bees fly to all the flowers, suck the goodness out of them and mix this in their honey. It will cure you, make your hair brown again, and your face fresh and red." The Irishman followed this advice and was soon as well as ever, and he never heard the evil voice again.[2]

The Creoles of Louisiana believe in the efficacy of smearing yourself over with honey from head to foot in order to drive away evil spirits, and they also say that doing this gives you an insight into the future.[3]

John Parkinson, that quaint old herbalist, whose book, the *Theatrum Botanicum*, was published in 1640, describes a tree, which he names the Indian Honytree, *Uhebebasou* (Fig. 31), and writes:

Thevet maketh mention of this tree among his other American singularities to be very tall, spreading the branches so uniformly, that it is a pleasure to behold. . . . In the hollow parts of this tree above other,

[1] Knortz, *Die Insekten*, p. 32.

[2] *Journal of American Folklore*, vol. ii, quoted by Knortz, *Die Insekten*, p. 31.

[3] Mary Owen, *Voodoo Tales*, quoted by Knortz, *Die Insekten*, p. 26.

the Bees doe make their Hony and Wax, whereoff the naturalls make
much account, for with it they season their foode made of roots, etc.
Unto this tree resorteth familiarly a certain beast somewhat like a cat,
but of a brown colour, called by them Heyrat, that is the Hony beast
to feed on the Hony, which it
carefully pulleth out with the
feet, without hurting the bees or
being stung or hurt by them.[1]

Vhebebasou. The Indian Hony tree.

The writer, whom Par-
kinson mentions, was André
Thevet, a Frenchman. His
book, *Les Singulaitiez de la
France Antarctique, autrement
nommée Amerique, et de plu-
sieurs Terres et Isles decou-
vertes de nostre temps,* was
published in 1558. He made
a short visit to Brazil in
1555–6, but is not considered
a very dependable authority,
as he is described as a "voya-
geur, connu par sa credu-
lité!" However, he makes a
few interesting remarks about
these bees, although he does
not state in what locality
they are to be found, and it
is impossible from his description to identify the Hony-

Fig. 31.—INDIAN HONYTREE
(John Parkinson: *Theatrum Botanicum,*
1640, p. 1648)

tree, the *Uhebebasou.* He noted two kinds of bees, who re-
sorted to these trees. One was the same size as our honey bee; it
only visited sweet-smelling flowers and made very good honey,
but its wax was not so yellow as ours; the other species was half as
small again, their honey was still better than that of the first kind,
and the natives called them *Hira;* their wax was black like coal.[2]

[1] *Theatrum Botanicum,* p. 1648. They were probably stingless bees!
[2] I am indebted to Mrs. Agnes Arber, the botanist, for this information
from Thevet's book.

CHAPTER XXI

RITUAL USES OF MILK AND HONEY

Honey much used in religious rites, and in India, Greece, and Rome, together with milk—Offerings to the dead and to chthonian divinities—Milk and honey in the mystery religions—Mithraic rites—First food for children—Golden Age—Apocalypse of Paul— Milk and honey in Christian rituals—Used at baptisms—Use in Egyptian and Ethiopian Churches—Not used in Syrian or Greek, but in Roman liturgies—Blessing used in "Sacramentarium Leoninum"—Use suddenly discontinued about A.D. 600—Story of Joseph and Asenath

WE have already mentioned many uses of honey in religious rites in Egypt, Sumeria, and Babylonia, and noted that in India, Greece, and Rome it was often used in conjunction with milk. This connection between milk and honey in ritual is a very ancient one, and was continued till about the end of the sixth century of our era; we have space here only to treat this interesting subject very briefly.

Looking back into the dim regions of the past we find that the offerings which man made to the spirits of his dead were exactly those things which were acceptable to himself, milk and honey, and later meal and wine. It was these which Odysseus offered when invoking the spirits of the dead (*Odyssey* XI 27; x. 515); Atossa, when calling on the shades of Darius, brings milk from the sacred cow, and the honey of the bees;[1] and in Euripides' *Iphigenia in Tauris* the offerings to the dead are poetically described:

> Milk of the mountain kine,
> The hallowed gleam of wine,
> The toil of murmuring bees.[2]

These offerings to the dead are possibly one of the oldest forms of ritual, then came the offerings to the Underworld Gods—the chthonian divinities—especially those to the Great-Mother goddesses like Rhea, Demeter, and Artemis, on whom all fertility, of man, animals, and of vegetable life, depended. It was to these

---

[1] See above, p. 121. [2] I, 158, Gilbert Murray's translation.

divinities, as we stated above, that the sober offerings, the *nephalia*, from which wine was excluded, were offered by the Greeks. Milk alone was not used in these cults, but was mixed with honey.[1] This mixture, *melikraton*, as the Greeks called it, was probably frequently used in everyday life; it may have been considered a delicacy, and men offered it as something specially good.

Probably milk and honey won a special place in the mystery religions thanks to their use in the chthonian cults. The old myth of Zeus being fed with milk and honey in the Cretan cave would be favourable to this development. In the Dionysian mysteries, as we have seen, honey played an important part. The coming of the god Dionysus was manifested by the streams of milk, honey, and wine:

> Then streams the earth with milk, yea streams
> With wine, and nectar of the bee.[2]

Porphyry notes the use of honey in the Orphic mysteries, and also says it was used in the rites of Mithras.[3]

In the Mithraic rites those who belonged to the three lowest grades were servers only, and could not participate in the higher mysteries. The fourth grade was that of the "Lion." The candidate for the "Lion" had honey, as a cleansing material, poured over his hands instead of water; the lion,

being the emblem of the principle of fire, the use of water the element hostile to fire was renounced, and in order to preserve the initiate from the blemish of sin, honey was poured on his hands and applied to his tongue, as was the custom with new-born children.[4]

The "Lions" were then allowed to share in the Mithraic feast or communion. The next grade was the "Persian," and at his initiation honey was presented to him as a preservative and as the food of the blessed, also because he was a husbandman and keeper of fruit. The "Persian" appears on the monuments wearing the Phrygian cap, characteristic of Mithra.[5]

---

[1] For milk in ritual, see Karl Wyss, *Die Milch im Kultus der Griechen und Römer*, Giessen, 1914, in *Religionsgeschichtliche Versuche*, vol. 15. For the gods to whom the *nephalia* were offered, see above, Chapter XI.

[2] Euripides, *Bac.*, 102.   [3] *De ant. nym.*, 15, 18.

[4] Franz Cumont, *The Mysteries of Mithra*, 1903, p. 157.

[5] L. Patterson, *Mithraism and Christianity*, Cambridge, 1921, p. 47.

Honey was regarded as a sacred substance by the Persians and magi of Asia Minor, so we can understand its introduction into the Mithraic rites, especially as during the centuries of the development of this religion the *bee* was regarded as being reproduced from the *bull*, which animal was intimately connected with Mithra himself.

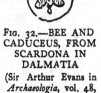

FIG. 32.—BEE AND CADUCEUS, FROM SCARDONA IN DALMATIA

(Sir Arthur Evans in *Archaeologia*, vol. 48, Fig. 9, 1884)

From Porphyry's account it appears that the bee was also regarded among the worshippers of Mithra as the special emblem of the soul, and in this connection three gems are of special interest. One is a red cornelian (Fig. 32) found by Sir Arthur Evans at Scardona in Dalmatia and depicts a bee, but in place of the proboscis there is the twisted end of a *caduceus*, the well-known symbol of Mercury. Sir Arthur writes:

> As bees, according to the ancient idea, were generated by Bulls' carcases, so bees, representing the vital principle, sprang from the Persian bull of Persian mythology. So too no fitter emblem could be found for the spirits of men that swarmed forth according to this creed (Mithraism) from the horned luminary of the heavens, the Moon, their primal dwelling-place, to migrate awhile for their earthly pilgrimage below;

FIG. 33.—RED JASPER CAMEO

(Reproduced by kind permission of the Open Court Publishing Company from Franz Cumont: *The Mysteries of Mithra*)

and he points out that this conjunction of the bee with the symbol of Mercury, the shepherd of departed souls, would therefore have a deep mystic significance.[1]

The second gem (Fig. 33) is a cameo of red jasper, which shows a bee, as a symbol of the soul, in the mouth of a lion, which beast

[1] Sir Arthur Evans drew my attention to this gem, which he describes in *Archaeologia*, vol. 48, p. 23.

was intimately connected with Mithra; above are seen seven stars, surrounded by magic Greek inscriptions.[1] The third gem shown on Plate XII, Fig. 4, is another example of this strange association of the lion and the bee. A coin of Sardis of the second century B.C., though probably not connected with the worship of Mithra, shows a bee resting on a lion (Fig. 34).

We have elsewhere alluded to the custom of smearing a newborn infant's lips with honey; it was a preservative, a divine substance, and solemnly gave them the right to live. It was probably given to them even before they tasted milk. Milk and honey were the first food of children, and therefore in the mystery cults they were given to the newly consecrated initiates as a sign of rebirth. In the *Berlin Magical Papyrus* the worshipper is told:

> Take the honey with the milk, drink of it before the rising of the sun, and there shall be something in thy heart that is divine.[2]

FIG. 34.—COIN OF SARDIS. LION AND BEE (British Museum Catalogue, Lydia, Pl. 24, Fig. 10)

Here we get a glimpse of the deeper meaning which was given to milk and honey when they were used by the early Christians, for it was probably from their use in the mystery religions that milk and honey passed into the Christian use. The Mithraic cult knew of a sacramental drink of immortality; honey was regarded as divine food, which gave the "Persian" new life and divinity; and we know the significance which honey and milk had in the Dionysian rites. Milk was the food of the physically born, as well as that of the reborn. The Christian use took over, perhaps unconsciously, some of the initiation rites of the old mysteries and carried them a step farther.[3]

Now milk and honey, besides their use in the chthonian cults and the mystery religions, were also connected in men's minds with the idea of the Golden Age, when, as so many of the poets— Hesiod, Vergil, Ovid, Horace, and many others—have told us, the honey dripped from the oaks and the milk pails overflowed; and

[1] From Cumont, *Textes et monuments figurés relatifs aux mystères de Mithra.*
[2] *Berliner Zauberpapyrus*, I, 20 (*Abt. Berl. Akad.*, 1865, s. 120).
[3] See Karl Wyss, *Die Milch im Kultus der Griechen und Römer*, p. 53, and Albrecht Dieterich, *Eine Mithrasliturgie*, Leipzig, 1910, p. 170 ff.

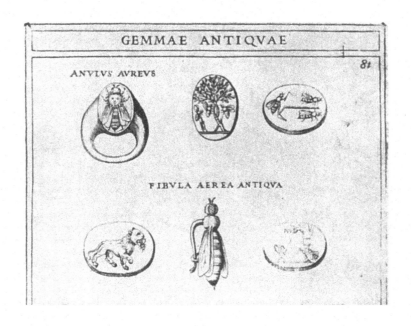

7. Grasshopper Ploughing with Team of Two Bees. (British Museum, No. 2548)

PLATE XII.—ANTIQUE GEMS

not only with the Golden Age, but also with the Isles of the Blest and the Land of the Gods, which are furnished with wells of milk and honey. This conception of the heavenly country is also found among the Hebrews; their idea of the Land of Promise was one of milk and honey, and in the heavenly Jerusalem there are said to have been twelve fountains flowing with milk and honey.[1] These wells or rivers appear later in Christian apocryphal writings.

In the Apocalypse of Paul,[2] which appeared at the end of the fourth century, but is made up of very early matter, Paul is taken by the angel to the Land of Promise:

And I looked around that land and saw a river flowing with milk and honey. . . . And the angel said, "follow me and I will bring thee unto the city of Christ." And he set me in a golden ship . . . and four rivers encompassed the city round about. There was a river of honey, and a river of milk, and a river of wine, and a river of oil. . . . But I went forward and the angel brought me to the river of honey, and I saw there Esaias and Jeremias and Ezekiel and Amos and Micheas and Zacharias, even the prophets lesser and greater, and they greeted me. . . . Again he led me where was the river of milk, and I saw in that place all the children whom the King Herod slew for the name of Christ and they greeted me.

Here we get the river of honey connected with the prophets, those men of eloquence whom the Greeks said had their lips touched with the honey of the sacred bees, and the river of milk connected with the innocent children.

We will now consider the use of milk and honey in the Christian Church.[3] The custom in the early Church was—and still is among the Copts and Ethiopians—to present newly baptized persons with mixed milk and honey after they had left the baptismal font. An old form of the service was discovered in the work, found at Verona, known as the *Didascalia Apostolorum*, the Apostles' Teachings.

Immediately after the completed service, the baptized persons were anointed by a presbyter with consecrated oil, and after they

---

[1] 2 Esdras ii. 19.

[2] Translated in the *Apocryphal New Testament* by Dr. M. R. James, 1924.

[3] For authorities, see H. Usener, "Milch und Honig," in *Kleiner Schriften*, 1913, vol. iv, p. 404. This interesting article was first published in *Rheinisches Museum* (1902), vol. lvii.

had put on their baptismal robes were taken into the church. There the bishop received them; he blessed them in the laying on of hands with consecrated oil and gave them the kiss, after which they took part in the prayers of the assembled congregation, and on their conclusion participated in the brethren's kiss. Then the Mass was said for them, and for that wine mixed with water, milk and honey mixed, and lastly water, were consecrated. Then the bishop instructed the newly baptized about the sacramental meaning of each element, broke the bread and gave it to them with the words "The bread of heaven in Jesus Christ," and they answered "Amen." Then three presbyters advanced (if there were not so many present, deacons took their place) one after the other, each provided with a chalice. In the chalice of the first was water, the second milk and honey, and the third wine mixed with water. At the first draught the priest said, "In God the Father Almighty," at the second "and in Jesus Christ our Lord," and at the third, "in the Holy Spirit," and at the end of each saying the candidates answered "Amen."[1]

The ritual use of milk and honey was known in the district round Alexandria, as is proved by Clement of Alexandria when he compares milk as the nourishment after the earthly birth with milk and honey as food after the spiritual birth, but its use was evidently not universal as the older epistle of Barnabas does not mention it, though he speaks of the land flowing with milk and honey. It is probable that the Egyptian Gnostics, known as the Naassenes, used milk and honey in their sacrament of baptism.[2]

When the use of these elements was discontinued or rather condemned by the Church, their use still continued in the Egyptian and Ethiopian Churches. The so-called Canons of Hippolytus, attributed to Hippolytus, Bishop of Rome (died about 240), which exist in an Arabic translation taken from a Coptic version of the original Greek, are valuable as they give information respecting the uses in these Churches.

Here is the description of the incidents after baptism in the Egyptian Church:

[1] Usener, *Kleiner Schriften*, p. 405. Here, as Professor Usener notes, are the three substances which had from time immemorial been used in the offerings to the dead.　　　　　　　　　　　　　[2] Ibid., p. 406.

Then the deacon begins to consecrate and the bishop completes the
Eucharist of the Body and Blood of the Lord; when he has finished the
congregation communicates, whilst he stands at the Table of the Lord's
Body and Blood, and the presbyters carry other chalices of milk and honey
to teach the communicants that they are born a second time as little
children, as little children partake of the milk and honey. . . . So the
bishop gives them of the body of the Anointed One and says, "This is
the body of Christ." They answer, "Amen." To those to whom he gives
the cup he says, "This is the blood of Christ," they answer, "Amen."
Then they communicate with the milk and honey as a foretaste of the
coming time and the sweetness of the treasures therein; that time which
does not turn to bitterness, and those treasures which do not disappear.
So they become perfect Christians, who have been fed on the Body of
Christ.[1]

This custom of receiving a chalice of milk and honey was still
extant in the times of Sophronios early in the sixth century.

Of the Ethiopian order of baptism the Canon says:

And afterwards they shall receive of the mysteries (the Eucharist) . . .
they shall eat of the flesh and drink of the precious blood of our Lord
and Saviour Jesus Christ. And after that shall be given to those who are
re-born in Christ, milk and pure honey.[2]

Milk and honey do not seem to have been used either in the
Syrian or Greek Churches, at least the Greek Fathers, John
Chrysostom and Cyril of Jerusalem, do not mention them, but they
appear in Roman liturgies.

The oldest Roman Sacramentary, compiled in the course of the
sixth century and known as the *Sacramentarium Leoninum*, is unfortunately mutilated and the section containing the Easter baptisms is missing, but in the Whitsuntide baptisms milk and honey
appear. The following blessing is ordered to be used:

Bless, O Lord, these thy creatures of the spring, of honey, of milk;
let thy servants drink out of this spring the invisible water of Life, which
is the spirit of Truth, and feed them with this milk and honey, as thou
hast promised to our fathers, Abraham, Isaac, and Jacob, to lead them
into the land of Promise, the land flowing with milk and honey. Unite
thy servants, O Lord, with the Holy Spirit, as here honey and milk are
united, as a sign that heavenly and earthly substance is united in Christ
Jesus our Lord.[3]

[1] Quoted by Usener, *Kleiner Schriften*, p. 407.
[2] Ibid.   [3] Ibid., p. 409.

This benediction is valuable confirmation of the rites mentioned above in the "Apostles' Teachings," for it shows that in Rome the three chalices of water, milk, and honey, and of course wine, were consecrated and given to the newly baptized. One other document, probably belonging to the first decade of the sixth century, also alludes to this custom. This is a letter sent by a Roman deacon of the common name of John to a noble called Senarius. This man had written to John asking for explanations on certain points, and among other questions had asked why "milk and honey was poured into the sacred chalice and was administered on Easter Sunday together with the sacrifice of the Mass."

The question and the full response show that the custom was still prevailing in the Roman Church. John calls the chalice "extremely holy," not because milk and honey were poured into the wine chalice of the Eucharist, but because the chalice which contained these fluids was administered as a constituent part of the sacrament: John especially emphasizes that. He tells Senarius that this form of the sacrament is administered to the candidates for baptism, so that they may know that only those who have partaken of the Body and Blood of the Lord will receive the Land of Promise; therefore they, on the commencement of their journey, are fed like sucklings with milk and honey. John was evidently acquainted with the "Apostles' Teaching," for he often uses the same words.[1]

Rome therefore kept up the custom for a long time, and then suddenly about 600, for some as yet unexplained reason, it completely disappears and is not found in any of the Sacramentaries of the seventh century. Perhaps it may some time be discovered who decreed the disuse of the milk and honey in the Roman liturgies.

From their use in the early cults, a use so natural to primitive man, an offering of gifts so acceptable both to the living and the dead, the use of milk and honey became symbolical in the mystery religions, and it was this aspect that the Christian Church emphasized. By baptism the Christian became the Son of God; he cast off the earthly in the waters of baptism and was re-born spiritually, and as a divine being was called to endless bliss. As a token of this

[1] Quoted by Usener, *Kleiner Schriften*, p. 411, from Mabillon, *Museum Italicum*, I. 2, pp. 69–76.

the newly baptized was fed, not only symbolically, but also sacramentally, with milk and honey.

We end this chapter with some quotations from a book called *Joseph and Asenath*, which was in existence before 569, and may have been written in the fifth century. The book was probably of Jewish origin, but revised by a Christian writer, as will be seen by the references to the sacred bread and cup, by which is undoubtedly meant the service of the Eucharist.[1]

Asenath has thrown all her idols away and prays to the God of Joseph to pardon her. The Archangel Michael appears and tells her that God has answered her prayer. Her sins shall be blotted out and "she shall eat the blessed bread of life and drink a cup filled with immortality and be anointed with the unction of incorruption." Asenath begs Michael to sit down and she will bring him bread and wine. "He said to her, 'Bring me also a honeycomb,' and she stood still and was perplexed and grieved for that she had not a bees' comb in her storehouse." So she told Michael that she would send a boy to fetch one. "The divine angel said to her, 'Enter thy storehouse and thou wilt find a bees' comb lying on the table; take it and bring it hither.' And she said, 'Lord, there is no bees' comb in my storehouse,' and he said, 'Go and thou shalt find.' And Asenath entered her storehouse and found a honeycomb lying upon the table, and the comb was great and white like snow and full of honey, and that honey was as the dew of heaven and the odour thereof was as the odour of life. Then Asenath said to hserself, 'Is this comb from the mouth of the man himself?' "

She took the comb to Michael and he said, " ' Why is it that thou saidest, there is no comb in my house? and lo thou hast brought it to me?' And she said, 'Lord, I never put a honeycomb in mine house but as thou saidest so hath it been made. Came this forth from thy mouth? for that the odour thereof is as the odour of ointment.' And the man smiled at her understanding . . . and said, 'Blessed art thou, Asenath, because the ineffable mysteries of God have been revealed to thee. . . . Blessed are all who cleave to the Lord God in penitence, because they shall eat of this comb, for that comb is the spirit of life, and this the bees of the paradise of delight have made from the dew of the roses of life that are in the Paradise of God, and of every flower, and of it eat

[1] *Joseph and Asenath*, trans. by E. W. Brook, S.P.C.K., 1918, Chapter XVI.

the angels and all the elect of God and all the sons of the Most
High, and whosoever shall eat of it shall not die for ever.' Then
the divine angel stretched forth his right hand, and took a small
piece from the comb and ate, and with his hand placed what was
left in Asenath's mouth and said to her, 'Eat,' and she ate. And the
angel said to her, 'Lo! now thou hast eaten the bread of life and
hast drunk the cup of immortality and been anointed with the
unction of incorruption.' . . . And the angel incited the comb,
and many bees arose from the cells of that comb, and the cells were
numberless, tens of thousands of tens of thousands and thousands
of thousands; and the bees were white like snow, and their wings
as purple and crimson stuff and as scarlet; and they had stings
and injured no man. Then all the bees encircled Asenath from head
to foot, and other great bees like their queens arose from the cells,
and they circled upon her face and upon her lips, and made a comb
upon her mouth and upon her lips like to the comb that lay before
the angel; and all the bees ate from the comb that was upon
Asenath's mouth. And the angel said to the bees, 'Go, now, to your
place.' Then all the bees rose and departed to heaven; but as many
as wished to injure Asenath all fell upon the earth and died.
Thereupon the angel stretched his staff over the dead bees and
said to them, 'Rise, and depart ye also to your place.' Then all the
bees rose and departed into the court that adjoined Asenath's
house and took up their lodging upon the fruit-bearing trees."

These quotations from this old tale seem a suitable ending to
our account of the bee in ancient times. They recall so many of the
beliefs mentioned in former chapters—the *divine bees*, whose
colour was *white*, who came from and returned to Paradise, except
for the few who, miraculously restored to life and whose colour
we feel sure, although it is not mentioned, must have been brown
or black, remain on earth to gladden men's hearts with the sweet
honey obtained from the fruit trees—it recalls the cup filled
with immortality, the old nectar and ambrosia of the gods, and yet
it emphasizes the deeper symbolic meaning which honey bore in
the many religions of the ancient world.

CHAPTER XXII

PRIMITIVE PEOPLES OF TO-DAY

Indian customs—The Veddas of Ceylon—Invocation of spirits before taking honey—Customs observed among the Nagas tribes—The Todas bee-souls—Beliefs among the Andaman Islanders—Bee-keeping in Borneo—Australian customs—Bee as tribe totem—Primitive beekeeping in Africa—Customs and superstitions of the A-Kamba—Uganda—Honey taboos among the Thonda—Stories of the honey-guide bird—Honey dance of the Bushman—Honey wine and bees—Customs in Morocco

In the previous chapters the habits and beliefs of the peoples of bygone ages have been considered. In this concluding chapter are noted a few of the beliefs and customs which still exist among backward peoples of to-day.

Whether primitive man resembled in some ways the backward peoples of to-day, whether any of the latter's beliefs can be traced back to the peoples of old, is a disputed question, which will not be discussed here; but we do find among some of the tribes of India, Africa, and Australia customs which recall the beliefs which we found in the far-off past. We find a belief in the purity of the bees, a belief which involves the chastity of those about to take part in honey gathering; we find certain taboos on honey; we find a belief that honey wards off evil spirits; we find that it is included in offerings to the dead; we find the belief in its magical properties and great medicinal virtues; and we also come across the belief in bee-souls.

In India honey is believed to have power over spirits, and is considered a great cleanser and purifier. Among the Deccan Hindus, when the bridegroom comes to the bride's house, honey and curds are given him to drink; this is the old mixture we found used in Vedic times, and the apparent object is to scare away evil from the bridegroom.[1]

Old honey is held to be a cure for coughs, wind, and bile; it also increases strength and virility. The Hindus use honey for

[1] J. M. Campbell, "Notes on the Spirit Basis of Belief and Custom," in *The Indian Antiquary*, vol. 24 (1885), p. 259.

washing their household gods; and the Deccan Brahman father drops honey into the mouth of his newborn child. Among higher-class Hindus, especially among Brahmans, when a child is born honey is dropped into his mouth from a gold ring or spoon.[1] This custom is one which was usual in early times, as we noted before.

These beliefs and customs are held by many of the civilized peoples of India, but in certain districts very primitive tribes are still found. Among these are the Veddas of Ceylon.

The Veddas live a wandering life for half the year, living in rock shelters and depending largely on honey for their food. This they get from bees' nests found in crevices of the rocks; each family is the recognized possessor of one or more rocky hills, but the whole community joins to collect honey from each hill, and the honey is always shared equally.

Honey-getting is a very important ceremony, for besides using much for food, the Vedda use it as an article of barter. Every year Mohammedan pedlars come to exchange goods for this much-prized honey. But it is a risky occupation, as the rock bees are very fierce, so spirits are invoked beforehand for protection.[2]

The *Maha Yakino* are the spirits of old Vedda women. One of them, Unapane Kiriamma, gives luck in honey-getting, and it is believed that somehow she causes bees to build good combs; in fact, all the *Maha Yakino* are connected with honey, because they are thought to haunt the rocky crests of the hills, and so offerings of honey are made to them.[3]

The spirits of dead Vedda, or *Yaka*, are also invoked to safeguard the men when they are collecting honey and to prevent them from falling. *Dola Yaka* is specially invoked for this purpose. The invocation can only be successful in the early afternoon when the bees are actively foraging. The following account of the ceremony is given by Dr. and Mrs. Seligmann.

A place is cleared for the dance and two arrows are placed in the centre. A betel leaf is put on the top of each and a small bead necklace looped over the leaf. These leaves are said to represent the large bundles

1 J. M. Campbell, "Notes on the Spirit Basis of Belief and Custom," in *The Indian Antiquary*, vol. 24 (1885), p. 259.

2 C. G. and B. Z. Seligmann, *The Veddas*, Cambridge, 1911, p. 42.

3 Ibid., p. 163.

of leaves which the Veddas use to smoke the bees from the comb, and the necklace the creeper by which the twigs would be tied together and by which it would be lowered over the cliff. Small leafy twigs are placed on the ground round the arrows, and on these a number of betel leaves and areca nuts are placed as an offering; the twigs are to keep the offering from touching the ground. The adult men take part in the dance, as only those who become possessed by *Dola Yaka* would obtain favour and help from him in gathering honey. The men walk round the arrows singing an invocation, bending their bodies towards the arrows as if listening for the hum of bees. Then they dance wildly round and cry, "We hear many bees, there will be plenty of honey!" They beat their bodies with their hands, driving away imaginary bees, even feigning to pick some off their bodies.[1]

Other spirits, the *Rahu Yaku*, are called upon to give good luck in collecting honey from *trees*, but it is only *Dola Yaka* who gives good fortune and protection when *rock* honey is sought.[2]

The Veddas also make ladders of cane by which they descend precipices to cut off the honeycombs adhering to their sides. They use smoke when doing this, but it is a dangerous task, only attempted by the most athletic; while doing it they sing special invocations to appease the spirit of the rock. A song is also chanted and a little honey sprinkled for the spirits before the combs are cut out from the rock.[3]

Other primitive tribes inhabiting the hills between Assam and Burmah are the Nagas. The Sama Nagas do not keep bees, but recognize private property in the wild rock bees, the first finder acquiring rights to the nest, which is taken yearly for the sake of the honey and also the grubs, which are eaten. If any person who has helped to take the nest dies during the year it is put down to the bees, and the nest is not disturbed again. Chastity must be observed the night before taking a bees' nest; if not the bees will sting the taker, and he would also be liable to be killed by his enemies. Before the bee-takers leave their houses early in the morning to secure the nest, nothing whatever must be taken out of the house. Should a domestic animal give birth to young, or a fowl hatch

[1] C. G. and B. Z. Seligmann, *The Veddas*, Cambridge, 1911, p. 252 f.

[2] Ibid., p. 254.

[3] Ibid., p. 327. Dr. Seligmann gives some of the songs used when collecting honey.

chickens within three days of going to take the bees, the owner cannot go. The Sama Nagas also taboo honey and the grubs of the bees to the first reaper (sometimes a man, sometimes a woman) during the duration of the harvest.[1]

In order to gain immunity from stings while gathering honey, the men of the Angami Nagas, from the day on which the expedition after bees' nests is arranged, must abstain from sexual intercourse. On the actual morning of taking the bees' nests, they are not allowed to speak. In absolute silence they go and make the ladders to take the combs. Under these circumstances they do not get stung, but any mistake leads to fearful stinging.[2] Among the Lhota Nagas a man who intends to take a bees' nest must also remain chaste the night before.

The Todas are a primitive people who live on the plateau of the Nilgiri Hills in Southern India. Some of their stories relate to bees. In one it is said that in a wood there stood a tree about eighty feet high. *Korateu*, one of their gods or spirits, ordered that honey bees should come out of this tree, and after a time there were about three hundred nests there, which made the tree bend with their weight. One day about twenty men came to collect honey, Todas, Kurumbas, and Irubas (these two last are wild, dwarfish tribes, feared by the Todas for their supposed magical powers). The Todas made a fire under the tree, while the Irudas and Kurumbas climbed it and collected the honey from the nests. When they had collected from all but three or four nests, the tree became so light that it sprang back and killed all the Irudas and Kurumbas, and the Todas returned triumphantly home![3]

Another of their stories brings in a spirit in the form of a bee. Great misfortune had been prophesied to a man called Teikuteidi unless he performed certain ceremonies for a whole year. On the very last day he forgot them and went to a place where he sat down under the shade of a *pulman* tree. This tree has a flower which blossoms only in the rainy season, and then the bees come to it. When Teikuteidi was sitting under this tree he was surprised to hear the humming of honey bees in it, for it was not the rainy season. The humming was caused by a *Kazun*, a spirit which brings

[1] J. H. Hutton, *The Sama Nagas*, 1921, p. 72.
[2] J. H. Hutton, *The Angami Nagas*, 1921, p. 236.
[3] W. H. R. Rivers, *The Todas*, 1906, p. 191.

death, and who had taken the form of a bee. The man looked up to see if there were any flowers to attract the bees, but he could see neither flowers nor bees. He then remembered the prophecy, got up, and went to attend a funeral with his companions. After the funeral he stopped and began to count his friends; he counted them, and like the wise man of Gotham, forgot to include himself, and said there were only nineteen instead of twenty. While looking for the twentieth man, a man passing shot him in the eye with an arrow and killed him.[1]

In Assam the spirits of men are said to become honey bees. An annual ceremony is held in honour of all who have died during the year, but the bodies of children dying in infancy are not represented at the ceremony, for their spirits are not supposed to become honey bees like those of other folk, but house flies, who live on the refuse of other spirits' plates in *Kazai-ram*, the abode of the dead.[2] Here we get the belief in *bee-souls*, which we have found in so many parts. This belief is also found in Timor, one of the East Indian islands, where it is said that the spirits of princes who fall in battle and those of warriors become bees;[3] and we find it, too, in Hindu ritual.

In his article on "The Spirit Basis of Belief," from which we quoted above, Mr. J. M. Campbell states that in India, at the ritual for setting up a god, Rama or any other god, in order that the deity may come and reside in it, the image is bathed, and butter and sesamum, both holy things, are scattered on the sacred fire. After making various offerings before the image, the officiant takes a small golden stick and *dips it in honey*, a mystic substance, being produced by *bees*, which are the *vehicles of the souls of the departed*, and applies it to the eyes of the image.[4]

Among the Andaman Islanders we find several beliefs about bees. Magical properties are attributed to beeswax, especially to black beeswax. It is used in medicine. In a case of pleurisy black wax was heated until it was soft and then smeared on to the

---

[1] W. H. R. Rivers, *The Todas*, 1906, p. 198.

[2] J. Shakespeare, in *Folklore*, vol. 23 (1912), p. 466.

[3] A. Bastian, *Indonesien, Timor und umliegende Inseln*, Berlin, 1885, p. 4.

[4] In *Indian Antiquary*, vol. 24, p. 363. For "external souls" in bee form, see Frazer, *Golden Bough*, XI, p. 101, and *Indian Antiquary*, 1885, p. 250.

patient's chest. It is believed to keep away the spirits of the forest.[1]

Honey is abundant during the hot season, which is from February to May, and the islanders melt all the wax to purify it and make it suitable for the many ways in which they employ it. During the rainy season scarcely any honey is to be found, and then only of an inferior variety. The Andaman Islanders believe that the burning or melting of wax arouses the anger of *Biliku*, a sort of goddess or storm spirit; the smell, they say, is especially obnoxious to her, and therefore causes her to make storms. Owing to this belief, it is a common practice to burn wax secretly when a person, against whom ill-will is borne, is engaged in fishing or hunting, the object being to make *Biliku* angry and so cause her to spoil the man's sport. If a storm suddenly arises the people say that someone must be burning wax. Stormy weather and the anger of *Biliku* are to the islanders the same thing, so that when they say that the anger of Biliku follows the melting of beeswax it is simply a statement of a natural fact.[2]

A very important ceremony among the Andaman Islanders is the *honey-eating*. The initiate sits cross-legged and honey is rubbed over his or her shoulder, and he or she is fed with it. When the honey fast is to be broken a quantity of honeycombs, according to the number of assembled people, are procured on the appointed day. The novice being placed in the midst of the group, the chief or another elder goes to him with a large honeycomb wrapped in leaves; after helping the novice to a large mouthful, which he does by means of a bamboo or iron knife, he presents the remainder to him and leaves him to devour it *in silence*. It is also an essential part of the ceremony that he should not use his fingers to break off pieces, but must eat it by holding the comb up to his mouth and attacking it with his teeth and lips. After eating what he can, he wraps up what is left in leaves to be eaten later. The chief then takes another comb and anoints the youth by squeezing it over his head, rubbing it well into his body. Then a bath follows to wash off the honey, which would otherwise attract ants. Beyond the observance of silence, and abstention from pigs' kidney fat, the youth may eat, drink, or sleep as he pleases. The only differ-

[1] A. R. Brown, *The Andaman Islanders*, 1922, p. 183.
[2] Ibid., pp. 152-3 and 357.

ence in the ceremony for a woman is that it cannot take place until after her first child is born; women are also required to abstain from honey during each succeeding pregnancy.[1]

In Borneo in many up-country villages the natives practise a primitive beekeeping. Hives are made of a section of a hollow tree-trunk, stopped top and bottom, with a hole bored at the side. These hives are fixed to the wall of the house, or sometimes in the house itself, but apparently the natives do not understand how to hive swarms; they hang the hives up and expect the bees to take possession of them.[2]

One of the tribes, the Dusuns, believe much in omens, good and bad, but pay more attention to the latter; and a flying swarm of bees is considered a bad omen,[3] which seems strange.

Some of the most primitive peoples are the aborigines of Australia, and honey is in great request among them. The native bee of Australia is stingless; our *Apis mellifica* was not introduced there until the nineteenth century. The honey they use is that of wild bees, which is collected by the men. N. W. Thomas gives an account of a game in which the children imitate their elders. He writes:

They play a game in which the girls squat on the ground, and place their hands, fingers downwards, one above the other, each bent at the knuckles so that a tree is represented by a pyramid of hands. Then each hand is knocked off from the top downwards, this is felling the tree. Before the last hand is knocked off, each space between the fingers is felt to see if any honey has dropped down into it. Then the arm of one of the girls is taken to represent the limb in which the honey is and they ask each other for a tomahawk. One of the players makes a chop at the elbow of the girl who represents the tree, and when the honey is secured, it is put into a trough represented by the cupped hands, there it is mixed with water. The reason why the arm is cut off at the elbow and not at the shoulder is curious; the upper part of the tree which contains the honey is *forbidden to the women*, and they have to content themselves with the lower part where the dirt and the droppings are.[4]

On the Bloomfield river if someone has sore eyes the natives say this is because he has cut down the upper branches of a certain

[1] A. R. Brown, *The Andaman Islanders*, 1922, pp. 104–6.

[2] Ivor H. N. Evans, *Among Primitive People in Borneo*, 1922, p. 99.

[3] Ibid., p. 165. Mr. Evans, on p. 179, relates a legend of how the Dusun learnt to use beeswax. [4] *The Natives of Australia*, 1906, p. 134.

tree sacred to *Baima* (or *Byamee*), the All-Father, in which a special kind of honey is found.[1] In order to get the honey from these trees the natives chop out the nest and kill the bees. The waxy stick which they have used to get the honey out they take home and throw into the fire; then they say all the dead bees go to a paradise in the skies, whence next season they will send the *Yarragerh Mayrah*, the spring wind, to blow the flowers open and then they will come down to earth again.[2]

In many parts of Australia the early European settlers found an intoxicating drink used by the natives, but only one traveller mentions that, in New South Wales, it was made of honey.

In Australia, as in India and Africa, bees and honey are tribe totems. In Northern Australia honey is the totem of the Mara tribes. In the banks of Barramunda Creek there is a big, heavy stone, which is believed to represent a honeycomb, carried about by the ancestor of the honey totem and left by him on the spot where he finally went down into the ground. The men who form that half of the tribe to which the honey totem belongs can increase the supply of bees, and therefore of honey, by scraping the big stone and blowing the powder in all directions, for this is supposed to turn into bees.[3] Honey is also the totem of the Kamilarvi in New South Wales,[4] and of one of the Manda tribes in India.[5]

Sir James Frazer notes that in India the *bee* is the totem of the Bhramada clan,[6] and of one of the Juang clans;[7] in Africa of one of the Suk clans,[8] and the bee and frog are the totems of a Nandi tribe. Men of this clan seem able to control bees. Mr. Hollis in his account of the Nandi, relates that he and his carriers had once been put to flight by bees, leaving their baggage behind them. A Nandi volunteered to quieten them, as he said he was of the bee totem and the bees were his. He said that Mr. Hollis was to blame for the attack as his men had lit a fire under the tree where the honey barrel was. (The Nandi place these barrels in trees for bees.) The man was practically naked, but started off to where the baggage was, whistling loudly all the time. The bees swarmed on him, but

[1] Geza Roheim, *Australian Totemism*, London, 1925, p. 65.

[2] K. Langloh Parker, *The Euahlayi Tribes*, 1905, p. 114.

[3] J. G. Frazer, *Totemism and Exogamy*, 1910, vol. i, p. 228.

[4] Ibid., p. 24.   [5] Ibid., vol. ii, p. 292.

[6] Ibid., p. 242.   [7] Ibid., p. 315.   [8] Ibid., p. 428.

he took no notice of them, but still whistling proceeded to the tree where their hive was. In a few minutes he was back and they were able to go and fetch the baggage.[1]

In Northern Rhodesia the bee is the totem of the Ba-Kaonda, who make a honey-beer;[2] in some of the other tribes certain family totems go in pairs. The Benang'onyi (birds) are paired with the Balemba (bees). The "birds" tease the "bees" by saying that one of their tribe (the honey-guide bird) devours bees and honey. This is considered a great joke.[3]

In Africa we find several customs relating to bees and honey, and beekeeping is practised by many peoples. Wild bees' nests are regularly emptied without being destroyed, and from this a primitive beekeeping is developed. In the Upper Nile district long plaited cylindrical hives are placed in trees, and in West Africa Livingstone noted that beekeeping was carried on in the same way as in the Nile district, from Lunda to Angola. The hives there were made of wooden cylinders of bark about five feet long; this bark preserved its original shape, and was joined where it had been cut with wooden needles. The hives were placed horizontally in high trees and a charm tied to the stem of the tree, as a protection against thieves.[4]

Mr. C. W. Hobley, writing of the Bantu tribes, notes that:

The A-Kamba (in Kenya Colony) are great beekeepers. When the Europeans first visited the country they found the industry fully established; as at the present day logs of wood were hollowed out and hung in trees for bees to hive in. They periodically collected the honey, brewed mead, and then threw away the combs. The Government officials have since then taught them to boil down the wax into cakes, which can be sold, and a large quantity is exported annually.

In Kikui when a man makes his first beehive, he does not hang it on a tree himself, but gets his uncle to do so; he believes that if he omitted to do this, the bees would not settle in it. The owner of the hive cannot cohabit with his wife until he sees that a swarm of bees has settled in the hive and is building there. Two nights after he is satisfied that this

---

[1] A. C. Hollis, *The Nandi*, 1909, p. 7.

[2] F. H. Melland, *In Witch-bound Africa*, 1923, p. 123.

[3] Ibid., p. 252. Many of the clans of Scotland are connected with animals, such as cats, dogs, mice, frogs, and the Mackenzies are the "Bees." It would be interesting to know if these names are a relic of totemism in the British Isles.

[4] Ratzel, *Völkerkunde*, vol. i, pp. 489 and 587.

is the case, he may resume marital relations. If on the first visit of inspection he finds the hive occupied, he brews beer and pours some on the ground as a libation to the *aiimu*, or ancestral spirits.

In a season when there is a dearth of honey the owners of the hives go to the woods in which they have put their hives and sacrifice a goat; the meat is eaten and the blood, mixed with beer, is poured on the ground as a propitiatory libation to the *aiimu* to secure a good honey crop. Among the Ulu A-Kamba the ceremonial varies and is apparently more elaborate.

When a man has hollowed out the log of wood which forms the beehive, he takes a shaving or chip of the wood, which is called *ikavu*, and gives it to his mother, who cooks beans, pigeon, peas and maize in a pot, and then places the chip, the *ikavu*, in the fire under the pot to assist in cooking the food. If he has lost his mother, the *ikavu* is given to his wife, who cooks the ceremonial meal. When the food is boiled, the villagers are summoned to eat it. The beehive is then hung on a tree, and when it is full the owner collects the honey and brings it to his village. Before the honey can be mixed with water to make beer or mead, the owner of the hive must present his mother with some of the honey.

When the first brew of the meal is ready, the father of the owner of the hive buys it for a goat, which may not be killed. On the second night after the purchase, the parents of the owner of the hive must cohabit.

They believe that the consumption of the beer in the succeeding ceremony ensures that the hive will always yield a good supply of honey, and that there will always be plenty of people to buy succeeding brews of mead made from the honey. The whole proceeding may therefore be considered as a magical fertility ceremony.

Among the Dorobo hunting tribes of the Kikuyu escarpment when a man makes a new beehive, beer is made and the old men and women drink it before it is hung in a tree. Then they ceremonially spit[1] on the hive and next morning place it on a tree; the inside of a hive is also smeared with beeswax to attract the bees.

The first crop of honey out of a new hive is only eaten by the children of the village or perhaps by very old women. The reason of this is said to be that if a young woman were to eat of it and then misconduct herself with a man, the honey crop would be spoilt, the bees would not enter any of the hives hung up that day.[2]

We have quoted this account fully as so many customs and superstitions are contained in it. These tribes always mark their

---

[1] Spitting is to avert evil and bring good luck. A Nandi spits when he takes a beehive. See Hollis, *The Nandi*, p. 79.

[2] C. W. Hobley, *Bantu Beliefs and Magic*, 1922, pp. 251-3.

hives with the clan's and the owner's marks, and also the trees used for the manufacture of the hives while they are still standing. A sketch of these marks is given in Fig. 35. The object of putting the mark of the clan as well as that of the owner seems to be a warning that if the hive is stolen the thief will have to reckon with the whole clan.[1] The Kikuyu and Kamba have also a kind of pictographic writing, which includes signs for bees, honey, and a beehive-maker (Fig. 35 (a, b, c)).[2]

In Uganda bees are kept by the Bakunta tribe. The hives are

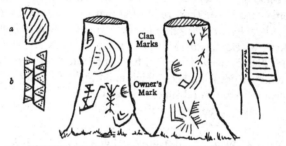

FIG. 35.—KIKUYU BEEHIVE MARKS ON TREES. PICTOGRAPHS
(a) Bees, a Swarm Settling on a Tree   (b) Honey   (c) A Beehive Maker
(C. W. Hobley: *Further Researches into Kikuyu and Kamba Beliefs*)

generally hollowed-out logs, but sometimes are cylinders of plaited papyrus about four feet long and twelve inches in diameter. Besides honey, they eat bee grubs and consider them a great delicacy. When a man is going to take honey, he must keep apart from his wife for a night. The next day he smokes the bees, driving them to one end of the long hive before taking the honey.[3]

Honey is also demanded as tribute by some of the tribes in Uganda. Mr. John Roscoe writes that in the district where he lived every year the chief had to bring two or three hundred large pots of honey, each holding some two gallons, to the king.[4]

There are many honey taboos among the Thonga in South

[1] C. W. Hobley, *Bantu Beliefs and Magic*, 1922, p. 254.

[2] Hobley, "Further Researches into Kikuyu and Kamba Beliefs," in *Journal of Anthropological Institute*, vol. 41, p. 412.

[3] J. Roscoe, *The Bagesu and other Tribes of the Uganda Protectorate*, 1924, p. 171.   [4] Ibid., p. 186.

Africa. During betrothal the suitor must not eat honey during his first visit to his future father-in-law, because honey slips away like a fish, and the girl he wishes to marry might slip through his hands.[1] When the man is married, he must not eat honey with his wife for a year, till she has had a child. The bride is allowed to eat honey at her father's house, but must not eat it in her new home or with her husband. The husband may eat it in the bush, but he must wash his hands before coming back, lest his wife should notice it; she would run home if she did. The reason is honey is too sweet and your wife is too sweet too—is it not your honeymoon or honey-year? Another reason is that when bees have eaten honey, they fly away from the hive, and the wife might do so too. After a year this misfortune is not to be feared.[2]

The Thonga have a magical horn into which honey is poured. This honey is got from bees which build their nests in the ground. The people have several superstitions about this honey. It may be eaten by anyone, but only certain families can see the nest and dig for it; to the others it is invisible. The horn into which some of this honey mixed with a drug is put is used for divination. It has a hole in it, and when war is imminent the stuff ferments and comes through the hole, and the people say, "It knows all about war," so they prepare themselves for it.[3]

In many parts of Africa stories are told of the honey-bird, which leads people by cries to hollow trees where the bees have collected honey. Amongst the Thonga the man may eat all the honey and give the bird all the wax, and if he wants to know where more honey is to be found he must burn the wax and the bird will lead him to another tree.[4] Among the Lango, a Nilotic tribe, the honey-bird flies singing before the hunters and directs them to the honey. After satisfying themselves some honey must be left for the bird, otherwise on the next occasion he will lead them to a lion's den out of revenge![5] The Lango also say that if you eat honey on the way to a hunt you will kill no game; and among one of their tribes, the Jo-Atekit, women may not eat honey.[6]

[1] Henri H. Junod, *Life of a South African Tribe*, London, 1912, vol. ii, p. 107.

[2] Ibid., vol. i, p. 239. It was the custom among the old Teutons to drink mead for thirty days after every wedding; hence arose the expression "honeymoon."　　　　[3] Ibid., p. 363.　　　　[4] Ibid., vol. ii, p. 319.

[5] J. H. Driburg, *The Lango*, 1923, p. 267.　　　　[6] Ibid., p. 194.

In Northern Rhodesia, among the Ba-Kaonda, the honey-guide bird is called Mayimba, and the following story is told:

Mayimba was sent by Lesa (God) to the first man and woman with three packets and told not to open them, but, like Pandora, he could not resist his curiosity and opened the boxes. In the first two he found seeds of various seed crops, but in the third death, sickness, fierce carnivores, and snakes. Lesa reproved him and he flew to the forest and dwelt there alone. But when hunger overtook him, he would go to the man and woman and call them to some honey which he had found, they would take the honey and leave a little on the ground for him.[1]

Another folk-tale, told by the Ila-speaking peoples of Northern Rhodesia, tells how "Honey-guide" came to have authority over honey, and another, which is given here, is called "Why Honey-guide betrays the Bees to people."

Honey-guide went to look for a wife in Bee-town. On his arrival there he said, "I want a wife." The Bees gave him a wife, but after a time they took her away from him. When they took her away, Honey-guide said, "Since you refuse me my wife, I shall simply go and tell tales about you to the people who pass along the road." Since he said that, to this day when a person passes he shows him the bees.[2]

This bird, *Cuculus indicator*, was mentioned by Livingstone in 1855. He said he often saw the bird, and inquired if it were true that it was sometimes a deceiver, and led you to wild beasts. Only one of one hundred and fourteen men who were with him could say he had been led to an elephant instead of a hive, and Livingstone came to the conclusion that in the majority of cases it led to honey.[3]

Other travellers say it is not to be depended upon. Of West Africa Major Tremearne writes that the honey-bird will lead you to hives of wild bees, but that according to some it is a bad bird, for:

Even if you have given it its share of honey on each occasion you have found a hive, one day it will lead you to a lion or a snake or something else dangerous and you may lose your life. When it takes you to a hive, it waits for its share of honey (which you place on the ground), but when

[1] F. H. Melland, *In Witch-Bound Africa*, p. 158.

[2] E. W. Smith and A. Murray Dale, *The Ila-speaking Peoples of Northern Rhodesia*, 1920, p. 357.   [3] *Missionary Travels*, p. 479.

it betrays you, it simply laughs at you and flies off, leaving you to get out of the danger as best you can.[1]

The Bushmen perform a dance with a sort of rattle, the *goin-goin*, in order that the bees may become abundant. They chant the following:

The people beat the goin-goin in order that the bees may become abundant for the people, in order that the bees may go into other peoples' places, that the people may eat honey. Therefore the people beat the goin-goin when they dance that the peoples' bees may go into other peoples' places, so that the people may eat honey, that they may put away honey into bags. And the people carry honey. And the people carrying honey bring the honey home. For the women are dying of hunger at home. Therefore the men take honey to the people at home; that the women may go to eat, for they feel that the women have been hungry at home, while they wish that the women may make them a drum, so that they may dance when the women are satisfied with food. For they do not frolic when they are hungry.[2]

Honey-wine or honey-beer is made in many parts of Africa. Among the Masai, persons brewing honey-wine must observe continence. A man and woman are chosen to brew it, and it is considered essential that they should both be chaste for two days before they begin to brew and during all the six days that the brewing lasts. If they break this rule, the Masai believe that not only would the brew be undrinkable, but the bees would also fly away.[3]

Among the Masai and the Akikuyu except at certain festivals the honey-wine is reserved for the elders. At the Masai circumcision ceremonies the honey-beer, which forms an important part of the feast, may be drunk only by the elders.[4]

There are many superstitions about bees and honey in Morocco. The inhabitants are firm believers in a mysterious wonder-working force, which they look upon as a blessing from God, and which they term *baraka*, a word meaning blessing or holiness. They believe that there is much *baraka* in the bee; therefore it is very

[1] A. J. N. Tremearne, *The Ban of the Bori*, 1914, p. 91.
[2] W. H. Bleek and L. C. Lloyd, *Bushman Folklore*, 1911, p. 353.
[3] Sir J. Frazer, *Totemism and Exogamy*, vol. ii, p. 411.
[4] S. Bagg, in *Journ. Anthrop. Inst.*, vol. 34, p. 127. For other examples, see *Hastings' Encyclopedia of Religion and Ethics*, under "Honey."

clever and knows everything. It predicts the weather by different ways of humming, and one tribe calls it a saint, for it is so small and yet produces so much sweetness. You must never kill a bee, even if it stings you, yet it will die in consequence. A story is told that the bee once said to the Prophet, "The people eat the food of my children; pray to God that if I sting anyone he may let me die." It said this by mistake; it meant "Let him die," but its first wish was fulfilled.[1]

As there is so much *baraka* in the bee, so there is also much in honey; indeed honey may be so full of *baraka* that it may increase of itself! In spite of its *baraka*, or rather in consequence of it, honey is looked upon as a somewhat dangerous article. If anyone enters another person's house or tent carrying honey, he must, before he takes it out again, give some of it to the people or smear a little on the door-post or tent-pole, lest some evil befall the household.

If you dream of bees you should offer food to the scribes of the mosque, as bees represent the Koran.[2] Another belief is that if you dream of bees entering your mouth and flying out again you will become a good singer; this dream is said to be a particularly trustworthy one.[3] It reminds us of the old belief that honey or bees bestowed the gift of song.

Among several of the tribes ceremonies are performed at midsummer in order to increase the supply of honey. In places where there are bees, the people will burn dry cowdung, the smoke of which, they say, will make the honey plentiful and prevent the bees from being killed by thunder. This custom is found in many Moroccan tribes. Another ceremony is to take earth from a place where three roads meet and throw it over the bees; this keeps them in good condition! Among another tribe a honeycomb is cut into two pieces on midsummer day and eaten if there is honey in it. Dr. Westermarck, who relates these ceremonies, states that he was told that if this ceremony were not performed the bees would have no honey.[4]

Thus all over Africa we find beekeeping of some kind carried

---

[1] Dr. E. Westermarck, *Ritual and Belief in Morocco*, 1926, vol. i, p. 104. In some districts they say that to kill a bee is as bad as to kill a man.

[2] Ibid., vol. ii, p. 47.   [3] Ibid., vol. ii, p. 49.

[4] In *Folklore*, vol. xvi, 1905, pp. 28–37.

on, and many ceremonies and superstitions concerning bees and honey still existing. It is remarkable that though there is not much honey obtained in Central Congoland and the densely forested regions, still it must exist in some degree and be appreciated everywhere, as there is a word for honey in every negro language.[1]

We have now surveyed the story of our Sacred Bees from the earliest times; the field is so wide that necessarily much has been omitted, but perhaps we can now realize in some slight degree how, among the animals which man has specially reverenced in past ages, the bee stands out pre-eminently. Scientists of to-day still spend much time in investigating her methods of working and of making herself intelligible to her fellow-workers; for it seems certain that in some marvellous way the bees do communicate with each other.

The unity of the hive, the harmonious life under one leader, the wonderfully sweet produce of the industrious community, led the Ancients to form an exalted idea of the bees' sacred origin, and thus Vergil, in his great *Epic of the Bees*, sang that some

Have declared that on bees is bestowed some share in the soul divine,
Some draughts of the airs of heaven, for that God moves everywhere
Through earth, the expanses of sea and the limitless depth of the air.

Yea, and to Him they return, for not unto Him do they die
At dissolution! there is no death; but they live and they fly
To the ranks of starland and enter the high-reared hall of the sky![2]

[1] Sir Harry Johnston, *George Grenfell and the Congo*, 1908, vol. ii, p. 612.
[2] *Geor.*, IV. 220 et seq. A. S. Way's translation.

NOTE.—"Telling the bees" in East Africa.

Since going to press the author has learnt that among the Akamba when the owner of beehives dies the nearest relatives go to the hives, throw small stones at them and say, "Wake up, you bees! Your owner is certainly dead, but because of that you must not cease to work and gather honey." (*Archives d'Études Orientales*, "The Akamba," by G. Lindblom, 1920, p. 499.)

INDEX

A CATALOG OF SELECTED
DOVER BOOKS
IN ALL FIELDS OF INTEREST

A CATALOG OF SELECTED DOVER BOOKS IN ALL FIELDS OF INTEREST

100 BEST-LOVED POEMS, Edited by Philip Smith. "The Passionate Shepherd to His Love," "Shall I compare thee to a summer's day?" "Death, be not proud," "The Raven," "The Road Not Taken," plus works by Blake, Wordsworth, Byron, Shelley, Keats, many others. 96pp. 5$\frac{3}{16}$ x 8$\frac{1}{4}$. 0-486-28553-7

100 SMALL HOUSES OF THE THIRTIES, Brown-Blodgett Company. Exterior photographs and floor plans for 100 charming structures. Illustrations of models accompanied by descriptions of interiors, color schemes, closet space, and other amenities. 200 illustrations. 112pp. 8$\frac{3}{8}$ x 11. 0-486-44131-8

1000 TURN-OF-THE-CENTURY HOUSES: With Illustrations and Floor Plans, Herbert C. Chivers. Reproduced from a rare edition, this showcase of homes ranges from cottages and bungalows to sprawling mansions. Each house is meticulously illustrated and accompanied by complete floor plans. 256pp. 9$\frac{3}{8}$ x 12$\frac{1}{4}$. 0-486-45596-3

101 GREAT AMERICAN POEMS, Edited by The American Poetry & Literacy Project. Rich treasury of verse from the 19th and 20th centuries includes works by Edgar Allan Poe, Robert Frost, Walt Whitman, Langston Hughes, Emily Dickinson, T. S. Eliot, other notables. 96pp. 5$\frac{3}{16}$ x 8$\frac{1}{4}$. 0-486-40158-8

101 GREAT SAMURAI PRINTS, Utagawa Kuniyoshi. Kuniyoshi was a master of the warrior woodblock print — and these 18th-century illustrations represent the pinnacle of his craft. Full-color portraits of renowned Japanese samurais pulse with movement, passion, and remarkably fine detail. 112pp. 8$\frac{3}{8}$ x 11. 0-486-46523-3

ABC OF BALLET, Janet Grosser. Clearly worded, abundantly illustrated little guide defines basic ballet-related terms: arabesque, battement, pas de chat, relevé, sissonne, many others. Pronunciation guide included. Excellent primer. 48pp. 4$\frac{3}{16}$ x 5$\frac{3}{4}$. 0-486-40871-X

ACCESSORIES OF DRESS: An Illustrated Encyclopedia, Katherine Lester and Bess Viola Oerke. Illustrations of hats, veils, wigs, cravats, shawls, shoes, gloves, and other accessories enhance an engaging commentary that reveals the humor and charm of the many-sided story of accessorized apparel. 644 figures and 59 plates. 608pp. 6 $\frac{1}{8}$ x 9$\frac{1}{4}$. 0-486-43378-1

ADVENTURES OF HUCKLEBERRY FINN, Mark Twain. Join Huck and Jim as their boyhood adventures along the Mississippi River lead them into a world of excitement, danger, and self-discovery. Humorous narrative, lyrical descriptions of the Mississippi valley, and memorable characters. 224pp. 5$\frac{3}{16}$ x 8$\frac{1}{4}$. 0-486-28061-6

ALICE STARMORE'S BOOK OF FAIR ISLE KNITTING, Alice Starmore. A noted designer from the region of Scotland's Fair Isle explores the history and techniques of this distinctive, stranded-color knitting style and provides copious illustrated instructions for 14 original knitwear designs. 208pp. 8$\frac{3}{8}$ x 10$\frac{7}{8}$. 0-486-47218-3

Browse over 9,000 books at www.doverpublications.com

ALICE'S ADVENTURES IN WONDERLAND, Lewis Carroll. Beloved classic about a little girl lost in a topsy-turvy land and her encounters with the White Rabbit, March Hare, Mad Hatter, Cheshire Cat, and other delightfully improbable characters. 42 illustrations by Sir John Tenniel. 96pp. 5³⁄₁₆ x 8¼. 0-486-27543-4

AMERICA'S LIGHTHOUSES: An Illustrated History, Francis Ross Holland. Profusely illustrated fact-filled survey of American lighthouses since 1716. Over 200 stations — East, Gulf, and West coasts, Great Lakes, Hawaii, Alaska, Puerto Rico, the Virgin Islands, and the Mississippi and St. Lawrence Rivers. 240pp. 8 x 10¾. 0-486-25576-X

AN ENCYCLOPEDIA OF THE VIOLIN, Alberto Bachmann. Translated by Frederick H. Martens. Introduction by Eugene Ysaye. First published in 1925, this renowned reference remains unsurpassed as a source of essential information, from construction and evolution to repertoire and technique. Includes a glossary and 73 illustrations. 496pp. 6⅛ x 9¼. 0-486-46618-3

ANIMALS: 1,419 Copyright-Free Illustrations of Mammals, Birds, Fish, Insects, etc., Selected by Jim Harter. Selected for its visual impact and ease of use, this outstanding collection of wood engravings presents over 1,000 species of animals in extremely lifelike poses. Includes mammals, birds, reptiles, amphibians, fish, insects, and other invertebrates. 284pp. 9 x 12. 0-486-23766-4

THE ANNALS, Tacitus. Translated by Alfred John Church and William Jackson Brodribb. This vital chronicle of Imperial Rome, written by the era's great historian, spans A.D. 14-68 and paints incisive psychological portraits of major figures, from Tiberius to Nero. 416pp. 5³⁄₁₆ x 8¼. 0-486-45236-0

ANTIGONE, Sophocles. Filled with passionate speeches and sensitive probing of moral and philosophical issues, this powerful and often-performed Greek drama reveals the grim fate that befalls the children of Oedipus. Footnotes. 64pp. 5³⁄₁₆ x 8 ¼. 0-486-27804-2

ART DECO DECORATIVE PATTERNS IN FULL COLOR, Christian Stoll. Reprinted from a rare 1910 portfolio, 160 sensuous and exotic images depict a breathtaking array of florals, geometrics, and abstracts — all elegant in their stark simplicity. 64pp. 8⅜ x 11. 0-486-44862-2

THE ARTHUR RACKHAM TREASURY: 86 Full-Color Illustrations, Arthur Rackham. Selected and Edited by Jeff A. Menges. A stunning treasury of 86 full-page plates span the famed English artist's career, from *Rip Van Winkle* (1905) to masterworks such as *Undine, A Midsummer Night's Dream,* and *Wind in the Willows* (1939). 96pp. 8⅜ x 11. 0-486-44685-9

THE AUTHENTIC GILBERT & SULLIVAN SONGBOOK, W. S. Gilbert and A. S. Sullivan. The most comprehensive collection available, this songbook includes selections from every one of Gilbert and Sullivan's light operas. Ninety-two numbers are presented uncut and unedited, and in their original keys. 410pp. 9 x 12. 0-486-23482-7

THE AWAKENING, Kate Chopin. First published in 1899, this controversial novel of a New Orleans wife's search for love outside a stifling marriage shocked readers. Today, it remains a first-rate narrative with superb characterization. New introductory Note. 128pp. 5³⁄₁₆ x 8¼. 0-486-27786-0

BASIC DRAWING, Louis Priscilla. Beginning with perspective, this commonsense manual progresses to the figure in movement, light and shade, anatomy, drapery, composition, trees and landscape, and outdoor sketching. Black-and-white illustrations throughout. 128pp. 8⅜ x 11. 0-486-45815-6

Browse over 9,000 books at www.doverpublications.com

THE BATTLES THAT CHANGED HISTORY, Fletcher Pratt. Historian profiles 16 crucial conflicts, ancient to modern, that changed the course of Western civilization. Gripping accounts of battles led by Alexander the Great, Joan of Arc, Ulysses S. Grant, other commanders. 27 maps. 352pp. 5⅜ x 8½. 0-486-41129-X

BEETHOVEN'S LETTERS, Ludwig van Beethoven. Edited by Dr. A. C. Kalischer. Features 457 letters to fellow musicians, friends, greats, patrons, and literary men. Reveals musical thoughts, quirks of personality, insights, and daily events. Includes 15 plates. 410pp. 5⅜ x 8½. 0-486-22769-3

BERNICE BOBS HER HAIR AND OTHER STORIES, F. Scott Fitzgerald. This brilliant anthology includes 6 of Fitzgerald's most popular stories: "The Diamond as Big as the Ritz," the title tale, "The Offshore Pirate," "The Ice Palace," "The Jelly Bean," and "May Day." 176pp. 5⅜ x 8½. 0-486-47049-0

BESLER'S BOOK OF FLOWERS AND PLANTS: 73 Full-Color Plates from Hortus Eystettensis, 1613, Basilius Besler. Here is a selection of magnificent plates from the *Hortus Eystettensis*, which vividly illustrated and identified the plants, flowers, and trees that thrived in the legendary German garden at Eichstätt. 80pp. 8⅜ x 11. 0-486-46005-3

THE BOOK OF KELLS, Edited by Blanche Cirker. Painstakingly reproduced from a rare facsimile edition, this volume contains full-page decorations, portraits, illustrations, plus a sampling of textual leaves with exquisite calligraphy and ornamentation. 32 full-color illustrations. 32pp. 9⅜ x 12¼. 0-486-24345-1

THE BOOK OF THE CROSSBOW: With an Additional Section on Catapults and Other Siege Engines, Ralph Payne-Gallwey. Fascinating study traces history and use of crossbow as military and sporting weapon, from Middle Ages to modern times. Also covers related weapons: balistas, catapults, Turkish bows, more. Over 240 illustrations. 400pp. 7¼ x 10⅛. 0-486-28720-3

THE BUNGALOW BOOK: Floor Plans and Photos of 112 Houses, 1910, Henry L. Wilson. Here are 112 of the most popular and economic blueprints of the early 20th century — plus an illustration or photograph of each completed house. A wonderful time capsule that still offers a wealth of valuable insights. 160pp. 8⅜ x 11. 0-486-45104-6

THE CALL OF THE WILD, Jack London. A classic novel of adventure, drawn from London's own experiences as a Klondike adventurer, relating the story of a heroic dog caught in the brutal life of the Alaska Gold Rush. Note. 64pp. 5³⁄₁₆ x 8¼. 0-486-26472-6

CANDIDE, Voltaire. Edited by Francois-Marie Arouet. One of the world's great satires since its first publication in 1759. Witty, caustic skewering of romance, science, philosophy, religion, government — nearly all human ideals and institutions. 112pp. 5³⁄₁₆ x 8¼. 0-486-26689-3

CELEBRATED IN THEIR TIME: Photographic Portraits from the George Grantham Bain Collection, Edited by Amy Pastan. With an Introduction by Michael Carlebach. Remarkable portrait gallery features 112 rare images of Albert Einstein, Charlie Chaplin, the Wright Brothers, Henry Ford, and other luminaries from the worlds of politics, art, entertainment, and industry. 128pp. 8⅜ x 11. 0-486-46754-6

CHARIOTS FOR APOLLO: The NASA History of Manned Lunar Spacecraft to 1969, Courtney G. Brooks, James M. Grimwood, and Loyd S. Swenson, Jr. This illustrated history by a trio of experts is the definitive reference on the Apollo spacecraft and lunar modules. It traces the vehicles' design, development, and operation in space. More than 100 photographs and illustrations. 576pp. 6¾ x 9¼. 0-486-46756-2

CATALOG OF DOVER BOOKS

A CHRISTMAS CAROL, Charles Dickens. This engrossing tale relates Ebenezer Scrooge's ghostly journeys through Christmases past, present, and future and his ultimate transformation from a harsh and grasping old miser to a charitable and compassionate human being. 80pp. 5³⁄₁₆ x 8¼. 0-486-26865-9

COMMON SENSE, Thomas Paine. First published in January of 1776, this highly influential landmark document clearly and persuasively argued for American separation from Great Britain and paved the way for the Declaration of Independence. 64pp. 5³⁄₁₆ x 8¼. 0-486-29602-4

THE COMPLETE SHORT STORIES OF OSCAR WILDE, Oscar Wilde. Complete texts of "The Happy Prince and Other Tales," "A House of Pomegranates," "Lord Arthur Savile's Crime and Other Stories," "Poems in Prose," and "The Portrait of Mr. W. H." 208pp. 5³⁄₁₆ x 8¼. 0-486-45216-6

COMPLETE SONNETS, William Shakespeare. Over 150 exquisite poems deal with love, friendship, the tyranny of time, beauty's evanescence, death, and other themes in language of remarkable power, precision, and beauty. Glossary of archaic terms. 80pp. 5³⁄₁₆ x 8¼. 0-486-26686-9

THE COUNT OF MONTE CRISTO: Abridged Edition, Alexandre Dumas. Falsely accused of treason, Edmond Dantès is imprisoned in the bleak Chateau d'If. After a hair-raising escape, he launches an elaborate plot to extract a bitter revenge against those who betrayed him. 448pp. 5³⁄₁₆ x 8¼. 0-486-45643-9

CRAFTSMAN BUNGALOWS: Designs from the Pacific Northwest, Yoho & Merritt. This reprint of a rare catalog, showcasing the charming simplicity and cozy style of Craftsman bungalows, is filled with photos of completed homes, plus floor plans and estimated costs. An indispensable resource for architects, historians, and illustrators. 112pp. 10 x 7. 0-486-46875-5

CRAFTSMAN BUNGALOWS: 59 Homes from "The Craftsman," Edited by Gustav Stickley. Best and most attractive designs from Arts and Crafts Movement publication — 1903–1916 — includes sketches, photographs of homes, floor plans, descriptive text. 128pp. 8¼ x 11. 0-486-25829-7

CRIME AND PUNISHMENT, Fyodor Dostoyevsky. Translated by Constance Garnett. Supreme masterpiece tells the story of Raskolnikov, a student tormented by his own thoughts after he murders an old woman. Overwhelmed by guilt and terror, he confesses and goes to prison. 480pp. 5³⁄₁₆ x 8¼. 0-486-41587-2

THE DECLARATION OF INDEPENDENCE AND OTHER GREAT DOCUMENTS OF AMERICAN HISTORY: 1775-1865, Edited by John Grafton. Thirteen compelling and influential documents: Henry's "Give Me Liberty or Give Me Death," Declaration of Independence, The Constitution, Washington's First Inaugural Address, The Monroe Doctrine, The Emancipation Proclamation, Gettysburg Address, more. 64pp. 5³⁄₁₆ x 8¼. 0-486-41124-9

THE DESERT AND THE SOWN: Travels in Palestine and Syria, Gertrude Bell. "The female Lawrence of Arabia," Gertrude Bell wrote captivating, perceptive accounts of her travels in the Middle East. This intriguing narrative, accompanied by 160 photos, traces her 1905 sojourn in Lebanon, Syria, and Palestine. 368pp. 5⅜ x 8½. 0-486-46876-3

A DOLL'S HOUSE, Henrik Ibsen. Ibsen's best-known play displays his genius for realistic prose drama. An expression of women's rights, the play climaxes when the central character, Nora, rejects a smothering marriage and life in "a doll's house." 80pp. 5³⁄₁₆ x 8¼. 0-486-27062-9

DOOMED SHIPS: Great Ocean Liner Disasters, William H. Miller, Jr. Nearly 200 photographs, many from private collections, highlight tales of some of the vessels whose pleasure cruises ended in catastrophe: the *Morro Castle, Normandie, Andrea Doria, Europa,* and many others. 128pp. 8⅞ x 11¾. 0-486-45366-9

THE DORÉ BIBLE ILLUSTRATIONS, Gustave Doré. Detailed plates from the Bible: the Creation scenes, Adam and Eve, horrifying visions of the Flood, the battle sequences with their monumental crowds, depictions of the life of Jesus, 241 plates in all. 241pp. 9 x 12. 0-486-23004-X

DRAWING DRAPERY FROM HEAD TO TOE, Cliff Young. Expert guidance on how to draw shirts, pants, skirts, gloves, hats, and coats on the human figure, including folds in relation to the body, pull and crush, action folds, creases, more. Over 200 drawings. 48pp. 8¼ x 11. 0-486-45591-2

DUBLINERS, James Joyce. A fine and accessible introduction to the work of one of the 20th century's most influential writers, this collection features 15 tales, including a masterpiece of the short-story genre, "The Dead." 160pp. 5³⁄₁₆ x 8¼. 0-486-26870-5

EASY-TO-MAKE POP-UPS, Joan Irvine. Illustrated by Barbara Reid. Dozens of wonderful ideas for three-dimensional paper fun — from holiday greeting cards with moving parts to a pop-up menagerie. Easy-to-follow, illustrated instructions for more than 30 projects. 299 black-and-white illustrations. 96pp. 8⅜ x 11. 0-486-44622-0

EASY-TO-MAKE STORYBOOK DOLLS: A "Novel" Approach to Cloth Dollmaking, Sherralyn St. Clair. Favorite fictional characters come alive in this unique beginner's dollmaking guide. Includes patterns for Pollyanna, Dorothy from *The Wonderful Wizard of Oz,* Mary of *The Secret Garden,* plus easy-to-follow instructions, 263 black-and-white illustrations, and an 8-page color insert. 112pp. 8¼ x 11. 0-486-47360-0

EINSTEIN'S ESSAYS IN SCIENCE, Albert Einstein. Speeches and essays in accessible, everyday language profile influential physicists such as Niels Bohr and Isaac Newton. They also explore areas of physics to which the author made major contributions. 128pp. 5 x 8. 0-486-47011-3

EL DORADO: Further Adventures of the Scarlet Pimpernel, Baroness Orczy. A popular sequel to *The Scarlet Pimpernel,* this suspenseful story recounts the Pimpernel's attempts to rescue the Dauphin from imprisonment during the French Revolution. An irresistible blend of intrigue, period detail, and vibrant characterizations. 352pp. 5³⁄₁₆ x 8¼. 0-486-44026-5

ELEGANT SMALL HOMES OF THE TWENTIES: 99 Designs from a Competition, Chicago Tribune. Nearly 100 designs for five- and six-room houses feature New England and Southern colonials, Normandy cottages, stately Italianate dwellings, and other fascinating snapshots of American domestic architecture of the 1920s. 112pp. 9 x 12. 0-486-46910-7

THE ELEMENTS OF STYLE: The Original Edition, William Strunk, Jr. This is the book that generations of writers have relied upon for timeless advice on grammar, diction, syntax, and other essentials. In concise terms, it identifies the principal requirements of proper style and common errors. 64pp. 5⅜ x 8½. 0-486-44798-7

THE ELUSIVE PIMPERNEL, Baroness Orczy. Robespierre's revolutionaries find their wicked schemes thwarted by the heroic Pimpernel — Sir Percival Blakeney. In this thrilling sequel, Chauvelin devises a plot to eliminate the Pimpernel and his wife. 272pp. 5³⁄₁₆ x 8¼. 0-486-45464-9

AN ENCYCLOPEDIA OF BATTLES: Accounts of Over 1,560 Battles from 1479 B.C. to the Present, David Eggenberger. Essential details of every major battle in recorded history from the first battle of Megiddo in 1479 B.C. to Grenada in 1984. List of battle maps. 99 illustrations. 544pp. 6½ x 9¼. 0-486-24913-1

ENCYCLOPEDIA OF EMBROIDERY STITCHES, INCLUDING CREWEL, Marion Nichols. Precise explanations and instructions, clearly illustrated, on how to work chain, back, cross, knotted, woven stitches, and many more — 178 in all, including Cable Outline, Whipped Satin, and Eyelet Buttonhole. Over 1400 illustrations. 219pp. 8⅜ x 11¼. 0-486-22929-7

ENTER JEEVES: 15 Early Stories, P. G. Wodehouse. Splendid collection contains first 8 stories featuring Bertie Wooster, the deliciously dim aristocrat and Jeeves, his brainy, imperturbable manservant. Also, the complete Reggie Pepper (Bertie's prototype) series. 288pp. 5⅜ x 8½. 0-486-29717-9

ERIC SLOANE'S AMERICA: Paintings in Oil, Michael Wigley. With a Foreword by Mimi Sloane. Eric Sloane's evocative oils of America's landscape and material culture shimmer with immense historical and nostalgic appeal. This original hardcover collection gathers nearly a hundred of his finest paintings, with subjects ranging from New England to the American Southwest. 128pp. 10⅝ x 9. 0-486-46525-X

ETHAN FROME, Edith Wharton. Classic story of wasted lives, set against a bleak New England background. Superbly delineated characters in a hauntingly grim tale of thwarted love. Considered by many to be Wharton's masterpiece. 96pp. 5³⁄₁₆ x 8 ¼. 0-486-26690-7

THE EVERLASTING MAN, G. K. Chesterton. Chesterton's view of Christianity — as a blend of philosophy and mythology, satisfying intellect and spirit — applies to his brilliant book, which appeals to readers' heads as well as their hearts. 288pp. 5⅜ x 8½. 0-486-46036-3

THE FIELD AND FOREST HANDY BOOK, Daniel Beard. Written by a co-founder of the Boy Scouts, this appealing guide offers illustrated instructions for building kites, birdhouses, boats, igloos, and other fun projects, plus numerous helpful tips for campers. 448pp. 5³⁄₁₆ x 8¼. 0-486-46191-2

FINDING YOUR WAY WITHOUT MAP OR COMPASS, Harold Gatty. Useful, instructive manual shows would-be explorers, hikers, bikers, scouts, sailors, and survivalists how to find their way outdoors by observing animals, weather patterns, shifting sands, and other elements of nature. 288pp. 5⅜ x 8½. 0-486-40613-X

FIRST FRENCH READER: A Beginner's Dual-Language Book, Edited and Translated by Stanley Appelbaum. This anthology introduces 50 legendary writers — Voltaire, Balzac, Baudelaire, Proust, more — through passages from *The Red and the Black, Les Misérables, Madame Bovary,* and other classics. Original French text plus English translation on facing pages. 240pp. 5⅜ x 8½. 0-486-46178-5

FIRST GERMAN READER: A Beginner's Dual-Language Book, Edited by Harry Steinhauer. Specially chosen for their power to evoke German life and culture, these short, simple readings include poems, stories, essays, and anecdotes by Goethe, Hesse, Heine, Schiller, and others. 224pp. 5⅜ x 8½. 0-486-46179-3

FIRST SPANISH READER: A Beginner's Dual-Language Book, Angel Flores. Delightful stories, other material based on works of Don Juan Manuel, Luis Taboada, Ricardo Palma, other noted writers. Complete faithful English translations on facing pages. Exercises. 176pp. 5⅜ x 8½. 0-486-25810-6

Browse over 9,000 books at www.doverpublications.com

FIVE ACRES AND INDEPENDENCE, Maurice G. Kains. Great back-to-the-land classic explains basics of self-sufficient farming. The one book to get. 95 illustrations. 397pp. 5⅜ x 8½. 0-486-20974-1

FLAGG'S SMALL HOUSES: Their Economic Design and Construction, 1922, Ernest Flagg. Although most famous for his skyscrapers, Flagg was also a proponent of the well-designed single-family dwelling. His classic treatise features innovations that save space, materials, and cost. 526 illustrations. 160pp. 9⅜ x 12¼. 0-486-45197-6

FLATLAND: A Romance of Many Dimensions, Edwin A. Abbott. Classic of science (and mathematical) fiction — charmingly illustrated by the author — describes the adventures of A. Square, a resident of Flatland, in Spaceland (three dimensions), Lineland (one dimension), and Pointland (no dimensions). 96pp. 5$\frac{3}{16}$ x 8¼. 0-486-27263-X

FRANKENSTEIN, Mary Shelley. The story of Victor Frankenstein's monstrous creation and the havoc it caused has enthralled generations of readers and inspired countless writers of horror and suspense. With the author's own 1831 introduction. 176pp. 5$\frac{3}{16}$ x 8¼. 0-486-28211-2

THE GARGOYLE BOOK: 572 Examples from Gothic Architecture, Lester Burbank Bridaham. Dispelling the conventional wisdom that French Gothic architectural flourishes were born of despair or gloom, Bridaham reveals the whimsical nature of these creations and the ingenious artisans who made them. 572 illustrations. 224pp. 8⅜ x 11. 0-486-44754-5

THE GIFT OF THE MAGI AND OTHER SHORT STORIES, O. Henry. Sixteen captivating stories by one of America's most popular storytellers. Included are such classics as "The Gift of the Magi," "The Last Leaf," and "The Ransom of Red Chief." Publisher's Note. 96pp. 5$\frac{3}{16}$ x 8¼. 0-486-27061-0

THE GOETHE TREASURY: Selected Prose and Poetry, Johann Wolfgang von Goethe. Edited, Selected, and with an Introduction by Thomas Mann. In addition to his lyric poetry, Goethe wrote travel sketches, autobiographical studies, essays, letters, and proverbs in rhyme and prose. This collection presents outstanding examples from each genre. 368pp. 5⅜ x 8½. 0-486-44780-4

GREAT EXPECTATIONS, Charles Dickens. Orphaned Pip is apprenticed to the dirty work of the forge but dreams of becoming a gentleman — and one day finds himself in possession of "great expectations." Dickens' finest novel. 400pp. 5$\frac{3}{16}$ x 8¼. 0-486-41586-4

GREAT WRITERS ON THE ART OF FICTION: From Mark Twain to Joyce Carol Oates, Edited by James Daley. An indispensable source of advice and inspiration, this anthology features essays by Henry James, Kate Chopin, Willa Cather, Sinclair Lewis, Jack London, Raymond Chandler, Raymond Carver, Eudora Welty, and Kurt Vonnegut, Jr. 192pp. 5⅜ x 8½. 0-486-45128-3

HAMLET, William Shakespeare. The quintessential Shakespearean tragedy, whose highly charged confrontations and anguished soliloquies probe depths of human feeling rarely sounded in any art. Reprinted from an authoritative British edition complete with illuminating footnotes. 128pp. 5$\frac{3}{16}$ x 8¼. 0-486-27278-8

THE HAUNTED HOUSE, Charles Dickens. A Yuletide gathering in an eerie country retreat provides the backdrop for Dickens and his friends — including Elizabeth Gaskell and Wilkie Collins — who take turns spinning supernatural yarns. 144pp. 5⅜ x 8½. 0-486-46309-5

HEART OF DARKNESS, Joseph Conrad. Dark allegory of a journey up the Congo River and the narrator's encounter with the mysterious Mr. Kurtz. Masterly blend of adventure, character study, psychological penetration. For many, Conrad's finest, most enigmatic story. 80pp. 5³⁄₁₆ x 8¼. 0-486-26464-5

HENSON AT THE NORTH POLE, Matthew A. Henson. This thrilling memoir by the heroic African-American who was Peary's companion through two decades of Arctic exploration recounts a tale of danger, courage, and determination. "Fascinating and exciting." — *Commonweal.* 128pp. 5⅜ x 8½. 0-486-45472-X

HISTORIC COSTUMES AND HOW TO MAKE THEM, Mary Fernald and E. Shenton. Practical, informative guidebook shows how to create everything from short tunics worn by Saxon men in the fifth century to a lady's bustle dress of the late 1800s. 81 illustrations. 176pp. 5⅜ x 8½. 0-486-44906-8

THE HOUND OF THE BASKERVILLES, Arthur Conan Doyle. A deadly curse in the form of a legendary ferocious beast continues to claim its victims from the Baskerville family until Holmes and Watson intervene. Often called the best detective story ever written. 128pp. 5³⁄₁₆ x 8¼. 0-486-28214-7

THE HOUSE BEHIND THE CEDARS, Charles W. Chesnutt. Originally published in 1900, this groundbreaking novel by a distinguished African-American author recounts the drama of a brother and sister who "pass for white" during the dangerous days of Reconstruction. 208pp. 5⅜ x 8½. 0-486-46144-0

THE HUMAN FIGURE IN MOTION, Eadweard Muybridge. The 4,789 photographs in this definitive selection show the human figure — models almost all undraped — engaged in over 160 different types of action: running, climbing stairs, etc. 390pp. 7⅞ x 10⅝. 0-486-20204-6

THE IMPORTANCE OF BEING EARNEST, Oscar Wilde. Wilde's witty and buoyant comedy of manners, filled with some of literature's most famous epigrams, reprinted from an authoritative British edition. Considered Wilde's most perfect work. 64pp. 5³⁄₁₆ x 8¼. 0-486-26478-5

THE INFERNO, Dante Alighieri. Translated and with notes by Henry Wadsworth Longfellow. The first stop on Dante's famous journey from Hell to Purgatory to Paradise, this 14th-century allegorical poem blends vivid and shocking imagery with graceful lyricism. Translated by the beloved 19th-century poet, Henry Wadsworth Longfellow. 256pp. 5³⁄₁₆ x 8¼. 0-486-44288-8

JANE EYRE, Charlotte Brontë. Written in 1847, *Jane Eyre* tells the tale of an orphan girl's progress from the custody of cruel relatives to an oppressive boarding school and its culmination in a troubled career as a governess. 448pp. 5³⁄₁₆ x 8¼.
0-486-42449-9

JAPANESE WOODBLOCK FLOWER PRINTS, Tanigami Kônan. Extraordinary collection of Japanese woodblock prints by a well-known artist features 120 plates in brilliant color. Realistic images from a rare edition include daffodils, tulips, and other familiar and unusual flowers. 128pp. 11 x 8¼. 0-486-46442-3

JEWELRY MAKING AND DESIGN, Augustus F. Rose and Antonio Cirino. Professional secrets of jewelry making are revealed in a thorough, practical guide. Over 200 illustrations. 306pp. 5⅜ x 8½. 0-486-21750-7

JULIUS CAESAR, William Shakespeare. Great tragedy based on Plutarch's account of the lives of Brutus, Julius Caesar and Mark Antony. Evil plotting, ringing oratory, high tragedy with Shakespeare's incomparable insight, dramatic power. Explanatory footnotes. 96pp. 5³⁄₁₆ x 8¼. 0-486-26876-4

Browse over 9,000 books at www.doverpublications.com

THE JUNGLE, Upton Sinclair. 1906 bestseller shockingly reveals intolerable labor practices and working conditions in the Chicago stockyards as it tells the grim story of a Slavic family that emigrates to America full of optimism but soon faces despair. 320pp. 5³⁄₁₆ x 8¼. 0-486-41923-1

THE KINGDOM OF GOD IS WITHIN YOU, Leo Tolstoy. The soul-searching book that inspired Gandhi to embrace the concept of passive resistance, Tolstoy's 1894 polemic clearly outlines a radical, well-reasoned revision of traditional Christian thinking. 352pp. 5³⁄₁₆ x 8¼. 0-486-45138-0

THE LADY OR THE TIGER?: and Other Logic Puzzles, Raymond M. Smullyan. Created by a renowned puzzle master, these whimsically themed challenges involve paradoxes about probability, time, and change; metapuzzles; and self-referentiality. Nineteen chapters advance in difficulty from relatively simple to highly complex. 1982 edition. 240pp. 5⅜ x 8½. 0-486-47027-X

LEAVES OF GRASS: The Original 1855 Edition, Walt Whitman. Whitman's immortal collection includes some of the greatest poems of modern times, including his masterpiece, "Song of Myself." Shattering standard conventions, it stands as an unabashed celebration of body and nature. 128pp. 5³⁄₁₆ x 8¼. 0-486-45676-5

LES MISÉRABLES, Victor Hugo. Translated by Charles E. Wilbour. Abridged by James K. Robinson. A convict's heroic struggle for justice and redemption plays out against a fiery backdrop of the Napoleonic wars. This edition features the excellent original translation and a sensitive abridgment. 304pp. 6⅛ x 9¼.
0-486-45789-3

LILITH: A Romance, George MacDonald. In this novel by the father of fantasy literature, a man travels through time to meet Adam and Eve and to explore humanity's fall from grace and ultimate redemption. 240pp. 5⅜ x 8½.
0-486-46818-6

THE LOST LANGUAGE OF SYMBOLISM, Harold Bayley. This remarkable book reveals the hidden meaning behind familiar images and words, from the origins of Santa Claus to the fleur-de-lys, drawing from mythology, folklore, religious texts, and fairy tales. 1,418 illustrations. 784pp. 5⅜ x 8½. 0-486-44787-1

MACBETH, William Shakespeare. A Scottish nobleman murders the king in order to succeed to the throne. Tortured by his conscience and fearful of discovery, he becomes tangled in a web of treachery and deceit that ultimately spells his doom. 96pp. 5³⁄₁₆ x 8¼. 0-486-27802-6

MAKING AUTHENTIC CRAFTSMAN FURNITURE: Instructions and Plans for 62 Projects, Gustav Stickley. Make authentic reproductions of handsome, functional, durable furniture: tables, chairs, wall cabinets, desks, a hall tree, and more. Construction plans with drawings, schematics, dimensions, and lumber specs reprinted from 1900s The Craftsman magazine. 128pp. 8⅛ x 11. 0-486-25000-8

MATHEMATICS FOR THE NONMATHEMATICIAN, Morris Kline. Erudite and entertaining overview follows development of mathematics from ancient Greeks to present. Topics include logic and mathematics, the fundamental concept, differential calculus, probability theory, much more. Exercises and problems. 641pp. 5⅜ x 8½. 0-486-24823-2

MEMOIRS OF AN ARABIAN PRINCESS FROM ZANZIBAR, Emily Ruete. This 19th-century autobiography offers a rare inside look at the society surrounding a sultan's palace. A real-life princess in exile recalls her vanished world of harems, slave trading, and court intrigues. 288pp. 5⅜ x 8½. 0-486-47121-7

THE METAMORPHOSIS AND OTHER STORIES, Franz Kafka. Excellent new English translations of title story (considered by many critics Kafka's most perfect work), plus "The Judgment," "In the Penal Colony," "A Country Doctor," and "A Report to an Academy." Note. 96pp. 5³⁄₁₆ x 8¼. 0-486-29030-1

MICROSCOPIC ART FORMS FROM THE PLANT WORLD, R. Anheisser. From undulating curves to complex geometrics, a world of fascinating images abound in this classic, illustrated survey of microscopic plants. Features 400 detailed illustrations of nature's minute but magnificent handiwork. The accompanying CD-ROM includes all of the images in the book. 128pp. 9 x 9. 0-486-46013-4

A MIDSUMMER NIGHT'S DREAM, William Shakespeare. Among the most popular of Shakespeare's comedies, this enchanting play humorously celebrates the vagaries of love as it focuses upon the intertwined romances of several pairs of lovers. Explanatory footnotes. 80pp. 5³⁄₁₆ x 8¼. 0-486-27067-X

THE MONEY CHANGERS, Upton Sinclair. Originally published in 1908, this cautionary novel from the author of *The Jungle* explores corruption within the American system as a group of power brokers joins forces for personal gain, triggering a crash on Wall Street. 192pp. 5⅜ x 8½. 0-486-46917-4

THE MOST POPULAR HOMES OF THE TWENTIES, William A. Radford. With a New Introduction by Daniel D. Reiff. Based on a rare 1925 catalog, this architectural showcase features floor plans, construction details, and photos of 26 homes, plus articles on entrances, porches, garages, and more. 250 illustrations, 21 color plates. 176pp. 8⅜ x 11. 0-486-47028-8

MY 66 YEARS IN THE BIG LEAGUES, Connie Mack. With a New Introduction by Rich Westcott. A Founding Father of modern baseball, Mack holds the record for most wins — and losses — by a major league manager. Enhanced by 70 photographs, his warmhearted autobiography is populated by many legends of the game. 288pp. 5⅜ x 8½. 0-486-47184-5

NARRATIVE OF THE LIFE OF FREDERICK DOUGLASS, Frederick Douglass. Douglass's graphic depictions of slavery, harrowing escape to freedom, and life as a newspaper editor, eloquent orator, and impassioned abolitionist. 96pp. 5³⁄₁₆ x 8¼. 0-486-28499-9

THE NIGHTLESS CITY: Geisha and Courtesan Life in Old Tokyo, J. E. de Becker. This unsurpassed study from 100 years ago ventured into Tokyo's red-light district to survey geisha and courtesan life and offer meticulous descriptions of training, dress, social hierarchy, and erotic practices. 49 black-and-white illustrations; 2 maps. 496pp. 5⅜ x 8½. 0-486-45563-7

THE ODYSSEY, Homer. Excellent prose translation of ancient epic recounts adventures of the homeward-bound Odysseus. Fantastic cast of gods, giants, cannibals, sirens, other supernatural creatures — true classic of Western literature. 256pp. 5³⁄₁₆ x 8¼. 0-486-40654-7

OEDIPUS REX, Sophocles. Landmark of Western drama concerns the catastrophe that ensues when King Oedipus discovers he has inadvertently killed his father and married his mother. Masterly construction, dramatic irony. Explanatory footnotes. 64pp. 5³⁄₁₆ x 8¼. 0-486-26877-2

ONCE UPON A TIME: The Way America Was, Eric Sloane. Nostalgic text and drawings brim with gentle philosophies and descriptions of how we used to live — self-sufficiently — on the land, in homes, and among the things built by hand. 44 line illustrations. 64pp. 8⅜ x 11. 0-486-44411-2

Browse over 9,000 books at www.doverpublications.com

ONE OF OURS, Willa Cather. The Pulitzer Prize–winning novel about a young Nebraskan looking for something to believe in. Alienated from his parents, rejected by his wife, he finds his destiny on the bloody battlefields of World War I. 352pp. 5³⁄₁₆ x 8¼.   0-486-45599-8

ORIGAMI YOU CAN USE: 27 Practical Projects, Rick Beech. Origami models can be more than decorative, and this unique volume shows how! The 27 practical projects include a CD case, frame, napkin ring, and dish. Easy instructions feature 400 two-color illustrations. 96pp. 8¼ x 11.   0-486-47057-1

OTHELLO, William Shakespeare. Towering tragedy tells the story of a Moorish general who earns the enmity of his ensign Iago when he passes him over for a promotion. Masterly portrait of an archvillain. Explanatory footnotes. 112pp. 5³⁄₁₆ x 8¼.
0-486-29097-2

PARADISE LOST, John Milton. Notes by John A. Himes. First published in 1667, *Paradise Lost* ranks among the greatest of English literature's epic poems. It's a sublime retelling of Adam and Eve's fall from grace and expulsion from Eden. Notes by John A. Himes. 480pp. 5³⁄₁₆ x 8¼.   0-486-44287-X

PASSING, Nella Larsen. Married to a successful physician and prominently ensconced in society, Irene Redfield leads a charmed existence — until a chance encounter with a childhood friend who has been "passing for white." 112pp. 5⅜ x 8½. 0-486-43713-2

PERSPECTIVE DRAWING FOR BEGINNERS, Len A. Doust. Doust carefully explains the roles of lines, boxes, and circles, and shows how visualizing shapes and forms can be used in accurate depictions of perspective. One of the most concise introductions available. 33 illustrations. 64pp. 5⅜ x 8½.   0-486-45149-6

PERSPECTIVE MADE EASY, Ernest R. Norling. Perspective is easy; yet, surprisingly few artists know the simple rules that make it so. Remedy that situation with this simple, step-by-step book, the first devoted entirely to the topic. 256 illustrations. 224pp. 5⅜ x 8½.   0-486-40473-0

THE PICTURE OF DORIAN GRAY, Oscar Wilde. Celebrated novel involves a handsome young Londoner who sinks into a life of depravity. His body retains perfect youth and vigor while his recent portrait reflects the ravages of his crime and sensuality. 176pp. 5³⁄₁₆ x 8¼.   0-486-27807-7

PRIDE AND PREJUDICE, Jane Austen. One of the most universally loved and admired English novels, an effervescent tale of rural romance transformed by Jane Austen's art into a witty, shrewdly observed satire of English country life. 272pp. 5³⁄₁₆ x 8¼.
0-486-28473-5

THE PRINCE, Niccolò Machiavelli. Classic, Renaissance-era guide to acquiring and maintaining political power. Today, nearly 500 years after it was written, this calculating prescription for autocratic rule continues to be much read and studied. 80pp. 5³⁄₁₆ x 8¼.   0-486-27274-5

QUICK SKETCHING, Carl Cheek. A perfect introduction to the technique of "quick sketching." Drawing upon an artist's immediate emotional responses, this is an extremely effective means of capturing the essential form and features of a subject. More than 100 black-and-white illustrations throughout. 48pp. 11 x 8¼.
0-486-46608-6

RANCH LIFE AND THE HUNTING TRAIL, Theodore Roosevelt. Illustrated by Frederic Remington. Beautifully illustrated by Remington, Roosevelt's celebration of the Old West recounts his adventures in the Dakota Badlands of the 1880s, from roundups to Indian encounters to hunting bighorn sheep. 208pp. 6¼ x 9¼.   0-486-47340-6

THE RED BADGE OF COURAGE, Stephen Crane. Amid the nightmarish chaos of a Civil War battle, a young soldier discovers courage, humility, and, perhaps, wisdom. Uncanny re-creation of actual combat. Enduring landmark of American fiction. 112pp. 5³⁄₁₆ x 8¼. 0-486-26465-3

RELATIVITY SIMPLY EXPLAINED, Martin Gardner. One of the subject's clearest, most entertaining introductions offers lucid explanations of special and general theories of relativity, gravity, and spacetime, models of the universe, and more. 100 illustrations. 224pp. 5⅜ x 8½. 0-486-29315-7

REMBRANDT DRAWINGS: 116 Masterpieces in Original Color, Rembrandt van Rijn. This deluxe hardcover edition features drawings from throughout the Dutch master's prolific career. Informative captions accompany these beautifully reproduced landscapes, biblical vignettes, figure studies, animal sketches, and portraits. 128pp. 8⅜ x 11. 0-486-46149-1

THE ROAD NOT TAKEN AND OTHER POEMS, Robert Frost. A treasury of Frost's most expressive verse. In addition to the title poem: "An Old Man's Winter Night," "In the Home Stretch," "Meeting and Passing," "Putting in the Seed," many more. All complete and unabridged. 64pp. 5³⁄₁₆ x 8¼. 0-486-27550-7

ROMEO AND JULIET, William Shakespeare. Tragic tale of star-crossed lovers, feuding families and timeless passion contains some of Shakespeare's most beautiful and lyrical love poetry. Complete, unabridged text with explanatory footnotes. 96pp. 5³⁄₁₆ x 8¼. 0-486-27557-4

SANDITON AND THE WATSONS: Austen's Unfinished Novels, Jane Austen. Two tantalizing incomplete stories revisit Austen's customary milieu of courtship and venture into new territory, amid guests at a seaside resort. Both are worth reading for pleasure and study. 112pp. 5⅜ x 8½. 0-486-45793-1

THE SCARLET LETTER, Nathaniel Hawthorne. With stark power and emotional depth, Hawthorne's masterpiece explores sin, guilt, and redemption in a story of adultery in the early days of the Massachusetts Colony. 192pp. 5³⁄₁₆ x 8¼.
0-486-28048-9

THE SEASONS OF AMERICA PAST, Eric Sloane. Seventy-five illustrations depict cider mills and presses, sleds, pumps, stump-pulling equipment, plows, and other elements of America's rural heritage. A section of old recipes and household hints adds additional color. 160pp. 8⅜ x 11. 0-486-44220-9

SELECTED CANTERBURY TALES, Geoffrey Chaucer. Delightful collection includes the General Prologue plus three of the most popular tales: "The Knight's Tale," "The Miller's Prologue and Tale," and "The Wife of Bath's Prologue and Tale." In modern English. 144pp. 5³⁄₁₆ x 8¼. 0-486-28241-4

SELECTED POEMS, Emily Dickinson. Over 100 best-known, best-loved poems by one of America's foremost poets, reprinted from authoritative early editions. No comparable edition at this price. Index of first lines. 64pp. 5³⁄₁₆ x 8¼. 0-486-26466-1

SIDDHARTHA, Hermann Hesse. Classic novel that has inspired generations of seekers. Blending Eastern mysticism and psychoanalysis, Hesse presents a strikingly original view of man and culture and the arduous process of self-discovery, reconciliation, harmony, and peace. 112pp. 5³⁄₁₆ x 8¼. 0-486-40653-9

SKETCHING OUTDOORS, Leonard Richmond. This guide offers beginners step-by-step demonstrations of how to depict clouds, trees, buildings, and other outdoor sights. Explanations of a variety of techniques include shading and constructional drawing. 48pp. 11 x 8¼. 0-486-46922-0

Browse over 9,000 books at www.doverpublications.com

SMALL HOUSES OF THE FORTIES: With Illustrations and Floor Plans, Harold E. Group. 56 floor plans and elevations of houses that originally cost less than $15,000 to build. Recommended by financial institutions of the era, they range from Colonials to Cape Cods. 144pp. 8⅜ x 11. 0-486-45598-X

SOME CHINESE GHOSTS, Lafcadio Hearn. Rooted in ancient Chinese legends, these richly atmospheric supernatural tales are recounted by an expert in Oriental lore. Their originality, power, and literary charm will captivate readers of all ages. 96pp. 5⅜ x 8½. 0-486-46306-0

SONGS FOR THE OPEN ROAD: Poems of Travel and Adventure, Edited by The American Poetry & Literacy Project. More than 80 poems by 50 American and British masters celebrate real and metaphorical journeys. Poems by Whitman, Byron, Millay, Sandburg, Langston Hughes, Emily Dickinson, Robert Frost, Shelley, Tennyson, Yeats, many others. Note. 80pp. 5³⁄₁₆ x 8¼. 0-486-40646-6

SPOON RIVER ANTHOLOGY, Edgar Lee Masters. An American poetry classic, in which former citizens of a mythical midwestern town speak touchingly from the grave of the thwarted hopes and dreams of their lives. 144pp. 5³⁄₁₆ x 8¼.
0-486-27275-3

STAR LORE: Myths, Legends, and Facts, William Tyler Olcott. Captivating retellings of the origins and histories of ancient star groups include Pegasus, Ursa Major, Pleiades, signs of the zodiac, and other constellations. "Classic." — *Sky & Telescope.* 58 illustrations. 544pp. 5⅜ x 8½. 0-486-43581-4

THE STRANGE CASE OF DR. JEKYLL AND MR. HYDE, Robert Louis Stevenson. This intriguing novel, both fantasy thriller and moral allegory, depicts the struggle of two opposing personalities — one essentially good, the other evil — for the soul of one man. 64pp. 5³⁄₁₆ x 8¼. 0-486-26688-5

SURVIVAL HANDBOOK: The Official U.S. Army Guide, Department of the Army. This special edition of the Army field manual is geared toward civilians. An essential companion for campers and all lovers of the outdoors, it constitutes the most authoritative wilderness guide. 288pp. 5³⁄₁₆ x 8¼. 0-486-46184-X

A TALE OF TWO CITIES, Charles Dickens. Against the backdrop of the French Revolution, Dickens unfolds his masterpiece of drama, adventure, and romance about a man falsely accused of treason. Excitement and derring-do in the shadow of the guillotine. 304pp. 5³⁄₁₆ x 8¼. 0-486-40651-2

TEN PLAYS, Anton Chekhov. *The Sea Gull, Uncle Vanya, The Three Sisters, The Cherry Orchard,* and *Ivanov,* plus 5 one-act comedies: *The Anniversary, An Unwilling Martyr, The Wedding, The Bear,* and *The Proposal.* 336pp. 5³⁄₁₆ x 8¼. 0-486-46560-8

THE FLYING INN, G. K. Chesterton. Hilarious romp in which pub owner Humphrey Hump and friend take to the road in a donkey cart filled with rum and cheese, inveighing against Prohibition and other "oppressive forms of modernity." 320pp. 5⅜ x 8½. 0-486-41910-X

THIRTY YEARS THAT SHOOK PHYSICS: The Story of Quantum Theory, George Gamow. Lucid, accessible introduction to the influential theory of energy and matter features careful explanations of Dirac's anti-particles, Bohr's model of the atom, and much more. Numerous drawings. 1966 edition. 240pp. 5⅜ x 8½. 0-486-24895-X

TREASURE ISLAND, Robert Louis Stevenson. Classic adventure story of a perilous sea journey, a mutiny led by the infamous Long John Silver, and a lethal scramble for buried treasure — seen through the eyes of cabin boy Jim Hawkins. 160pp. 5³⁄₁₆ x 8¼.
0-486-27559-0

Browse over 9,000 books at www.doverpublications.com

THE TRIAL, Franz Kafka. Translated by David Wyllie. From its gripping first sentence onward, this novel exemplifies the term "Kafkaesque." Its darkly humorous narrative recounts a bank clerk's entrapment in a bureaucratic maze, based on an undisclosed charge. 176pp. 5³⁄₁₆ x 8¼. 0-486-47061-X

THE TURN OF THE SCREW, Henry James. Gripping ghost story by great novelist depicts the sinister transformation of 2 innocent children into flagrant liars and hypocrites. An elegantly told tale of unspoken horror and psychological terror. 96pp. 5³⁄₁₆ x 8¼. 0-486-26684-2

UP FROM SLAVERY, Booker T. Washington. Washington (1856-1915) rose to become the most influential spokesman for African-Americans of his day. In this eloquently written book, he describes events in a remarkable life that began in bondage and culminated in worldwide recognition. 160pp. 5³⁄₁₆ x 8¼. 0-486-28738-6

VICTORIAN HOUSE DESIGNS IN AUTHENTIC FULL COLOR: 75 Plates from the "Scientific American – Architects and Builders Edition," 1885-1894, Edited by Blanche Cirker. Exquisitely detailed, exceptionally handsome designs for an enormous variety of attractive city dwellings, spacious suburban and country homes, charming "cottages" and other structures — all accompanied by perspective views and floor plans. 80pp. 9¼ x 12¼. 0-486-29438-2

VILLETTE, Charlotte Brontë. Acclaimed by Virginia Woolf as "Brontë's finest novel," this moving psychological study features a remarkably modern heroine who abandons her native England for a new life as a schoolteacher in Belgium. 480pp. 5³⁄₁₆ x 8¼. 0-486-45557-2

THE VOYAGE OUT, Virginia Woolf. A moving depiction of the thrills and confusion of youth, Woolf's acclaimed first novel traces a shipboard journey to South America for a captivating exploration of a woman's growing self-awareness. 288pp. 5³⁄₁₆ x 8¼. 0-486-45005-8

WALDEN; OR, LIFE IN THE WOODS, Henry David Thoreau. Accounts of Thoreau's daily life on the shores of Walden Pond outside Concord, Massachusetts, are interwoven with musings on the virtues of self-reliance and individual freedom, on society, government, and other topics. 224pp. 5³⁄₁₆ x 8¼. 0-486-28495-6

WILD PILGRIMAGE: A Novel in Woodcuts, Lynd Ward. Through startling engravings shaded in black and red, Ward wordlessly tells the story of a man trapped in an industrial world, struggling between the grim reality around him and the fantasies his imagination creates. 112pp. 6⅛ x 9¼. 0-486-46583-7

WILLY POGÁNY REDISCOVERED, Willy Pogány. Selected and Edited by Jeff A. Menges. More than 100 color and black-and-white Art Nouveau–style illustrations from fairy tales and adventure stories include scenes from Wagner's "Ring" cycle, *The Rime of the Ancient Mariner, Gulliver's Travels,* and *Faust.* 144pp. 8⅜ x 11. 0-486-47046-6

WOOLLY THOUGHTS: Unlock Your Creative Genius with Modular Knitting, Pat Ashforth and Steve Plummer. Here's the revolutionary way to knit — easy, fun, and foolproof! Beginners and experienced knitters need only master a single stitch to create their own designs with patchwork squares. More than 100 illustrations. 128pp. 6½ x 9¼. 0-486-46084-3

WUTHERING HEIGHTS, Emily Brontë. Somber tale of consuming passions and vengeance — played out amid the lonely English moors — recounts the turbulent and tempestuous love story of Cathy and Heathcliff. Poignant and compelling. 256pp. 5³⁄₁₆ x 8¼. 0-486-29256-8

Browse over 9,000 books at www.doverpublications.com